D1351396

THE LITERATURE
OF FANTASY

GARLAND REFERENCE LI[
OF THE HUMANITIES
(VOL. 176)

THE LITERATURE OF FANTASY

A Comprehensive, Annotated Bibliography of Modern Fantasy Fiction

Roger C. Schlobin

GARLAND PUBLISHING, INC. • NEW YORK & LONDON
1979

Library of Congress Cataloging in Publication Data

Schlobin, Roger C
    The literature of fantasy.

    (Garland reference library of the humanities ; v. 176)
    Includes bibliographical references and indexes.
    1. Fantastic fiction, English—Bibliography.   2. Fantastic
fiction, American—Bibliography.   I. Title.
Z2014.F4S33   [PR830.F3]   016.823′0876   78-68287
ISBN 0-8240-9757-2

Printed on acid-free, 250-year-life paper
Manufactured in the United States of America

To Eugene B. Cantelupe,
Mentor, Muse, Friend:
". . . stand me now and ever in good stead."

CONTENTS

PREFACE

Purpose of the Work

Despite the vast popular success of adult fantasy literature among the reading public, until ten years ago the only major studies of modern fantasy literature were E.M. Forster's chapter on fantasy in *Aspects of the Novel and Related Writings* (1927) and J.R.R. Tolkien's often-cited essay, "On Fairy-Stories" (1947).[1] Fortunately, beginning with Tzvetan Todorov's *The Fantastic: A Structural Approach to a Literary Genre*[2] in 1970, there have been a number of serious studies published. The important contributions of Robert Crossley, L. Sprague de Camp, W.R. Irwin, Colin N. Manlove, Jane Mobley, Eric S. Rabkin, and Gary K. Wolfe[3] indicate that the examination of fantasy in fiction has become an important preoccupation among academics.

Bibliographic study has lagged even further behind popular acclaim and critical examination. Most of the existing checklists and bibliographies have concentrated on juvenile fantasy[4] or on fantasy as part of science-fiction, horror, and/or weird literature.[5] To date, adult fantasy as an area of bibliographic attention has been neglected.[6] This volume is an attempt to fill the bibliographic void that currently exists. I hope that it can serve as a touchstone for all those who are interested in pursuing the literature of fantasy, be they scholars, librarians, teachers, students, and/or fans. While this volume does not pretend to be a substitute for individual author bibliographies, I have attempted to comprehensively list and annotate all major modern fantasy authors and works.

An introduction, "Fantasy and Its Literature," precedes the bibliographic sections. It sets forth the principles used in selecting the titles included in the bibliography and examines the psychological nature of fantasy and its manifestation in literature.

Scope of the Work

For the purpose of this volume, "modern fantasy fiction" is chronologically defined as beginning with the publication of George MacDonald's *Phantastes: A Faerie Romance for Men and Women* in 1858 (a small number of significant earlier works are cited, e.g., Sara Coleridge's *Phantasmion* in 1837 and George Meredith's *The Shaving of Shagpat* in 1856). Listings include titles published through April, 1979. The titles selected are restricted to adult fantasy and juvenile fantasy with strong adult appeal. The citations are primarily limited to prose works originally published in book form in the English language; the only foreign-language authors and titles included are those that have conspicuously contributed to the Anglo-American literary tradition (e.g., Italo Calvino, E.T.A. Hoffmann, and Isaac Bashevis Singer). Horror, science-fiction, and weird literature is excluded unless it contains material that would be of particular interest to the fantasy reader.

Over 800 authors, 100 editors, 721 novels, 244 collections, 100 anthologies, 3610 short stories, and 165 author bibliographies are cited and indexed here, and, except as indicated, all have been directly examined.

Arrangement of the Work

The Literature of Fantasy is divided into two sections: (1) Novels and Collections and (2) Anthologies. The first section is arranged alphabetically by author, and the second alphabetically by editor. In all cases, works are listed by the author's or editor's true name; pseudonyms are cross-referenced both in the bibliographic sections and in the Author, Compiler, Editor, and Translator Index.

In both sections, works are cited by first edition, unless otherwise noted, with additional citation of reprints appropriate for library acquisition. The form of each citation follows the guidelines set forth by the Modern Language Association. Each citation includes, as appropriate, author, pseudonym, full title, variant titles, variant editions, translator and/or editor, place of publication, publisher, and date of publication. If the title was originally published in paperback, this information is also included.

Each author entry in the novel and collection section is arranged as follows: Listed first, in alphabetical order, are individual novels and/or collections, each with its own annotation. Second, series are identified, with novels and collections in the series listed *in reading order*, and with a single annotation presented for the entire series. Third, author bibliography or bibliographies are cited, when available, for those readers who would like to further explore each author's canon.

Within each individual editor listing in the anthology section, titles are listed alphabetically; when anthology selections are excerpts from larger works, these larger works have been noted.

The novel annotations are primarily descriptive and only secondarily critical, and, where necessary, publishing details and background information are provided. The collection and anthology annotations, because of the frequent variation among the collection and anthology contents, are primarily restricted to the listing of contents. However, when certain generalizations are possible, they are included. Individual short stories in collections and anthologies are designated by letter for ease of access through the title index.

The two indices appended to the volume access its entire contents. The first index includes the names of authors, compilers, editors, and translators; it also cross-references names mentioned in the annotations and pseudonyms. The second index accesses the titles of all individual volumes and all short story titles, as well as cross-referencing all substantive references to titles in the annotations and all title variations. It should be noted that this is the first time the contents of this many fantasy collections and anthologies have been indexed.

Acknowledgments

The Literature of Fantasy has been formally in progress for over three years, and informally under way for a much longer period of time. Many, many more titles have been discarded than included, and much of this selection process has been the result of the support of colleagues and friends, of book dealers who have been far more helpful than mercenary, of a number of publishers who have generously supplied review copies of their publications, and of various libraries and their staffs. While it would be impossible to mention all those who have helped with this volume, there are a number of people whose contributions should be acknowledged.

Miss Andre Norton loaned her entire fantasy library and gave freely of her substantial knowledge of fantasy.

The Director of the Lilly Library at Indiana University, William R. Cagle, and his staff, most particulary Susan Godlewski and Stephen H. Cape, went well beyond the mandates of normal service in making their significant holdings in fantasy accessible.

John J. Pappas, Chairman of the Department of English at the North Central Campus of Purdue University, has been consistently supportive, and his continual confidence has been an inspiration.

Marshall B. Tymn of the English Department of Eastern Michigan University was instrumental in the conception of this project and has generously given of his bibliographic expertise.

Ann M. Berg, Donna E Williams, and Charles M. Schaeve of the Purdue University Library System have readily and graciously responded to the most obscure and esoteric requests.

A number of colleagues have shared their significant knowledge of specific authors and topics. Robert A. Collins, Florida Atlantic University, helped with Thomas Burnett Swann, and Kathy Spencer, Wright State University, with Charles W.S. Williams. Gary K. Wolfe, Roosevelt University, not only helped with George MacDonald and David Lindsay, but also acquainted me with many of the psychological studies that are cited in the introduction.

I have also drawn on *A Research Guide to Science Fiction Studies* (New York and London: Garland, 1977), compiled by Marshall B. Tymn, L.W. Currey, and this author, and "The Year's Scholarship in Science Fiction and Fantasy" (annually in

Extrapolation), edited by Marshall B. Tymn and this author, for some of the author bibliographies cited in this volume. I am grateful for the shared expertise and on-going and quality companionship of my collaborators.

Miss Susan E. Howard, my typist and friend, has labored long over the camera-ready copy and portions of the indices. Without her diligence and sacrifice, this volume would never have been completed.

Finally, while I have tried to make *The Literature of Fantasy* as comprehensive and useful as possible, my bibliographic explorations of fantasy will not cease here. I would welcome the assistance of anyone who thinks that valuable titles have been omitted or that others have been inappropriately included. Such information is necessary for the success of future bibliographies.

ROGER C. SCHLOBIN
Department of English
Purdue University
North Central Campus
Westville, Indiana 46391

Notes

1. E.M. Forster, "Fantasy," in *Aspects of the Novel and Related Writings* (1927; rpt. London: Edward Arnold, 1974), pp. 73–85; J.R.R. Tolkien, "On Fairy-Stories," in *Essays Presented to Charles Williams*, ed. C.S. Lewis (London: Oxford University Press, 1947), pp. 38–89.

2. Tzvetan Todorov, *The Fantastic: A Structural Approach to a Literary Genre*, trans. Richard Howard (Cleveland and London: The Press of Case Western Reserve University, 1973). Originally published as *Introduction à la littérature fantastique*, 1970.

3. Robert Crossley, "Education and Fantasy," *College English*, 37, No. 3 (1975), 281–293; L. Sprague de Camp, *Literary Swordsmen and Sorcerers: The Makers of Heroic Fantasy* (Sauk City, WI: Arkham House, 1976); W.R. Irwin, *The Game of the Impossible: A Rhetoric of Fantasy*

(Urbana: University of Illinois Press, 1976); C.N. Manlove, *Modern Fantasy: Five Studies* (Cambridge: Cambridge University Press, 1976); Jane Mobley, "Toward a Definition of Fantasy Fiction." *Extrapolation*, 15, No. 2 (1974), 117–128; Eric S. Rabkin, *The Fantastic in Literature* (Princeton: Princeton University Press, 1976); Gary K. Wolfe, "Symbolic Fantasy," *Genre*, 8 (1975), 194–209.

4. Among the bibliographies and checklists that cite primarily juvenile fantasy, the following specific and general works are noteworthy: Naomi Lewis, *Fantasy Books for Children* (London: National Book League, 1975); D.L. Kirkpatrick, ed., *Twentieth-Century Children's Writers* (New York: St. Martin's Press, 1978); and Diana Waggoner, *The Hills of Faraway: A Guide to Fantasy* (New York: Atheneum, 1978).

5. A number of bibliographies and checklists that include both science fiction and fantasy are important to note: Everett F. Bleiler, *The Checklist of Fantastic Literature: A Bibliography of Fantasy, Weird and Science Fiction Books Published in the English Language* (Chicago: Shasta, 1948; rpt. West Linn, OR: FAX Collector's Editions, 1972; [2nd rev. ed.] as *The Checklist of Science-Fiction & Supernatural Fiction*, Glen Rock, NJ: Firebell Books, 1978); Joseph H. Crawford, *"333": A Bibliography of the Science-Fiction Novel* (Providence, RI: Grandon, 1953); Bradford M. Day, *The Supplemental Checklist of Fantastic Literature* (Denver, NY: Science-Fiction & Fantasy Publications, 1963; rpt. New York: Arno, 1975); Robert Reginald, pseud. [Michael Burgess], *Stella Nova: The Contemporary Science Fiction Authors* (Los Angeles: Unicorn & Son, 1970; [2nd ed.] as *Contemporary Science Fiction Authors*, New York: Arno, 1975) and *Science Fiction and Fantasy Literature, with Contemporary Science Fiction Authors II* (Detroit: Gale Research, forthcoming [1979]); Donald H. Tuck, *The Encyclopedia of Science Fiction and Fantasy Through 1968*, 2 vols. (Chicago: Advent, 1974, 1978); Marshall B. Tymn, *American Fantasy and Science Fiction: Toward a Bibliography of Works Published in the United States, 1948–1973* (West Linn, OR: FAX Collector's Editions, 1979); and Stuart W. Wells III, *The Science Fiction and Heroic Fantasy Author Index* (Duluth, MN: Purple Unicorn Books, 1978).

Readers who choose to consult these works will find additional information concerning some of the authors cited in *The Literature of Fantasy*.

In addition, readers desiring more information than cited above should consult the following research and reference works: Thomas

Clareson, *Science Fiction Criticism: An Annotated Checklist* (Kent, OH: Kent State University Press, 1972); Marshall B. Tymn, Roger C. Schlobin, and L.W. Currey, *A Research Guide to Science Fiction Studies: An Annotated Checklist of Primary and Secondary Sources for Fantasy and Science Fiction* (New York and London: Garland, 1977); and Roger C. Schlobin and Marshall B. Tymn, "The Year's Scholarship in Science Fiction and Fantasy: 1974–," annually in *Extrapolation*, 1976–, and its first cumulation in book form as *The Year's Scholarship in Science Fiction and Fantasy, 1972–1975* (Kent, OH: Kent State University Press, 1979).

6. There are some indications that the bibliographic neglect of adult fantasy is being corrected. In addition to the Waggoner bibliography (see note 4 above), which does include some adult titles, Robert H. Boyer and Kenneth J. Zahorski published a brief guide, *An Annotated Bibliography of Fantasy Literature*, in 1978 (River Falls, WI: Wisconsin Council of Teachers of English Service Bulletin No. 35), that briefly annotates eighty-five works of fantasy fiction and also lists a variety of scholarly and support publications and services.

The January, 1978, issue of the *CEA Critic* is also devoted to fantasy, and in addition to a number of scholarly essays, it contains two bibliographies of fantasy fiction and reference materials by this author and Marshall B. Tymn, respectively.

In June, 1978, Paul Allen began publishing the *Fantasy Newsletter*. This is an invaluable tool for keeping aware of new publications in the field. It is available from Paul Allen (1015 West 36th St., Loveland, CO 80537) at a rate of five dollars for twelve issues in the United States, six dollars in Canada, and nine dollars elsewhere.

In the Summer of 1979, Marshall B. Tymn and the aforementioned Professors Boyer and Zahorski will be publishing *Fantasy Literature: A Core Collection and Reference Guide* (New York: R.R. Bowker). This volume is reported to annotate three hundred "all-ages" titles and to provide an annotated guide to secondary resources.

INTRODUCTION
Fantasy and Its Literature

Fantasy was born neither in literature nor art. It is one of the original qualities that distinguished man from the flora and fauna of his first beginnings. In some dark cave—perhaps in Africa, perhaps in Asia—an odorous organism felt the first stirrings of that mental activity that was to metamorphose him from survivor into creator. Much has been made of his fellows who discovered fire and wheel, but his nascent discoveries of self, mind, and idea relegate their mechanistic achievements to the level of simple crudities. It was for this primitive caveman—understanding so little of himself—to create and develop man's most precious characteristic: the power of fantasy, the power to create *ex nihilo*, out of nothing. It is difficult for the modern mind to comprehend the measureless achievement of his primitive forebear. Concepts such as "I," "you," "mate," "friend," and "time" are so automatic as to be allied with breathing. Yet for anyone who has ever watched a baby begin to stir to self-awareness and consciousness, some small empathy may exist with primitive man's triumphant movement from organism to cave painter, from single entity to social being, from existence to consciousness. It must have been an agonizing process, one conceived in necessity, forged in isolation. Fortunately, man progressed from necessary preoccupation with externals to awareness of the internal and began to shape and interrelate his world. He distinguished between the inner and outer, between inner reality and outer appearance, and it was upon inner reality that he built himself and his relationships, societies, civilizations, and, most importantly, his cultures.

Man lives in this inner awareness. Besieged by externals and simultaneously shaping these externals through his mind, he is constantly the creator, and in the eons that have passed since that first burgeoning of awareness, he has distinguished himself as "*homo fantasia*, the visionary dreamer and myth-maker."[1] In this role, he has populated the cosmos with spirits and demons, religions and philosophies, social orders and political systems, rituals and myths, laws and mores, boundaries and belongings, hopes and expectations—all created first in the mind. And these vitally important involvements have arisen from the inner man, all without initial external actuality. Erich Neumann, in *Depth Psychology and a New Ethic*, accurately summarizes the enormity of these activities:

> The decisive part played by psychic reality—as depth psychology is just beginning to discover—is a more powerful influence behind the scenes than the naive consciousness of average Western man has ever dreamt of. Individuals and groups—and nations, too, and movements of history—are conditioned by the power of inner psychic realities which often enough appear in the first place as fantasies in the mind of an individual. This influence of the inner world is to be found at work in such diverse spheres as politics and religion, technology and art. War and destruction are repeatedly let loose to devastate the world at the behest of men driven by fantasies of power; at the same time, the inner images of creative artists become the cultural possession of the whole human race.[2]

Although Neumann perceptively elevates fantasy to a grand level, this is not to say that its creative power is not present on the mundane plane. By means of perception, "Fantasy helps determine what we consider to be fact just as surely as the other way around."[3] It is an essential quality, along with some sense of identity and place, in every man, but unlike the sense of identity and place that maintains existence, fantasy is the characteristic that creates existence:

> Fantasy-images are both the raw materials and finished products of psyche, and they are the privileged mode of access to knowledge of soul. Nothing is more primary. Every notion in our minds, each perception of the world and sensation in ourselves must go through a psychic organization in order to "happen" at all. Every single feeling or observation occurs as a psychic event by first forming a fantasy-image.[4]

Thus, no one stands alone. Through participation in what C.G. Jung has labeled the "collective unconscious,"[5] every man inherits the sum total of the species' experience. Occasionally confused or identified with instinct, this legacy is inherited and manifests itself through archetypes visible through major symbols that characterize the natures and activities of all societies and all cultures and that are coordinated in patterns. Whether they be the patterns of rites of passage and initiation or the persuasive symbol of the "Great Mother,"[6] they work through the activity of fantasy to create myth, art, religion, and behavior:

> Just as the archetypes occur on the ethnological level as myths, so also they are found in every individual, and their effect is always strongest, that is, they anthropomorphize reality most, where consciousness is weakest and most restricted, and where fantasy can overrun the facts of the outer world.[7]

Fantasy, then, is an everyday, natural activity that summons and creates images and converts them into external manifestations. As imaginative activity, it is the "direct expression of psychic life."[8] Fantasy recognizes all possibilities in man's nature.[9] Mankind's capacities for tool-making and system-making have been legitimately applauded, but if these activities had not been conceived internally first and if the external world of meaning had not evolved, mankind would be indistinguishable from highly sophisticated social insects. The visible world is simply the "subcreation" of the inner, for fantasy gives "form to thought" and is the "richest source of human creativity."[10] As a social activity, it is the well-spring of myth, ritual, religion, and play; as a cultural activity, it is the source of art. Universally, it supplies the will with needed content, purpose, and focus. On one hand, fantasy brings man closest to his oldest self[11] through the collective unconscious and archetypes, but on the other, it is the essence of imaginative culture, which "transcends the limits of both the naturally possible and of the morally acceptable."[12] When individuals participate in their fantasies or share the most disciplined imaginings of artists, they travel, as gods, on a road where the world is created *ex nihilo*. They experience rare dreams or

sensations for the first time; break traditions and violate ritual;
open non-empirical, visionary doors; and find that, as the journey
continues, their minds expand and are enriched by their
capacities and their links with the most essential past.[13]

Moreover, as the mythopoetic force that it is, fantasy shares
myth's capacity to impinge upon "that awesome ultimate mystery which is both beyond and within himself [man] and all
things. . . ." Intellectually, it is the state from which words turn
back, where "mythological symbols touch and exhilarate centers
of life beyond the reach of the vocabularies of reason and coercion."[14] Fantasy, as a personal and artistic experience, involves
its practitioners in a quest in which archetypes and primordial
images come alive. In this process, they participate in the collective unconscious[15] and the suspension of everyday concerns and
preoccupations. Thus, fantasy lures its followers into an examination of their own natures, the seminal truths of their existences,
and an extension of the frontiers of their futures.[16] For the fantasist, life is psychological, and its purpose is to find the connection
between life and soul. This activity is not the foolishly esoteric;
rather it is "the activity that makes events esoteric."[17]

Yet fantasy as a valid and truthful mode is in peril. It produces
a truth of pure forms[18] that is antithetical to contemporary, mate-
rialistic, empirical, phenomenological, and technological society.
Despite its formalized support of the arts, twentieth-century
Western society "has consistently been antagonistic to the flow-
ering of the life of fantasy."[19] Anyone who has had the misfortune to laud a fantasy work or express a fantasy before one of the
all-too-frequently "realistic" audiences knows the crippled
snobbery that is summoned. Anyone who has taught fantasy
probably will sympathize with Eric S. Rabkin's description of his
uninitiated students:

> Before they ever enter the classroom, our students "know" the
> following about fantasy: fantasy is for kids (so it's got to be sim-
> ple); fantasy is unreal (so life's problems won't bother us here);
> and fantasy is popular (so we don't need to learn anything from the
> teacher).[20]

Sadly, even though "fantasy is a self-justifying biological function," it is brought into question, on the grounds of usefulness, only by those who mistakenly believe in the absolute existence of a "concrete reality."[21] In its appropriate frame, its autonomy from everyday makes it the final "refuge of dignity,"[22] and the charge that fantasy is "escape" only reinforces man's need for the ability to disengage the mind from the mundane.

Yet today the right to fantasy is clearly being challenged by philosophies and orientations that would prefer security to advancement, technology to invention, and acceptance to thought. Numerous warnings have been sounded against the empirical stance. Harvey Cox, in *The Feast of Fools*, dramatically states that "without fantasy a society cuts itself off from the visceral fonts of renewal" and that "the survival of mankind also has been placed in jeopardy by the repression of festivity and fantasy."[23] Erich Neumann, in *Depth Psychology and a New Ethic*, examines the Judeo-Christian dualism's inability to cope with man's nature. He assesses the modern age as follows:

> The modern age is an epoch in human history in which science and technology are demonstrating beyond doubt the capacity of the conscious mind to deal with physical nature and to master it to a very great extent—at any rate, to a greater degree than in any earlier period in human history. But it is also an epoch in which man's incapacity to deal with psychic [adj. from psyche] nature, with the human soul, has become more appallingly obvious than ever before [p. 25].

Ursula K. Le Guin, the noted science-fiction and fantasy writer, may be correct when she says that Americans fear fantasy because it is too true and threatens "all that is false, . . . phony, unnecessary and trivial in the life they [adults] have let themselves be forced into living. They are afraid of dragons, because they are afraid of freedom."[24] It would be interesting to see what the American public would do if it were stripped of its condominiums and Cadillacs and had to rely on some non-economic system of immaterial values as a measure of success, or if there were a general understanding that history demonstrates that wealth is a very poor method of seeking immortality. Certainly material wealth generates security, but at a high price, for it severely limits psychological freedom and growth. Security and stability attempt to negate change and produce a static, rather than a dynamic, society. The signs of such general stagnation are clear. Secularization, socialization, and nominalism have reduced the invigorating rebirth of the mythic experience and the liberating mind-play of festivity and games to socially acceptable and "inferior" portions of the "superior" utilitarian world. Art is subordinated to "real" waking experience.[25] Ideas, visions, truths, and rigorous concepts have been reduced to ideologies and fads, which depend more on slogans and ephemeral appeal than on important, articulated systems.[26] Everywhere, marketing glorifies the consumable and caters to the uneducated and superficial. This is no surprise: mass participation requires a collective with as few distinctive qualities as possible, one that does as little by itself as possible. The creative individual, the mind that accepts fantasy as a viable and major portion of life, simply does not conform to the collective; he or she leads it:

> . . . the archetypal canon is always created and brought to birth by "eccentric" individuals. These are the founders of religions, sects, philosophies, political sciences, ideologies, and spiritual movements, in the security of which the collective man lives without needing to come into contact with the primordial fire of direct revelation, or to experience the throes of creation.[27]

It is one of the functions of society, by definition, to foster uniformity of behavior and thought, and this is the major reason why society and culture are inherently antagonistic. Socialized religion, for example, is not prepared to accept any new prophets, and the established faiths will rise wrathfully and righteously against any "new" systems of belief. Closed systems of religion "have an undoubted tendency to suppress the unconscious in the individual as much as possible, thus paralyzing his fantasy activity."[28] This is because the original fantasy creations of religions have been placed in the category of inviolate fact and have been socialized into the realm of empirical data. Thus, every-Christian has no fantasies; other people have fantasies. Every-Christian's world is rigidly ruled by externals he or she has been taught to accept as actuality. This is why fantasy is inaccessible to the socialized Christian writer. He cannot achieve the Keatsian "negative capability" necessary to respond to, and empathize with, fantasy's often amoral, asocial, and mysterious qualities, especially in its pagan, heroic form.[29] The few exceptions to this—such authors as Charles Williams, C.S. Lewis, and James Blish—clearly are able to write Christian fantasies because their understandings return to religion in its mythic essence rather than in its social form.

Such reliance on the seemingly actual and on rational empiricism creates a hierarchy of values that considers the intellect and science supreme and that, like all established systems, is self-protective and self-perpetuating:

> The intellect remains imprisoned in itself just so long as it does not willingly sacrifice its supremacy by recognizing the value of other aims. It shrinks from the step which takes it out of itself and which denies its universal validity, since from the standpoint of the intellect everything else is *nothing but fantasy*. But what great thing ever came into existence that was not first fantasy? Inasmuch as the intellect rigidly adheres to the absolute aim of science it cuts itself off from the springs of life. For it [the intellect] fantasy is nothing but a wish dream, and herein is expressed all that depreciation of fantasy which for science is so welcome and so necessary.

Most of all, fantasy threatens personal and social complacency through its apparently uncontrollable quality. It is "an irrational, instinctive function"[30] that—like its child, art—leads mankind away from reason to intuition and graphically illuminates all that is shallow, superficial, and conventional in rational or scientific truth.[31] This can be a disquieting and world-shaking experience. James Hillman, the contempory humanistic psychologist, expresses this at length:

> Fantasies are incompatible with my usual ego, and because they are uncontrollable and "fantastic"—that is, away from the relation to ego reality—we feel them alien. We are not embarrassed in the

same way by our will and intelligence; indeed, we proudly exhibit their accomplishments. But what breeds in the imagination we tend to keep apart and to ourselves. Imagination is an inner world—not spatially inside, but kept in, esoteric, the inner aspect of consciousness. These affections and fantasies are the imaginal or unconscious aspect of everything we think and do. This part of the soul that we keep to ourselves is central to analysis, to confession, to prayer, central between lovers and friends, central in the work of art, central to what we mean by "telling the truth," and central to our fate. What we hold close in our imaginal world are [sic] not just images and ideas but living bits of soul; when they are spoken, a bit of soul is carried with them. When we tell our tales, we give away our souls. The shame we feel is less about the content of the fantasy than it is that there is fantasy at all, because the revelation of the imagination is the revelation of the uncontrollable, spontaneous spirit, an immortal, divine part of the soul, the *memoria Dei*. Thus the shame we feel refers to a sacrilege: the revelation of fantasies exposes the divine, which implies that *our fantasies are alien because they are not ours*. They arise from the transpersonal background, from nature or spirit or the divine, even as they become personalized through our lives, moving our personalities into mythic enactments.[32]

Fantasy, like creative mythology, "springs not, like theology, from the dicta of authority, but from the insights, sentiments, thought, and vision of an adequate individual, loyal to his own experience of value."[33] It is infortunate that this loyalty to, and dignity of, self is so distasteful to the modern mind, for fantasy does represent an effort to make sense of areas of experience that "have not been lived through directly to any great extent."[34]

This vicarious experience is, of course, the key to art, and fantasy is the prime progenitor of art, just as fantasy is the inner world of the artist, and artistic manifestation is the outer symbol of fantasy's inner activity. As a symbol, art is not simply a nominalistic representation. Art is, rather, the symbol that "must be understood in an immanent—not in a transcendant sense."[35] It represents a mode of thought that "takes an inside event and puts it outside, at the same time making this content alive, personal, and even divine."[36] Creative fantasy produces symbols of actuality—fantasms that are *idées-forces* and represent the sum of the libido—that "touch and exhilarate centers of life beyond the vocabularies of reason and coercion," and that are products of a mode that recognizes that all realities are "primarily symbolic or metaphorical.[37] Within this mode, the role of the creative artist and fantasist is well described by Joseph Campbell in *The Masks of God: Creative Mythology*:

> Creative artists . . . are mankind's wakeners to recollection: summoners of our outward mind to conscious contact with ourselves, not as participants in this or that morsel of history, but as spirit, in the consciousness of being. Their task, therefore, is to communicate directly from one inward world to another, in such a way that an actual shock of experience will have been rendered: not a mere statement for the information or persuasion of a brain, but an effective communication across the void of space and time from one center of consciousness to another [pp. 92–93].

Fantasy, then, occupies a very elemental place in literary art and art in general. It is, however, incorrect to identify it as a literary genre. Such an edict is far too constrictive. While a number of recent critics have supported the view that fantasy must not be seen as a genre, most notably Eric S. Rabkin in *The Fantastic in Literature* and W.R. Irwin in *The Game of the Impossible*,[38] the initial and definitive statement of fantasy's pervasive quality belongs to E.M. Forster:

> There is more in the novel than time or people or logic or any of their derivatives, more even than fate. And by "more" I do not mean something that excludes these aspects nor something that includes them, embraces them. I mean something that cuts across them like a bar of light, that is intimately connected with them at one place and patiently illumines all the problems, and at another place shoots over or through them as if they did not exist. We shall give that bar of light two names, fantasy and prophecy.[39]

While fantasy can occur as an element in any literary work, regardless of genre, the literature that can be identified as fantasy is that corpus in which the impossible is primary in its quantity or centrality. A fantasy work must present "the persuasive establishment and development of an impossibility, an arbitrary construct of the mind. . . ."[40] Within these limits, fantasy literature, the "clearest expression of the specific activity of psyche,"[41] is what could never have been, cannot be, and can never be within the actual, social, cultural, and intellectual milieu of its creation. The impossibilities of fantasy must be recognized within their social, cultural, and historical context, or there is the danger of turning fantasy literature into a panacea, offering perspectives on, and solutions to, whatever the twentieth-century mind finds unbelievable, regardless of its origins. The creation of fantasy in literature is non-accidental; fantasy does demand an intellectual rejection of the experiential, external world.[42] The criteria for fantasy are not dependent on the sophistication of the individual reader, but on the sophistication of "the culture which a work of art simultaneously reflects and is received by. . . ." If this context were avoided, a modern reader would view the unicorns, dragons, basilisks, and other creatures included in the classical and medieval encyclopedias and bestiaries as products of fantasy rather than as examples of the periods' perceived natural histories. Thus, one of the essential characteristics of fantasy literature is that "it contradicts our experience, not the limited experience we can attain as individuals, but the totality of our knowledge of what our culture regards as real."[43]

Obviously, such a movement away from the experiential world makes a special demand. As an asocial and non-causal mode, fantasy literature compels its readers to make an adjustment that is required by all art:

> For art arises from other and deeper sources [than logical ones]. In order to discover these sources we must first forget our common standards, we must plunge into the mysteries of our unconscious life.[44]

However, the appreciation and apprehension of fantasy require an additional adjustment beyond that of art.[45] This necessary and *a priori* departure from the actual world of data and measurable phenomena has been variously labelled. Samuel Taylor Coleridge called it "the willing suspension of disbelief," a term adopted by T.S. Eliot and one which has gained wide acceptance; J.R.R. Tolkien named it the "literary belief" in "sub-creation"; E.M. Forster, "acceptance"; Tzvetan Todorov, rational "uncertainty" or "hesitation"; and W.R. Irwin, "credence."[46] All of these labels or tags point to a rigorous detachment from the ordinary and to a union with fiction, which Harvey Cox amplifies by saying that "In fantasy, our physical body is left behind and an imaginary body, often differing markedly from the physical one, takes over."[47] Through this shift, fantasy as literature demands that its readers enter into a "complex and dynamic relationship"[48] in which creative inner realities are paradoxically made manifest and the internal is externalized and made visible through art as symbol.[49] In this effort "to make non-fact appear as fact," the "writer and reader knowingly enter upon a conspiracy of intellectual subversiveness. . . ."[50]

The immediate result of the game of "non-fact" that the reader and writer engage in is the evocation of wonder. This wonder may range

> from crude astonishment at the marvellous, to a sense of "meaning-in-the-mysterious" or even the numinous. Wonder is of course generated by fantasy purely from the presence of the supernatural or impossible, and from the element of mystery and lack of explanation that goes with it.

This is a wonder generated by the admiration for the human mind, and fantasy is the animate symbol of the mind's creative function. This is why fantasy literature is distinct from horror literature. Horror inspires "numinous rage"[51] and fear because it maims and distorts creation. Fantasy celebrates creation, and, like romance,

> turns fear at a distance, or terror, into the adventurous; fear at contact, or horror, into the marvellous, and fear without object, or dread (*Angst*), into a pensive melancholy. It turns pity at a distance, or concern, into the theme of chivalrous rescue; pity at contact, or tenderness, into a languid and relaxed charm, and pity

without an object (which has no name but is a kind of animism, or treating everything in nature as though it had human feelings) into creative fantasy.[52]

Often, this wonder is produced through the devices of the supernatural, the numinous, and the mysterious. Paradoxically, fantasy does this in its capacity as a bridge spanning the gap between the known and the unknown. And it is this giving of concrete form to the unknown that gives fantasy a portion of its delightful appeal and its verisimilitude. For while a literature like science fiction always runs the risk of its science and technology becoming obsolete, magic never grows old and acquires "a unique place in a [positivistic] world from which all supernatural forces are excluded."[53] Moreover, the movement away from the actual, be it through the supernatural or through other means, which makes fantasy elemental rather than moral, frequently gives it the form of the mythic psychomachia and allows fantasy to confront the non-effectable and to transcend mundane limitations and causality.

As a result, the fictive setting that fantasy creates "is more than a backdrop; it is integral to the events themselves, a kind of spiritual landscape in which even the least element might carry a moral meaning."[54] This event-oriented, temporarily non-causal fantasy realm, along with fantasy's often picaresque and estranged characters, fantasy shares in common with its intimate mate, myth:

> The world of myth is a dramatic world—a world of actions, of forces, of conflicting powers. In every phenomenon of nature it sees the collision of these powers. Mythical perception is always impregnated with these emotional qualities. Whatever is seen or felt is surrounded by a special atmosphere—an atmosphere of joy or grief, of anguish, of excitement, of exultation or depression. Here we cannot speak of "things" as a dead or indifferent stuff. All objects are benign or malignant, friendly or inimical, familiar or uncanny, alluring and fascinating or repellent and threatening. We can easily reconstruct this elementary form of human experience, for even in the life of the civilized man it has by no means lost its original power.[55]

As extreme in their departure from the actual as the worlds of fantasy may seem in their mythopoetic magnitude, they are not a full denial of, or departure from, the "normal," work-a-day world. Dependent on the empirical and causal expectations of the actual world for its impossibilities, fantasy is also bound by semantics and perspective. A complete fantasy world can no more exist than a purely empirical one could. "Even the wildest and most wanton fantasy" is governed by "inflexible universal laws."[56] In addition, fantasy creation is not quite the 180-degree reversal from the ground rules of everyday which Eric S. Rabkin depicts.[57] Fantasy's laws, even though they are impulsive rather than factual, are often more internally consistent, "conventionalized,"[58] rigorous, and ethical than those of the mundane world, especially when fantasy is allied with the epic and produces heroic or sword & sorcery fantasy. Fantasy must be this way. Without an internally lawful system, it would have no credibility, the willing suspension of disbelief notwithstanding. The lack of internal order would disrupt the intellectual game of the new set of "continuous and coherent" facts that the reader has "willfully and speculatively accepted, against the established facts, which he only pretends to reject."[59] Such lawlessness would destroy the mental play that allows the reader to accept the new world of the fantasy.[60] Thus, just as the involvement in the release of festivity and holiday operates by the lawful reversal of everyday, so too fantasy literature conforms to its own strictures, and the resultant liberation from actuality generates purposeful and joyful play, allowing the reader's mind to seek and explore its own capacities for appreciation.

Fantasy literature, through its rejection of the mundane world, its wonder, and its coherent and liberating new worlds, creates a fantastic duality for the reader. Quality fantasy "may by virtue of the strength and skill with which it is created make us feel simultaneously that it does and does not have reality."[61] The reader is aware that he or she still exists in the world of accepted actuality but, at the same time, ventures into another, impossible place. Within this duality, the reader's mind is free to play upon both the actual and fictive experiences. And while it is not necessary for the existence of the fantasy experience, the fantasy writer "may really hope that his story will have some lasting effect of modifying the way in which his readers accept the norm that he has playfully violated."[62] Robert Scholes calls this possible cognitive return "fabulation" and defines it as "fiction that offers us a world clearly and radically discontinuous from the one we know, yet returns to confront that known world in some cognitive way."[63]

Apart from the great pleasure that fantasy literature bestows upon its reader, this cognitive reflection is its most utilitarian benefit. In the conflict between creation and social, religious, and cultural restrictions, fantasy as thought and art maintains mankind's sense of itself and its capacities, denying the separation from self that must result from purely external determinants of behavior and thought. As C.G. Jung vividly explains:

> It [fantasy] is, pre-eminently, the creative activity from which the answers to all answerable questions come; it is the mother of all possibilities, where, like all psychological opposites, the inner and outer worlds are joined together in living union. Fantasy it was and ever is which fashions the bridge between the irreconcilable claims of subject and object, introversion and extraversion. In fantasy alone both mechanisms are united.[64]

Within the state of enchantment and wonder it creates through its embodiment of psychic unity, fantasy ignores the inconsequential distraction of the immediate and embraces the elemental and the whimsical, rejects the social and the moralistic, and confronts the essential and universal potentialities of art and mind. Since its reality is formed in the mind but bound to the external world, fantasy confronts, materializes, and unifies the paradoxical, the ambiguous, and the non-effectable common to the human condition. As it transcends mundane limitations, it becomes more and more irreducible, frequently promoting growth and enhancing existence, forming an interface with basic historical and human realities.

What would the world be like without fantasy? Since it is such a basic element of humanity, such a question is as difficult to entertain as the reality of our own inevitable deaths. However, J.B. Priestley, in his short story "The Grey Ones," comes very close to stating the consequences of such a world. One character, Mr. Patson, has become aware of a conspiracy by the "Evil Principle" and its minions, the "grey ones," to gain control of mankind. Not knowing that he is talking to one of the grey ones, Priestley's character captures the nature of a world without fantasy:

> "The main object, I gathered from what Firbright said," Mr. Patson replied earnestly, "is to make mankind go the way the social insects went, to turn us into automatic creatures, mass beings without individuality, soulless machines of flesh and blood."
> The Doctor seemed amused, "And why should the Evil Principle want to do that?"
> "To destroy the soul of humanity," said Mr. Patson, without an answering smile. "To eliminate certain states of mind that belong essentially to the Good. To wipe from the face of this earth all wonder, joy, deep feeling, the desire to create, to praise life."[65]

Notes

1. Harvey Cox, *The Feast of Fools: A Theological Essay on Festivity and Fantasy* (Cambridge, MA: Harvard University Press, 1969), p. 11.

2. Erich Neumann, *Depth Psychology and a New Ethic*, trans. Eugene Rolfe (1949; rpt. New York: Harper & Row, 1973), p. 107.

3. Cox, p. 79.

4. James Hillman, *Re-Visioning Psychology* (New York: Harper & Row, 1975), p. xi.

5. C.G. Jung, *The Archetypes and the Collective Unconscious*, 2nd ed., trans. R.F.C. Hull, The Collected Works of C.G. Jung, Vol. 9, pt. I (Princeton: Princeton University Press, 1968), p. 155.

6. Cf. Erich Neumann, *The Great Mother: An Analysis of the Archetype*, 2nd ed., trans. Ralph Manheim (Princeton: Princeton University Press, 1963).

7. Jung, *The Archetypes and the Collective Unconscious*, p. 67.

8. C.G. Jung, *Psychological Types*, trans. H.G. Baynes, rev. R.F.C. Hull, The Collected Works of C.G. Jung, Vol. 6 (Princeton: Princeton University Press, 1971), p. 433.

9. Hillman, *Re-Visioning Psychology*, p. xi.

10. J.R.R. Tolkien, "On Fairy-Stories," in *Essays Presented to Charles Williams*, ed. C.S. Lewis (London: Oxford University Press, 1947; rev. ed. in *The Tolkien Reader*, New York: Ballantine, 1966), p. 47 [74]; George MacDonald, "The Imagination. Its Functions and Its Culture," in *The Imagination and Other Essays* (Boston: Lothrop, [1883], p. 2; Cox, p. 59.

11. Jung, *Psychological Types*, p. 115; C.G. Jung, *Symbols of Transformation: An Analysis of the Prelude to a Case of Schizophrenia*, 2nd ed., trans. R.F.C. Hull, The Collected Works of C.G. Jung, Vol. 5, pt. I (Princeton: Princeton University Press, 1967), p. 29.

12. Northrop Frye, *The Anatomy of Criticism: Four Essays* (Princeton: Princeton University Press, 1971), p. 127.

13. C.S. Lewis, "On Science Fiction," in *Of Other Worlds: Essays and Stories*, ed. Walter Hooper (New York: Harcourt, Brace & World, 1966), p. 70; Robert Scholes and Robert Kellogg, *The Nature of Narrative* (London: Oxford University Press, 1966), p. 14; Cox, p. 12; Joseph Campbell, *The Masks of God: Creative Mythology* (1968; rpt. New York: Penguin, 1976), p. 649.

14. Campbell, pp. 6, 609, 4.

15. Jung, *The Archetypes and the Collective Unconscious*, pp. 66–67; Jung, *Psychological Types*, p. 52; *The Archetypes and the Collective Unconscious*, p. 155.

16. Cox, p. 8.

17. Hillman, *Re-Visioning Psychology*, pp. ix, 154.

18. Ernst Cassirer, *An Essay on Man: An Introduction to a Philosophy of Human Culture* (1944; rpt. New Haven: Yale University Press, 1962), p. 164.

19. Herbert Fingarette, *The Self in Transformation: Psychoanalysis, Philosophy, and the Life of the Spirit* (1963; rpt. New York: Harper & Row, 1965), p. 190.

20. Eric S. Rabkin, "Fantasy Literature: Gut with a Backbone," *The CEA Critic*, 40, No. 2 (January 1978), 6–7.

21. C.G. Jung, "Forward to Wickes: 'Von der inneren Welt des Menschen' " (1953), rpt. in *The Symbolic Life: Miscellaneous Writings*, trans. R.F.C. Hull, The Collected Works of C.G. Jung, Vol. 18 (Princeton: Princeton University Press, 1976), p. 527.

22. Hillman, *Re-Visioning Psychology*, p. 39.

23. Cox, pp. 69, 12.

24. Ursula K. Le Guin, "Why Are Americans Afraid of Dragons?" *P[acific] N[orthwest] L[ibrary] A[ssociation] Quarterly*, Winter 1974, p. 18.

25. Fingarette, p. 189.

26. Hillman, *Re-Visioning Psychology*, p. 119.

27. Erich Neumann, *The Origins and History of the Consciousness*, trans. R.F.C. Hull (1954; rpt. Princeton: Princeton University Press, 1970), p. 376.

28. Jung, *Psychological Types*, p. 53.

29. Charles Moorman, *Kings & Captains: Variations on a Heroic Theme* (Lexington: University Press of Kentucky, 1971), p. 132.

30. Jung, *Psychological Types*, pp. 59, 115.

31. Cassirer, p. 161.

32. James Hillman, *The Myth of Analysis: Three Essays in Archetypal Psychology* (Evanston, IL: Northwestern University Press, 1972), p. 182.

33. Campbell, pp. 6–7.

34. Jerome L. Singer, *The Inner World of Daydreaming* (New York: Harper & Row, 1976), p. 185.

35. Cassirer, p. 157.

36. Hillman, *Re-Visioning Psychology*, p. 12; also discussed by Neumann, *The Origins and History of the Consciousness*, p. 369.

37. Jung, *Psychological Types*, p. 433; Campbell, p. 4; Hillman, *Re-Visioning Psychology*, p. x.

38. Eric S. Rabkin, *The Fantastic in Literature* (Princeton: Princeton University Press, 1976), p. 29; W.R. Irwin, *The Game of the Impossible: A Rhetoric of Fantasy* (Urbana: University of Illinois Press, 1976), pp. 8–9.

39. E.M. Forster, *Aspects of the Novel and Related Writings* (1927; rpt. London: Edward Arnold, 1974), p. 74.

40. Irwin, p. 9.

41. Jung, *Psychological Types*, p. 52.

42. Irwin, p. 60.

43. Rudolf B. Schmerl, "Fantasy as Technique," in *SF: The Other Side of Realism: Essays on Modern Fantasy and Science Fiction*, ed. Thomas D. Clareson (Bowling Green, OH: Bowling Green University Popular Press, 1971), p. 106.

44. Cassirer, pp. 160–161.

45. Forster, p. 75.

46. Tolkien, pp. 36–37 [63–64]; Forster, p. 75; Tzveton Todorov, *The Fantastic: A Structural Approach to a Literary Genre*, trans. Richard Howard (Ithaca, NY: Cornell University Press, 1975), pp. 25, 31; Irwin, p. 66.

47. Cox, p. 73.

48. Irwin, p. 55.

49. Neumann, *The Origins and History of the Consciousness*, p. 369.

50. Irwin, p. 9.

51. C.N. Manlove, *Modern Fantasy: Five Studies* (Cambridge: Cambridge University Press, 1975), pp. 7, 9.

52. Frye, *The Anatomy of Criticism,* p. 37.

53. Julius Kagarlitski, "Realism and Fantasy," in *SF: The Other Side of Realism: Essays on Modern Fantasy and Science Fiction*, ed. Clareson, p. 39.

54. Gary K. Wolfe, "Symbolic Fantasy," *Genre*, 8 (1975), 201.

55. Cassirer, pp. 76–77.

56. C.G. Jung, *Two Essays on Analytical Psychology*, 2nd ed., trans. R.F.C. Hull, The Collected Works of C.G. Jung, Vol. 7 (Princeton: Princeton University Press, 1966), p. 201.

57. Rabkin, *The Fantastic in Literature*, pp. 12, 41.

58. Northrop Frye, *The Secular Scripture: A Study of the Structure of Romance* (Cambridge, MA: Harvard University Press, 1976), p. 36.

59. Irwin, pp. 9, 67.

60. Cassirer, p. 164.

61. Manlove, p. 2.

62. Irwin, p. 183.

63. Robert Scholes, *Structural Fabulation: An Essay on Fiction of the Future*, University of Notre Dame Ward-Phillips Lectures in English Language and Literature, Vol. 7 (Notre Dame and London: University of Notre Dame Press, 1975), p. 29.

64. Jung, *Psychological Types*, p. 52.

65. J.B. Priestley, "The Grey Ones," in *The Other Place and Other Stories of the Same Sort* (Melbourne, London, and Toronto: William Heinemann, 1953); rpt. in *The Unknown*, ed. Marvin Allen Karp (New York: Popular Library, 1965), p. 26.

NOVELS AND COLLECTIONS

EDWIN ABBOTT ABBOTT

1. Square, A., pseud. *Flatland: A Romance of Many Dimensions.* London: Selley, 1884.

    A two-dimensional being ponders the possibility of a one-dimensional realm and attempts to share his knowledge of the three-dimensional "spaceland" with his doubting fellows. The classical mathematical fantasy and a biting satire on women and education.

    Bibliography

2. Watson, George, ed. *The New Cambridge Bibliography of English Literature.* Cambridge: Cambridge University Press, 1969, III (1800-1900), 1611.

RICHARD ADAMS

3. *Shardik.* London: Allen Lane, 1974.

    The principal character, Kelderick, is saved from death by a bear. He believes that the bear is a god, names it Shardik, and adopts it as his totem. Through this and other circumstances, he becomes his people's leader and spends most of the novel as a pawn to political and social forces. Ultimately, he escapes these external pressures and discovers that his metaphysical and religious beliefs are not true perspectives on himself or his society. Instead, he adopts a more successful rational and realistic view in his search for self and truth.

4. *Watership Down.* London: Rex Collings, 1972.

    In this beast epic, a group of rabbits, terrorized by man's impersonal progress and at odds with other groups of their own kind, searches for utopia and their particular joys. Filled with excellent anecdotal and epic digressions as the "rabbit's eye" view lends unusual per-

1

spectives and identifies its own special brands of heroes and villains.

ROBERT ADAMS

The Horseclan Series

5. *Horseclans Odyssey*. In progress.

6. *The Coming of the Horseclans*. New York: Pinnacle, 1975 [paper].

7. *Swords of the Horseclans*. New York: Pinnacle, 1977 [paper].

8. *Revenge of the Horseclans*. Los Angeles: Pinnacle, 1977 [paper].

9. *A Cat of Silvery Hue*. Forthcoming from New American Library.

10. *The Silver Goddess*. Forthcoming from New American Library.

11. *The Patrimony*. Forthcoming.

While not as barbaric as Treece's *The Green Man* (see below), this twenty-seventh century, sword and sorcery series has more than its share of blood and battles. The action centers on the militaristic and political conquests of Milo, an immortal warrior, as the series explores man's attempts to share his world with telepathic animals and to rebuild shattered civilization. Throughout, Milo and his companions are opposed by the machinations of the last vestiges of the scientific community. The characterization of Milo's mistress, Mara, is particularly strong as she comes to terms with her own newly discovered immortality and asserts herself in a violent and masculine world.

A.E., pseud. See GEORGE WILLIAM RUSSELL

BRIAN [WILSON] ALDISS

12. *The Malacia Tapestry*. London: Faber & Faber, 1976.

A highly descriptive and picaresque tale that

is set in the fantastic city, Malacia, where
humans, soothsayers, strange beings, and dino-
saurs roam about amid splendor and squalor.
The novel focuses on the career of an itinerant
actor, Perion de Chirolo; his quest for love,
fame and wealth; and his final confrontation
with a "devil jaw" on his paramour's estate,
the resolution of all his quests. Strongly
reminiscent of the eighteenth-century picaresque novel and the engravings of Hogarth.

Bibliography

13. Aldiss, Margaret. *Item Eighty-Three: Brian W.
Aldiss, 1954-1972.* Oxford: Bocardo Press,
1973 [paper].

KINGSLEY AMIS

14. *The Alteration.* London: Jonathan Cape, 1976.

An alternate history in which the Reformation
did not take place. Martin Luther has been
Pope, and a Machiavellian Pope from Yorkshire
now rules England and most of the world. The
novel focuses on Herbert Anvil, the best boy
soprano in memory, who flees castration (to
preserve his voice) into a world where piety
is rampant and science condemned.

15. *The Green Man.* London: Jonathan Cape, 1969.

Bibliography

16. Gohn, Jack Benoit. *Kingsley Amis: A Checklist.*
Kent, OH: Kent State University Press, 1976.

POUL ANDERSON

17. *The Broken Sword.* New York: Abelard-Schuman, 1954.
Rev. ed. New York: Ballantine, 1971 [paper].

Set in Elfland and its neighboring kingdoms,
this classic fantasy involves a changeling's
attempt to reconcile his humanity with his
training and conditioning as an elf prince.
Valgard the changeling—originally stolen by
Imric, elf earl, and replaced by a necromanti-
cally conceived elf-troll—continually doubts
his own value as he judges himself in relation

to the graceful and magical elves. However,
he does discover his true worth when he must
confront the evil and perverse elf-troll who
replaced him in the human realm.

18. *High Crusade.* New York: Doubleday, 1960.

In this comic, pseudo-historical work, a group
of Medieval knights capture an alien spaceship
in 1345 A.D. Arriving at the center of the
aliens' civilization, they use their force of
arms to conquer the existing order and institute English feudalism throughout the galaxy.

19. *Hrolf Kraki's Saga.* New York: Ballantine, 1973
[paper].

A robust imitation and reconstruction of the
early Norse and Icelandic sagas, set in the mid-
sixth century, A.D. Hrolf Kraki, mentioned in
Beowulf and King of the Geats, and the heroes
of his court--Bjarki, with his magic sword,
Lövi; Svipelag, who slays berserkers; and the
youthful Hjalti, with his magic blade Goldhilt--
are featured in this interlocking series of
brutal adventures.

20. *A Midsummer Tempest.* Garden City, NY: Doubleday,
1974.

Another of Anderson's pseudo-historical novels,
based on the principle that Shakespeare was a
historian recording actual events and personages in his plays. Prince Rupert of the Rhine
battles against Charles I of England, Oberon
and Titania lament the coming of science and
Christianity, Puck sorrows under the "wintry"
faith of Puritanism, Ariel and Caliban continue
their conflict as the aging Caliban searches
for his lost Miranda, and Anderson adds his
patent "creative anachronisms" (e.g., Rupert
avoids a conflict with the Puritans by escaping
on a steam engine) in this stylistic *tour de
force* that captures the content and flavor of
Shakespeare's plays.

21. *Operation Chaos.* Garden City, NY: Doubleday, 1971.

In a realm where magic is an everyday, mundane
reality, a werewolf and a witch meet in the
army during wartime while they are using their
special talents to combat an equally magical

enemy. After the conflict is over, they are mustered out of the special "corps" and marry. Shortly after, they must harrow hell to recover their stolen child. A humorous and ingenious fantasy with a very well-conceived setting that contains such things as "rune keys" to start cars and open locks. Many of the minor characters, particularly the denizens of hell, are delightfully drawn.

22. *Three Hearts and Three Lions*. Garden City, NY: Doubleday, 1961.

One of the better examples of the sword and sorcery sub-genre of fantasy and yet another example of Anderson's affection for pseudo-historical settings. Drawn from Medieval French, Danish, and Authurian legends and using the concepts of the parallel universe and the immortal hero, this is the tale of a 20th-century man who becomes a knight in a Medieval realm; allies himself with a wereswan and a dwarf; and battles a werewolf, a dragon, and the evil Morgan le Fay. Sadly, when his tasks are done, he must return to his own mundane world, leaving behind a legend promising his return. For a comparable work, see Robert A. Heinlein's *Glory Road* (below).

Bibliography

23. "Poul Anderson: Bibliography." *The Magazine of Fantasy and Science Fiction*, April 1971, pp. 56-63.

STELLA BENSON [ANDERSON]
(Mrs. J. C. O'Gorman)

24. Benson, Stella, pseud. *The Awakening: A Fantasy*. San Francisco: J.W. Arrowsmith, 1889 [paper-- not seen]. Rpt. San Francisco: Latern Press, 1925.

25. _____. *Living Alone*. London: Macmillan, 1919.

The quaint tale of a witch with a sentimental weakness for collecting stray animals and beings.

STELLA BENSON [ANDERSON] continued

Bibliography

26. Gawsworth, John, pseud. [Terence Ian Fytton Arm-
strong]. *Ten Contemporaries: Notes Toward
Their Definitive Bibliography*. Second Series.
London: Joiner and Steele, 1933.

ANONYMOUS

27. O. Henry's Ghost, pseud. *My Tussle With the Devil
and Other Stories*. New York: I.M.Y., 1918.

    a. "My Tussle With the Devil"
    b. "The Contest"
    c. "Sleeping"
    d. "Yearning"
    e. "Animals"
    f. "Flowers"
    g. "Jewels"
    h. "Remembrances"
    i. "Munitions"
    j. "Going Home"
    k. "My Hearth"
    l. "The Three H's"
    m. "The Senses"
    n. "Fancies"
    o. "Yesterday--Today"
    p. "Action--Reaction"
    q. "A Vision"

F. ANSTEY, pseud. See THOMAS ANSTEY GUTHRIE

PIERS ANTHONY, pseud. See PIERS ANTHONY DILLINGHAM JACOB

MARTIN [DONISTHORPE] ARMSTRONG

28. *The Fiery Dive and Other Stories*. London: Victor
Gollancz, 1929.

    a. "The Fiery Dive"
    b. "The Widow of Ephesus"
    c. "Portrait of the Misses Harlowe"
    d. "Sombrero"
    e. "In the Wilds"
    f. "Saint Hercules"

MARTIN [DONISTHORPE] ARMSTRONG continued

Bibliography

29. Bristol Public Libraries. *Martin Armstrong: Poet and Novelist: A Bibliography*. Bristol: [Public Libraries, 1937].

30. Mégroz, R.L. *Five Novelist Poets*. London: Joiner and Steele, 1933.

ELEANOR ARNASON

31. *The Sword Smith*. New York: Condor, 1978 [paper].

A light tale concerning a smith who flees the frivolity and tyranny of the King of Eshgorin. Limper the Smith and his companion, a baby dragon named Nargri, endure cannibals, escape a seductive temptress, and are joined by a young girl as Limper tries to find freedom and the mystical truth of his craft.

EDWIN LESTER [LINDEN] ARNOLD

32. *Phra the Phoenician*. 3 vols. London: Chatto & Windus, 1891 [issued in 1890].

33. *The Story of Ulla*. London: Longmans, 1895.

Bibliography

34. Watson, George, ed. *The New Cambridge Bibliography of English Literature*. Cambridge: Cambridge University Press, III (1800-1900), 607-608.

FRANK ATKINS

35. Aubrey, Frank, pseud. *A Queen of Atlantis: A Romance of the Caribbean Sea*. London: Hutchinson, 1899 [issued in 1898?]. Rpt. New York: Arno Press, 1975.

A group of marooned Americans rediscover Atlantis. A woman in the group, Vanina, is identified as the long-awaited queen of Atlantis. The Americans join forces with Vanina's supporters and Monella, a strange godlike figure, to overcome the Karanda and the king, Kara. However, the defeated King Kara bewitches Vanina. Monella, Vanina's boyfriend, and a race of

7

winged elves must again come to the rescue.

36. _____. *The Devil Tree of El Dorado: A Novel.*
London: Hutchinson, 1896. Rpt. New York: Arno
Press, 1978 [not seen].

Although published earlier, this is the sequel
to *A Queen of Atlantis* . . . (see above). The
enigmatic Monella reappears and gathers a group
to rediscover the lost city of El Dorado. In
fact, she leads the group to the Kingdom of
Manoa where she overthrows a tyrannical government and destroys a carnivorous tree. Finally,
it is learned that Monella is the two-thousand-
year-old Queen of Manoa who has returned to
resume her reign.

FRANK AUBREY, pseud. See FRANK ATKINS

MICHAEL AYRTON

37. *Tittivulus or the Verbiage Collector.* London:
Max Reinhardt, 1953.

A satire in which Tittivulus, a minor demon,
is assigned to collect all the negligences,
pomposities, and vanities uttered throughout
the world. His collection is quoted for the
reader's amusement from actual political
speeches, arguments, philosophies, and literary
opinions.

JOHN KENDRICK BANGS
(See also ANONYMOUS ANTHOLOGIES: BARON MUCHAUSEN)

38. *Alice in Blunderland: An Iridescent Dream.* New York:
Doubleday, Page, 1907.

One of the many parodies of Dodgson's *Alice in
Wonderland* (see below).

39. *Over the Plum-Pudding.* New York and London: Harper
& Brothers, 1901.

a. "'Over the Plum-Pudding'"
b. "Bills, M.D."
c. "The Flunking of Watkin's Ghost"
d. "An Unmailed Letter"
e. "The Amalgamated Brotherhood of Spooks"

     f.   "A Glance Ahead"
     g.   "Hans Pumpernickel's Vigil"
     h.   "The Affliction of Baron Humpfelhimmel"
     i.   "The Great Composer"
     j.   "How Fritz Became a Wizard"
     k.   "Rise and Fall of Pope Gregory"
     l.   "The Loss of the 'Gretchen B'"

40. *The Water Ghost and Others.* New York: Harper & Brothers, 1894.

     a.   "The Water Ghost of Harrowby Hall"
     b.   "The Spectre Cook of Bangletop"
     c.   "The Speck on the Lens"
     d.   "A Midnight Visitor"
     e.   "A Quicksilver Cassandra"
     f.   "The Ghost Club"
     g.   "A Psychical Prank"
     h.   "The Literary Remains of Thomas Bragdon"

The Houseboat Books

41. *A House-Boat on the Styx: Being Some Account of the Divers Doings of the Associated Shades.* New York: Harper & Brothers, 1896.

42. *The Pursuit of the House-Boat: Being Some Further Account of the Divers Doings of Associated Shades, Under the Leadership of Sherlock Holmes, Esq.* New York: Harper & Brothers, 1897.

Accounts of the meetings, gossiping, and inter-actions of the ghosts of famous personages as they meet in a club based in a house boat on the river Styx. Characters included, among others in these delightful books, are Baron Muchausen, Charles Darwin, Hamlet, William Shakespeare, Nero, Samuel Johnson, Cicero, Jonah, Napoleon Bonaparte, Diogenes, Christopher Columbus, George Washington, Confucius, Queen Elizabeth, Walter Raleigh, Demosthenes, Cassius, Artemus Ward, Ophelia, Xanthippe, Adam, Homer, Oliver Goldsmith, Robert Burns, Shem, Shylock, Captain Kidd, Sherlock Holmes, and Cassandra.

Bibliography

43. Bangs, Francis H. "John Kendrick Bangs, Humorist of the Nineties." *Yale University Library Gazette*, 7 (January 1933), 53-76.

44. *The Glass Mender and Other Stories*. London: James
    Nisbet, 1910.

    a.   "The Glass Mender"
    b.   "The Blue Rose"
    c.   "The Story of Vox Angelica and Lieblich
          Gedacht"
    d.   "The Vagabond"
    e.   "The Minstrel"
    f.   "The Hunchback, the Pool, and the Magic Ring"
    g.   "The Silver Mountain"
    h.   "The Ring"
    i.   "The Merchant's Daughter"
    j.   "The Cunning Apprentice"
    k.   "Orestes and the Dragon"
    l.   "The Wise Princess"

45. *Half a Minute's Silence*. London: William Heinemann,
    1925.

    a.   "Half a Minute's Silence"
    b.   "Pogrom"
    c.   "The Antichrist"
    d.   "'Dirge in Marriage'"
    e.   "The Governor's Niece"
    f.   "'What is Truth?'"
    g.   "A Police Officer"
    h.   "Russalka"
    i.   "The Flute of Chang Liang"
    j.   "Chun wa"
    k.   "'Habent Sua Fata Libelli'"
    l.   "The Alternative"
    m.   "A Luncheon-Party"
    n.   "The Island"
    o.   "The Shadow of a Midnight"
    p.   "Fête Galante"
    q.   "The Garland"
    r.   "Venus"
    s.   "Dr. Faust's Last Day"
    t.   "The Ikon"
    u.   "The Thief"
    v.   "The Cricket Match"
    w.   "The Man Who Gave Good Advice"
    x.   "The Prodigal Who Came Back Too Late"
    y.   "The Brass Ring"

Bibliography

46. Chaundy, Leslie. *A Bibliography of the First
    Editions of the Works of Maurice Baring*.
    London: Dulac, 1925.

LESLIE BARRINGER

The Neustrian Cycle

47. *Gerfalcon*. New York: Doubleday, Page; London:
    William Heinemann, 1927. Rpt. Van Nuys, CA:
    Newcastle, 1976 [paper].

48. *Joris of the Rock*. London: William Heinemann,
    1928. Rpt. North Hollywood, CA: Newcastle,
    1976 [paper].

49. *Shy Leopardess*. London: Methuen, 1948. Rpt. North
    Hollywood, CA: Newcastle, 1977 [paper].

    Set geographically in Neustria, once a place in
    early medieval, Merovingian France, and set
    chronologically during the 100 Years War in the
    14th and 15th centuries, this trilogy reconstructs
    much of the period with fanciful characters. The
    Neustrian Cycle is most interesting for the over-
    lapping coverage of events among the three vol-
    umes and the variety of narrative perspectives
    that result. In *Gerfalcon*, Raoul, a young baron
    with affections for swordsmanship, music, and
    excessive morality, becomes involved with a
    witches' coven and its leader, Red Anne; recovers
    his title; falls in love; defeats a band of
    robbers; and is besieged in a church tower by
    the rogue and robber Joris of the Rock. Joris,
    along with Red Anne and his illegitimate son,
    Jubal, are the main characters of *Joris of the
    Rock*, which begins earlier and ends later than
    Gerfalcon. It begins with Joris' biography and
    his early murder of a priest and his mother's
    burning as a witch. Before he is slain by his
    son, who doesn't know of their relationship,
    Joris and Red Anne are embroiled in a struggle
    between two aspirants to the throne, Thorismund
    and Conrad. It is most interesting to read the
    siege of Raoul in the tower from the opposing
    point of view. *Shy Leopardess* is the history of
    a young woman, Yolande, who becomes a pawn in
    her uncle's political machinations and is the
    victim of an arranged marriage to her uncle's
    sadistic son, Balthasor. After adventures and
    conflicts, she is saved by two pages, Lionel
    and Diomede, with the help of Raoul of the
    first volume in the cycle, and all combine to
    thwart a plot against the king. Both squires
    become Yolande's lovers, a dilemma Barringer
    resolves with devices that echo Chaucer's
    "Knight's Tale."

50. *Chimera*. New York: Random House, 1972.

Divided into three sections, this novel uses
The Thousand Nights and One Night and the two
Greek myths of Perseus and Bellerophon as its
points of departure. The first section,
"Dunyazadiad," follows *The Thousand Nights and
One Night* as Scheherezade's sister, after whom
the section is titled, sits at the foot of the
bed and listens to her elder sister tell tales
to King Shahryar and watches them make love.
In Barth's version of the ancient tale collection, Scheherezade is an ardent defender of her
sex and needs the help of a literary genie to
continue the tales. She and her sister eventually marry the King and his brother on a
literal razor's edge. Section two, "Perseid,"
focuses on Perseus, a star in the heavens, as
he relates his youthful exploits to Medusa,
another star. His tale is told from the dis-
illusionment of middle age, and the original
myth's content and Perseid's successes are markedly altered by his bitter perspective.
"Bellerophoniad," the third section, continues
Barth's theme of middle-age perspective. Sur-
rounded by loving family and subjects, Bellerophon rules his kingdom in peace. However,
Pegasus can no longer fly, and Bellerophon questions his status as a mythical hero. In an attempt to recover his past, he leaves his Amazon
lover and journeys to discover a drug that will
restore flight to his aged, winged steed. Gaining the drug from Melanippe, an Amazon spy, he
flies to Olympus to receive immortality from the
gods, but he is thwarted and doomed to eternally
relive the story of his life. This conclusion
reflects a major theme of the novel: the effect
of fiction on the nature of life and myth.

Bibliography

51. Walsh, Thomas P., and Cameron Northouse. *John Barth,
Jerzy Kosinski, and Thomas Pynchon: A Reference
Guide*. Boston: G.K. Hall, 1977.

52. Weixlmann, Joseph John. *John Barth: A Descriptive
Primary and Secondary Bibliography, Including a
Descriptive Catalog of Manuscript Holdings in
United States Libraries*. New York: Garland,
1976.

H[ERBERT] E[RNEST] BATES

53. *The Seekers*. London: John and Edward Bumpus, 1926.

54. *Seven Tales and Alexander*. London: Scholartis Press, 1929.

      a.   "Alexander"
      b.   "The Barber"
      c.   "The Child"
      d.   "A Comic Actor"
      e.   "The Peach Tree: A Fantasy"
      f.   "A Tinker's Donkey"
      g.   "The King Who Lived on Air: A Child's Tale"
      h.   "Lanko's White Mare"

Bibliography

55. [Armstrong, Terence Ian Fytton]. Gawsworth, John, pseud. *Ten Contemporaries: Notes Toward Their Definitive Bibliography*. London: Joiner and Steele, 1933.

L[YMAN] FRANK BAUM

56. *The Purple Dragon and Other Fantasies*. Lakemont, GA: Fictioneer Books, 1976.

A collection of the shorter fantasies, published from 1892 to 1905.

      a.   "The King's Head and the Purple Dragon"
      b.   "The Ruby Casket"
      c.   "The Wicked Wizard and the Princess Truella"
      d.   "Prince Fiddlecumdoo and the Giant"
      e.   "Old King Cole"
      f.   "The Wondrous Wise Man"
      g.   "Three Wise Men of Gotham"
      h.   "The Glass Dog"
      i.   "The Queen of Quok"
      j.   "The Magic Bonbons"
      k.   "The Dummy That Lived"
      l.   "The King Who Changed His Mind"
      m.   "The Forest Oracle"
      n.   "The Transformation of Bayal the Porcupine"
      o.   "The Enchanted Buffalo"

The Oz Series

57. *The Wonderful Wizard of Oz*. Chicago and New York: Geo M. Hill, 1900 [later reprinted, without change, as a "revised edition" as *The New Wizard of Oz*. Indianapolis: Bobbs-Merrill, 1903].

58. *The Marvelous Land of Oz*. Chicago: Reilly & Britton, 1904.

59. *Ozma of Oz*. Chicago: Reilly & Britton, 1907.

60. *Dorothy and the Wizard of Oz*. Chicago: Reilly & Britton, 1908.

61. *The Road to Oz*. Chicago: Reilly & Britton, 1909.

62. *The Emerald City of Oz*. Chicago: Reilly & Britton, 1910.

63. *The Patchwork Girl of Oz*. Chicago: Reilly & Britton, 1913.

64. *Tik-Tok of Oz*. Chicago: Reilly & Britton, 1914.

65. *The Scarecrow of Oz*. Chicago: Reilly & Britton, 1915.

66. *Rinkitink in Oz*. Chicago: Reilly & Britton, 1916.

67. *The Lost Princess of Oz*. Chicago: Reilly & Britton, 1917.

68. *The Tin Woodman of Oz*. Chicago: Reilly & Britton, 1918.

69. *The Magic of Oz*. Chicago: Reilly & Britton, 1919.

70. *Glinda of Oz*. Chicago: Reilly & Britton, 1920.

> Strictly, Baum's Oz books should not appear in a volume devoted to adult fantasy, as this one is. They are clearly juvenile. However, as America's first major fantasy writer, Baum's influence on and contribution to the development of contemporary fantasy cannot be slighted. His works and Judy Garland's rendition have made the Oz adventures an American fixture that has done much for the acceptance of fantasy literature and cinema in this country. Partial evidence of this is the number of authors, fully cited in Peter F. Hanff and Douglas G. Greene's *Bibliographia Oziana* . . . (see below), who continued the Oz books: Ruth Plumly Thompson, John R. Neill, Jack Snow, Rachel R. Cosgrove, Eloise Jarvis McGraw and Lauren McGraw Miller, W.W. Denslow, and Frank [Joslyn] Baum.

Bibliography

71. Gardner, Martin, and Russel B. Nye. *The Wizard of Oz and Who He Was*. East Lansing: Michigan State University Press, 1957.

72. Hanff, Peter E., and Douglas G. Greene. *Bibliographia Oziana: A Concise Bibliographical Checklist of the Oz Books by L. Frank Baum and His Successors: Founded on and Continuing the "Baum Bugle Checklist" by Dick Martin, James E. Haff, and David L. Greene*. [Demorest, GA]: International Wizard of Oz Club, 1976 [paper].

PETER S[OYER] BEAGLE

73. *The Fantasy Worlds of Peter Beagle*. New York: Viking, 1978.

    a.   *A Fine and Private Place*
    b.   *The Last Unicorn*
    c.   "Lila the Werewolf"
    d.   "Come, Lady Death"

74. *A Fine and Private Place*. New York: Viking, 1960.

An unusual variation on the theme of eternal love in which the barrier between life and death vanishes in a Bronx cemetery. A special comic role is played by a world-wise and caustic raven.

75. *The Last Unicorn*. New York: Viking, 1968.

The poignant quest of the last unicorn for her ensorcered fellows that is filled with wonder, magic, and emotion. The characterization of the unicorn's companions--Molly Grue and Schmendrick the magician--is particularly noteworthy.

76. *Lila the Werewolf*. Capra Chapbook Series, No. 17. Santa Barbara, CA: Capra, 1974.

A young liberal tries to maintain a tolerant position when he discovers that the young girl he is living with is a werewolf. Frequently anthologized; see the title index.

PETER S[OYER] BEAGLE continued

Bibliography

77. Bruccoli, Mathew J., and C.E. Frazer Clark, eds.
    First Printings of American Authors: Contribu-
    tions Toward Definitive Checklists. Detroit:
    Gale Research, 1978, II, 33.

HENRY N. BEARD AND DOUGLAS C. KENNEY

78. *Bored of the Rings: A Parody of J.R.R. Tolkien's*
    The Lord of the Rings. New York: New American
    Library, 1969 [paper].

    The *Harvard Lampoon*'s parody of J.R.R. Tolkien's
    classic trilogy (see below), featuring such
    characters as Frito the Boggie, Dildo Bugger,
    Goodgulf the Wizard, Sorhed with his dread
    Narcs, Spam the faithful, and Arrowroot the
    King. Not for those who take their fantasy too
    seriously.

CHARLES BEAUMONT

79. *The Hunger and Other Stories*. New York: G.P.
    Putnam's Sons, 1957.

        a.   "Miss Gentilbelle"
        b.   "The Vanishing American"
        c.   "A Point of Honor"
        d.   "Fair Lady"
        e.   "Free Dirt"
        f.   "Open House"
        g.   "The Train"
        h.   "The Dark Music"
        i.   "The Customers"
        j.   "Last Night the Rain"
        k.   "The Crooked Man"
        l.   "Nursery Rhyme"
        m.   "The Murderers"
        n.   "The Hunger"
        o.   "Tears of the Madonna"
        p.   "The Infernal Bouillabaisse"
        q.   "Black Country"

L[ILLY MORESBY] ADAMS BECK

80. *The Ninth Vibration and Other Stories*. New York:
    Dodd, Mead, 1922.

a. "The Ninth Vibration"
b. "The Interpreter: A Romance of the East"
c. "The Incomparable Lady: A Story of China
   With a Moral"
d. "The Hatred of the Queen: A Story of Burma"
e. "Fire of Beauty"
f. "The Building of the Taj Mahal"
g. "How Great is the Glory of Kwannon!"
h. "The Round-Faced Beauty"

81. *The Perfume of the Rainbow and Other Stories.* New
    York: Dodd, Mead, 1923.

a. "The Man and the Lesser Gods"
b. "Juana"
c. "The Courtesan of Vaisali"
d. "The Flute of Krishna"
e. "The Emperor and the Silk Goddess"
f. "The Loveliest Lady of China"
g. "The Ghost Plays of Japan"
h. "The Marvels of Xanadu"
i. "From the Ape to the Buddha"
j. "The Sorrow of the Queen"
k. "The Perfect One"
l. "The Way of Attainment"
m. "The Day Book of a Court Lady of Old Japan"
n. "The Courtesan Princess"
o. "The Happy Solitudes"
p. "The Desolate City"

WILLIAM BECKFORD

82. *An Arabian Tale from an Unpublished Manuscript
    with Notes Critical and Explanatory* [later
    titles: *The House of the Caliph Vathek* and
    Vathek]. London: J. Johnson, 1786.

    Vathek, a caliph, commits the sin of excessive
    pride, *superbia*, and seeks wealth in the sub-
    terranean fire. His sin causes him to be sum-
    moned by Elbis, the fire god, and Vathek is
    condemned to have his heart eternally enshroud-
    ed in flame. Originally published in French.

Bibliography

83. Chapman, Guy, and J. Hodgkin. *A Bibliography of
    William Beckford of Fonthill.* London: Con-
    stable, 1930.

84. Gennett, Robert. "An Annotated Checklist of the Works of William Beckford." *Papers of the Bibliographic Society of America*, 61 (1967), 243-258.

85. Graham, Kenneth W. "*Vathek* in English and French." *Studies in Bibliography*, 28 (1975), 153-166.

[SIR HENRY] MAX[IMILLIAN] BEERBOHM

86. *The Dreadful Dragon of Hay Hill*. London: William Heinemann, 1928.

    A comic and farcical fantasy in which a dragon is revived, slain, and impersonated. This work also has strong elements of the didactic fable as it shows mankind's basic antagonistic nature.

87. *The Happy Hypocrite: A Fairy Tale for Tired Men*. Bodley Booklets, No. 1. New York and London: John Lane, The Bodley Head, 1897 [paper].

    A mock fairy tale that illustrates the belief that if someone adopts the appearance or seeming of goodness, the pose can lead to inner goodness.

88. *More*. London: John Lane, The Bodley Head; New York: John Lane, 1907.

    a. "Some Words on Royalty"
    b. "Punch"
    c. "Actors"
    d. "Madame Tussaud's"
    e. "Groups of Myrmidons"
    f. "Pretending"
    g. "An Infamous Brigade"
    h. "The Sea-Side in Winter"
    i. "If I Were Ædile"
    j. "Sign-Boards"
    k. "Ouida"
    l. "The Blight on the Music Halls"
    m. "Prangley Valley"
    n. "Arise, Sir — — !"
    o. "Fashion and Her Bicycle"
    p. "Going Back to School"
    q. "'A. B.'"
    r. "A Cloud of Pinafores"
    s. "At Covent Garden"
    t. "The Case of Prometheus"

89. *Zuleika Dobson or An Oxford Love Story*. London:
     William Heinemann, 1911.

     In this tale of the preposterous, the most
     beautiful woman in the world (so beautiful sta-
     tues sweat when she passes) comes to Oxford
     where she entrances all the undergraduates to
     such an extent that they all drown themselves
     for her at the conclusion of the crew races.

     Bibliography

90. Gallatin, A.E., and L.M. Oliver. *A Bibliography
     of the Works of Max Beerbohm*. London: Rupert
     Hart-Davis, 1952.

91. Riewald, J.G. *Sir Max Beerbohm: Man and Writer.
     A Critical Analysis with a Brief Life and a
     Bibliography*. Brattleboro, VT: Stephen Greene
     Press, 1952.

                    JOHN BELLAIRS

92. *The Face in the Frost*. London: Macmillan, 1969.

     Roger Bacon and Prospero seek to ward off evil
     and protect the original spell that bound the
     four elements and which maintains order in the
     world. Set in the 20th century and suitable
     for juveniles.

                 STEPHEN VINCENT BENÉT

93. *The Devil and Daniel Webster*. Weston, VT:
     Countryman Press, 1937.

     The classic tale of how Daniel Webster outwitted
     the Devil.

94. *Thirteen O'Clock: Stories of Several Worlds*. New
     York and Toronto: Farrar & Rinehart, [1937].

          a.   "By the Waters of Babylon"
          b.   "The Blood of the Martyrs"
          c.   "The King of the Cats"
          d.   "A Story by Angela Poe"
          e.   "The Treasure of Vasco Gomez"
          f.   "The Curfew Tolls"
          g.   "The Sobbin' Women"
          h.   "The Devil and Daniel Webster"

                         19

STEPHEN VINCENT BENÉT continued

      i.   "Daniel Webster and the Sea Serpent"
      j.   "Glamour"
      k.   "Everybody Was Very Nice"
      l.   "A Death in the Country"
      m.   "Blossom and Fruit"

Bibliography

95. Maddocks, Gladys Louise. "Stephen Vincent Benét: A Bibliography." *Bulletin of Bibliography*, 20 (September-December 1951), 142-146; 20 (January-April 1952), 158-160.

GERTRUDE BARROWS BENNETT

96. Stevens, Francis, pseud. *The Citadel of Fear*. New York: Paperback Library, 1970 [paper] [not seen].

Originally published in *Argosy*, September 14-October 19, 1918.

97. _____. *Claimed*. New York: Avalon, 1966.

98. _____. *The Heads of Cerberus*. Reading, PA: Polaris Press, 1952 [probably written in 1917]. Rpt. New York: Arno Press, 1978 [not seen].

Andrew Powers is transported by the "Dust of Purgatory" through "Ulithia and the Gateway of the Moon" into the realm of Ulithia with its wraith-like riders, moon gate, ritual dancers, and goddess--the white Weaver. He is then transported to a twenty-second century Philadelphia, which is drastically transformed into a religious dictatorship by the great god Penn. After rebelling against the tyranny, Powers and his fellows are returned to their original and normal world.

PIERRE BENOIT

99. *L'Atlantide*. Paris: Albin Michel, 1919.

A well-written imitation of H. Rider Haggard's *She* (see below).

STELLA BENSON, pseud. See STELLA BENSON ANDERSON

MICHEL BERNANOS

100. *The Other Side of the Mountain*. Trans. Elaine P.
Halperin. New York: Dell, 1970 [paper]. Originally published as *La Montagne morte de la
vie*. Paris: Jean-Jacques Pauvert, 1967 [not
seen].

A macabre work, this short novel begins with
what seems to be a straight-forward account of
a nineteenth-century shanghai. However, after
the ship is becalmed and its crew become drunk-
en cannibals, the young protagonist and his
protector, the cook, finally gain what they
think is salvation on a blood-red island.
After journeying for many days and undergoing
great privation, they come to a mountain, de-
corated with the alarmingly life-like human
statues they have observed throughout their
travels. The existential ending marks the cul-
mination of a physiological change both men have
been only vaguely noticing amid their thirst and
hunger: they turn to stone and become part of
the mountain.

WALTER BESANT AND JAMES RICE

101. *The Case of Mr. Lucraft and Other Tales*. Library
ed. New York: Dodd, Mead, [1888]. [An 1886,
2 vol., London edition has been cited in other
bibliographies.]

a. "The Case of Mr. Lucraft"
b. "The Mystery of Joe Morgan"
c. "An Old, Old Story"
d. "Lady Kitty"
e. "The Old Four-Poster"
f. "My Own Experience"
g. "Titania's Farewell"

Plus five pieces of non-fiction.

DAVID BISCHOFF

102. *Nightworld*. New York: Ballantine, 1979 [paper].

Like Christopher Stasheff's Gramarye series
(see below) and Poul Anderson's "The Queen of
Air and Darkness," this is an example of the
use of fantasy devices in the science-fiction
genre. A young noble accompanies a mandroid,
a being made in the image of H.G. Wells by a

fallen galactic empire, to overthrow Satan and
his night creatures on a forgotten and backward
planet called Styx. Actually Satan is the old
governor of the planet, gone quite mad after he
engineered the construction of the planet's
imitation of Victorian England for the pleasure
of the galaxy's ruling classes. Satan creates
vampires, werewolves, dragons, griffins, demons,
and various other creatures with the help of
the planet's computer and terrorizes the degen-
erated population. He is finally defeated by
the 500-year-old Wells, his young companion, and
a spoiled daughter of the new galactic empire.

ODD BJERKE AND MEREDITH MOTSON

103. *The Search for Trollhaven*. Boise, ID: Beatty
Book, 1977 [paper].

A charming and delightful juvenile, well illustrated by Marvin Wood, that chronicles in prose
and poetry the Trolls' search for an utopia
they have seen in a dream. Following a voice
borne on the west wind, they are aided and delayed by the creatures of the desolate Arctic
as they seek their dream.

CHRISTOPHER BLAYRE, pseud. See EDWARD HERON-ALLEN

JAMES BLISH

The After Such Knowledge Tetralogy

104. *Doctor Mirabilis*. New York: Dodd, Mead, 1971.

105. *Black Easter or Faust Aleph-Null*. Garden City,
NY: Doubleday, 1968.

106. *The Day After Judgment*. Garden City, NY: Doubleday, 1971.

107. *A Case of Conscience*. New York: Ballantine, 1958
[paper].

In the "Afterword" to *The Day After Judgment*,
Blish points to a speech in the novel which
explains the rationale of his loosely connected
tetralogy: "'maybe,' Baines said, 'A large part
of the mystic tradition says that the possession

and use of secular knowledge--or even the desire for it--is in itself evil ..." (p. 103).
Within this philosophic premise, the series
operates within a wide variety of settings and
circumstances. *Dr. Mirabilis* is a fictional
biography of Roger Bacon that is a vivid portrait of thirteenth-century attitudes and beliefs. *Black Easter* focuses on the activities
of a master sorcerer and his client, a mater-
ialistic industrialist. Together, they con-
spire to release a number of devils and demons
upon the world and, as a result, bring about
Armageddon. In *The Day After Judgment*, the
direct sequel to *Black Easter*, the world has
ended and the remnants of mankind and its
armies struggle against Satan and his minions
as the city of Dis comes to earth. In *A Case
of Conscience*, a space-faring Jesuit priest
must decide if an alien race is totally good or
totally evil since it appears that the aliens
have avoided original sin.

Bibliography

108. Owings, Mark. "James Blish: Bibliography."
Magazine of Fantasy and Science Fiction, April
1972, pp. 78-83.

ROBERT BLOCH

109. *Dragons and Nightmares: Four Short Novels.* Baltimore: Mirage Press, 1968.

A collection of humorous and fantastic tales of
necromancy that combine the everyday with
fantasy:

a.   "A Good Knight's Work"
b.   "The Eager Dragon"
c.   "'Nursemaid to Nightmares' including
'Black Barter'"

Bibliography

110. Hall, Graham. *Robert Bloch Bibliography*. Tewkes-
bury, Gloucestershire: Graham M. Hall, 1965
[paper].

HANNES BOK*
See also A[BRAHAM] MERRITT AND HANNES BOK

111.   *The Blue Pagoda*. New York: New Collectors' Group,
       1946. A completion of and bound with A.
       Merritt's *The Fox Woman*. See the A. MERRITT
       entry for the annotation.

112.   *The Sorcerer's Ship*. New York: Ballantine, 1969
       [paper].

       Highly indebted to A. Merritt's *Ship of Ishtar*
       (see below), although not as effective in tech-
       nique or plot. Nonetheless, this is a good
       illustration of the use of alternate worlds in
       fantasy literature. The characterization of
       the fish creature wizard, Yanuk, and the god,
       Orcher, are intriguing. Unfortunately, the
       conception of the romance between Gene, the
       twentieth-century transposed man, and Siwara,
       the princess, is pedestrian and overly stylized.
       This tale was originally published in *Unknown
       Worlds* in 1942. Bok's other novel, *Beyond the
       Golden Stair*, first published in Lin Carter and
       Ballantine Books' Adult Fantasy Series in 1970,
       is an example of the combination of lost-race
       literature and science fiction.

   *N.B. Stuart W. Wells III, in his *The Science
       Fiction and Heroic Fantasy Author Index* (Duluth,
       MN: Purple Unicorn Books, 1978), cites Hannes
       Bok as a pseudonym for Wayne Woodward, a conten-
       tion that I have been unable to verify.

ANTHONY BOUCHER, pseud. See WILLIAM ANTHONY PARKER WHITE

ELIZABETH [DOROTHRA COLE] BOWEN
(Mrs. A.C. Cameron)

113.   *The Dream Lover and Other Stories*. London:
       Jonathan Cape, 1945.

       a.   "In the Square"
       b.   "Sunday Afternoon"
       c.   "The Inherited Clock"
       d.   "The Cheery Soul"
       e.   "Songs My Father Sang to Me"
       f.   "The Demon Lover"
       g.   "Careless Talk"
       h.   "The Happy Autumn Fields"
       i.   "Ivy Gripped the Steps"
       j.   "Pink May"

ELIZABETH [DOROTHRA COLE] BOWEN continued

      k.   "Green Holly"
      l.   "Mysterious Kôr"

    Bibliography

114. Heath, William Webster. *Elizabeth Bowen: An Introduction to Her Novels*. Madison, WI: University of Wisconsin Press, 1961, pp. 170-3.

115. Sellery, J'nan. "Elizabeth Bowen: A Check List." *Bulletin of the New York Public Library*, 74 (1970), 219-274.

              MARJORIE BOWEN, pseud.
   See GABRIELLE MARGARET VERE [CAMPBELL] LONG

  EDWARD P. BRADBURY, pseud. See MICHAEL MOORCOCK

        RAY[MOND DOUGLAS] BRADBURY

116. *Dark Carnival*. Sauk City, WI: Arkham House, 1947.

      a.   "The Homecoming"
      b.   "Skeleton"*
      c.   "The Jar"*
      d.   "The Lake"*
      e.   "The Maiden"
      f.   "The Tombstone"
      g.   "The Smiling People"
      h.   "The Emissary"*
      i.   "The Traveler"
      j.   "The Small Assassin"*
      k.   "The Crowd"*
      l.   "Reunion"
      m.   "The Handler"
      n.   "The Coffin"
      o.   "Interim"
      p.   "Jack-in-the-Box"*
      q.   "The Scythe"*
      r.   "Let's Play 'Poison'"
      s.   "Uncle Einar"*
      t.   "The Wind"*
      u.   "The Night"
      v.   "There Was an Old Woman"*
      w.   "The Dead Man"
      x.   "The Man Upstairs"*
      y.   "The Night Sets"
      z.   "Cistern"*
      aa. "The Next in Line"*

RAY[MOND DOUGLAS] BRADBURY continued

*For revisions of these short stories, see *The October Country* below.

117. *Dark Carnival*. London: Hamish Hamilton, 1948.

The first British edition that omits the following stories that were included in the first and American edition above:

a. "The Maiden"
b. "Reunion"
c. "The Coffin"
d. "Interim"

118. *The Day It Rained Forever*. London: Rupert Hart-Davis, 1959.

Supposedly a reprint of *A Medicine for Melancholy* (see below), but this edition adds and omits a number of short stories and changes one title:

Additions:
a. "Referent"
b. "Almost the End of the World"
c. "Perchance to Dream"
d. "And the Rock Cried Out"

Omissions:
e. "The First Night of Lent"
f. "All Summer in a Day"
g. "The Great Collision of Monday Last"

Title Change:
h. "The Shore Line at Sunset" is called "The Sunset Harp" in this collection.

119. *The Golden Apples of the Sun*. Garden City, NY: Doubleday, 1953.

a. "The Fog Horn"
b. "The Pedestrian"
c. "The April Witch"
d. "The Wilderness"
e. "The Fruit at the Bottom of the Bowl"
f. "Invisible Boy"
g. "The Flying Machine"
h. "The Murderer"
i. "The Golden Kite, the Silver Wind"
j. "I See You Never"
k. "Embroidery"
l. "The Big Black and White Game"

    m.   "A Sound of Thunder"
    n.   "The Great Wide World Over There"
    o.   "Powerhouse"
    p.   "En la Noche"
    q.   "Sun and Shadow"
    r.   "The Meadow"
    s.   "The Garbage Collector"
    t.   "The Great Fire"
    u.   "Hail and Farewell"
    v.   "The Golden Apples of the Sun"

According to Nolan's Bradbury bibliography (see below), the British first edition (London: Rupert Hart-Davis, 1953) is slightly abridged.

120.   *The Illustrated Man*. Garden City, NY: Doubleday, 1951.

    a.   "Prologue: The Illustrated Man"
    b.   "The Veldt"
    c.   "Kaleidoscope"
    d.   "The Other Foot"
    e.   "The Highway"
    f.   "The Man"
    g.   "The Long Rain"
    h.   "The Rocket Man"*
    i.   "The Fire Balloons"*
    j.   "The Last Night of the World"
    k.   "The Exiles"*
    l.   "No Particular Night or Morning"
    m.   "The Fox and the Forest"
    n.   "The Visitor"
    o.   "The Concrete Mixer"*
    p.   "Marionettes, Inc."
    q.   "The City"
    r.   "Zero Hour"
    s.   "The Rocket"
    t.   "Epilogue"

The British edition (London: Rupert Hart-Davis, 1952) omits the stories that are asterisked above and adds one story:

    u.   "Usher II"

121.   *The Martian Chronicles*. Garden City, NY: Doubleday, 1950 [British title: *The Silver Locusts*. See below].

    a.   "January 1999: Rocket Summer"
    b.   "February 1999: Ylla"
    c.   "August 1999: The Summer Night"

    d. "August 1999: The Earth Men"
    e. "March 2000: The Tax Payer"
    f. "June 2001: — And the Moon Be Still as Bright"
    g. "August 2001: The Settlers"
    h. "December 2001: The Green Morning"
    i. "February 2002: The Locusts"
    j. "August 2002: Night Meeting"
    k. "October 2002: The Shore"
    l. "February 2003: Interim"
    m. "April 2003: Way in the Middle of the Air"
    n. "2004-2005: The Naming of Names"
    o. "April 2005: Usher II"
    p. "August 2005: The Old Ones"
    q. "September 2005: The Martian"
    r. "November 2005: The Luggage Shore"
    s. "November 2005: The Off Season"
    t. "November 2005: The Watchers"
    u. "December 2005: The Silent Towns"
    v. "April 2026: The Long Years"
    w. "August 2026: There Will Come Soft Rains"
    x. "October 2026: The Million-Year Picnic"

122. *A Medicine for Melancholy*. Garden City, NY: Doubleday, 1959 [See the revised and altered British edition — *The Day It Rained Forever* — above].

    a. "In a Season of Calm Weather"
    b. "The Dragon"
    c. "A Medicine for Melancholy"
    d. "The End of the Beginning"
    e. "The Wonderful Ice Cream Suit"
    f. "Fever Dream"
    g. "The Marriage Mender"
    h. "The Town Where No One Got Off"
    i. "A Scent of Sarsaparilla"
    j. "Icarus Montgolfier Wright"
    k. "The Headpiece"
    l. "Dark They Were, and Golden-eyed"
    m. "The Smile"
    n. "The First Night of Lent"
    o. "The Time of Going Away"
    p. "All Summer in a Day"
    q. "The Gift"
    r. "The Great Collision of Monday Last"
    s. "The Little Mice"
    t. "The Shore Line at Sunset"
    u. "The Strawberry Window"
    v. "The Day It Rained Forever"

RAY[MOND DOUGLAS] BRADBURY continued

123. *The October Country*. New York: Ballantine, 1955.

>   Revisions of selected short stories from *Dark Carnival* (as asterisked above) plus five additional titles:
>
>   a.   "The Dwarf"
>   b.   "The Watchful Poker Chip of H. Matisse"
>   c.   "Touched with Fire"
>   d.   "Homecoming"
>   e.   "The Wonderful Death of Dudley Stone"

124. *The Silver Locusts*. London: Rupert Hart-Davis, 1951. [First and American edition: *The Martian Chronicles*. See above.]

>   This British first edition adds stories and omits others that were in *The Martian Chronicles*:
>
>   Additions:
>   a.   "April 2000: The Third Expedition"
>   b.   "November 2002: The Fire Balloons"
>   c.   "April 2003: The Musicians"
>
>   Omissions:
>   d.   "April 2003: Way in the Middle of the Air"
>   e.   "April 2005: Usher II"

125. *Something Wicked This Way Comes*. New York: Simon and Schuster, 1962.

>   In this tale, two boys encounter a strange, macabre, traveling carnival that has appeared every October for at least one hundred years. The carnival affects the boys and the people around it in peculiar and unusual ways as Mr. Dark weaves his spell of evil amid lightning rods and shape changing.

Bibliography

126. Nolan, William F. *The Ray Bradbury Companion: A Life and Career History, Photolog, and Comprehensive Checklist of Writings with Facsimiles from Ray Bradbury's Unpublished and Uncollected Work in All Media*. Detroit: Gale Research, 1975.

J.S. BRADFORD

127. *Even A Worm*. London: Arthur Barker, 1936.

>   The animal kingdom unites to fight its common

enemy, Man, and freely sacrifices individuals
to the greater good of the many species.

ERNEST BRAMAH, pseud. See ERNEST BRAMAH SMITH

E[DITH] NESBIT [BRAND]

128. Nesbit, E., pseud. *The Story of the Amulet*.
      London: T. Fisher Unwin, 1906.

      Although Edith Nesbit Brand's books are clearly
      juveniles, she does appear to have a following
      among adults. In this novel, the sequel to
      Five Children and It (1902), five children are
      again allied with the lovable and irascible
      Sand Fairy, Psammead, and travel through time
      to ancient Egypt and Babylon to complete a magic
      amulet. Other juvenile titles are listed below
      without annotation.

129. _____. *Five Children and It*. London: T. Fisher
      Unwin, 1902.

130. _____. *Harding's Luck*. London: Hodder & Stough-
      ton, 1909.

131. _____. *The House of Arden: A Story for Children*.
      London: T. Fisher Unwin, 1908.

132. _____. *The Magic City*. London: Macmillan, 1910.

133. _____. *The Phoenix and the Carpet*. London:
      George Newnes, 1904.

MARY CHAVELITA CLAIRMONTE BRIGHT

134. Egerton, George, pseud. *Fantasias*. London and
      New York: John Lane: Bodley Head, 1898.

      a. "The Star-Worshiper"
      b. "The Elusive Melody"
      c. "The Mandrake Venus"
      d. "The Futile Quest"
      e. "The Kingdom of Dreams"
      f. "The Well of Truth"

Bibliography

135. Gawsworth, John, pseud. [Terence Ian Fytton Arm-
        strong]. *Ten Contemporaries: Notes Toward
        Their Definitive Bibliography*. London: E.
        Benn, 1932.

DAMIEN BRODERICK

136. *Sorcerer's World*. New York: Signet, 1970 [paper].

> A hero is transported to a parallel world as a
> side effect of an experiment conducted by three
> super beings attempting to transform and revive
> Earth in the far distant future. He becomes
> their tool. Pretty average stuff.

TERRY BROOKS

137. *The Sword of Shannara*. New York: Ballantine;
        New York: Random House, 1977.

> A disappointing post-holocaust, Tolkien-like
> tale of the quest for a magical sword by a
> company of heroes amid a struggle between the
> dark powers and the elves.

JEAN BRULLER

138. Vercors, pseud. *Sylva*. Paris: Bernard Grasset,
        1961 [paper].

> A fox, fleeing from the hunt, is transformed
> into a woman. As the fox, Sylva, becomes more
> human, another woman, Dorothy, becomes less and
> less human as a result of drug addiction. Thus,
> this novel is an examination of the validity of
> humanity regardless of shape and the nature of
> the distinction between man and animal.

JOHN BRUNNER

139. *The Devil's Work*. New York: W.W. Norton, 1970.

> A haunting, poignant novel, written partially
> in the stream of consciousness, in which a young
> English boy is seduced by the devil and a
> succuba. Stephen, suffering the death of his

elegant mother and the crudity of his father,
comes to a small town after graduating high
school. Confused about his future and yearning
for the graciousness of his mother, he is easy
prey for the devil's material inducements. A
noteworthy feature is Brunner's fun with the
names of the characters: the devil is Mr. Some-
body; the succuba, Moira Morgan; Stephen's
father's crude housekeeper-mistress, Mrs. Lowe;
the effeminate curate, Jimmy Lavender; the avar-
icious parson, Mr. Unthank; the town tough,
Jack Wildspin; and the ripe, young protagonist,
Stephen Green.

140. *Father of Lies*. New York: Belmont, 1968 [paper].
Bound with Bruce Duncan's *Mirror Magic*.

An emotionally crippled child uses mind power to
create an Arthurian realm complete with dragons,
knights, and maidens. He rules it with a dement-
ed hand until he is outwitted.

141. *Times Without Number*. New York: Ace, 1969 [paper].

While this appears to be a typical, science-
fiction, time-paradox adventure, in actuality
its setting is in an unreal time frame that has
never existed, one in which the Spanish Armada
was victorious and the Catholic Church has re-
mained a major political power. However, a
group of conspirators is attempting to alter
this "present" by manipulating the past. They
are successful and the world returns to normal
history, based on the Armada's defeat. Revised
from a serial that appeared in *Science Fiction
Adventures* in 1962.

142. *The Traveler in Black*. New York: Ace, 1971 [paper].

A series of stories centered on the traveler in
black, a mysterious, god-like figure who moves
about the land bringing order out of chaos. His
physical identity varies, but his nature is always the same: in bringing order, his pronounce-
ments and actions are both just and ironic,
offering surprising truths to the mistakenly
self-righteous.

a. "Imprint of Chaos"
b. "Break the Door of Hell"
c. "The Wager Lost by Winning"
d. "Dread Empire"

Bibliography

143. DeBolt, Joe, and Denise DeBolt. "A Brunner Bibliography." In *The Happening Worlds of John Brunner: Critical Explorations in Science Fiction*. Ed. Joe DeBolt. Port Washington, NY and London: Kennikat Press, 1975, pp. 195-209.

JOHN BUCHAN

144. *The Moon Endureth: Tales and Fancies*. Edinburgh and London: William Blackwood and Sons, 1912.

Tales alternating with poems (*):

a. "From the Pentlands Looking North and South"*
b. "The Company of the Marjolaine"
c. "Avignon, 1759"*
d. "A Lucid Interval"
e. "The Shorter Catechism (Revised Version)"*
f. "The Lemnian"
g. "Atta's Son"*
h. "Space"
i. "Stocks and Stones"*
j. "Streams of Water in the South"
k. "The Gypsy's Song to the South"*
l. "The Grove of Ashtaroth"
m. "Wood Magic"*
n. "The Riding of Ninemileburn"
o. "Plain Folk"*
p. "The Kings of Orion"
q. "Babylon"*
r. "The Green Glen"
s. "The Wise Years"*
t. "The Rime of True Thomas"

Bibliography

145. Archibald, Hanna, Jr. *John Buchan: 1875-1940: A Bibliography*. Hamden, CT: Shoe String Press, 1953.

[HENRY] KENNETH BULMER

146. *Swords of the Barbarians*. New York: Belmont, 1970.

A sword and sorcery novel involving twins: a brother who is a mixture of thinker and bar-barian and a sister who must strip naked to perform her magic. The novel contains a number of well-contrived villains and some special moments that involve Frelgar the Pragmatist, a wizard who has forsworn magic.

147. *Kandar*. New York: Paperback Library, 1969.

A mediocre tale in which a young scholar-prince is forced into action by the capture and ensorcering of his beloved and his city. He must find a number of magical tomes that contain the information needed to break the spell.

EDWARD GEORGE EARLE BULWER-LYTTON

148. *A Strange Story*. 2 vols. London: Sampson Low, Son, 1862. [An earlier edition--Leipzig: Tauchnitz, 1861--is cited in a number of bibliographies.]

A strangely vital man, Margrave, attempts to draw a pastor, Fenwick, into the dark world of witchcraft. Margrave hopes to use Fenwick to renew an evil elixir of life. However, Fenwick gains a magic wand that helps him temporarily halt Margrave who has kidnapped Fenwick's fiancée. Fenwick and the girl flee to Austria to start a new life, but Margrave pursues them in his search for the elixir. At the moment that Margrave discovers the couple, he suddenly begins to degenerate and is seized by the dark powers he has served.

Bibliography

149. Stevenson, Lionel, ed. *Victorian Fiction: A Guide to Research*. Cambridge, MA: Harvard University Press, 1964.

KAY [KATHERINE] BURDEKIN

150. *The Burning Ring*. London: Butterworth, 1927; New York: William Morrow, 1929.

An eternal life story similar in a number of respects to H. Warner Munn's *Merlin's Ring* (see below). A youth uses a magic ring to continue to live through several centuries.

ANTHONY BURGESS, pseud. See JOHN ANTHONY BURGESS WILSON

JOSEPH BURGO

151. *The Lights of Barbrin*. New York: Pocket Books,
      1978 [paper].

      Character development is usually one of the
      weakest aspects of works that are predominantly
      fantasy. Such is not the case with this unusual
      work. Ehred, a young boy living in the squalor
      of a village in a dying land, has his unusual
      nature identified in a remote haven called
      Nabrilehr. In this place, humanity is still
      noble and recognizes the psychic power of the
      mind. Ehred and three other young "misfits"
      must form a Haziad, a four-person mind web in
      which each member represents and has power over
      one of the four elements, to fully realize them-
      selves. Each member must overcome his or her
      personal tragedy and flaws to find union; with-
      out this union and personal evolution, their
      world, their haven, and mankind's hope will fall
      before the dread power of the evil Rand, Ehred's
      boyhood friend, and their own weakness.

JOHN BURKE

152. *The Devil's Footsteps*. London: Weidenfeld and
      Nicolson, 1976.

      An occult mystery that might appeal to fantasy
      readers for its supernatural content. The enig-
      matic Dr. Caspian and the lovely Bronwen Powys
      are united in love as they confront an ancient
      evil that possesses the inhabitants of a late
      nineteenth-century British town. Compares very
      favorably with the works of Dennis Wheatley and
      Charles Evelyn Vivian (see below). Sequel:
      The Black Charade: A Dr. Caspian Story. London:
      Weidenfeld and Nicolson, 1977.

EDGAR RICE BURROUGHS

      The Mars of Barsoom Series

153. *A Princess of Mars*. Chicago: A.C. McClurg, 1917.

154. *The Gods of Mars*. Chicago: A.C. McClurg, 1918.

155. *The Warlord of Mars*. Chicago: A.C. McClurg, 1919.

35

156. *Thuvia, Maid of Mars*. Chicago: A.C. McClurg, 1920.

157. *The Chessman of Mars*. Chicago: A.C. McClurg, 1922.

158. *The Master Mind of Mars*. Chicago: A.C. McClurg, 1928.

159. *A Fighting Man of Mars*. New York: Metropolitan, 1931.

160. *Swords of Mars*. Tarzana, CA: E.A. Burroughs, 1936.

161. *Synthetic Men of Mars*. Tarzana, CA: E.A. Burroughs, 1940.

162. *John Carter of Mars*. New York: Canaveral, 1964.

163. *Llana of Gathol*. Tarzana, CA: E.A. Burroughs, 1948.

Although traditionally considered science fiction, this series lacks the necessary ingredient of extrapolation that would make it part of that genre. Rather, it is a rationalized fantasy, and Burroughs has used occasional scientific pretenses to ease the reader's willing suspension of disbelief. Moreover, it would be impossible to measure the influence of this series on the development of contemporary sword and sorcery fantasy. In the series, an earthman, John Carter, is astrally transported in answer to a beautiful princess's appeal. He uses his superior earthly muscles and his cunning to become warlord of Mars and marries the princess. Throughout the series, John Carter, his wife, family, and companions are continually involved in bizarre adventures, most of which involve the divergent races and constant warfare of Mars.

Bibliography

164. Harwood, John. *The Literature of Burroughsiana: A Listing of Magazine Articles, Book Commentaries, News Items, Book Reviews, Movie Reviews, Fanzines, Amateur Publications, and Related Items Concerning the Life And/Or Works of Edgar Rice Burroughs*. Baton Rouge, LA: Camille Cazedessus, 1963 [paper].

165. Heins, Henry Hardy. *A Golden Anniversary Bibliography of Edgar Rice Burroughs*. West Kingston, RI: Donald M. Grant, 1964.

166. Porges, Irwin. *Edgar Rice Burroughs: The Man Who Created Tarzan*. Provo, UT: Brigham Young University Press, 1975.

ALICE ELIZABETH BURTON

167. Kerby, Susan Alice, pseud. *Miss Carter and the Ifrit*. London: Hutchinson, [1945]. Rpt. New York: Arno Press, 1978 [not seen].

An old spinster burns a log in her fireplace and releases a Muslim demon, an Ifrit, who had been imprisoned there by King Sulayman. In gratitude, the Ifrit enthusiastically and magically responds to the woman's every whim. While her needs are simple and she is somewhat overwhelmed, the Ifrit does reunite her with a past paramour, she is married, and releases the Ifrit from his bondage to mankind.

JAMES BRANCH CABELL

The Biography of the Life of Manuel

168. *Beyond Life: Dizaine des Demiurges*. New York: McBride, 1919.

169. *Figures of Earth: A Comedy of Appearances*. New York: McBride, 1921.

170. *The Silver Stallion: A Comedy of Redemption*. New York: McBride, 1926.

171. *The Witch Woman: A Trilogy About Her*. New York: Farrar, Straus, 1948.

    a. "A Note as to Ettarre"
    b. "The Music from Behind the Moon"
    c. "The Way of Ecben"
    d. "The White Robe"

172. *The Soul of Melicent*. New York: Frederick A. Stokes, 1913. Rev. ed. as *Domnei: A Comedy of Woman-Worship*. New York: McBride, 1920.

173. *Chivalry*. New York: Harper, 1909. Rev. ed. New York: McBride, 1921.

    a. "The Prologue"
    b. "The Story of the Sestina (1906)"

      c.   "The Story of the Tenson (1906)"
      d.   "The Story of the Rat-Trap (1907)"
      e.   "The Story of the Choices (1908)"
      f.   "The Story of the Housewife (1906)"
      g.   "The Story of the Satraps (1909)"
      h.   "The Story of the Heritage"
      i.   "The Story of the Scabbard (1908)"
      j.   "The Story of the Navarrese (1907)"
      k.   "The Story of the Fox-Brush (1905)"
      l.   "The Epilogue"

174. *Jurgen: A Comedy of Justice*. New York: McBride, 1919 [paper].

175. *The Line of Love*. New York: Harper, 1905. Rev. ed. New York: McBride, 1921.

      a.   "The Episode Called Adhelmar at Puysange"
      b.   "The Episode Called Love Letters of Falstaff"
      c.   "The Episode Called 'Sweet Adelais'"
      d.   "The Episode Called In Necessity's Mortar"
      e.   "The Episode Called the Conspiracy at Arnaye"
      f.   "The Episode Called the Castle of Content"
      g.   "The Episode Called In Ursula's Garden"
      h.   "Envoi"

176. *The High Place: A Comedy of Disenchantment*. New York: McBride, 1923.

177. *Gallantry: An Eighteenth Century Dizain in Ten Comedies with an Afterpiece*. New York: Harper, 1907. Rev. ed. as *Gallantry: Dizaine des Fetes Galantes*. New York: McBride, 1922.

      a.   "The Epistle Dedicatory"
      b.   "The Prologue"
      c.   "Simon's Hour"
      d.   "Love at Martinmas"
      e.   "The Casual Honeymoon"
      f.   "The Rhyme to Porringer"
      g.   "Actors All"
      h.   "April's Message"
      i.   "In the Second April"
      j.   "Heart of Gold"
      k.   "The Scapegoats"
      l.   "The Ducal Audience"
      m.   "Love's Alumni"
      n.   "The Epilogue"

178. *Something About Eve: A Comedy of Fig-Leaves*. New York: McBride, 1927.

179. *The Certain Hour (Dizaine des Poetes)*. New York: McBride, 1916.

     a.   "Ballad of the Double-Seal"
     b.   "Auctorial Induction"
     c.   "Belh's Cavaliers"
     d.   "Balthazar's Daughter"
     e.   "Judith's Creed"
     f.   "Concerning Corinna"
     g.   "Olivia's Pottage"
     h.   "A Brown Woman"
     i.   "Pro Honoria"
     j.   "The Irresistible Ogle"
     k.   "A Princess on Grub Street"
     l.   "The Lady of All Our Dreams"
     m.   "'Ballad of Plagiary'"

180. *The Cords of Vanity: A Comedy of Shirking*. New York: Doubleday, Page, 1909. Rev. ed. New York: McBride, 1920.

181. *From the Hidden Way: Being Seventy-five Adaptations*. New York: McBride, 1916. Rev. ed. New York: McBride, 1924.

182. *The Jewel Merchants: A Comedy in One Act*. New York: McBride, 1921.

183. *The Rivet in Grandfather's Neck: A Comedy of Limitations*. New York: McBride, 1923.

184. *The Eagle's Shadow*. New York: Doubleday, Page, 1904. Rev. ed. New York: McBride, 1923.

185. *The Cream of the Jest: A Comedy of Evasions*. New York: McBride, 1917. Rev. ed. New York: McBride, 1922.

186. *The Lineage of Lichfield: An Essay in Eugenics*. New York: McBride, 1922.

187. *Straws and Prayer Books: Dizain des Diversions*. New York: McBride, 1922.

     a.   "The Author of Jurgen"
     b.   "A Note on Alcoves"
     c.   "The Way of Wizardry"
     d.   "Minions of the Moon"
     e.   "The Thin Queen of Elfhame"

f.   "Celestial Architecture"
g.   "Romantics About Them"
h.   "Diversions of the Anchorite"
i.   "The Delta of the Anchorite"
j.   "A Theme with Variations"
k.   "Flaws in the Spur"
l.   "The Author of the Eagle's Shadow"

Cabell's twenty-volume Life of Manuel is the most massive series in a genre that has a great affection for multi-volume works. Combining poetry and prose, the series has three major themes: chivalry, gallantry, and poetry itself. Set in the mythic, neo-medieval kingdom Poictesme and often starkly realistic in its treatment of human nature, the major focus is on the rise, life, fall, and deification of its central figure. The most acclaimed volumes are *Figures of Earth*, concerning the early adventures of Manuel and the formation of a group of comrades, the Fellowship of the Silver Stallion; *The Silver Stallion*, examining the reactions of the various members of the Fellowship of the Silver Stallion to Manuel's death and his deification; and *Jurgen*, concerning a journey through various bizarre environments and various amorous encounters with unusual women, such as Mrs. Satan.

Bibliography

188. Brewer, Frances Joan. *James Branch Cabell: A Bibliography of His Writings, Biography and Criticism*. Charlottesville, VA: University of Virginia Press, 1957.

189. Bruccoli, Matthew J. *Notes on the Cabell Collection at the University of Virginia*. Charlottesville, VA: University of Virginia Press, 1957.

190. Hall, James N. *James Branch Cabell: A Complete Bibliography*. New York: Revisionist Press, 1974.

191. Holt, Guy. *A Bibliography of the Writings of James Branch Cabell*. Philadelphia: Centaur Book Shop, 1924. Rpt. New York: Haskell House, 1972.

MOYRA CALDECOTT

192. *The Tall Stones*. New York: Hill and Wang, 1977.

> Two children, Kyra and Karne, befriend the town
> priest, Maal, in Bronze-Age Britain. Maal
> draws his powers from a circle of standing
> stones, much like Stonehenge, and is a member
> of a group of *numina* who are highly trained and
> who operate for the good of all. However, Maal
> is dying and preparing to join a type of Jung-
> ian "oversoul." When his replacement arrives,
> he and the children realize that the new
> priest, Wardyke, is evil and has never been
> properly sealed to the powers of good. Using
> her own burgeoning powers, Kyra communicates
> with Maal's companions through the circle of
> stones and aids Maal in the defeat of Wardyke
> and the salvation of the village. Suitable
> for juveniles. Second in this proposed trilogy:
> *The Temple of the Sun* (1977).

ITALO CALVINO

193. *Il Cavaliere Inesistente and Il Visconte Dimezzato*
     [American title: *The Nonexistent Knight* and
     The Cloven Viscount]. Torino: Giulio Einandi,
     1957.

> *Il Cavaliere Inesistente*: The being Agiluf is
> a white suit of armor with nothing inside it.
> A paladin in Charlemagne's army, he exists be-
> cause he remains constantly aware of himself
> and his virtue. In juxtaposition, his squire,
> an idiot, is constantly in personal peril be-
> cause he is completely unaware of himself. For
> example, he nearly drowns in a bowl of soup
> because he's not sure if he's to eat the soup
> or if the soup is to eat him. This farcical
> adventure is loosely unified by Agilulf's
> absurd quest to confirm the virginity of a woman
> he saved from rape many years prior.

> *Il Visconte Dimezzato*: A viscount is halved by
> a cannonball. One half, after being sealed
> with pitch, returns to his estate and establish-
> es a reign of macabre terror. The other half,
> containing all the virtuous qualities, arrives
> later, saves a young maiden from the evil half,
> and fights a fantastic duel with the evil half.
> A delightful parody of the psychomachia tradi-
> tionally associated with the fantasy genre.

41

194.   *Il Barone Rampante* [American title: *The Baron in the Trees*]. Torino: Giulio Eiuandi, 1957.

   A young Italian nobleman rebells against his parents and spends the rest of his life in the trees. He adjusts well, invents appropriate games and pursuits, engages in love affairs, and writes philosophy.

BERNARD [EDWARD JOSEPH] CAPES

195.   *From Door to Door: A Book of Romances, Fantasies, Whimsies and Levities*. New York: Frederick A. Stokes, 1900.

   a.   "The Sword of Corporal Lacoste"
   b.   "An Ugly Customer"
   c.   "The Cursing Bell (A Dream Story)"
   d.   "A Coward"
   e.   "The Foot of Time"
   f.   "The Meek Shall Inherit the Earth"
   g.   "The Chapter's Doom"
   h.   "Jemmy Jessama, the Runner"
   i.   "The Scatterling and the Aurelian"
   j.   "The Writer and the Prince"
   k.   "Solomon's Seal"
   l.   "A True Princess"
   m.   "The Widow's Clock"
   n.   "Above Proof"
   o.   "Doña Pollonia's Corset"
   p.   "The Lady-Killer"
   q.   "A Doll and A Moral"

CHRIS CARLSEN

Berserker Series

196.   *Berserker: Shadow of the Wolf*. London: Sphere Books, 1977 [paper].

197.   *Berserker: The Bull Chief*. London: Sphere Books, 1977 [paper].

   The first and second in an expected series that is distinguished primarily by its gore and violence. Young Harald Swiftaxe or Harald the Innocent is possessed by the god Odin and becomes a berserker: a warrior of super-human strength and vitality who cannot distinguish between friend or foe. After ravaging his

young betrothed and savaging his family, he joins
with a group of berserkers who hate him and com-
mits a variety of senseless brutalities. Sadly,
he does enjoy moments of sanity of varying dura-
tion, and he does also quest for release from
his hideous burden. The second volume is particularly characterized by the introduction of an
Irish and Welsh setting, its imitation of the
chronicle form, and its characterizations of
King Arthur and Niall of the Nine Tails.

[JAMES CARNEGIE]
[NINTH] EARL OF SOUTHESK

198. *Suomiria: A Fantasy.* Edinburgh: [By the Author],
      1899.

A man saves a sphinx from evil subterranean creatures and returns with her to the underworld.
Her father allows her to become human, and she
and the man are married. However, he misses
his former life too much and returns to the surface where he falls in love and marries again.
Later, the sphinx, in an act of selfless love,
rescues the man and his new wife, but through
this act, the sphinx forfeits her humanity.

LEWIS CARROLL, pseud. See CHARLES LUTWIDGE DODGSON

ANGELA CARTER

199. *Heroes and Villains.* New York: Simon & Schuster,
      1969.

A post-holocaust, sword and sorcery novel concerning a professor's daughter who becomes the
mistress of a leader of a wandering tribe of nomads. An interesting examination of the intellectual versus the physical in a survival-orient-
ed, shattered environment, which is often brutal
in its vivid descriptions and event orientation.

200. *The Infernal Desire Machines of Doctor Hoffman*
      [American title: *The War of Dreams*]. London:
      Rupert Hart-Davis, 1972.

Machines driven by sexual desire create macabre
and total delusion for an entire population in
this grotesque fantasy. The protagonist, a

civil servant, finally destroys the machines and his own innocence amid a kaleidoscope of shifting identities and allegiances.

201. *The Passion of New Eve*. London: Victor Gollancz, 1977.

LIN[WOOD VROOMAN] CARTER
See also ROBERT E[RVIN] HOWARD: Conan Series

202. *Thongor and the Wizard of Lemuria*. New York: Berkley, 1969 [paper]. Abr. ed. as *The Wizard of Lemuria*. New York: Ace, 1965 [paper].

The first volume in Carter's six-volume Thongor series. Thongor is allied with Sharajsha, the Wizard of Lemuria, in this run-of-the-mill sword and sorcery novel. Together, they confront the attempted vengeance of the last remnants of the evil and alien Dragon Kings and save mankind. Certainly, Carter must be recognized as one of the major, if not the major, reason why fantasy has enjoyed a renaissance in the last twenty years. His editorship of the Ballantine Adult Fantasy series and his many anthologies (see Anthology Section) have popularized and gained acceptance for numerous authors who might easily have been unnoticed by many readers. However, as is the danger of editing, his fiction too often only imitates other authors and never attains its own distinctive or attractive identity.

In addition to the Thongor series, Carter's large output includes the following other series: Green Star (five volumes as of 1976), Zarkon: Lord of the Unknown (three volumes as of 1976), and Godwane (five volumes as of 1977).

203. *Thongor and the Dragon City*. New York: Berkley, 1970 [paper]. Abr. ed. as *Thongor of Lemuria*. New York: Ace, 1966 [paper].

204. *Thongor Against the Gods*. New York: Paperback Library, 1967 [paper].

205. *Thongor in the City of the Magicians*. New York: Paperback Library, 1968 [paper].

206. *Thongor Fights the Pirates of Tarkakus*. New York: Berkley, 1970 [paper].

207. *Thongor at the End of Time*. New York: Paperback
     Library, 1970 [paper].

ROBERT W[ILLIAM] CHAMBERS

208. *In Search of the Unknown*. New York: Harper and
     Brothers, 1904. Rpt. Westport, CT: Hyperion,
     1974.

     A time-lost novel by the author of the classic
     horror short story collection *The King in Yellow*
     (1895). A young scientist enters a realm where
     prehistoric creatures have survived and have
     maintained their delightful and bizarre per-
     sonalities.

Bibliography

209. Hornberger, Theodore. "American First Editions
     at Texas University: Robert William Chambers
     (1865-1933)." *Library Chronicle of the Uni-
     versity of Texas*, 2 (Spring 1947), 193-195.

JOY CHANT

210. *The Grey Mane of Morning*. London: George Allen
     & Unwin, 1977.

     Set in the same fantasy environment as *Red Moon
     and Black Mountain* (see below) and preceding it
     in chronological sequence, this is the tale of
     the first hero in Chant's fantasy cosmos. The
     tribes of the "Great Plain" are ruled by the
     "Golden People" of the cities. This dictator-
     ial situation continues unquestioned until the
     Golden People steal the sister of a young war-
     rion, Mor'anh, of the Alnei. While this is a
     common practice, Mor'anh refuses to accept it,
     and in a quickly moving and often poignant nar-
     rative with less magical content than *Red Moon
     and Black Mountain*, he overthrows the rule of
     the oppressors and creates a new life for the
     people of his world.

211. *Red Moon and Black Mountain: The End of the House
     of Kendreth*. London: Allen & Unwin, 1970.

     Oliver Powell and his younger brother and sis-
     ter are summoned to "The Starlit Land" to con-
     front Fendral, the fell enchanter and perverter

of the ethereal star magic. Oliver becomes
Li'vanh, Lord of Warriors, and is allied with
the High King Kiron, the Princess In'serinna,
and their human and animal following. An excellent epic fantasy that concludes with Oliver
facing the necessity of human sacrifice with
him as the victim. Suitable for juveniles.

VERA CHAPMAN

The Three Damosels or Arthurian Trilogy

212. *The Green Knight*. London: Rex Collings, 1975.

213. *The King's Damosel*. London: Rex Collings, 1976.

214. *King Arthur's Daughter*. London: Rex Collings, 1976.

Much of Chapman's material is elaborated from
Sir Thomas Malory's account of the Arthurian
legend, with the exception of her own creation,
Ursulet, in *King Arthur's Daughter*. However, to
indicate that her trilogy is another mere retelling of the legend would be a serious error. In
the first place, all her tales are narrated by
female characters: Vivian, grand-daughter of
Merlin's Nimuë, in *The Green Knight*; Lynett,
King Arthur's messenger, in *The King's Damosel*;
and Ursulet, the small bear and princess of all
England, in *King Arthur's Daughter*. The tales
are set generations apart, but are unified by
characters who age and reappear and by the ever-
boding personage of Arthur's arch-enemy, Morgan
le Fay. Throughout, they are marked by the magical events of the Arthurian legend--e.g., Berti-
lak's shape-changing beneath the wand of Morgan,
Ursulet's achievement of the Holy Grail, the
sleeping Arthur, and many more--and by Chapman's
vivid portrayals of young women growing, learning,
and loving in complex, trying, and sorcerous
times.

G[ILBERT] K[EITH] CHESTERTON

215. *The Man Who Was Thursday: A Nightmare*. London:
J.W. Arrowsmith, 1908.

A very atypical work that successfully treads
the fine line between absurdity and seriousness.
Mutability and the nature of the cosmos are the

themes as six philosophic London spies unwitting-
ly form a council of anarchists that they believe
they are actually infiltrating. Little do they
realize that the seventh and final member of
their group is the only true anarchist, the
awesomely enigmatic Sunday.

Bibliography

216. Sullivan, John. *G.K. Chesterton: A Bibliography.*
London: University of London Press, 1958. Rpt.
Westport, CT: Greenwood Press, 1974.

217. Sullivan, John. *Chesterton Continued. A Bibliographical Supplement.* London: University of
London Press; New York: Barnes and Noble, 1968.

218. Sullivan, John. "Chesterton Bibliography Continued." *Chesterton Review,* 2 (1975), 94-98; 2
(1976), 267-272; 3 (1976-1977), 141-147; 4
(1978), 269-284.

ARTHUR C[HARLES] CLARKE

219. *Tales of the White Hart.* New York: Ballantine,
1957 [paper].

    a.   "Silence Please"
    b.   "Big Game Hunt"
    c.   "Patent Pending"
    d.   "Armaments Race"
    e.   "Critical Mass"
    f.   "The Ultimate Melody"
    g.   "The Pacifist"
    h.   "The Next Tenants"
    i.   "Moving Spirit"
    j.   "The Man Who Ploughed the Sea"
    k.   "The Reluctant Orchid"
    l.   "Cold War"
    m.   "What Goes Up"
    n.   "Sleeping Beauty"
    o.   "The Defenestration of Ermintrude Inch"

REGOR CLARKK

220. *The Last of the Sorcerer-Dragons.* Trans. [from
the Welsh] Philip D. Baugher. West Hempstead,
NY: Grail Press, 1944.

In this poignant and bittersweet love story, a

young professor, on leave in the Gobi Desert, discovers the last of a race of sorcerous dragons. The dragons have guarded mankind since its beginnings. The beautiful and compassionate reptile tells the young man the story of man's beginning--a tale stripped of its Christian overtones that is influenced by the medieval love story, *Tristan and Iseult*, and which retells the Eden myth in a totally new and delightful way. Throughout, the tragedy of the slowly dying race of benevolent dragons is intertwined, and their powers are gradually explained and transferred to the young professor. As she ends her tale, the dragon dies and the man suddenly realizes that he is now the one with the power to aid mankind. One of the least read and least noticed of all fantasy works.

SAMUEL LANGHORNE CLEMENS

221. Twain, Mark, pseud. *The Mysterious Stranger: A Romance*. New York and London: Harper & Brothers, 1916.

222. _____. *The Mysterious Stranger and Other Stories*. New York and London: Harper & Brothers, 1922.

    a. "The Mysterious Stranger"
    b. "A Horse's Tale"
    c. "Extract From Captain Stormfield's Visit to Heaven"
    d. "A Fable"
    e. "My Platonic Sweetheart"
    f. "Hunting the Deceitful Turkey"
    g. "The McWilliamses and the Burglar Alarm"

Bibliography

223. Johnson, Merle DeVore. *A Bibliography of the Works of Mark Twain, Samuel Langhorne Clemens*. Rev. and enl. ed. New York: Harper, 1935. Rpt. Westport, CT: Greenwood Press, 1972.

SARA COLERIDGE

224. *Phantasmion*. London: William Pickering, 1837.

A heroic fantasy whose scope is later echoed in Tolkien's *Lord of the Rings* (see below).

Bibliography

225. Watson, George, ed. *The New Cambridge Bibliography of English Literature*. Cambridge: Cambridge University Press, 1969, III (1800-1900), 515.

JOHN [HENRY NOYES] COLLIER

226. *Defy the Foul Fiend or the Misadventures of the Heart*. London: Macmillan, 1934.

227. *The Devil and All*. n.p.: Nonesuch Press, 1934.

    a. "Possession of Angela Bradshaw"
    b. "The Right Side"
    c. "Half Way to Hell"
    d. "After the Ball"
    e. "The Devil, George, and Rosie"
    f. "Hell Hath No Fury"

228. *Fancies and Goodnights*. Garden City, NY: Doubleday, 1951.

    a. "Bottle Party"
    b. "De Mortuis"
    c. "Evening Primrose"
    d. "Witchs Money"
    e. "Are You Too Late or Was I Too Early"
    f. "Fallen Star"
    g. "The Touch of Nutmeg Makes It"
    h. "Three Bears Cottage"
    i. "Pictures in the Fire"
    j. "Wet Saturday"
    k. "Squirrels Have Bright Eyes"
    l. "Halfway to Hell"
    m. "The Lady on the Grey"
    n. "Incident on a Lake"
    o. "Over Insurance"
    p. "Old Acquaintance"
    q. "The Frog Prince"
    r. "Season of Mists"
    s. "Great Possibilities"
    t. "Without Benefit of Galsworthy"
    u. "The Devil George and Rosie"
    v. "Ah the University"
    w. "Back for Christmas"
    x. "Another American Tragedy"
    y. "Collaboration"

z.   "Midnight Blue"
aa. "Gavin O Leary"
bb. "If Youth Knew Age Could"
cc. "Thus I Refute Beelzy"
dd. "Special Delivery"
ee. "Rope Enough"
ff. "Little Memento"
gg. "Green Thoughts"
hh. "Romance Lingers Adventure Lives"
ii. "Bird of Prey"
jj. "Variation on a Theme"
kk. "Night Youth Paris and the Moon"
ll. "The Steel Cat"
mm. "Sleeping Beauty"
nn. "Interpretation of a Dream"
oo. "Mary"
pp. "Hell Hath No Fury"
qq. "In the Cards"
rr. "The Invisible Dove Dancer of Strathpheen
      Island"
ss. "The Right Side"
tt. "Spring Fever"
uu. "Youth from Vienna"
vv. "Possession of Angela Bradshaw"
ww. "Cancel All I Said"
xx. "The Chaser"

229. *His Monkey Wife Or, Married To A Chimp*. London:
      Peter Davis, 1930.

      In this mockery of pretense, Collier extends to
      its logical end the traditional loyalty of
      animals while providing an on-going and comic
      commentary on the triviality of fashion and
      society.

230. *No Traveller Returns*. London: White Owl Press,
      1931.

231. *Pictures in the Fire*. London: Rupert Hart-Davis,
      1958.

      a. "Interpretation of a Dream"
      b. "And Who, With Eden ..."
      c. "Little Moments"
      d. "Are You Too Late or Was I Too Early?"
      e. "Think No Evil"
      f. "Incident on a Lake"
      g. "Old Acquaintance"
      h. "Mademoiselle Kiki"
      i. "Without Benefit of Galsworthy"
      j. "Spring Fever"

k. "Back for Christmas"
l. "Pictures in the Fire"
m. "Romance Lingers, Adventure Lives"
n. "The Steel Cat"
o. "In the Cards"
p. "Wet Saturday"
q. "Season of Mists"
r. "Over Insurance"
s. "De Mortuis"
t. "Ah, the University"
u. "Three Bears Cottage"
v. "Gavin O'Leary"
w. "The Tender Age"

232. *Presenting Moonshine.* New York: Viking, 1941.

a. "Evening Primrose"
b. "Witch's Money"
c. "Green Thoughts"
d. "Mary"
e. "Rope Enough"
f. "Thus I Refute Beelzy"
g. "Variation on a Theme"
h. "Old Acquaintance"
i. "The Frog Prince"
j. "Special Delivery"
k. "Half-Way to Hell"
l. "Bird of Prey"
m. "Collaboration"
n. "The Right Side"
o. "Night! Youth! Paris! And the Moon"
p. "Another American Tragedy"
q. "Bottle Party"
r. "If Youth Knew If Age Could"
s. "The Devil, George, and Rosie"
t. "Squirrels Have Bright Eyes"
u. "Sleeping Beauty"
v. "Possession of Angela Bradshaw"
w. "The Invisible Dove Dancer of Strathpheen Island"
x. "The Chaser"

233. *The Touch of Nutmeg and More Unlikely Stories.*
      New York: The Press of the Readers Club, 1943.

a. "The Touch of Nutmeg Makes It"
b. "De Mortuis"
c. "Wet Saturday"
d. "Little Moments"
e. "Mary"
f. "Midnight Blue"
g. "Back for Christmas"

    h.   "Evening Primrose"
    i.   "The Frog Prince"
    j.   "Rope Enough"
    k.   "The Chaser"
    l.   "The Devil, George, and Rosie"
    m.   "Great Possibilities"
    n.   "Half-Way to Hell"
    o.   "Possession of Angela Bradshaw"
    p.   "The Right Side"
    q.   "Another American Tragedy"
    r.   "Bird of Prey"
    s.   "Thus I Refute Beelzy"
    t.   "Night! Youth! Paris! And the Moon!"
    u.   "Variation on a Theme"
    v.   "Old Acquaintance"
    w.   "Ah, the University!"
    x.   "After the Ball"
    y.   "Hell Hath No Fury"
    z.   "Green Thoughts"

234.   *Witch's Money*. New York: Viking, 1940.

Bibliography

235.   Gawsworth, John, pseud. [Terence Ian Fytton Armstrong]. *Ten Contemporaries: Notes Toward Their Definitive Bibliography*. Second Series. London: Joiner and Steele, 1933.

EDMUND COOPER

236.   "The Firebird" in *Double Phoenix*. Ed. Lin Carter. New York: Ballantine, 1971 [paper].

A slight novella, that Carter presents as an allegory, that concerns a young boy's pursuit of the phoenix into an alternate wonder-world. The boy must overcome various temptations and reject various kinds of love to confront the phoenix in an irritatingly vague climax that seems to symbolize the ambiguities of wisdom, age, innocence, youth, and purity. Roger Lancelyn Green's "From the World's End" is the companion novella in this volume.

LOUISE COOPER

237.   *The Book of Paradox*. New York: Dell, 1975 [paper]; New York: Delacorte Press, 1973 [not seen].

Based on the Major Arcana of the Tarot, this

disappointing and slow-moving fantasy chronicles the supernatural pursuit of his beloved Aloethe by Varka with all the attendant paraphernalia and happenings.

SUSAN COOPER

The Dark is Rising Series

238. *Over Sea, Under Stone*. New York: Harcourt, Brace & World, 1965.

239. *The Dark is Rising*. New York: Atheneum, 1973.

240. *Greenwitch*. Atheneum, 1975.

241. *The Grey King*. New York: Atheneum, 1975.

242. *Silver on the Tree*. New York: Atheneum, 1977.

Like Ursula K. LeGuin's Wizard of Earthsea series (see below), this is one of those marvelous "juvenile" series that seems to be read more by adults than children.

In Cornwall, a young boy, Will Stanton, discovers that he is the lastborn of the "Old Ones," a confederation of sorcerers. As an Old One, he must use his special powers and the "High Magic" to recover the ancient treasures of Britain and to battle the evil Dark and its minions. Amid an interweaving of Celtic, Welsh, and Arthurian legends, Will's world becomes a dual one in which the mundane is overlaid with wondrous visions of a more elemental struggle, one that supersedes even Christianity. Will is joined, at various times in the series, by his brother and sister and various friends--including his uncle Merriman (Merlin) and a strange Albino boy, Bran (the Blessed)--before he can find the timeless "Lost Land" and recover the crystal sword so King Arthur may rise again and Herne the Hunter thwart the Dark Rider.

ROBERT COOVER

243. *Pricksongs & Descants: Fictions*. New York: E.P. Dutton, 1969.

a. "The Door: A Prologue of Sorts"

    b.   "The Magic Poker"
    c.   "Morris in Chains"
    d.   "The Gingerbread House"
    e.   "Seven Exemplary Fictions"
        1. "Panel Game"
        2. "The Marker"
        3. "The Brother"
        4. "In a Train Station"
        5. "Klee Dead"
        6. "J's Marriage"
        7. "The Wayfarer"
    f.   "The Elevator"
    g.   "Romance of the Thin Man and the Fat Lady"
    h.   "Quenby and Ola, Swede and Carl"
    i.   "The Sentient Lens"
    j.   "Scene for 'Winter'"
    k.   "The Milkmaid of Samaniego"
    l.   "The Leper's Helix"
    m.   "A Pedestrian Accident"
    n.   "The Babysitter"
    o.   "The Hat Act"

Bibliography

244.   Bruccoli, Mathew J. and C.E. Frazer Clark, eds.
        First Printings of American Authors: Contribu-
        tions Toward Definitive Checklists. Detroit:
        Gale Research, 1977, I, 71-74.

A[LFRED] E[DGAR] COPPARD

245.   *Adam & Eve & Pinch Me*. Waltham, Saint Lawrence,
        Berkshire: Golden Cockerel Press, 1921.

    a.   "Marching to Zion"
    b.   "Dusky Ruth"
    c.   "Weep Not My Wanton"
    d.   "Piffingcap"
    e.   "The King of the World"
    f.   "Adam & Eve & Pinch Me"
    g.   "The Princess of Kingdom Gone"
    h.   "Communion"
    i.   "The Quiet Women"
    j.   "The Trumpeters"
    k.   "The Angel & the Sweep"
    l.   "Arabesque: The Mouse"

246.   *The Black Dog and Other Stories*. London: Jonathan
        Cape, 1923.

    a.   "The Black Dog"

      b.   "Alas, Poor Bollington!"
      c.   "The Ballet Girl"
      d.   "Simple Simon"
      e.   "The Tiger"
      f.   "Mordecai and Cocking"
      g.   "The Man from Kilsheelan"
      h.   "Tribute"
      i.   "The Handsome Lady"
      j.   "The Fancy Dress Ball"
      k.   "The Cat, the Dog, and the Bad Old Dame"
      l.   "The Wife of Ted Wickham"
      m.   "Tanil"
      n.   "The Devil in the Churchyard"
      o.   "Huxley Rustem"
      p.   "Big Game"
      q.   "The Poor Man"
      r.   "Luxury"

247. *Clorinda Walks in Heaven*. Walthem, Saint Lawrence,
     Berkshire: Golden Cockerel Press, 1922.

      a.   "The Hurly-Burly"
      b.   "Clorinda Walks in Heaven"
      c.   "The Cherry Tree"
      d.   "The Elixir of Youth"
      e.   "Felix Tineler"
      f.   "Craven Arms"
      g.   "A Broadsheet Ballad"
      h.   "Cotton"
      i.   "Pomona's Babe"

248. *Dark-Eyed Lady: Fourteen Tales*. London: Methuen,
     1947.

      a.   "The Ring of Trouble"
      b.   "The Kisstruck Bogey"
      c.   "Apes Don't Shave"
      d.   "Hail Columbia!"
      e.   "Not Wanted"
      f.   "The Nameless One"
      g.   "Dark-Eyed Lady"
      h.   "Woman Versus Women"
      i.   "No Oats for Joseph"
      j.   "The Sullens Sisters"
      k.   "The Gold Watch"
      l.   "Polly and the Pikeys"
      m.   "A Study in Chalk"
      n.   "Tapsters' Tapestry"

249. *Dunky Fitlow: Tales*. London: Jonathan Cape, 1933.

    a.   "The Smith of Pretty Peter"
    b.   "Paste Restante"
    c.   "Ahoy! Sailor Boy"
    d.   "Crotty Shinkwin"
    e.   "The Watchman"
    f.   "The Beauty Spot"
    g.   "'Cheefou'"
    h.   "Corridors"
    i.   "Perfect Fool"
    j.   "Vincent's Pride"
    k.   "Dunky Fitlow"
    l.   "The Foggy Foggy Due"
    m.   "Groggo's Chimney"
    n.   "Abel Staple Disapproves"
    o.   "Due"

250. *Fearful Pleasures*. Sauk City, WI: Arkham House, 1946.

The collected fantasies

    a.   "Adam and Eve and Pinch Me"
    b.   "Clorinda Walks in Heaven"
    c.   "The Elixir of Youth"
    d.   "Simple Simon"
    e.   "Old Martin"
    f.   "The Bogie Man"
    g.   "Polly Morgan"
    h.   "The Gollan"
    i.   "The Post Office and the Serpent"
    j.   "Crotty Shinkwin"
    k.   "Ahoy, Sailor Boy!"
    l.   "Gone Away"
    m.   "Rocky and the Bailiff"
    n.   "Ale Celestial?"
    o.   "The Fair Young Willowy Tree"
    p.   "Father Raven"
    q.   "The Drum"
    r.   "Cheese"
    s.   "The Homeless One"
    t.   "The Kisstruck Bogie"
    u.   "The Tiger"
    v.   "The Gruesome Fit"

251. *Nixley's Harlequin: Tales*. London: Jonathan Cape, 1931.

    a.   "The Green Drake"
    b.   "Count Stefan"
    c.   "The Limping Lady"

      d.   "Wilt Thou Leave Me Thus?"
      e.   "The Gollan"
      f.   "The Idle Frumkin"
      g.   "The Post Office and the Serpent"
      h.   "My Hundredth Tale"
      i.   "Nixley's Harlequin"
      j.   "Dark Knowledge"

252. *Polly Oliver: Tales*. London: Jonathan Cape, 1935.

      a.   "Gone Away"
      b.   "The Two Nurses"
      c.   "Old Rascal"
      d.   "Look Before You Leap"
      e.   "Ring the Bells of Heaven"
      f.   "Hallo, Beaver!"
      g.   "What Can I Do?"
      h.   "Uncle Hobart"
      i.   "Crippled Bloom"
      j.   "The Banns"
      k.   "Emergency Exit"
      l.   "The Council of Seven"

253. *Ugly Anna and Other Tales*. London: Methuen, 1944.

      a.   "Father Raven"
      b.   "Ugly Anna"
      c.   "Coat of Many Colours"
      d.   "The Cream of Creation"
      e.   "Return March"
      f.   "Home Guard"
      g.   "Amy, Agatha, and Ruth"
      h.   "The Three Captains"
      i.   "Jubal and Jackson"
      j.   "Smulvey at the Junction"
      k.   "The Drum"
      l.   "Cobbler Butticass"
      m.   "Sweet Enemy"
      n.   "The Family Tree"
      o.   "Chinfeather"
      p.   "The Other Woman's Story"
      q.   "Barber's Rash"
      r.   "Cheese"

254. *You Never Know, Do You? and Other Tales*. London: Methuen, 1939.

      a.   "You Never Know, Do You?"
      b.   "The Cheese-Cutter Hat Man"
      c.   "Prompt Payment"
      d.   "The Gruesome Fit"
      e.   "Rocky and the Bailiff"

    f.   "Miss Milly"
    g.   "The Prince's Portrait"
    h.   "I Know a Bank"
    i.   "Keeper Cuffley"
    j.   "Secret Business"
    k.   "A Devil of a Cook"
    l.   "The Claudy Affair"
    m.   "Knight-Errant"
    n.   "Pedestrian Fancy"
    o.   "The Fair Young Willowy Tree"
    p.   "Homeward Bound"
    q.   "Ale Celestrial"
    r.   "Cheque-Mate"
    s.   "Pit-a-Pat"
    t.   "Time's Sweet Use"
    u.   "Tigers Alive"
    v.   "Proud Rollo"
    w.   "Kiss-the-Book Beezer"

Bibliography

255.   Fabes, Gilbert Henry. *The First Editions of A.E.
       Coppard, A.P. Herbert and Charles Morgan, with
       Values and Bibliographic Points*. London:
       Myers, 1933.

256.   Schwartz, Jacob. *The Writings of Alfred Edgar
       Coppard: A Bibliography*. London: Ulysses
       Bookshop, 1931.

DONALD CORLEY

257.   *The Fifth Son of the Shoemaker*. New York: Robert
       M. McBride, 1930.

       It is difficult to categorize Corley's glowing
       prose. *The Fifth Son of the Shoemaker* contains
       no magic, and from a purely objective viewpoint,
       the novel is just the story of the rise of a
       Muscovite family of shoemakers from obscurity
       in a cellar on New York's Orchard Street to
       world-wide fame and fortune. Yet, Corley en-
       dows the everyday with a sorcery that transports
       the reader into a realm of beauty, creation,
       art, and love. Ivan, the family's patriarch
       and the master shoemaker, seemingly becomes
       Dedaleus; Alexey, the capitalist, is the foil
       to the sensitive Pyotr, virtuoso, growing
       artist, and the creative center of the novel.
       The enigmatic Nischka, actress and goddess,
       is the family's spiritual matriarch, and the

dancing Cinderella and the silver Altierce
are Pyotr's inspiration as he explores a world
of love rich beyond experience. In all ways,
this novel is a celebration of nobility and the
elemental origins of art.

258. *The Haunted Jester*. New York: Robert M. McBride,
1931.

a. "Seven Knights in Silver"
b. "The God from the Shelf"
c. "The Dance of the Drowned"
d. "The Red Lacquer Box of Nirr-Lo-Fan"
e. "The Bride's Feast"
f. "The Lama, the Lady, and the Topaz"
g. "The Road to Benachie"
h. "The Troubled Promises of Kings"
i. "The Eyes of Compassion"
j. "*Que le Diable!*"
k. "The Daughter of the Moon"
l. "*Droit de Seigneur*"
m. "Fifteen Annas in the Rupee"
n. "The Bird with the Golden Beak"

259. *The House of Lost Identity*. Intro. James Branch
Cabell. New York: McBride, 1927.

A fine collection of charming and whimsical
tales that are paragons of Cabell's assessment
in the introduction: the unique "property of
magic is its pleasing ability to coerce 'nature' . . . ."

a. "The House of Lost Identity"
b. "The Price of Reflection"
c. "The Daimyō's Bowl"
d. "Figs"
e. "The Manacles of Youth"
f. "The Ghost-Wedding"
g. "The Glass Eye of Throgmorton"
h. "The Legend of the Little Horses"
i. "The Tale that the Ming Bell Told"
j. "The Book of Debts"
k. "The Song of the Tombelaine"

BARON CORVO, pseud. See FREDERICK WILLIAM ROLFE

JUANITA COULSON

260. *The Web of Wizardry.* New York: Ballantine Books, 1978 [paper].

In this sword and sorcery epic, an evil wizard unleashes his zombie-like armies upon the disunified land of Krantin. It falls to a young desert nomad, Danaer, to be the agent of harmony among his people's varied ways of life, religions, beliefs, and hatreds. Through his love of the young Lira, a nubile young apprentice sorceress and a member of a web of wizardry that attempts to combat the fell wizard, Danaer and his people are victorious and the way is established for the rise of the leader who will unite all the divergent elements of Krantin.

F[RANCIS] MARION CRAWFORD

261. *Khaled: A Tale of Arabia.* 2 vols. New York: Collier, 1890.

A djinn is allowed to become a man but can only gain a soul and the true paradise of Allah if he wins the love of a self-centered and petulant princess. Interesting for its action and pseudo-orientalism.

MICHAEL CRICHTON

262. *Eaters of the Dead: The Manuscript of Ibn Fadlan, Relating His Experiences with the Northmen in A.D. 922.* New York: Alfred E. Knopf, 1976 [not seen]. Rpt. New York: Bantam, 1977 [paper].

A sometimes comic and often brutal recreation of the travels of the emissary of the Caliph of Bagdad, an excessively civilized man, among the "ferocious hairy demons of the Northland." Ibn Fadlan's incredulity at the religious and social customs of his "hosts" and his often ironic narration provide much of the interest. The Bantam edition features Ian Miller's superbly detailed illustrations.

JOHN KEIR CROSS

263. *The Other Passenger.* Philadelphia and New York:

J.B. Lippincott, 1946.

a. "The Glass Eye"
b. "Petronella Pan"
c. "The Last of the Romantics"
d. "Clair de Lune"
e. "Absence of Mind"
f. "Hands"
g. "Another Planet"
h. "Liebestraum"
i. "Miss Thing and the Surrealist"
j. "Valdemosa"
k. "Amateur Gardening"
l. "The Little House"
m. "Esmeralda"
n. "Music, When Soft Voices Die"
o. "Cyclamen Brown"
p. "Couleur de Rose"
q. "The Lovers"
r. "The Other Passenger"

BRIAN DALEY

264. *The Doomfarers of Coramonde*. New York: Ballantine, 1977 [paper].

An uneven, neo-medieval, sword and sorcery novel,
with a touch of alternate worlds. A young Viet-
nam veteran, transported to a fantasy realm,
aids Prince Starbuck in recovering his throne
and discovering his manhood. The highpoint of
the adventure is the battle between the fell
dragon, Chaffinch, and an armored personnel
carrier.

265. *The Starfollowers of Coramonde*. New York: Ballantine, 1979 [paper].

The sequel to *The Doomfarers of Coramonde* and the
further adventures of Prince Starbuck and Gil
MacDonald, the transported soldier. MacDonald,
while seeking a magic sword, confronts Yardiff
Bey, the master sorcerer who attempted to usurp
Starbuck's throne. Even after a duel of magic
is won, Gil is captured, and Starbuck must battle the "Host of the Dead" to rescue his friend.

266. *Peregrine: Primus*. New York: Walker, 1971.

> A picaresque sword and sorcery novel that was to
> be the first in a trilogy that has yet to be con-
> tinued. It is the episodic and loosely connected
> quest by the young bastard of a pagan king for
> his brother. Set in a society gone dogmatically
> Christian, the novel is chiefly distinguished
> by the protagonist's traveling companions:
> Atilla the Fourth, king of a horde of about ele-
> ven warriors; Stingy Gus, caesar of a city-state;
> Eudoxia, a madame; Claude, who acts the idiot;
> and Appledore, philosopher and sorcerer.

267. *The Phoenix and the Mirror [or The Enigmatic
     Speculum]*. Garden City, NY: Doubleday, 1969.

> Vergil Magus, a sorcerer, is commissioned to
> construct a major speculum--a virgin mirror
> that reveals more than just reflection--to dis-
> cover the whereabouts of a kidnapped maiden.
> The excellent alchemical adventure of the cons-
> truction of the speculum almost overshadows
> Vergil's love quest for the maiden and his
> final confrontation with the legendary Phoenix.

268. *The Island Under the Earth*. New York: Ace, 1969
     [paper].

> Between Earthflux and Starflux lies the island
> under the earth, a chaotic realm that was to be
> presented in a trilogy with other yet unpub-
> lished titles: "The Six-Limbed Folk" and "The
> Cap of Grace." Its main characters include an
> eunuch, a sea captain and his slave wife, an
> old centaur, a merchant, and a thief. Their
> fortunes are subject to the eternal conflict
> between centaur and man and the catastrophic
> arrivals of earthflux and starflux with their
> disorienting effects.

269. *Ursus of Ultima Thule*. New York: Avon, 1973
     [paper].

> In some ways as elemental and as violent as
> Treece's *The Green Man* (see below) and concern-
> ed with the same archetypal, primitive forces,
> this is the tale of shape changers and, more
> specifically, of Arnten the Bear as he searches
> for his true father and his own destiny.

L[YON] SPRAGUE DE CAMP
See also ROBERT E[RVIN] HOWARD, Conan Series, and
FLETCHER PRATT AND L[YON] SPRAGUE DE CAMP

270. *The Clocks of Iraz*. New York: Pyramid, 1971 [paper].

The sequel to *The Goblin Tower* (see below) and
the continued adventures of the fugitive king
and jack-of-all-trades Jorian. He still cannot
overcome his attraction to the least attractive
member of his former harem and continues to
search for her. As is expected in de Camp's
fiction, there are many fine moments of magic,
action, and characterization.

271. *The Fallible Fiend*. New York: Signet, 1973 [paper].

A fiend from a parallel plane is summoned by
magic. Delightful episodes occur as the fiend
misunderstands his commands and tries to function in a totally alien environment, which is,
of course, quite normal for the reader. Deter-
iorates somewhat at the end as the fiend becomes
a hero and saves civilization.

272. *The Goblin Tower*. New York: Pyramid, 1968 [paper].

A highly episodic sword and sorcery fantasy
that is part of de Camp's loosely connected
novels that focus on the device of alternate
planes of existence. As is typical of de Camp's
fiction, this is filled with fine secondary
characters: a lusty girl, a doddering sorcerer,
and a strong lout. The novel reaches an effective dénouement as the young king who has fled
his kingdom to avoid a ritual beheading and his
companions deliver a chest of magic scrolls
that has become incidental in light of the
happenings along the way.

273. *The Reluctant Shaman and Other Fantastic Tales*.
New York: Pyramid, 1970 [paper].

    a.   "The Reluctant Shaman"
    b.   "The Hardwood Pile"
    c.   "Nothing in the Rules"
    d.   "The Ghost of Melvin Pye"
    e.   "The Wisdom of the East"
    f.   "Mr. Arson"
    g.   "Ka the Appalling"

274. *The Tritonian Ring*. New York: Twayne, 1953.

An above-average sword and sorcery, quest fantasy about the conflict between a prince and the gods that compares favorably with Leiber's Fafhrd and the Gray Mouser series (see below).

275. "The Undesired Princess." In *The Fantasy Twins*. Los Angeles: Fantasy Publishing, 1951 [Bound with Stanley Weinbaum's "The Dark Other" and de Camp's "Mr. Arson"].

Rollin Hobart, "the most unwilling knight-errant that this world of noble heroes and dastardly villains had ever seen" (p. 100), is transported into a medieval realm that has only extreme morals or ethics. He is persuaded by a talking and violently faithful lion to rescue his mistress, a princess; lead the princess's father's armies; and defeat an "andro-sphinx" and an evil sorcerer. After his reluctant successes, Hobart is offered the opportunity to replace the Greek Zeno of Elea as the presiding god of the two-value realm (just good and evil), but he decides to return to the mixed values of the mundane world.

276. *The Virgin & the Wheels*. New York: Popular Library, 1976 [paper].

A reprint of two earlier novelettes. "The Virgin" (1962 in *Thrilling Wonder Stories* as "The Virgin of Zesh") is a pedestrian sword and sorcery tale in which a warrior repeatedly saves a lush maiden from danger. "The Wheels" (1940 in *Unknown* as "The Wheels of If") is a far better effort and is based on the premises that the South won the Civil War and that America developed under the influence of Vinland.

L[YON] SPRAGUE DE CAMP AND FLETCHER PRATT
See also FLETCHER PRATT AND L[YON] SPRAGUE DE CAMP

277. *The Carnelian Cube: A Humorous Fantasy*. New York: Gnome Press, 1948.

A marble cube--a dream stone--allows the protagonist to journey to what he believes to be the best of all possible worlds, all of which are unsatisfactory. A panorama of varied egotistical attempts at utopia.

The Incomplete Enchanter Series

278. *The Incomplete Enchanter*. New York: Henry Holt, 1941.

279. *The Castle of Iron: A Science Fantasy Adventure*. New York: Gnome Press, 1950.

280. *The Wall of Serpents*. New York: Avalon, 1960.

Harold Shea and his companions learn that they can transport themselves to various literary realms through a combination of magic and mathematics. In *The Incomplete Enchanter*, the characters journey first into Norse mythology and then into Edmund Spenser's *Faerie Queene*. In *The Castle of Iron*, the setting is Ariosto's *Orlando Furioso*. *The Wall of Serpents* collects two earlier short stories--"Wall of Serpents" (1953) and "The Green Magician" (1954). They are set in the realms of the *Kalevala* and Irish mythology, respectively. Throughout the series, a comic tone is maintained as characters lose their memories, inadvertently change into wolves, confront awesome sorcerers and beasts, and, in *The Incomplete Enchanter*, are even present for Ragnarok, the final battle of Norse mythology when the gods and all things are destroyed. An omnibus volume, *The Compleat Enchanter: The Magical Adventures of Harold Shea* (Garden City, NY: Nelson Doubleday [The Science Fiction Book Club], 1975), contains *The Incomplete Enchanter* and *The Castle of Iron* but omits *The Wall of Serpents*.

ALEXANDER DE COMEAU

281. *Fires of Isis*. London: A.H. Stockwell, [1927].

282. *Monk's Magic*. London: Methuen, 1931. Rpt. New York: Arno Press, 1978 [from a 1931 New York edition that, along with this reprint, has not been seen].

Dismas, a Medieval monk, is ordered by his abbot to search for the elixer of life. His search is filled with fantastic adventures, strange and faithful helpers, and miraculous talismans. When he befriends a young orphan, he doesn't realize that what he thinks is a boy is actually a girl. Rescuing she/he from a

coven's black mass in the land of the dead,
Dismas must struggle with his own "love" for
the orphan and, after fruitlessly searching
for the elixer, must return to face the darkest
of all challenges, the Devil himself.

WARWICK DEEPING

283. *The Man Who Went Back*. New York: Alfred A. Knopf,
1940 [first American edition].

A classic allegorical fantasy novel in which a
modern Englishman is transported back to Roman
Britain, which faces an invasion by barbaric
German tribes, to live as a soldier, lover, and
adventurer, who finally returns to his own time
with a new perspective.

284. *Uther & Igraine*. London: Grant Richards, 1973.

A retelling of the Arthurian love story, involving Pelleas, Uther, and Igraine, that
relates the conception of King Arthur.

Bibliography

285. Watson, George, ed. *The New Cambridge Bibliography of English Literature*. Cambridge: Cambridge University Press, 1972, IV (1900-1950),
559-560.

WALTER [JOHN] DE LA MARE

286. *A Penny A Day*. New York: Alfred A. Knopf, 1960.

  a. "A Penny A Day"
  b. "The Three Sleeping Boys of Warwickshire"
  c. "The Lovely Myfanwy"
  d. "The Dutch Cheese"
  e. "Dick and the Beanstalk"
  f. "The Lord Fish"

287. *The Collected Tales of Walter de la Mare*. Ed.
Edward Wagenknecht. New York: Alfred A.
Knopf, 1950.

  a. "The Riddle"
  b. "The Almond Tree"
  c. "In the Forest"
  d. "The Talisman"

    e.   "Miss Duveen"
    f.   "The Bowl"
    g.   "The Tree"
    h.   "An Ideal Craftsman"
    i.   "Seaton's Aunt"
    j.   "Limpet, Lispett and Vaine"
    k.   "The Three Friends"
    l.   "Willows"
    m.   "Missing"
    n.   "The Connoisseur"
    o.   "The Nap"
    p.   "All Hallows"
    q.   "The Wharf"
    r.   "The Orgy: An Idyll"
    s.   "Cape Race"
    t.   "Physic"
    u.   "The Trumpet"
    v.   "The Creature"
    w.   "The Vats"
    x.   "Strangers and Pilgrims"

288.   *The Connoisseur and Other Stories*. London: W. Collins Sons, 1926.

    a.   "Mr. Kempe"
    b.   "Missing"
    c.   "The Connoisseur"
    d.   "The Nap"
    e.   "Pretty Poll"
    f.   "All Hallows"
    g.   "The Wharf"
    h.   "The Lost Track"

289.   *Henry Brocken: His Travels & Adventures in the Rich, Strange, Scarce-Imaginable Regions of Romance*. New York: Alfred A. Knopf, 1924.

A young man goes on an imaginary journey and meets the characters of literature, including Lucy Gray, Jane Eyre, Electra, Bottom, Titania, Sleeping Beauty, Lemuel Gulliver, La Belle Dame sans Merci, Annabel Lee, and Criseyde.

290.   *Limpet, Lispett, and Vaine*. London: [The Morland Press], 1923.

291.   *On the Edge: Short Stories*. London: Faber and Faber, 1930.

    a.   "A Recluse"
    b.   "Willows"
    c.   "Crewe"

        d.   "At First Sight"
        e.   "The Green Room"
        f.   "The Orgy: An Idyll"
        g.   "The Picnic"
        h.   "The Ideal Craftsman"

292.   *The Riddle and Other Stories*.   London: Selwyn & Blount, 1923.

        a.   "The Almond Tree"
        b.   "The Count's Courtship"
        c.   "The Looking Glass"
        d.   "Miss Duveen"
        e.   "Selina's Parable"
        f.   "Seaton's Aunt"
        g.   "The Bird of Travel"
        h.   "The Bowl"
        i.   "The Three Friends"
        j.   "Limpet, Lispett, and Vaine"
        k.   "The Tree"
        l.   "Out of the Deep"
        m.   "The Creature"
        n.   "The Riddle"
        o.   "The Vats"

293.   *Snow-White*.   London: Hulton Press, 1952.

294.   *The Three Mulla-Mulgars*.   London: Duckworth, 1910.

A beast fable in which three personified animals have their purity and courage rewarded when they return to their homes and kingships after a long quest. This is typical of all of de la Mare's fiction with its emphasis on dreams and children to create portals into imaginary realms and situations and his contention that imaginative tales are more real for the reader than unimaginative ones.

295.   *The Wind Blows Over*.   London: Faber and Faber, 1936.

        a.   "What Dreams May Come"
        b.   "Cape Race"
        c.   "Physic"
        d.   "The Talisman"
        e.   "In the Forest"
        f.   "'A Froward Child'"
        g.   "Miss Miller"
        h.   "The House"
        i.   "A Revenant"

        j.   "'A Nest of Singing Birds'"
        k.   "The Trumpet"

    Bibliography

296. Clark, Leonard. "A Handlist of the Writings in
        Book Form, 1902-1953, of Walter de la Mare."
        Studies in Bibliography, 6 (1954), 197-218.

297. _____. "Addendum: A Checklist of Walter de la
        Mare." *Studies in Bibliography*, 8 (1956),
        269-270.

                    SAMUEL R. DELANY

298. *The Jewels of Aptor*. Abr. ed. New York: Ace
        [bound dos-a-dos with James White's *Second
        Ending*], 1962 [paper]. Cmpl. ed. New York:
        Ace, 1968 [paper]. Rpt. Boston: Gregg, 1976.

        An interesting sword and sorcery, quest novel
        in which a high priestess, a young thief, a
        poet, and a soldier search for the jewels that
        figure prominently in an atypical conflict bet-
        ween two cultures in a post-holocaust environ-
        ment.

                    GRAHAM DIAMOND

    Haven Series

299. *The Haven*. Chicago: Playboy Press, 1977 [paper].

300. *Lady of the Haven: Adventures of the Empire Princess*.
        Chicago: Playboy Press, 1978 [paper].

301. *Dungeons of Kuba*. Chicago: Playboy Press, forth-
        coming.

        In the far distant future, mankind has with-
        drawn to a small, dying empire centered around
        the fortress known as the Haven. Their numbers
        shrinking, they battle talking dogs, furious
        beasts who have finally been united under the
        leadership of the Master, Toland, and who have
        allied themselves with the Night-Birds (vampire
        bats). While mankind struggles against their
        foes, the Lord Nigel endures hardship to find
        his way through the Endless Forest to the New
        Lands and salvation. Allied with talking birds,

wolves, and snakes, mankind is temporarily successful in this strong example of action and description with its strikingly effective characterizations of man, animals, and love.

Although *Lady of the Haven* has been billed as a sequel to *The Haven*, it is actually a bit more. Relating the youth of Lady Anastasia, Nigel's daughter, who is raised by the wolves, it is the first volume in what is a projected trilogy. Fascinated by the tale of an old white wolf, Anastasia decides to lead an expedition across the sea to find a new land, but first she must convince her father and the ruling council.

PETER DICKINSON

302. *The Blue Hawk*. London: Victor Gollancz, 1976 [simultaneous publication: Boston: Little, Brown ?].

A young boy becomes the center of a mystic and political struggle in a country like ancient Egypt by befriending a blue hawk, the symbol of kingly power, and by fulfilling the archetypal role of the "nay-sayer" in a ritual of succession. His rite of passage and his often tortured decisions that follow make for an intriguing search for self and truth.

303. *The Weathermonger*. London: Victor Gollancz, 1968.

Two children, Geoffrey (a young weathermonger) and Sally, are driven out of England by unusual changes in the country, much of it having been returned to the Middle Ages. Sent back from France and using a 1909 Rolls Royce for transportation to investigate, they discover that the changes are being produced by the mind of a reawakened, but drugged, Merlin. The children persuade Merlin to deny the drug and return to his rightful rest. Two other of Dickinson's novels are also novels concerned with regressive "changes" and can be read separately or in conjunction with *The Weathermonger*: *Heartsease* [London: Victor Gollancz; Boston: Little, Brown, 1969] and *The Devil's Children* [London: Victor Gollancz; Boston: Little, Brown, 1970].

GORDON R[UPERT] DICKSON

304. *The Dragon and the George*. Garden City, NY: Nelson
     Doubleday [The Science Fiction Book Club], 1976.

     A fine fantasy romp concerning a maiden who is
     lost in an oppressively mundane everyday and
     found in a world of magic, wonder, and knight-
     hood. Her boyfriend's mind is projected into
     the body of a talking dragon to effect her res-
     cue, and the company he accumulates on his quest
     and their often burlesque adventures make this
     one of the most pleasing examples of rational-
     ized fantasy.

Bibliography

305. "Gordon R. Dickson Bibliography." In *Gordon R.
     Dickson's SF Best*. Ed. James R. Frenkel. New
     York: Dell, 1978, pp. 223-236 [paper].

CHARLES LUTWIDGE DODGSON

306. Carroll, Lewis, pseud. *Alice's Adventures in
     Wonderland*. London: Macmillan, 1865.

307. _____. *Through the Looking-Glass, and What Alice
     Found There*. London: Macmillan, 1872 [actually
     released in 1871].

308. _____. *The Wasp in a Wig: A "Suppressed" Episode
     of Through the Looking Glass and What Alice
     Found There*. Ed. Martin Gardner. Carroll
     Studies No. 2. New York: The Lewis Carroll
     Society of North America, 1977.

     Through the artistry of Walt Disney, the adven-
     tures of Alice have become enormously popular,
     and it is rare to find someone who is not aware
     of her journeys through Dodgson's "fairy tale"
     settings. However, examination of the two
     books from an adult and/or scholarly point of
     view reveals that Alice's adventures often are
     excursions into the darker portions of human
     consciousness, and that *Alice's Adventures in
     Wonderland* with its major theme of change and
     Through the Looking Glass with its structural
     model of the chess game are dark narratives
     focusing on a repressed Victorian child over-
     whelmed and intimidated by capricious and
     illogical adults and authority figures.
     Dodgson uses this repressive situation to illus-
     trate the essential honesty and straightfor-

wardness of children.

Bibliography

309. Williams, Sidney Herbert, and Falconer Maden.
*The Lewis Carroll Handbook: Being a New Version
of the Literature of the Rev. C.L. Dodgson ...
Now Revised, Augmented and Brought Up to 1960.*
Rev. Roger Lancelyn Green. London: Oxford
University Press, 1962.

STEPHEN R. DONALDSON

The Chronicles of Thomas Covenant, the Unbeliever

310. *Lord Foul's Bane: The Chronicles of Thomas
Covenant, the Unbeliever. Book One.* Garden
City, NY: Nelson Doubleday [Science Fiction
Book Club], 1977.

311. *The Chronicles of Thomas Covenant, the Unbeliever:
The Illearth War.* New York: Holt, Rinehart
and Winston, 1977.

312. *The Chronicles of Thomas Covenant, the Unbeliever:
The Power That Preserves.* New York: Holt,
Rinehart and Winston, 1977.

A twentieth-century leper is transported into
the midst of a titantic psychomachia in a
fantasy realm where magic functions and the
inhabitants are deeply bound to the health of
the sentient land. He must overcome his own
doubts, find the courage to try to do more
than survive his leprosy (which initially disappears in the fantasy environ), and come to
terms with his own scepticism and despondency
before he can aid the people who become so dear
to him. The series is distinguished by its
characterization, the delineations of evil and
its representatives, its settings and descriptions, and its depiction of the protagonist's
inner torment. One of the best of the recent
fantasy series.

NORMAN DOUGLAS

313. *Nerinda (1901).* Florence: G. Florence, 1929.

A young man seeks a destructive reunion with

his soul mate, who was killed when Pompeii was
destroyed.

314. *South Wind*. London: Martin Secker, 1917.

Set in the imaginary Mediterranean realm of
Nepenthe, this is a tale of dark conversion.
A young bishop of the Church of England,
exhausted from his evangelistic efforts in
Africa, finds the pagan natives of Nepenthe
irresistible. Their amorality and paganism
convince the bishop that he will not return to
the church, but will embrace the clarity of
the natives' pantheism.

Bibliography

315. McDonald, Edward David. *A Bibliography of the
Writings of Norman Douglas, With Notes by
Norman Douglas*. Philadelphia: Centaur Book-
shop, 1927.

DIANE DUANE

316. *The Door Into Fire*. New York: Dell, 1979 [paper].

Despite an overly cute "Overture," by David
Gerrold, Duane's first book publication effectively combines a diverse number of elements
within a sword and sorcery frame. Herewiss
is the first man in eons to possess an internal,
magical flame of enormous power. However, the
various instruments that women use to focus and
control their flames shatter whenever Herewiss
attempts to use them. Futilely, he attempts to
forge a sword that will focus and develop the
nascent flame, and when this fails, he finds
aid through the carnal visitation of a goddess
and the company of a fire elemental, Sunspark.
Ultimately, it is the portals into other worlds
contained in a fortress built by a long-for-
gotten race that resolve his dilemma. Through
his tampering, he releases an alien and elemental evil and must find his power to save his
friends from a horrible death. Interwoven
into the plot are Duane's excellent descriptions
of settings; her skillful handling of the
homo- and heterosexual triangle among Herewiss,
his friend Prince Freelorn, and Segnbora, a
woman who is trying to control her flame also;
and her deft characterization of Sunspark, the

fire elemental, who becomes increasingly human through his contact with Herewiss.

LORD DUNSANY, pseud.
See EDWARD JOHN MORETON DRAX PLUNKETT

EARL OF SOUTHESK, pseud. See JAMES CARNEGIE

GEORG [MORITZ] EBERS

317. *The Elixir and Other Tales*. Trans. Edward Hamilton Bell. New York: W.S. Gottsberger, 1890 [first English translation of the original German].

   a.   "The Elixir"
   b.   "The Greylock, A Fairy Tale"
   c.   "The Nuts, A Christmas Story"

E[RIC] R[UCKER] EDDISON

318. *The Worm Ouroboros: A Romance*. London: Jonathon Cape, 1922.

A psychomachia that is set on an imaginary Mercury and fought by the forces of Demonland and Witchland. King Gorice XII, a necromancer, of Witchland is in conflict with the Lords of Demonland: three brothers--Lord Juss, Goldry Gluszco, and Spitfine--and their cousin, Lord Brandoch Daha. Gorice kidnaps Goldry through sorcery and imprisons him on a distant mountain; his kinsmen must attempt to rescue him while Gorice attacks their homeland. Juss and Brandoch Daha seek the aid of the immortally youthful Queen Sophonisba, whose castle had been sacked by one of Gorice's ancestors. From her, Juss learns that he can rescue Goldry only by flying to the mountain on a hippogriff. After the failure of a land rescue, the Lords recover a hippogriff egg from the bottom of a lake in Demonland. In the meantime, Gorice's forces are laying waste to Demonland, and Brandoch Daha's sister, Mevrian, escapes capture only with the help of a traitor to Gorice's cause, Lord Gro. After Goldry is rescued with the help of the hippogriff, the reunited Lords drive Gorice's forces out of Demonland, capture

his castle, and kill the witch lords. This
work is considered by many to be an allegory
of the fall of Lucifer (the sorcerer-king of
Witchland) and to be one of the best examples
of a non-extrapolated environment. As its
title--a major symbol of the eternal cycle--
indicates, the novel has no resolution but
ends with the realization that struggle must
continue for eternity.

The Zimiamvian Novels

319. *Mistress of Mistresses*. New York: E.P. Dutton,
     1935.

320. *A Fish Dinner in Memison*. New York: E.P. Dutton,
     1941.

321. *Mezentian Gate*. Plaistow, England: Curwen Press,
     1958.

Set in Zimiamvia, a paradise mentioned by Lords
Juss and Brandoch Daha in Chapter 12 of *The
Worm Ouroboros* (see above), this incomplete
trilogy draws heavily from *Orkneyinga Saga*,
Virgil, and the Homeric Hymns.

Mistress of Mistresses begins with the death of
Edward Lessingham at age ninety. He is rein-
carnated in Zimiamvia as a young captain and
becomes active in politics after the death of
King Mezentius. Despite his honorable nature,
Lessingham supports his Machiavellian cousin,
Horius Parry, the regent to the late king's
daughter, Antiope, against the king's bastard
son and the honorable Duke Barganax. Throughout the novel lurks the dreadful and beautiful
Aphrodite. Typical of the novel's ruthless and
aristocratic characters, she operates through a
number of guises: Florinda, Barganax's mistress;
Queen Antiope; Barganax's mother, the Duchess
of the Kingdom of Memison; and Lessingham's
dead wife, Mary. It is Aphrodite who has
allowed Lessingham to enter Zimiamvia as her
lover and who, in fact, created it for him to
occupy.

A Fish Dinner in Memison, although written
later than *Mistress of Mistresses*, takes place
earlier in Zimiamvia during the lifetime of
King Mezentius. It concerns Barganax's court-
ship of Florinda/Aphrodite; King Mezentius'

early involvement with Amalie/Aphrodite,
Duchess of Memison; and Edward Lessingham's
involvement with his wife, Mary Scarnside/Aphro-
dite. The relationships are treated in alter-
nation with Florinda's awareness of the goddess
within her the unifying element. At the banquet the novel draws its title from, a question
is posed: If any of the partakers were gods,
what kind of a world would they create? The
answer is, of course, created by Eddison in
Mistress of Mistresses.

Mezentian Gate was unpublished and only two-
thirds complete when Eddison died, but Eddison
did have the entire book outlined and summarized.
These summaries are substituted for the missing
chapters. While the other two volumes cover
relatively short lengths of time, *Mezentian
Gate* spans three-quarters of a century and
chronicles the domestic and political intrigues
of three kingdoms: Meszria, Rerek, and Fingiswold. Featured are Lessingham's recollection
of his childhood, adulthood, and death; of
eighteenth and nineteenth century Britain; the
members of the Parry Clan of Rerek and the Royal
House of Fingiswold; and the murder of Mary
Scarnside's father. A highly complex series
that should be read in reverse order of publication to maintain internal chronology.

H.M. EGBERT, pseud. See VICTOR ROSSEAU EMANUEL

GEORGE EGERTON, pseud.
See MARY CHAVELITA CLAIRMONTE BRIGHT

PHYLLIS EISENSTEIN

322. *Sorcerer's Son*. New York: Ballantine, 1979
      [paper].

Delivev, a sorceress, admits what appears to be
a wounded knight to Castle Spinweb. However,
the knight, Gildrum, is actually a demon, and,
after a brief and passionate affair, he leaves
her pregnant, and unaware that he had fallen
in love with her. When the child, Cray, is
grown, he goes in search of his father, not
knowing that Gildrum has been enslaved by the
evil sorcerer, Rezhyk, and has been prevented

from returning. When Cray attempts to use
sorcery to find his father, he falls under
Rezhyk's sway, and Rezhyk is his mother's sworn
enemy.

GORDON EKLUND

323. "The Twilight River." In *Binary Star No. 2.*
New York: Dell, 1979 [paper]. Bound with F.
Paul Wilson's science-fiction novella, "The
Tery."

Earth in the far future has been invaded and
conquered by aliens known as the Rangels; towns
are ruled by puppet governors called Warlocks.
Sam, one of a few remaining free men, lives a
wandering life until he saves the beautiful
Trina, a warlock's daughter, from the wrath of
the Rangels after she has slain one of them.
They attempt to journey to the realm of the
Free Men, a seemingly mythic place, but are
delayed when they meet a true wizard (actually
Sam's father) who helps them and must destroy
Sam's mother, a vampire. When they finally do
find their goal, they are dismayed to find it
is peopled by man's successor on earth, highly
evolved and intelligent dogs.

PAUL ELDRIDGE
See GEORGE SYLVESTER VIERECK AND PAUL ELDRIDGE

HARLAN ELLISON

324. *The Beast That Shouted Love at the Heart of the
World.* New York: Avon, 1969 [paper].

a. "Introduction: The Waves of Rio"
b. "The Beast That Shouted Love at the Heart
of the World"
c. "Along the Scenic Route" (original title:
"Dogfight on 101")
d. "Phoenix" (original title "Phoenix Land")
e. "Asleep: With Still Hands"
f. "Santa Claus vs. S.P.I.D.E.R."
g. "Try a Dull Knife"
h. "The Pitll Pawob Division"
i. "The Place With No Name"
j. "White on White"
k. "Run for the Stars"

    l.   "Are You Listening?"
    m.   "S.R.O."
    n.   "Worlds to Kill"
    o.   "Shattered Like a Glass Goblin"
    p.   "A Boy and His Dog"

325. *Deathbird Stories: a pantheon of modern gods.* New York: Harper & Row, 1975.

    a.   "Introduction: Oblations at Alien Altars"
    b.   "The Whimper of Whipped Dogs"
    c.   "Along the Scenic Route"
    d.   "On the Downhill Side"
    e.   "O Ye of Little Faith"
    f.   "Neon"
    g.   "Basilisk"
    h.   "Pretty Maggie Moneyeyes"
    i.   "Corpse"
    j.   "Shattered Like a Glass Goblin"
    k.   "Delusion for a Dragon Slayer"
    l.   "The Face of Helene Bournouw"
    m.   "Bleeding Stones"
    n.   "At the Mouse Circus"
    o.   "The Place with No Name"
    p.   "Paingod"
    q.   "Ernest and the Machine God"
    r.   "Rock God"
    s.   "Adrift Just Off the Islets of Langerhans: Latitude 38° 54'N, Longitude 77° 00'W"
    t.   "The Deathbird"

326. *Strange Wine: Fifteen New Stories From the Nightside of the World.* New York: Harper & Row, 1978.

    a.   "Croatoan"
    b.   "Working With the Little People"
    c.   "Killing Bernstein"
    d.   "Mom"
    e.   "In Fear of K"
    f.   "Hitler Painted Roses"
    g.   "The Wine Has Been Left Open Too Long and the Memory Has Gone Flat"
    h.   "From A to Z, in the Chocolate Alphabet"
    i.   "Lonely Women Are the Vessels of Time"
    j.   "Emissary from Hamelin"
    k.   "The New York Review of Bird"
    l.   "Seeing"
    m.   "The Boulevard of Broken Dreams"
    n.   "Strange Wine"
    o.   "The Diagnosis of Dr. D'*arque*Angel"

Bibliography

327. Swigart, Leslie Kay. *Harlan Ellison: A Bibliograph-ical Checklist*. Dallas: Williams, 1973 [paper].

328. Swigart, Leslie Kay. "Harlan Ellison: An F&SF Checklist." *The Magazine of Fantasy and Science Fiction*, July 1977, 80-89.

VICTOR ROUSSEAU EMANUEL

329. Egbert, H.M., pseud. *Eric of the Strong Heart*. London: John Long, 1925.

Set in a tropical land at the North Pole, this is both a lost-race and sword and sorcery novel.

EVANGELINE WALTON ENSLEY

The Mabinogion Series

330. Walton, Evangeline, pseud. *Prince of Annwn: The First Branch of the Mabinogion*. New York: Ballantine, 1974 [paper].

331. _____. *The Children of Llyr: The Second Branch of the Mabinogion*. New York: Ballantine, 1971 [paper].

332. _____. *The Song of Rhiannon: The Third Branch of the Mabinogion*. New York: Ballantine, 1972 [paper].

333. _____. *The Virgin and the Swine: The Fourth Branch of the Mabinogion*. Chicago and New York: Willet, Clark, 1936. Rpt. as *The Island of the Mighty: The Fourth Branch of the Mabinogion*. New York: Ballantine, 1970 [paper].

A retelling of the Welsh *Mabinogion*. While this version is easier, more coherent reading than the original, the original's rough and vital prose; its event, rather than character or plot orientation; and its often barbaric power of human interaction, politics, and love are re-tained.

HANNS HEINZ EWERS

334. *The Sorcerer's Apprentice*. Trans. Ludwig Lewisohn. New York: John Day, 1927.

> Set in a small Italian village, this work was highly thought of by H.P. Lovecraft and is considered a classic black arts novel.

PAUL W. FAIRMAN

335. Jorgensen, Ivar, pseud.* *Whom the Gods Would Slay*. New York: Belmont, 1968 [paper].

> A brief, unassuming sword and sorcery novel concerning an ancient viking's magical quest to destroy an alien space craft.

> *N.B. This pseudonym has also been connected with Robert Silverburg and/or Harlan Ellison by various sources. Fairman seems to be the best possibility.

ELEANOR FARJEON

336. *The Fair of St. James: A Fantasia*. London: Faber and Faber, 1932.

> In this light and fanciful tale, two young visitors to a French cathedral town become so enthralled by the festive atmosphere that they enter the land of dreams and participate in a fair. While there, they observe and are involved with royalty, a crystal gazer, various beggars, and many internal fantasy tales.

337. *Humming Bird: A Novel*. New York: Frederick A. Stokes, 1937.

338. *The Soul of Kol Nikon*. London: Collins, 1923.

> A young boy grows up as an outcast because his mother has labelled him as a fairy changeling. Believing it himself, he spends much of the novel in a bittersweet quest to steal a soul, thus making himself human and hoping to gain his mother's love. An interesting exploration into the nature of identity and self-knowledge.

Bibliography

339. Zeeman, Denise Avril. *Eleanor Farjeon: A Biblio-*

graphy. Johannesburg: University of Wtwaters-
rand, Department of Bibliography, Librarianship
and Typography, 1970.

PHILIP JOSÉ FARMER

340. *Flesh.* Garden City, NY: Doubleday, 1968.

What begins as a seeming science-fiction story,
in which a group of astronauts return to Earth
eight-hundred years after their departure, is
quickly transformed into a primitive and socially expansive fantasy involving the rites of
passage, kingship, and godhood. In the future,
post-holocaust world, the population has
committed itself to an orgastic cult that
transforms one of the astronauts into a human
stag, the sun hero, who becomes subject to the
brutal and elemental laws of procreation and
rebirth.

341. *Inside Outside.* New York: Ballantine, 1964 [paper].

An inhabitant of Hell and his companion escape
from their damnation, explore the nature of
their environment, and discover what exists
beyond the afterlife.

342. *Night of Light.* New York: Berkley, 1966 [paper].
Rpt. New York: Garland, 1975.

John Carmody, a vicious criminal, is transformed
into a priest by the miraculous "night of
light" (a periodic solar flare) and fathers a
new god to replace the one he'd slain in his
previous evil existence. This, like other
Farmer novels, is distinguished by the mixture
of the real and the unreal, the mystical and
the mundane.

The Riverworld Series

343. *To Your Scattered Bodies Go: A Science Fiction
Novel.* New York: G.P. Putnam's Sons, 1971.

344. *The Fabulous Riverboat: A Science Fiction Novel
in the Riverworld Series.* New York: G.P.
Putnam's Sons, 1971.

345. *The Dark Design: The Third Novel in the Riverworld
Series.* New York: Berkley, 1977.

346. *The Magic Labyrinth*. Forthcoming.

> In the unfinished Riverworld series (at least
> one more volume is promised), earth's dead are
> reborn along the shores of a seemingly endless
> river, and personages from all geographic areas
> and time periods are brought together to begin
> new lives and establish new societies. The
> Riverworld has been created and is maintained
> by a group of super beings called the Ethicals,
> and much of the action of the series focuses
> on the attempt by the characters to sail to the
> head waters of the river and discover the
> nature of the Ethicals' dark tower that is
> located there. Farmer's expert use of histori-
> cal figures (Richard Burton and Mark Twain are
> the protagonists of the first two books; the
> enigmatic Peter Jairus Frigate -- the Farmer
> persona -- of the third) and his understanding
> of human motivations and society are two of
> the most noteworthy aspects of the series.

The World of Tiers Series

347. *Maker of Universes*. New York: Ace, 1965 [paper].
     Rpt. New York: Garland, 1975.

348. *Gates of Creation*. New York: Ace, 1966 [paper].

349. *A Private Cosmos*. New York: Ace, 1968 [paper].

350. *Behind the Walls of Terra*. New York: Ace, 1970
     [paper].

351. *The Lavalite World*. New York: Ace, 1977 [paper].

> The World of Tiers series, also known as the
> Pocket Universe series, focuses on a race of
> superior beings who create totally new uni-
> verses for their personal toys. Jadawin, also
> known as Robert Wolff, has created the pocket
> universe that most of the action takes place
> in. Humanized by his contact with mankind,
> Jadawin is converted from a typical, scheming,
> arrogant, and uncaring "Lord" to a more invol-
> ved and compassionate individual. Much of the
> action of the series is generated by Jadawin's
> conflicts with Kickaha the Trickster, also
> known as Paul James Finnegan and probably a
> Farmer self-portrait, as the two struggle for
> control of Jadawin's desirable pocket universe.
> This is a complicated and fascinating series

in which Farmer explores the nature of artistic
and literary creation, often expressing his
views through the female Lord Anana, Jadawin's
sister.

Bibliography

352. Brizzi, Mary. *A Reader's Guide to Philip José
Farmer*. West Linn, OR: Starmont House, 1979
[paper].

353. Knapp, Lawrence. *The First Editions of Philip
José Farmer*. Menlo Park, CA: David G. Turner,
1976 [paper].

354. Wymer, Thomas. "Speculative Fiction, Bibliographies, & Philip José Farmer." *Extrapolation*,
18 (1976), 65-72.

HENRY FIELDING

355. *A Journey From This World to the Next*. London:
Harrison, 1783. Rpt. New York: Arno, 1976,
from the 1930 Golden Cockerel Press edition.

In a mock memoir, the soul of a dead man is
escorted, along with other souls, to Elysium
by the god Mercury. As they travel in a coach,
stops are made and homage paid at the City of
Diseases and the Palace of Death. When the
souls arrive at the River Cocytus, they are
passed by many pitiable souls, judged unfit
for the afterlife, and sent back to Earth for
another existence, new lives selected by the
wheel of fortune. The narrator, fortunately,
is accepted by Minos, the great judge, for
entry into Elysium. In Elysium, he meets and
converses with numerous famous figures from
history. This was originally intended as a
contemporary satire of British customs and
society.

Bibliography

356. Henley, William Ernest, ed. *The Complete Works of
Henry Fielding*. New York: Crosscup & Sterling,
1902, XVI, xlvii-lxii.

357. Dudden, Frederick Hoines. *Henry Fielding, His
Life, Works and Times*. Oxford: Oxford University Press, 1952, II, 1126-1151.

358. *The Circus of Dr. Lao.* New York: Viking, 1935.

> The inhabitants of Abalone, Arizona, are enter-
> tained by the wonders of Dr. Lao's circus: a
> medusa, a chimera, a werewolf, and a satyr, all
> authentic. The circus's finale is a ritual
> offering to an ancient and unknown god, and
> each spectator experiences an ironic, personal,
> and horrible vision of self during the ceremony.
> Long considered a classic of weird fantasy.

359. *The Ghosts of Manacle.* New York: Pyramid, 1964
      [paper].

> a. "The Iowan's Curse"
> b. "The Horsenapping of Hotspur"
> c. "The Life and Death of a Western Gladiator"
> d. "The Gilashrikeys"
> e. "The Black Retriever"
> f. "The Captivity"
> g. "The Door"
> h. "The End of the Rainbow"

360. "The Magician Out of Manchuria." In *Unholy City
      and Magician Out of Manchuria.* New York:
      Pyramid, 1968 [paper].

> Finney's magician is a lazy and dishonest bri-
> gand and con man who sheds his skin at various
> inopportune intervals because of his serpent
> lineage. Along with a queen made beautiful by
> magic, an ass, and an assistant, the magician
> is involved in adventures and hair-breadth
> escapes. His dalliances and rescue of the
> Queen of Lust are among the best moments in
> this novelette, which also includes such items
> as the magician's paraphrase of James Joyce's
> *A Portrait of the Artist as a Young Man* to the
> ass. Funny, often esoteric, and a heavy-handed
> criticism of socialism.

361. *The Unholy City.* New York: Vanguard, 1937.

> Though not as successful as *The Circus of Dr.
> Lao* or "The Magician Out of Manchuria," *The
> Unholy City* is a representative example of
> Finney's creation of the picaresque and delight-
> ful rascal. In this tale, the only survivor
> of a plane crash and a resident of Abalone,
> Arizona (the setting for *The Circus of Dr. Lao*),
> is taken in hand by a free-spending inhabitant
> of the unholy city of Heilar-wey. Much of the

novel is devoted to their adventures in this futuristic city as Finney sustains a constant parody of social materialism.

Bibliography

362. Burke, W.J., Will D. Howe, Irving Weiss, and Anne Weiss. *American Authors and Books: 1640 to the Present*. 3rd rev. ed. New York: Crown, 1972, p. 212.

[ARTHUR ANNESLEY] RONALD FIRBANK

363. *The Artificial Princess*. London: Duckworth, 1934.

364. *Caprice*. London: Grant Richards, 1917.

365. *The Flower Beneath the Foot: Being a Record of the Early Life of St. Laura de Nazianz; and the Times in Which She Lived*. London: Grant Richards, 1923.

In this burlesque parody of courtly life, a young woman, Laura Lita Carmen Etoile de Nazianzi, is disappointed in love when her beloved, His Weariness Prince Yousef, marries another. She returns to the convent of her youth, the Convent of the Flaming-Hood, and, after lamenting her misfortune, she embarks upon a life devoted to sanctity and the pursuit of sainthood. This delightful parody is further distinguished by its criticisms of Roman Catholic piety and by the names of its characters: Her Gaudiness, the Mistress of the Robes (Laura's mother); Her Dreaminess (the Queen); the Marquesa Pizzi-Parma; Lord Limpness; April Flowers; Count Cabinet; Mrs. Chilleywater; Father Nostradamns, etc.

366. *Odette D'Antrevernes and A Study in Temperament*. London: Elkin Matthews, 1905.

367. *The Princess Zoubaroff: A Comedy*. London: Grant Richards, 1920.

368. *Vainglory*. London: Grant Richards, 1915.

369. *Valmouth: A Romantic Novel*. London: Grant Richards, 1919.

Bibliography

370. Benkowitz, Miriam Jeanette. *A Bibliography of Ronald Firbank*. London: Rupert Hart-Davis, 1963.

VIOLET MARY FIRTH

371. Fortune, Dion, pseud. *The Secrets of Doctor Taverner*. London: Noel Douglas, 1926.

A collection of fantasy-occult tales featuring Dr. Taverner, an alturistic initiate into the arcane mysteries of antiquity. Like Firth's other works, this reflects her intense interest in the unseen, the mystical, and the psycho-analytic.

a. "Blood Lust"
b. "The Return of the Ritual"
c. "The Man Who Sought"
d. "The Soul That Would Not Be Born"
e. "The Scented Poppies"
f. "The Death Hound"
g. "A Daughter of Pan"
h. "The Subletting of the Mansion"
i. "Recalled"
j. "The Sea Lure"
k. "The Power House"

A number of Firth's other works follow, with the caution that they may contain too much horror and occult to be truly considered fantasy.

372. _____. *The Demon Lover*. London: Noel Douglas, 1927.

373. _____. *The Goat Foot God*. London: Williams & Norgate, 1936.

374. _____. *Moon Magic: Being the Memoirs of a Mistress of That Art*. London: Aquarian Press, 1956.

The posthumously published sequel to *The Sea Priestess* (see below).

375. _____. *The Sea Priestess*. London: By the Author, 1938.

376.   _____. *Winged Bull*. London: Williams & Norgate,
         1935.

GENE FISHER

The Godkiller Series.

377. Lancour, Gene, pseud. *The Lerios Mecca*. Garden
     City, NY: Doubleday, 1973.

     A young man, Dirshan, accepts a quest from the
     major religion, "The Order," to escape a death
     sentence, and pursues a renegade priest.   In
     his quest, he falls in love with a warrior-prin-
     cess, Karinth, and goes to a hidden valley
     where he discovers the secret of a religious
     prophet, older and wiser than any member of The
     Order.

378.   _____. *The War Machines of Kalinth*. Garden City,
         NY: Doubleday, 1977.

     The sequel to *The Lerios Mecca* and the con-
     tinued adventures of Dirshan as he battles the
     Kalinthian Horde.

379.   _____. *Sword for the Empire*. Garden City, NY:
         Doubleday, 1978.

GEORGE U. FLETCHER, pseud. See FLETCHER PRATT

E[DWARD] M[ORGAN] FORSTER

380. *The Celestial Omnibus and Other Stories*. London:
     Sedgwick & Jackson, 1911.

         a.   "The Story of a Panic"
         b.   "The Other Side of the Hedge"
         c.   "The Celestial Omnibus"
         d.   "Other Kingdom"
         e.   "The Curate's Friend"
         f.   "The Road from Colonus"

381. *The Eternal Moment and Other Stories*. New York:
     Harcourt, Brace, 1928.

         a.   "The Machine Stops"
         b.   "The Point of It"
         c.   "Mr. Andrews"

      d.   "Co-ordination"
      e.   "The Story of the Siren"
      f.   "The Eternal Moment"

382. *A Room With a View*. London: Edward Arnold, 1908.

Bibliography

383. Kirkpatrick, Brownlee Jean. *A Bibliography of E.M. Forster*. London: Rupert Hart-Davis, 1965.

DION FORTUNE, pseud. See VIOLET MARY FIRTH

GARDNER F[RANCIS] FOX

The Llarn Series

384. *Warrior of Llarn*. New York: Ace, 1964 [paper].

385. *Thief of Llarn*. New York: Ace, 1966 [paper].

Both of these novels are heavily influenced by Edgar Rice Burroughs' Mars series (see above), although they use parallel universes as their setting.

The Kothar Series

386. *Kothar Barbarian Swordsman*. New York: Belmont, 1969 [paper].

      a.   "The Sword of the Sorcerer"
      b.   "The Treasure of the Labyrinth"
      c.   "The Woman in the Witch-Wood"

387. *Kothar of the Magic Sword!* New York: Belmont, 1969 [paper].

      a.   "The Helix From Beyond"
      b.   "A Plague of Demons"

388. *Kothar and the Demon Queen*. New York: Tower, 1969 [paper].

389. *Kothar and the Conjurer's Curse*. New York: Belmont, 1970 [paper].

390. *Kothar and the Wizard Slayer*. New York: Belmont, 1970 [paper].

> Fox's Kothar series is very much in the blood-thirsty tradition of Robert E. Howard's Conan series (see below) in its swordplay, wizards, and heroic endeavors. It is distinguished, however, by the characterization of the sorceress, Red Lori, who maintains a love-hate relationship with Kothar.

Kyrik Series

391. *Kyrik: Warlock Warrior*. New York: Leisure Books, 1975 [paper].

392. *Kyrik Fights the Demon World*. New York: Leisure Books, 1975 [paper].

393. *Kyrik and the Wizard's Sword*. New York: Leisure Books, 1976 [paper].

394. *Kyrik and the Lost Queen*. New York: Leisure Books, 1976 [paper].

> A sword and sorcery series set in pre-history that chronicles the adventures of Kyrik, warrior and wizard. Returning after a thousand years of enchanted sleep, Kyrik struggles to regain his kingdom, wields the sword Bluefang, and is involved with Illis, the seductive demon-goddess he loved and worshipped.

MARY E. WILKINS [FREEMAN]

395. *The Wind in the Rose Bush and Other Tales of the Supernatural*. Garden City, NY: Doubleday, Page, 1903.

    a. "The Wind in the Rose-Bush"
    b. "The Shadows on the Wall"
    c. "Luella Miller"
    d. "The Southwest Chamber"
    e. "The Vacant Lot"
    f. "The Lost Ghost"

ARTHUR O. FRIEL

396. *Tiger River*. New York: Harper, 1923 [not seen].

ARTHUR O. FRIEL continued

>Rpt. New York: Centaur Press, 1971 [paper].
>
>In a quest for a vast hoard of gold, a group of
>Americans and a Peruvian outlaw venture into
>the South American jungles and, particularly,
>to an area known as Tigre Yacu, "the River of
>Missing Men." After confronting races of white
>Indians and green men, they are turned into
>beasts by the wine of a "Circe" in a valley in
>the Andes before they gain unexpected help,
>are freed, and find the gold. Friel's other
>major novel, *The Pathless Trail* (1922. Rpt.
>New York: Centaur Press, 1969 [paper]) is a
>lost-race, adventure story.

GANPAT, pseud. See MARTIN LOUIS ALAN GOMPERTZ

JOHN [CHAMPLIN] GARDNER, [JR.]

397. *Grendel*. New York: Alfred E. Knopf, 1971.

>A retelling of the *Beowulf* epic from the mon-
>ster's point of view. An interesting tour-de-
>force of sympathetic characterization as the
>shift to Grendel's perspective puts Hrothgar
>and Beowulf in a different, more modern light.
>Grendel gains humanity through its admiration
>and envy of humankind.

398. *In the Suicide Mountains*. New York: Alfred A.
>Knopf, 1977.

>Three people meet in the Suicide Mountains.
>Each is intent on self-destruction: a black-
>smith's daughter, Amanda, who has committed
>unfortunate acts for the sake of a false role
>of weak maidenhood; an ugly dwarf, Chudu the
>Goat's Son, whose magic powers have made him
>suspect of horrible acts until he finally
>believes himself capable of them; and a crown
>prince, Christopher the Sullen, who prefers
>poetry and music to being a knight. At the
>conclusion of the tale, they all gain and
>learn from each other's tolerance, from a battle
>with a dragon, and from the tales of an enig-
>matic abbot. This work draws heavily on var-
>ious Russian folk tales.

399. *Jason and Medeia*. New York: Alfred A. Knopf, 1973.

    An epic retelling of the Jason and Medeia myth, in verse and in imitation of Homer and Virgil, that spans a period of time from the classic age to New York to the end of the world. A rollicking account as Jason is portrayed as a politician and an intellectual from the west, and Medeia is characterized as the intuitive and passionate figure from the east. Among this novel's wonders are Jason's talking ship and Medeia's sinister ravens.

400. *The King's Indian: Stories and Tales*. New York: Alfred A. Knopf, 1974.

    a. "Pastoral Care"
    b. "The Ravages of Spring"
    c. "The Temptation of St. Ivo"
    d. "The Warden"
    e. "John Napper, Sailing Through the Universe"
    f. "Queen Louisa"
    g. "King Gregor and the Fool"
    h. "Muriel"
    i. "The King's Indian: A Tale"

Bibliography

401. Bruccoli, Mathew J., and C.E. Frazer Clark, eds. *First Printings of American Authors: Contributions Toward Definitive Checklists*. Detroit: Gale Research, 1978, II, 117-123.

ALAN GARNER

402. *Elidor*. London: William Collins & Sons, 1965.

    This work is not as otherworldly as *The Moon of Gomrath* and *The Weirdstone of Brisingamen*. Most of the action takes place in this world and revolves around the keeping of the four treasures of Elidor by four children. The major theme is the conflict among the children between rationalism and wonder.

403. *The Moon of Gomrath*. London: William Collins & Sons, 1963.

    The sequel to *The Weirdstone of Brisingamen* which continues Garner's excellent amalgamation of Western and Northern European mythology and the geography of his hometown, Alderley in Cheshire. Susan, one of the young protagonists, finds herself the focus of the yet undefeated evil forces due to a magical bracelet she wears. The episodes involving the Wild Hunt and the "Old Magic," the seemingly ill-advised powers that the children summon, comprise two of the most effective portions of the book.

404. *The Owl Service*. London: William Collins Sons, 1967.

Darker and less narratively cogent than Garner's other fantasies, this is nonetheless interesting for its use of material from the Welsh *Mabinogion* (see Evangeline Walton Ensley above). A valley holds the residue and accumulated power of a myth focusing on Lleu, Blodenwedd, and Gronw Pebyr--figures from Welsh legend. The myth must be re-enacted over and over again until three modern young people are able to break the spell.

405. *The Weirdstone of Brisingamen: A Tale of Alderley*. London: William Collins Sons, 1960. Rev. ed. London: Penguin, 1963.

Although considered primarily as a juvenile, this is one of the few books that evokes a sense of wonder comparable to Tolkien's Trilogy (see below). Two 20th-century children and the immortal Merlin seek a talisman that is essential to the safety of the world and to the preservation of the sleeping King Arthur. Sequel: *The Moon of Gomrath* (see above).

DAVID GARNETT

406. *Lady Into Fox*. London: Chatto & Windus, 1922.

An attractive young wife unexpectedly begins to turn into a vixen, a female fox, and her husband, baffled, attempts to deal with her remaining vestiges of humanity until he too begins to lose his humanity. For a comparable work, see Jean Bruller's *Sylva* above.

407. *A Man in the Zoo*. London: Chatto & Windus, 1924. [simultaneous publication in New York by Alfred

DAVID GARNETT continued

        A. Knopf?].

        A young man thwarted in love donates himself to
        a zoo as an example of homo sapiens until his
        young lady recognizes his value and allows his
        love.

408.   *Two by Two: A Story of Survival*. London: Longmans,
        Green, 1963 [simultaneous publication in New
        York by Atheneum?].

        Bibliography

409.   Watson, George, ed. *The New Cambridge Bibliography
        of English Literature*. Cambridge: Cambridge
        University Press, 1972, IV (1900-1950), 586.

                        RICHARD GARNETT

410.   *The Twilight of the Gods and Other Tales*. London:
        T. Fisher Unwin, 1888.

        a.   "The Twilight of the Gods"
        b.   "The Potion of Lao-Tsze"
        c.   "Abdallah the Adite"
        d.   "Ananda the Miracle-Worker"
        e.   "The City of Philosophers"
        f.   "The Demon Pope"
        g.   "The Cupbearer"
        h.   "The Dumb Oracle"
        i.   "Duke Virgil"
        j.   "Madam Lucifer"
        k.   "The Elixir of Life"
        l.   "The Poet of Panopolis"
        m.   "The Purple Head"
        n.   "The Bell of St. Euschemon"
        o.   "Bishop Adds and Bishop Gadds"
        p.   "The Poison-Maid"

        Bibliography

411.   Pollard, Alfred William. "Richard Garnett."
        English Illustrated Magazine, New Series, 30
        (February 1904), 553-555, 559.

412.   Texas University Humanities Research Center. *The
        Garnetts, A Literary Family: An Exhibition*.
        Austin: Texas University, 1959.

[GORDON] RANDALL [PHILIP DAVID] GARRETT

413. *Murder and Magic*. New York: Ace Books, 1979
      [paper].

      The further adventures of the detective Lord
      Darcy and his sidekick, Master Sean O Lochlainn,
      a forensic sorcerer, in a realm where magic
      exists and the British Empire still rules most
      of the world and struggles against the insidious
      Polish Empire. Psychic and sorcerous mysteries
      at their best:

      a.   "The Eyes Have It"
      b.   "A Case of Identity"
      c.   "The Muddle of the Woad"
      d.   "A Stretch of the Imagination"

414. *Too Many Magicians*. New York: Doubleday, 1966.
      Rpt. Boston: Gregg Press, 1978.

      An excellent whodunit, featuring the perceptive
      Lord Darcy, set in an alternate Britain where
      the Plantagenets still rule and magic is a
      reality, which in its appropriate usage exists
      in harmony with the church. The main thrust of
      this Darcy adventure is the solution of a
      seemingly sorcerous murder that takes place at
      a magicians' and sorcerers' convention. For a
      similar work, see James Gunn's *The Magicians*
      (below).

JANE GASKELL, pseud. See JANE DENVIL LYNCH

FRANCIS GERARD

415. *Secret Sceptre*. New York: E.P. Dutton, 1939.

      A British detective discovers and joins an an-
      cient order of Knights in the Black Mountains
      of Wales. Their responsibility is to guard the
      Holy Grail and prevent it and other reliques
      that maintain Britain from falling into the
      hands of an anti-Christ.

MARK S. GESTON

416. *The Siege of Wonder*. Garden City, NY: Doubleday,
      1976.

      An end-of-time, post-holocaust struggle is be-

ing waged between the proponents of magic and
science. A science spy is corrupted when he
attempts to penetrate the wizard's inner cycle
and place an electronic eye in a unicorn.
Ultimately, he must confront the fact and fancy
of his own mixed nature.

W[ILLIAM] S[CHWENCK] GILBERT

417. *Foggerty's Fairy and Other Tales.* London: George
     Routledge and Sons, 1890.

     a. "Foggerty's Fairy"
     b. "An Elixir of Love"
     c. "Johnny Pounce"
     d. "Little Mim"
     e. "The Triumph of Vice"
     f. "My Maiden Brief"
     g. "Creatures of Impulse"
     h. "Maxwell and I"
     i. "Actors, Authors, and Audiences"
     j. "Angela"
     k. "Wide Awake"
     l. "A Stage Play"
     m. "The Wicked World"
     n. "The Finger of Fate"
     o. "A Tale of a Dry Plate"
     p. "The Burglar's Story"
     q. "Unappreciated Shakespeare"
     r. "Comedy and Tragedy"
     s. "Rosencrantz and Guildenstern"

Bibliography

418. Searle, R. Townley. *Sir William Schwenck Gilbert:
     A Topsy-Turvy Adventure.* London: Alexander-
     Ouseley, 1931.

419. Dubois, Arthur Edwin. "Additions to the Biblio-
     graphy of W.S. Gilbert's Contributions to
     Magazines." *Modern Language Notes*, 47 (May
     1932), 308-314.

WILLIAM GOLDMAN

420. *The Princess Bride: S. Morgenstern's Classic
     Tale of True Love and High Adventure. The
     "Good Parts" Version, Abridged.* New York:

Harcourt Brace Jovanovich, 1973.

This novel, by a popular mainstream author
(*Butch Cassidy and the Sundance Kid,* 1969;
Soldier in the Rain, 1960; *Marathon Man,* 1974),
manages to successfully jam almost every con-
ceivable fantasy device and dilemma between
its covers. All is for naught, however, for in
the time-honored tradition of 18th-century
domestic comedy, the hero, Westley, and the
heroine, Buttercup, are reunited. They even
manage to overcome Goldman's tiresome textual
comments as he "revises" the text.

MARTIN LOUIS ALAN GOMPERTZ

421. Ganpat, pseud. *The Voice of Dashin: A Romance of
Wild Mountains.* London: Hodder & Stoughton,
1926.

Gompertz is best known as a writer of lost-race
adventure tales. *The Voice of Dashin,* however,
has a number of fantasy elements as, in true
lost-race fashion, the intrepid Britisher and
his comrades aid the Tibetan People of the Hand
in recapturing their lost City of Fairy Towers by
introducing the miracles of modern warfare.
Fantasy content includes crystals that show
the past and future plus various mythopoetic
and magic elements surrounding the return of a
long-dead prince and his now-aged beloved.

For those readers with an affection for lost-
race fiction who would like to search some
other Gompertz works for fantasy elements, a
selection follows:

422. _____. *Dainra.* London: Hodder and Stoughton, 1929.

423. _____. *Fairy Silver, a Traveller's Tale.* London:
Hodder and Stoughton, 1932.

424. _____. *Harilek: A Romance of Modern Central Asia.*
Edinburgh and London: William Blackwood, 1923.
Rpt. in a omnibus volume with *Wrexham's Romance:
Adventures in Sakaeland, Comprising Harilek: A
Romance* [from the 1923 Boston, Houghton Mifflin
edition] *and Wrexham's Romance, Being a Contin-
uation of "Harilek."* New York: **Arn**o, 1978 [not
seen].

425. _____. *Mirror of Dreams: A Tale of Oriental My-
      stery.* Garden City, NY: Doubleday, Doran, 1928.

426. _____. *The Snow Rubies.* Boston: Houghton Mifflin,
      1925.

427. _____. *The Speakers in Silence.* London: Hodder
      and Stoughton, 1929.

428. _____. *Walls Have Eyes.* London: Hodder and
      Stoughton, 1930.

429. _____. *Wrexham's Romance.* London: Hodder and
      Stoughton, 1935. Rpt. as noted above in the
      Harilek entry.

KENNETH GRAHAME

430. *Dream Days.* New York and London: John Lane: The
      Bodley Head, 1899.

      a.   "The Twenty-First of October"
      b.   "Dies Iræ"
      c.   "Mutabile Semper"
      d.   "The Magic Ring"
      e.   "Its Walls Were as of Jasper"
      f.   "A Saga of the Seas"
      g.   "The Reluctant Dragon"
      h.   "A Departure"

431. *The Golden Age.* London: John Lane; Chicago: Stone
      and Kimball, 1895.

      a.   "Prologue: The Olympians"
      b.   "A Holiday"
      c.   "A Whitewashed Uncle"
      d.   "Alarums and Excursions"
      e.   "The Finding of the Princess"
      f.   "Sawdust and Sin"
      g.   "'Young Adam Cupid'"
      h.   "The Burglars"
      i.   "A Harvesting"
      j.   "Snowbound"
      k.   "What They Talked About"
      l.   "The Argonauts"
      m.   "The Roman Road"
      n.   "The Secret Drawer"
      o.   "'Exit Tyrannus'"
      p.   "The Blue Room"
      q.   "A Falling Out"
      r.   "'Lusisti Satis'"

432. *Pagan Papers*. London: Elkin Mathews and John
     Lane; Chicago: Stone and Kimball, 1894.

    a. "The Romance of the Road"
    b. "The Romance of the Rail"
    c. "Non Libri Sed Liberi"
    d. "Loafing"
    e. "Cheap Knowledge"
    f. "The Rural Pan"
    g. "Marginalia"
    h. "The Eternal Whither"
    i. "Deus Terminus"
    j. "Of Smoking"
    k. "An Autumn Encounter"
    l. "The White Poppy"
    m. "A Bohemian in Exile"
    n. "Justifiable Homicide"
    o. "The Fairy Wicket"
    p. "Aboard the Galley"
    q. "The Lost Centaur"
    r. "Orion"
    s. "The Olympians"
    t. "A White-Washed Uncle"
    u. "The Finding of the Princess"
    v. "'Young Adam Cupid'"
    w. "The Burglars"
    x. "Snowbound"

433. *The Wind in the Willows*. London: Methuen, 1908.

A classic among contemporary beast fables with
an adventuresome toad, a mole, a water rat, and
a badger as its well characterized protagonists.
In a variety of ways, the novel is the celebration of the English countryside and an examination of the relationships between the worlds of
man and nature. While the Toad's adventures
have been more frequently remembered than the
other protagonists', such episodes as how Mole
learns to love the river, Rat's infatuation with
the life of a sailor, Mole's night in the Wild
Wood, and the vision of Pan on the river bank
are of equal, if not greater, value.

Interested readers should also see *The First
Whisper of "The Wind in the Willows."* Ed.
Elspeth Grahame. London: Methuen, 1944.

Bibliography

434. Green, Peter [Morris]. *Kenneth Grahame, 1859-1932:
     A Study of His Life, Work, and Times*. London:

John Murray, 1959, pp. 377-380.

ROBERT [RANKE] GRAVES

435. *Watch the North Wind Rise*. New York: Creative Age
Press, 1949. British title: *Seven Days in New
Crete*. London: Cassell, 1949 [follows the
American edition by six months].

Bibliography

436. Higginson, Fred H. *A Bibliography of the Works of
Robert Graves*. Hamden, CT: Archon Books, 1966.

NICHOLAS STUART GRAY

437. *The Stone Cage*. London: Dennis Dobson, 1963.

An amplification of the Brothers Grimm tale of
Rapunzel. The child Rapunzel is taken by guile
from her parents by a witch who attempts to
raise the child as a witch. With the protection
of a cynical cat, Tomlyn, and an idealistic
raven, Marshall, Rapunzel grows to womanhood
unaffected by the spells and machinations of
the witch, Mother Gothel. However, before the
beautiful maiden can be united with her beloved
prince, she, Tomlyn, and Marshall, with the aid
of the wizard Macpherson, must defeat the witch
and endure a necromantic exile to the dark side
of the moon.

While Gray's novels are interesting, they may
be too juvenile for many adult readers. The
titles that follow are listed without annotation with this caution.

438. *The Apple-Stone*. London: Dennis Dobson, 1965.

439. *Down in the Cellar*. London: Dennis Dobson, 1961.

440. *Grimbold's Other World*. London: Faber and Faber,
1963.

441. *Mainly by Moonlight*. London: Faber and Faber, 1965.

442. *Over the Hills to Fabylon*. London: Oxford University Press, 1954.

443. *The Seventh Swan: An Adventure Story*. London: Dennis Dobson, 1962.

ROGER [GILBERT] LANCELYN GREEN

444. *From the World's End: A Fantasy*. Leicester, U.K.: Edmund Ward, 1948.

> A dark tale of two lovers who spend a night in the house on the edge of the world. They are separated and drawn into the unacceptable extremes of *caritas* and *cupiditas* by visitations from the fairy folk. The book parallels C.S. Lewis' use of the celestial and earthly Venus in *That Hideous Strength* (see below) and is distinguished by Green's knowledge of Celtic and Welsh mythology, as well as his knowledge of the English literary tradition and English mythology. It culminates in the realization of the necessity of the co-existence of both spiritual and physical love.

> *From the World's End* is included with Edmund Cooper's *The Firebird* in *Double Phoenix*, ed. Lin Carter.

445. *The Land Beyond the North*. London: Bodley Head, 1958.

> Melas, the hereditary guardian of the Golden Fleece, joins Jason and the Argonauts as they voyage to free themselves of the curse that has resulted from Medea's slaying of her brother. They journey to the Kingdom of the North Wind and beyond to the Land Beyond the North. The tale culminates with a mid-summer sacrifice at Stonehenge.

ROLAND GREEN

Wandor Series

446. *Wandor's Ride*. New York: Avon, 1973 [paper].

447. *Wandor's Journey*. New York: Avon, 1975 [paper].

448. *Wandor's Voyage*. New York: Avon, forthcoming 1979.

> Wandor is an orphan who has grown to be a Master of Duelists. His horizons expand very quickly

as he becomes a King's messenger and begins to
journey throughout his medieval-like world.
Soon he discovers that he might be the fulfillment of a prophecy and sorcerous expectations.
He is charged by a spirit, the Guardian of the
Mountain, to pursue a number of quests, most
notably, the alliances of a Conan-like warrior
and a red-haired sorceress. He is to be
affirmed the King of Five Crowns when his quests
are achieved.

JAMES [EDWIN] GUNN

449. *The Magicians*. New York: Charles Scribner's Sons,
     1976.

     A fantasy-mystery set in the 20th century in
     which a detective joins forces with a fetching
     sorceress and a mathematical wizard to discover
     the true name of the leader of a magical "con-
     vention." Only by gaining the control of the
     true name can the three protagonists defeat the
     evil wizard's plan to unleash Satan and his
     minions on the world.

NEIL [MILLER] GUNN

450. *The Green Isle of the Great Deep*. London: Faber
     and Faber, 1944.

     A boy and an old man descend into a subterranean
     world, discover the Green Isle, and recover the
     immortal fruit for mankind. Sequel to *Young
     Art and Old Hector* (see below).

451. *The Silver Bough*. London: Faber and Faber, 1948.

452. *The Well at the World's End*. London: Faber and
     Faber, 1951.

     A man and a woman, touring the Scottish high-
     lands, discover a well that leads him on a
     quest for the well at the World's End where a
     visionary union of male and female is revealed.

453. *Young Art and Old Hector*. London: Faber and Faber,
     1942.

NEIL [MILLER] GUNN

454. Aitken, William Russell. "Neil Miller Gunn."
Bibliotheck, 3, No. 3 (1961), 89-95.

THOMAS ANSTEY GUTHRIE

455. Anstey, F., pseud. *Humor & Fantasy: Vice Versa,
The Tinted Venus, A Fallen Idol, The Talking
Horse, Salted Almonds, The Brass Bottle*. London: John Murray, 1931. Rpt. New York: Arno
Press, 1978 [from a 1931 New York edition that,
along with this reprint, has not been seen].

An influential collection of six humorous fantasy novels, as listed above in the title,
written from 1882 to 1906.

Bibliography

456. Turner, Martin John. *Bibliography of the Works of
F. Anstey*. London: privately printed, 1931.

H[ENRY] RIDER HAGGARD
Also see H[ENRY] RIDER HAGGARD AND ANDREW LANG

457. *Allan and the Ice-Gods: A Tale of Beginnings*.
[London]: Hutchinson, [1927]. Rpt. New York:
Arno Press, 1976 [reprinted from the Garden
City, NY: Doubleday, Page, 1927, edition].

One of Haggard's numerous novels featuring
Allan Quartermain (for another, see *She and
Allan* in the She series below). Allan is
mysteriously transported back through time by
the use of a strange drug and awakens in the
body of Wi, a hunter. Defeating the cruel
leader of a primitive, Ice Age tribe, Allan
becomes its leader and introduces many of the
advantages of "civilization." Befriending a
member of the tribe, Pag, and gaining the
friendship of a witch, the beautiful Laleela,
he attempts to save the tribe from a descend-
ing glacier. However, his attempts are doomed
to failure when, as he is trying to prevent
the tribe from indulging in its annual blood
sacrifice, the tip of the glacier falls and
kills most of the tribe. Wi, Pag, Laleela,
and a few others escape, but shortly thereafter
Allan awakens in his own time as the drug wears
off.

458. *The Mahatma and the Hare: A Dream Story.* London: Longmans, Green, 1911.

> Supposedly inspired by a dream Haggard had, this dream fantasy is a strong condemnation of hunting and blood sports. A depressed writer is saved from suicide by an occult adept, who teaches him to love himself through various occult philosophies. The writer has a dream and is told by a slain hare of the terrors and agonies of the hunt.

459. *People of the Mist.* London: Longmans, Green, 1894.

> A lost-race novel in which a young English adventurer rescues a Caucasian girl and discovers a ruby-rich, lost culture in Central Africa. His and his beloved's salvation is ultimately the result of the help of the pygmy Otter. Incorrectly considered a fantasy since its inclusion in the Ballantine Adult Fantasy series in 1973.

460. *The Saga of Eric Brighteyes.* London: Longmans, Green, 1891. Rpt. Hollywood, CA: Newcastle, 1974 [paper].

> A highly stylized attempt to duplicate an Icelandic saga that focuses on love and the functions and roles of the Icelandic bard or *skald*.

> The Newcastle reprint contains a noteworthy history of Haggard's career by Douglas Menville.

The She Series

461. *Wisdom's Daughter: The Life and Love Story of She-Who-Must-Be-Obeyed.* London: Hutchinson, [1923]. Rpt. New York: Arno Press, 1978 [from the 1923 Doubleday Page edition that, along with the reprint, has not been seen].

462. *She: A History of Adventure.* Harper's Franklin Square Library No. 558. New York: Harper & Brothers, 1886 [paper]. This edition precedes the London 1887 one, from Longmans, Green, by eight days: December 24, 1886, versus January 1, 1887.

463. *Ayesha: The Return of She.* London: Ward Lock, 1905.

464. *She and Allan*. New York: Longmans, Green, 1921.
Rpt. Van Nuys, CA: Newcastle, 1976 [paper].

While the style and devices of these 19th-cen-
tury, lost-race romances are a bit difficult
for the 20th-century reader, the She series
continues to maintain an unusual appeal and
literary influence through its immortal white
goddess and her search for the reincarnation
of her long dead lover, Kallikrates, plus its
invariable true-blue, confused male protagonists.
While *Wisdom's Daughter* is published last, it
is the background novel for the series and recounts Ayesha's origin, youth, and murder of
her lover. A related novel is *She and Allan*.
In this combination of two of Haggard's most
popular protagonists, Allan Quartermain journeys
into the spirit world in search of his dead wife
and meets Ayesha. Although he rejects Ayesha's
offer of immortality, he does aid her in putting
down a revolt against her rule.

Bibliography

465. Scott, J.E. *A Bibliography of the Works of Sir
Henry Rider Haggard 1856-1925*. Takeley,
Bishop's Stortford, Herts., England: Elkin
Matthews, 1947.

466. Day, Bradford M. *Bibliography of Adventure: Mundy,
Burroughs, Rohmer, Haggard*. Denver, NY: Science
Fiction and Fantasy Publications, 1964 [paper].
Rpt. New York: Arno Press, 1978.

H[ENRY] RIDER HAGGARD AND ANDREW LANG

467. *The World's Desire*. New York: Longmans, Green,
1890.

A continuation of the *Odyssey* in which Odysseus,
finding everyone at home dead of a plague,
travels to Egypt in search of the world's desire,
the immortal Helen of Troy. Odysseus' cunning
is overcome by Pharaoh's wife and sister--the
sorceress Meriamun--and by court intrigue. He
and Helen find their love thwarted by death
and the fates.

ISIDORE HAIBLUM

468. *The Tsaddik of the Seven Wonders.* New York: Ballantine, 1971 [paper].

A farcical Yiddish fantasy that must contain every cliché ever associated with the Jewish stereotype. A Hebrew wise man and time traveler, the tsaddik, and his homunculus, Greenburg, join forces with a dimensional civil servant and combine their magic and technology to close an interdimensional rift caused by a greedy, interplanetary real estate agent.

LINDA HALDEMAN

469. *The Lastborn of Elvinwood.* Garden City, NY: Doubleday, 1978.

After a seemingly autobiographical and unfortunately slow beginning, this tale of fairies and changelings does generate some interest. To save the fairy folk, Mompen, a cross-eyed and unsuccessful fairy, agrees to change places with a human child, a girl. Aided by a group of humans, particularly the actor Ian James, the transfer is accomplished despite the necessity for the human child's approval. However, Ian must confront and challenge Merlin, the archimage, to accomplish the final master spell that will allow the human changeling full acceptance by the fairies and the rascal fairy prince, Puck.

E[DWARD] E[LTON] Y[OUNG] HALES

470. *Chariot of Fire.* Garden City, NY: Doubleday, 1977.

The publisher's notes fictionally identify this as the diary of Henry Brock, a British railway worker, begun after his death in a sea disaster and recounting his experiences in a terminal where the dead are issued tickets to Heaven or Hell. Scheduled to go to the second circle of Hell, Brock exchanges his ticket for one held by a dozing cleric and goes to Heaven instead. Completely uncomfortable in Heaven, he requests and gets a return ticket to Hell where he joins a conspiracy led by Marc Anthony and Cleopatra and involving Satan and the Archangel Michael. This fantasy of the afterlife draws heavily on Milton, Virgil, and Dante. Some of its de-

vices--e.g. celestial airports and a railroad
called the Limbo Line--are strongly reminiscent
of Poul Anderson's *Operation Chaos* (see above).

EDWARD EVERETT HALES

471. *His Level Best and Other Stories*. Boston: James
R. Osgood, 1873.

   a.   "His Level Best"
   b.   "The Brick Mason"
   c.   "Water Talk"
   d.   "Mouse and Lion"
   e.   "The Modern Sinbad"
   f.   "A Tale of a Salamander"
   g.   "The Queen of California"
   h.   "Confidence"

Bibliography

472. Holloway, Jean. "A Checklist of the Writings of
Edward Everett Hales." *Bulletin of Bibliography*, 21 (May-August 1954), 89-92; 21 (September-December 1954), 114-120; 21 (January-May 1955),
140-143.

M. Y. HALIDOM, pseud.
See ANONYMOUS ANTHOLOGIES: *Tales of the Wonder Club*

EDMOND [MOORE] HAMILTON

473. *The Valley of Creation*. New York: Lancer, 1964
[paper].

A lost-race and creation novel that begins as
a fantasy and turns into science fiction. In
this rationalized fantasy, Eric Nelson, an
American mercenary, is drawn into the valley
of L'Lan and a dispute between a human group
and the Brotherhood, a mixture of humans,
eagles, horses, tigers and wolves--all intelligent and telepathic. Ultimately, it is discovered that all life on earth is derived from
an alien mind transference originating in the
distant past.

474. *Dragon Winter*. New York: Popular Library, 1978
      [paper].

      A group of personified animals--otters, beavers,
      badgers, and squirrels--must flee killer wolves,
      man, a wizard committed to conquering all
      creation, and their own doubts and weaknesses
      to escape the coming of the dread "Dragon Win-
      ter." Guided by a "High Lord," one of the
      animal gods, they must endure hardship and fear
      to find their way to Old Bark, a virtuous wizard
      who often takes the shape of a silver bear, to
      find peace in the idyllic realm "Below the
      Falls."

      The Circle of Light Tetralogy

475. *Circle of Light - 1: Greyfax Grimwald*. New York:
      Popular Library, 1977 [paper].

476. *Circle of Light - 2: Faragon Fairingay*. New York:
      Popular Library, 1977 [paper].

477. *Circle of Light - 3: Calix Stay*. New York:
      Popular Library, 1977 [paper].

478. *Circle of Light - 4: Squaring the Circle*. New
      York: Popular Library, 1977 [paper].

      A bear, an otter, an elf, a dwarf, and two rus-
      tic men hold the future of Atlanton Earth in
      their hands as they become the bearers of a
      talisman, the Arkenchest, and its five secrets.
      Broco, the dwarf, is the principal bearer, and
      like the One Ring in Tolkien's *Lord of the
      Rings*, the Arkenchest poisons the mentality of
      its owner. The six companions, aided by the
      wizards of the Circle of Light, particularly by
      Greyfax Grimwald and Faragon Fairingay, must
      defeat the Queen of the Dark, Dorini, and save
      their world and its inhabitants for the final
      joyful union with the creator, the High Lord
      of Windameir. Fate plays a major role as the
      actions of the main characters are predetermined
      by divine will, and the series is marred by the
      failure of its potentially excellent settings--
      the world across the river Calix Stay, the
      edenic "Home," and "The World Before Time"--to
      ever really materialize for the reader. The
      sub-plot of the love of Cybelle and Fairingay
      does add interest to this Tolkien imitation as
      does the animal personification.

M. JOHN HARRISON

479. *The Pastel City*. New York: Doubleday, 1971.

In the far future, a medieval civilization rises
from the holocaust of past technology. Tegeus-
Cromis, a member of a chivalric order named
after Methvon, their dead leader, reunites the
order to aid in the power struggle between the
two women who claim to be queen. An excellent
mixture of sword, sorcery, and politics.

FRANZ HARTMANN

480. *Among the Gnomes: An Occult Tale of Adventure in
the Untersberg*. London: Occult Publishing,
1896. Rpt. New York: Arno Press, 1978 [the
reprint, which has not been seen, is reported
to be of an 1895 edition that could not be
verified].

Herr Schneider enters the Untersberg in the
Austrian Alps, an area reported to be inhabited
by various good and evil spirits. In a cave
he encounters the Princess Adalga, the daughter
of the Gnome King. Both he and the inhabitants
regard each other as spirits, a fact that
quickly loses credibility as Schneider becomes
embroiled in a conflict between the gnomes and
the elemental spirits of the air. After a frog
idol is destroyed, evil is vanquished and
Schneider is restored to the world, wondering
if it all ever really happened.

LAFCADIO HEARN

481. *Fantastics and Other Fancies*. Ed. Charles Woodward Hutson. Boston and New York: Houghton
Mifflin, 1914. Rpt. New York: Arno, 1979
[not seen].

a. "All in White"
b. "The Little Red Kitten"
c. "The Night of All Saints"
d. "The Devil's Carbuncle"
e. "Les Coulisses"
f. "The Stranger"
g. "Y Porqué?"
h. "A Dream of Kites"
i. "Hereditary Memories"
j. "The Ghostly Kiss"
k. "The Black Cupid"

l. "When I Was a Flower"
m. "Metempsychosis"
n. "The Undying One"
o. "The Vision of the Dead Creole"
p. "The Name on the Stone"
q. "Aphrodite and the King's Prisoner"
r. "The Fountain of Gold"
s. "A Dead Love"
t. "At the Cemetery"
u. "'Aida'"
v. "El Vomito"
w. "The Idyl of a French Snuff-Box"
x. "Spring Phantoms"
y. "A Kiss Fantastical"
z. "The Bird and the Girl"
aa. "The Tale of a Fan"
bb. "A Legend"
cc. "The Gipsy's Story"
dd. "The One Pill-box"
ee. "A River Reverie"
ff. "His Heart is Old"
gg. "MDCCCLIII"
hh. "Hiouen-Thsang"
ii. "L'Amour après la Mort"
jj. "The Post-Office"

Bibliography

482. Perkins, P.D., and Ione Perkins. *Lafcadio Hearn: A Bibliography of His Writings,* 1934. Rpt. New York: Burt Franklin, 1968.

BEN HECHT

483. *A Book of Miracles.* New York: Viking, 1939 [paper].

a. "A Lost Soul"
b. "The Little Candle"
c. "The Missing Idol"
d. "Death of Eleazer"
e. "Remember Thy Creator"
f. "The Heavenly Choir"
g. "The Adventures of Professor Emmett"

Bibliography

484. Burke, W.J., Will D. Howe, Irving Weiss, and Anne Weiss. *American Authors and Books: 1640 to the Present.* 3rd rev. ed. New York: Crown, 1972, p. 288.

ROBERT A[NSON] HEINLEIN

485. *Glory Road*. New York: G.P. Putnam's, 1963.

In this robust sword and sorcery adventure, a
disenchanted and purposeless Oscar Gordon is
recruited by the devastatingly attractive em-
press of the twenty universes and takes to hero-
ing and the glory road. The characters are
frolicsome, and there is a constant interchange
between the practical and the philosophical,
the flesh and the spirit. The flesh wins frequently. Uniquely Heinlein in its combinations
of romanticism and scepticism, magic and science,
gruffness and sentimentality.

486. "Magic, Inc." In *Waldo and Magic, Inc*. Garden
City, NY: Doubleday, 1950.

A matter-of-fact look at magic as a business in
a realm that accepts magic shops as easily as
supermarkets. As in any business community,
there is competition and crime. The protagonist
must deal with a protection racket run by the
devil, and to do so, he enlists the help of an
erudite African witch doctor, a charming old
witch, and a government agent.

Bibliography

487. Owings, Mark. *Robert A. Heinlein: A Bibliography*.
Baltimore: Croatan House, 1973 [paper].

FRANK HERBERT

488. *The God Makers*. New York: G.P. Putnam's, 1972.

What begins as a straight-forward science fiction novel soon becomes a mystical and religious
fantasy as a young explorer dies, undergoes
rites of passage, and is reborn as a god of
awesome power.

EDWARD HERON-ALLEN

489. Blayre, Christopher, pseud. *The Princess Daphne*.
London: H.J. Drane, [1885].

490. _____. *The Strange Papers of Dr Blayre*. London:
Philip Allan, 1932 [see note at the end of

annotation for an earlier citation].

a. "The Purple Sapphire (Mineralogy)"
b. "The House on the Way to Hell"
c. "Aalila (Psychology)"
d. "The Mirror that Remembered (Mathematics)"
e. "Purpura Lapillus (History)"
f. "Mano Pantea (Fine Arts)"
g. "The Thing that Smelt (Zoology)"
h. "The Blue Cockroach (Chemistry)"
i. "The Man Who Killed the Jew"
j. "The Demon"
k. "The Book"
l. "The Cosmic Dust (Chemistry)"

This collection--alleged to contain items "of too fantastic and inexplicable a nature to be published" that were left in the files of a "Registrar in a great university"--has also been cited, by George Medhurst in *Ferret Fantasy's Christmas Annual for 1973* (London: Ferret Fantasy, 1974), as *The Purple Sapphire, and Other Posthumous Papers: Selected from the Unofficial Records of the University of Cosmopoli by Christopher Blayre, sometime Registrar of the University.* London: Philip Allan, 1921. This edition, as reported, contains four fewer tales but has resisted all efforts toward verification.

JAMES HILTON

491. *Lost Horizons.* New York: William Morrow; London: Macmillan, 1933.

A classic among lost-race fantasies and the subject of two feature-length films (1937, 1978) that has made the term "Shangri-La" part of the lexicon of the language through its explorations of Tibetan mysteries and the lure of eternal youth and peace.

Bibliography

492. "Checklist Bibliographies of Modern Authors: James Hilton." *Book Trade Journal,* 62 (July 1936), 20.

HAROLD HOBSON

493. *The Devil in Woodford Wells: A Fantastic Novel.*
London: Longmans, Green, 1946.

Drawing on the fictions of Max Beerbohm and his
character Enoch Soames, this is a domestic fantasy set in a small village on the northeast
edge of London and concerns the reactions of
the village folk to a visit by Satan.

WILLIAM HOPE HODGSON

494. *The Boats of the 'Glen Carrig': Being an Account
of their Adventures in the Strange Places of
the Earth, After the Foundering of the Good
Ship Glen Carrig Through Striking upon a Hidden
Rock in the Unknown Sea to the Southward. As
Told by John Winterstraw, Gent., to His Son
James Winterstraw, in the Year 1757, and by Him
Committed Very Properly to Manuscript.* London:
Chapman & Hall, 1907. Rpt. Westport, CT:
Hyperion, 1976 [from a 1920 edition].

A significant novel in the contemporary redis-
covery of Hodgson's canon: A ship's boats drift
to an uncharted island where the crew confronts
a series of skillfully drawn monstrosities.

495. *Deep Waters.* Sauk City, WI: Arkham House, 1967.

a.   "The Sea Horses"
b.   "The Derelict"
c.   "The Thing in the Weeds"
d.   "From the Tideless Sea"
e.   "The Island of the Ud"
f.   "The Voice in the Night"
g.   "The Adventure of the Headland"
h.   "The Mystery of the Derelict"
i.   "The Shamraken Homeward-Bounder"
j.   "The Crew of the Lancing"
k.   "The Habitants of Middle Islet"
l.   "The Call in the Dawn"

496. *The Ghost Pirates.* London: Stanley Paul, 1909.
Rpt. Westport, CT: Hyperion, 1976.

Only one sailor escapes to tell the tale of a
cursed ship, the Mortzestus, that seems to draw
horror and evil from the sea. The ship and its
crew meet their final doom at the hand of the
"ghost pirates," terrible sea demons. A highly
descriptive and suspenseful work.

112

497. *The House on the Borderland; from the Manuscript, discovered in 1877 by Mesors. Tonnison and Berroggnog, in the Ruins that Lie to the South of the Village of Kraighten in the West of Ireland. Set Out Here with Notes.* London: Chapman & Hall, 1908. Rpt. Westport, CT: Hyperion, 1976.

The protagonist-narrator discovers a hidden cavern behind the wall of his home. After entering and winning his way past pig-like monsters, he finds a bottomless pit. His soul is then transported throughout the cosmos, and he witnesses the final destruction of the solar system. He returns home and awaits his own horrible end.

498. *The Nightland: A Love Tale.* London: Nash, 1912. Rpt. Westport, CT: Hyperion, 1976.

A far-future novel centered on the dying remnants of humanity and the quest of a strangely transported 19th-century man to rescue a girl who is the reincarnation of his previous lost love. His journey between the only two remaining havens of humanity in a land gone dark and evil is the most effective portion of the book; the return trip with the girl dissolves into an exposé of Victorian sexual inhibitions and urges. There is a revised and condensed version, titled *The Dream of X*, which was printed in paperback by Harold Page of New York to protect Hodgson's American copyright (1912). It includes thirteen of Hodgson's poems that were not in the first edition and has been reprinted by Donald Grant (West Kingston, RI, 1977).

499. *Out of the Storm: Uncollected Fantasies . . .* Ed. Sam Moskowitz. West Kingston, RI: Donald M. Grant, 1975.

a. "A Tropical Horror"
b. "Out of the Storm"
c. "The Finding of the Graiken"
d. "Eloi Eloi Laura Sabachthani"
e. "The Terror of the Water Tank"
f. "The Albatross"
g. "The Haunting of the Lady Shannon"

E[RNST] T[HEODOR] A[MADEUS] HOFFMANN
(born: Ernst Theodor Wilhelm Hoffmann)

500. *The Best Tales of Hoffmann.* Ed. E.F. Bleiler. New York: Dover Publications, 1967 [various translators] [paper].

    a.   "The Golden Flower Pot"
    b.   "Automata"
    c.   "A New Year's Eve Adventure"
    d.   "Nutcracker and the King of Mice"
    e.   "The Sand-Man"
    f.   "Rath Krespel"
    g.   "Tobias Martin, Master Cooper, and His Men"
    h.   "The Mines of Falun"
    i.   "Signor Formica"
    j.   "The King's Betrothed"

501. *E.T.A. Hoffmanns Werke.* Ed. Hermann Leber. Band I. Salzburg/Stuttgart: Das Bergland Buch, [1965].

    a.   *Phantasiestücke in Callots Manier*
        1.   "Hinweise"
        2.   "Ritter Gluck"
        3.   "Kreisleriana"
        4.   "Don Juan"
        5.   "Nachricht von den neuesten Schicksalen des Hundes Berganza"
        6.   "Der Magnetiseur"
        7.   "Der goldne Topf"
        8.   "Die Abenteuer der Silvesternacht"
        9.   "Kreisleriana"

    b.   *Die Elixiere des Teufels*

    c.   *Nachtstücke*
        1.   "Hinweise"
        2.   "Der Sandmann"
        3.   "Das Sanctus"
        4.   "Das öde Haus"
        5.   "Das Majorat"
        6.   "Das Gelübde"

    d.   *Klein Zaches Genannt Zinnober*

    e.   *Die Serapionsbrüder*
        1.   "Der heilige Serpion"
        2.   "Rat Krespel"
        3.   "Die Fermate"
        4.   "Der Dichter und der Komponist"
        5.   "Ein Fragment aus dem Leben dreier Freunde"

6.   "Der Artushof"
7.   "Die Bergwerke zu Falun"
8.   "Nussknacker und Mausekönig"

502.   *E.T.A. Hoffmanns Werke*. Ed. Hermann Leber.   Band
       II.   Salzburg/Stuttgart: Das Bergland Buch,
       [1965].

   a.   *Die Serapionsbrüder*   (continued)
        9.   "Der Kampf der Sänger"
       10.   "Die Automate"
       11.   "Doge und Dogaressa"
       12.   "Meister Martin der Küfner und seine
             Gesellen"
       13.   "Das fremde Kind"
       14.   "Die Brautwahl"
       15.   "Der unheimliche Gast"
       16.   "Das Fräulein von Scuderi"
       17.   "Spielergluck"
       18.   "Signor Formica"
       19.   "Die Konigsbraut"

   b.   *Prinzessin Brambilla*

   c.   *Lebensansichten des Kater Murr*

   d.   *Letzte Erzahlungen/Meister Floh*
        1.   "Des Vetters Eckfenster"
        2.   "Der Elementargeist"

503.   *The King's Bride*.   Trans. Paul Turner.   London:
       John Calder, 1959.

504.   *Selected Writings of E.T.A. Hoffmann*. Vol. I:
       Tales.   Ed. and trans. Leonard J. Kent and
       Elizabeth C. Knight.   Chicago & London: The
       University of Chicago Press, 1969.

   a.   "Ritter Gluck"
   b.   "The Golden Pot"
   c.   "The Sandman"
   d.   "Councillor Krespel"
   e.   "The Mines of Falun"
   f.   "Mademoiselle de Scudéri"
   g.   "The Doubles"

505.   *Three Märchen of E.T.A. Hoffmann*.   Trans. Charles
       E. Passage.   Columbia, SC: University of South
       Carolina Press, 1971.

   a.   "Little Zaches, Surnamed Zinnober"
   b.   "Princess Brambilla"

E[RNST] T[HEODOR] A[MADEUS] HOFFMANN continued

        c.   "Master Flea"

Bibliography

506. Salomon, Gerhard. *E.T.A. Hoffmann: Bibliographie.*
      Hildesheim, Germany: Georg Olms Verlagsbuch-
      handlung, 1963.

CLAUDE HOUGHTON, pseud. See CLAUDE HOUGHTON OLDFIELD

LAURENCE HOUSMAN

507. *Gods and Their Makers.* London: John Lane, The
      Bodley Head, 1897.

508. *Strange Ends and Discoveries: Tales of this World
      and the Next.* London: Jonathan Cape, 1948.

        a.   "The Distorting Mirror"
        b.   "The Great Adventure"
        c.   "The Return Journey"
        d.   "The Impossible Penitent"
        e.   "The Finish Touch"
        f.   "The Fall of the Sparrow"
        g.   "The New Dispensation"
        h.   "Vessels of Clay"
        i.   "The Catch of the Cherub"
        j.   "Improved Relations"
        k.   "The Cry of the Parrot"
        l.   "An Unexpected Miracle"
        m.   "The Flag of Peace"
        n.   "A Striking Incident"
        o.   "Hidden Identity"
        p.   "Weighed in the Balance"
        q.   "Changa-Ranga"
        r.   "Dead Man's Lane"
        s.   "The Widow"
        t.   "The Return of the Prodigal"
        u.   "Oranges and Lemons"
        v.   "Maggie's Bite"
        w.   "Camouflage"
        x.   "Little Pear-Blossom"

Bibliography

509. Rudolf, Anna. *Die Dichtung Von Laurence Housman.*
      Breslam: Priebatschs, 1930, pp. 85-89.

510. *The Dark Man and Others*. Sauk City, WI: Arkham House, 1963 [not seen]. Rpt. New York: Lancer, n.d. Title change: *Pigeons from Hell*. New York: Zebra, 1976 [paper].

     a.   "Pigeons from Hell"
     b.   "The Gods of Bal-Sagoth"
     c.   "People of the Dark"
     d.   "The Children of the Night"
     e.   "The Dead Remember"
     f.   "The Man on the Ground"
     g.   "The Garden Fear"
     h.   "The Hyena"
     i.   "Dig Me No Grave"
     j.   "The Dream Snake"
     k.   "In the Forest of Villèfere"
     l.   "Old Garfield's Heart"
     m.   "The Voice of El-Lil"

511. *The Illustrated Gods of the North*. West Warwick, R.I.: Necronomicon Press, 1977 [paper]. Originally appeared in the March, 1934, *Fantasy Fan*.

512. *Skull-Face*. New York: Berkley, 1978 [paper].

     a.   "Skull-Face"
     b.   "Lord of the Dead"
     c.   "Names in the Black Book"
     d.   "Taverel Manor"

     Includes an introduction by Richard A. Lupoff and should not be confused with *Skull-Face and Others* (Sauk City, WI: Arkham House, 1946 [not seen]), a much larger collection.

513. *The Sword Woman*. New York: Zebra, 1977 [paper].

     The adventures of Agnes de Chastillon, woman warrior in the tradition of C.L. Moore's Jirel of Jorey (see below).

     a.   "Sword Woman"
     b.   "Blades for France"
     c.   "Mistress of Death" (with Gerald W. Page)
     d.   "The King's Service"
     e.   "The Shadow of the Hun"

     The Conan Series and Related Volumes by Other Authors

514. *Conan the Conquerer: The Hyborean Age*. New York:

ROBERT E[RVIN] HOWARD continued

Gnome, 1950.

515. *The Sword of Conan*. New York: Gnome, 1952.

    a.   "The People of the Black Circle"
    b.   "The Slithering Shadow"
    c.   "The Pool of the Black One"
    d.   "Red Nails"

516. *King Conan*. New York: Gnome, 1953.

    a.   "Jewels of Gwahlur"
    b.   "Beyond the Black River"
    c.   "The Treasure of Tranicos"
    d.   "The Phoenix on the Sword"
    e.   "The Scarlet Citadel"

517. *The Coming of Conan*. New York: Gnome, 1953.

    a.   "The Shadow Kingdom"
    b.   "The Mirrors of Tuzun Thune"
    c.   "The King and the Oak"
    d.   "The Tower of the Elephant"
    e.   "The God in the Bowl"
    f.   "Rogues in the House"
    g.   "The Frost-Giant's Daughter"
    h.   "Queen of the Black Coast"

This collection also includes a letter from
Howard to P. Schuyler Miller, a letter from H.P.
Lovecraft to Donald A. Wollheim, an informal
biography of Howard by J.D. Clark and P.
Schuyler Miller, and a running commentary on
the tales by L. Sprague de Camp.

518. *Conan the Barbarian*. New York: Gnome Press, 1954.

    a.   "Black Colossus"
    b.   "Shadows in the Moonlight"
    c.   "A Witch Shall Be Born"
    d.   "Shadows in Zamboula"
    e.   "The Devil in Iron"

519. *Tales of Conan* with L. Sprague de Camp. New York:
Gnome, 1955.

    a.   "The Blood-Stained God"
    b.   "Hawks Over Shem"
    c.   "The Road of the Eagles"
    d.   "The Flame-Knife"

520. *Conan* with L. Sprague de Camp and Lin Carter.
New York: Lancer, 1967 [paper].

    a.   "The Thing in the Crypt" (Carter and de Camp)
    b.   "The Tower of the Elephant" (Howard)
    c.   "The Hall of the Dead" (Howard and de Camp)
    d.   "The God in the Bowl" (Howard)
    e.   "Rogues in the House" (Howard)
    f.   "The Hand of Nergal" (Howard and Carter)
    g.   "The City of Skulls" (Carter and de Camp)

This collection also includes a letter from Howard to P. Schuyler Miller, an introduction by de Camp, and part one of Howard's essay "The Hyborian Age."

521. *Conan of Cimmeria* with L. Sprague de Camp and Lin Carter. New York: Lancer, 1969 [paper].

    a.   "The Curse of the Monolith" (de Camp and Carter)
    b.   "The Bloodstained God" (Howard and de Camp)
    c.   "The Frost Giant's Daughter" (Howard)
    d.   "The Lair of the Ice Worm" (de Camp and Carter)
    e.   "Queen of the Black Coast" (Howard)
    f.   "The Vale of Lost Women" (Howard)
    g.   "The Castle of Terror" (de Camp and Carter)
    h.   "The Snout in the Dark" (Howard, de Camp and Carter)

522. *Conan the Freebooter* with L. Sprague de Camp.
New York: Lancer, 1968 [paper].

    a.   "Hawks Over Shem" (Howard and de Camp)
    b.   "Black Colossus" (Howard)
    c.   "Shadows in the Moonlight" (Howard)
    d.   "The Road of the Eagles" (Howard and de Camp)
    e.   "A Witch Shall Be Born" (Howard)

523. *Conan the Wanderer* with L. Sprague de Camp and Lin Carter. New York: Lancer, 1968 [paper].

    a.   "Black Tears" (de Camp and Carter)
    b.   "Shadows of Zamboula" (Howard)
    c.   "The Devil in Iron" (Howard)
    d.   "The Flame Knife" (Howard and de Camp)

524. *Conan the Adventurer* with L. Sprague de Camp.

New York: Lancer, 1966 [paper].

a. "The People of the Black Circle" (Howard)
b. "The Slithering Shadow" (Howard)
c. "Drums of Tombalku" (Howard, edited by de Camp)
d. "The Pool of the Black One" (Howard)

525. *Conan the Buccaneer* by L. Sprague de Camp and Lin Carter. New York: Lancer, 1971 [paper].

a. "Prologue: Dream of Blood"
b. "An Old Zingaran Custom"
c. "A Knife in the Dark"
d. "Death of the *Sea Queen*"
e. "The Nameless Isle"
f. "At the World's Edge"
g. "Flaming Eyes"
h. "The Toad-Thing"
i. "The Cobra Crown"
j. "Wind in the Rigging"
k. "The Black Coast"
l. "Web of Doom"
m. "City of the Warrior Women"
n. "The Queen of the Amazons"
o. "Under the Lash"
p. "The Black Labyrinth"
q. "The Devouring Tree"
r. "The Wreak of the *Wastrel*"
s. "A Kingdom in the Balance"
t. "King Thoth-Amon"
u. "Red Blood and Cold Steel"

526. *Conan the Warrior*. Ed. L. Sprague de Camp. New York: Lancer, 1967 [paper].

a. "Red Nails"
b. "Jewels of Gwahlur"
c. "Beyond the Black River"

527. *Conan the Usurper* with L. Sprague de Camp. New York: Lancer, 1967 [paper].

a. "The Treasure of Tranicos" (by Howard, but originally published and revised by de Camp as "The Black Stranger," 1953)
b. "Wolves Beyond the Border" (Howard, edited by de Camp)
c. "The Phoenix on the Sword" (Howard)
d. "The Scarlet Citadel" (Howard)

528. *Conan the Conqueror*. Ed. L. Sprague de Camp. New

York: Lancer, 1967 [paper].

529. *Conan the Avenger* by Björn Nyberg. New York: Gnome, 1957. Rev. ed. with L. Sprague de Camp. New York: Lancer, 1968 [paper].

Contains Howard's essay "The Hyborian Age, Part 2."

530. *Conan of Aquilonia* by L. Sprague de Camp and Lin Carter. New York: Ace, 1977 [paper].

a. "The Witch of the Mists"
b. "Black Sphinx of Nebthu"
c. "The Moon of Zembabwei"
d. "Shadows in the Skull"

531. *Conan of the Isles* by L. Sprague de Camp and Lin Carter. New York: Lancer, 1968 [paper].

a. "Red Shadows"
b. "The Black Heart of Golamira"
c. "The Cup and Trident"
d. "Scarlet Tortage"
e. "The Black Kraken"
f. "Magic Fire"
g. "The Phantom Warriors"
h. "The Casket from Atlantis"
i. "Voyage on an Unknown Sea"
j. "Lost City"
k. "Thieves of Ptahuacan"
l. "The Black Labyrinth"
m. "Dungeon of Despair"
n. "In the Dragon's Lair"
o. "A Day of Blood and Fire"
p. "Gates of Doom"
q. "The Crystal Talisman"
r. "Gods of Light and Darkness"

Original Conan Series from *Weird Tales*

532. *Conan: The Hour of the Dragon*. Ed. Karl Edward Wagner. New York: Berkley, 1977 [paper].

533. *Conan: The People of the Black Circle*. Ed. Karl Edward Wagner. New York: Berkley, 1977 [paper].

a. "The Devil in Iron"
b. "The People of the Black Circle"
c. "A Witch Shall Be Born"
d. "Jewels of Gwahlur"

534. *Conan: Red Nails*. Ed. Karl Edward Wagner. New
York: Berkley, 1977 [paper].

    a.   "Beyond the Black River"
    b.   "Shadows in Zamboula"
    c.   "Red Nails"
    d.   "The Hyborian Age" (essay)

Immensely popular, Howard's sword and sorcery
novels and collections featuring Conan the Barbarian have had a significant influence on the
development of contemporary fantasy. These adventures pit the barbaric and guileless warrior
against wizards, ghouls, mad kings, sorceresses,
beasts, gods and mere mortals. Most of Howard's
tales were written in the late 1940's and
appeared originally in *Weird Tales*, but since
the 1950's other authors--most notably L.
Sprague de Camp and Lin Carter--have completed
unfinished Howard manuscripts or adopted the
barbarian for their own imitative creations.
There is even a parody of Howard by Poul Anderson, "The Barbarian," in the May, 1956, issue
of *The Magazine of Fantasy and Science Fiction*.
Most recently, Karl Edward Wagner has been editing the tales as they originally appeared in
Weird Tales for Berkley Publications, 1977
[paper].

The Solomon Kane Tales

535. *The Moon of Skulls*. New York: Centaur, 1969 [paper].

    a.   "The Moon of Skulls"
    b.   "Skulls in the Stars"
    c.   "The Footfalls Within"

536. *The Hand of Kane*. New York: Centaur, 1970 [paper].

    a.   "The Hills of the Dead"
    b.   "Hawk of Basti"
    c.   "Wings in the Night"
    d.   "The Children of Asshur"

537. *Solomon Kane*. New York: Centaur, 1971 [paper].

    a.   "The Right Hand of Doom"
    b.   "Red Shadows"
    c.   "Rattle of Bones"
    d.   "The Castle of the Devil"
    e.   "Blades of the Brotherhood"
    f.   "The Return of Sir Richard Grenville"

g.   "Solomon Kane's Homecoming"

Published in the late 1920's and the early
1930's in *Weird Tales*, these are the tales of
Howard's other heroic protagonist: Solomon Kane,
an oppressively puritan figure and Howard's
first sword and sorcery hero. The stories are
set in a sixteenth-century locale complete with
black magic, fiends, monsters, sorcerers, and,
for the virtuous Kane, maidens-that-must-be-
denied. Many of these stories, if not all,
appeared in *Red Shadows*. West Kingston, R.I.:
Donald M. Grant, 1968 [not seen].

Bibliography

538. Lord, Glenn. *The Last Celt: A Bio-bibliography of
      Robert Ervin Howard*. West Kingston, R.I.:
      Donald M. Grant, 1976.

539. Miller, P. Schuyler, and John D. Clark. "A Pro-
      bable Outline of Conan's Career." In *The
      Hyborian Age*. Los Angeles: Los Angeles-New
      York Cooperative Publications, 1938 [paper];
      revised and enlarged by Clark for the paragraphs
      between tales in the Gnome Press Conan books,
      1950-1954; further revised and enlarged by
      Clark, Miller, and L. Sprague de Camp for "An
      Informal Biography of Conan of Cimmeria." *Amra*,
      2, No. 4 (1959); further enlarged by de Camp
      for the paragraphs between the tales in the
      Lancer Conan books, 1966-1969; rpt. de Camp,
      L. Sprague, and George Scithers, eds. *The
      Conan Swordbook: 27 Examinations of Heroic
      Fiction*. Baltimore: Mirage, 1969, pp. 227-255.

FERGUS HUME

540. *Chronicles of Fairy Land*. Philadelphia and London:
      J.B. Lippencott, 1911 [earlier edition: London:
      Griffith, Farrar, 1892?].

a.   "King Oberon's Library"
b.   "The Red Elf"
c.   "Shadowland"
d.   "The Water-Witch"
e.   "Moon Fancies"
f.   "The Rose-Princess"
g.   "Sorrow-Singing"
h.   "The Golden Goblin"
i.   "The Enchanted Forest"

FERGUS HUME continued

541. *The Dwarf's Chamber and Other Stories*. London:
     Ward, Lock & Bowden, 1896.

     a.   "The Dwarf's Chamber"
     b.   "Miss Jonathon"
     c.   "The Dead Man's Diamonds"
     d.   "'The Tale of the Turquoise Skull'"
     e.   "The Green-Stone God and the Stockbroker"
     f.   "The Jesuit and the Mexican Coin"
     g.   "The Rainbow Camellia"
     h.   "The Ivory Leg and the Twenty-Four Diamonds"
     i.   "My Cousin from France"

JAMES [GIBSON] HUNEKER

542. *Visionaries*. New York: Charles Scribner's Sons;
     London: T. Laurie, 1905 [simultaneous publi-
     cation? T. Laurie edition not seen].

     a.   "A Master of Cobwebs"
     b.   "The Eighth Deadly Sin"
     c.   "The Purse of Aholibah"
     d.   "Rebels of the Moon"
     e.   "The Spiral Road"
     f.   "A Mock Sun"
     g.   "Antichrist"
     h.   "The Eternal Duel"
     i.   "The Enchanted Yodler"
     j.   "The Third Kingdom"
     k.   "The Haunted Harpsichord"
     l.   "The Tragic Wall"
     m.   "A Sentimental Rebellion"
     n.   "Hall of the Missing Footsteps"
     o.   "The Cursory Light"
     p.   "An Iron Fan"
     q.   "The Woman Who Loved Chopin"
     r.   "The Tune of Time"
     s.   "Nada"
     t.   "Pan"

Bibliography

543. De Casseres, Benjamin. *James Gibson Huneker*. New
     York: Joseph Lawren, 1925, pp. 41-62.

C[HARLES] J[OHN] CUTCLIFFE [WRIGHT] HYNE

544. *The Lost Continent*. New York: Harper; London:

Hutchinson, 1900 [simultaneous publication?].

A young Atlantean returns to his homeland to
find a heartless and evil usurper on the throne.
His initial attempt at revolt fails and his beloved is buried alive. Seven years later he
returns, tries to lead another revolt, and
restores his beloved to life. However, the
virtuous priesthood realizes that the evil
queen, Phorenice, cannot be destroyed by force
and that they must destroy the entire island
to rid the world of her insanity. A few of the
valiant rebels are sent off on an ark with the
accumulated wisdom of Atlantis to found a new
world. A highly descriptive work that enjoyed
significant popularity when it was serialized
in *Pearson's* in 1899.

Bibliography

545. Watson, George, ed. *The New Cambridge Bibliography
of English Literature*. Cambridge: Cambridge
University Press, 1969, III (1800-1900), 1105.

DAHLOV IPCAR

546. *A Dark Horn Blowing*. New York: Viking, 1978.

Told from the viewpoints of four characters--
Nora, a mother; Eben, a father; Owen, their son;
and Eelie, the Prince of Erland--and based in
part on ballads selected from Francis James
Child's *The English and Scottish Popular Ballads*
and Norse mythology, this is a tale of identity
and discovery. Nora is stolen by the magical,
elvin folk of Erland to nurse the young prince.
Victimized by the witch Bab Magga, Nora is lost
to her husband and child, and Bab possesses and
torments them both. After the Queen of Erland
dies, never having been able to care for her
own child, the King of Erland covets Nora.
Through trickery, he nearly conquers her, but
Nora is saved by her own wit and Elver's (the
young prince) discovery of his true nature and
shape: a golden eagle. Nora is restored to the
normal world and her family; her husband Eben,
having been changed into a goat by Bab Magga,
is restored through Elver's efforts as the new
king of Erland, following his lecherous father's
death. The final trial, however, is Elver's as
he must dominate the spirit ghost of his father,

blow the dark horn, and lead the Wild Hunt.

547. *The Warlock of Night*. New York: Viking, 1969.

Much less successful than the later *A Dark Horn
Blowing* and based on a classic chess match played in 1949 by two grandmasters. The forces of
the Land of Day struggle against the armies of
the Land of Night. The pivotal places in this
psychomachia belong to Ploy, apprentice to the
powerful Warlock of Night; his informal tutor,
the wanderer Magaw; and a raven, Corbie. After
Ploy has succeeded in conquering one of the
major strongholds of the Land of Day, he too
quickly realizes the futility of conflict.

ERIC IVERSON

The Gerin the Fox Series

548. *Wereblood*. New York: Belmont Tower, 1979 [paper].

549. *Werenight*. New York: Belmont Tower, 1979 [paper].

A sword and sorcery series featuring Gerin,
called the Fox, as he struggles to save his empire from the barbaric Trokmo and their evil
sorcerer-king, Balamung. With the giant Van
and the beautiful Elise, he fights his way to
the City of Elabon in a futile attempt to defeat
the werebeasts and find a wizard powerful enough
to defeat Balamung.

PIERS ANTHONY DILLINGHAM JACOB

550. Piers Anthony, pseud. *Hasan*. San Bernardino, CA:
Borgo Press, 1977 [paper].

An Eastern fantasy reminiscent of the *Arabian
Nights*. Hasan, a gullible young man, is tricked
by an evil merchant into believing that he can
make gold. Kidnapped, Hasan encounters numerous
adventures in this slow-moving narrative that
culminates in his search for his princess-bride
in a matriarchal country where men are usually
slain.

The Chameleon Series

551. _____. *A Spell for Chameleon*. New York: Ballan-

tine, 1977 [paper].

552. _____. *The Source of Magic*. New York: Ballantine, 1979 [paper].

553. _____. *Castle Roogna*. New York: Ballantine, scheduled for release in July, 1979 [paper].

Everyone in the magical realm of Xanth has a sorcerous talent except Bink of the North Village. Bink, clearly a deviant, is exiled and his further search for his own true spell-- the yet unsuspected immunity from all magic harm--embroils him and his comrades in a quest for the evil magician Trent and in numerous conflicts with elves, dwarves, krakans, dragons, and a sphinx. In Bink's further adventures in *The Source of Magic*, he goes in search of the source of Xanth's magic. In the company of Chester the Centaur and Crombie, a soldier transformed into a griffin, and with the aid of Humfrey, the good magician, Bink is harried by an unseen enemy. Finally, abandoned by his comrades, Bink does discover the "source of all magic," only to let it be destroyed. The series is distinguished by three of the better female characterizations in contemporary fantasy: Iris, Chameleon, and Franchon.

JOHN [WILLIAM] JAKES

554. *The Last Magicians*. New York: Signet, 1969 [paper].

A tale of wonder and psychomachia that centers on Cham, the last of the evil red magicians, who has denounced his final vows to the fell god of his order, "The Unborn." Trapped within a new order that is antithetical to magic and to him, he is forced to confront his past master to survive in the new world. The characterization of Cham and his dilemma is unusually well done. For comparable works that feature an evil protagonist, see Michael Moorcock's Elric series and Karl Edward Wagner's Kane series below.

555. *Mention My Name in Atlantis*. New York: DAW, 1972 [paper].

Hoptor the Vintner, a whimsical conniver, joins forces with the barbarian Conax of Chimeria

(clearly a relative of Howard's Conan) to bring
chaos to Atlantis. Both Hoptor's uproarious
machinations and Jakes' unusual explanation for
the disappearance of Atlantis combine well to
make this a good example of comic, sword and
sorcery fantasy.

Brak the Barbarian Series

556. *Brak the Barbarian*. New York: Avon, 1968 [paper].

    a.   "The Unspeakable Shrine"
    b.   "Flame-Face"
    c.   "The Courts of the Conjurer" (originally:
         "Silk of Shaitan")
    d.   "Ghosts of Stone" (originally: "Pillars
         of Chambalor")
    e.   "The Barge of Souls"

557. *Brak Versus the Mark of the Demons*. New York:
Paperback Library, 1969 [paper].

558. *Brak the Barbarian Versus the Sorceress*. New
York: Paperback Library, 1969 [paper].

559. *Brak: When the Idols Walked*. New York: Pocket
Books, 1978? [not seen].

Although indebted to Howard's Conan, Brak is
basically an innocent good guy, quick to help,
quick to suffer for his naive approach to life.
The series is highly episodic and is loosely
unified by Brak's attempt to travel to a city,
Khurdisan the Golden. The series' main appeals
are in its undisguised brutality, lusty women,
and excellently conceived villains and monsters.

Bibliography

560. Allen, Paul C. "Of Swords & Sorcery No. 3."
Fantasy Crossroads, No. 10-11 (March 1977),
42-46.

G. JEFFERY

561. *Erinord*. London: Rex Collings, 1976.

Erinord, prince of the magical kingdom of
Solaris, loses his memory through the machina-
tions of a witch and her woodcutter husband.
Their misplaced need for a son delays Erinord's

quest for the Orb of Light, the necessary weapon against an enigmatic and fell sorcerer, the Shadow Seeker. Erinord ultimately recovers his memory with the help of the leader of a Shangri La-like kingdom, and he and his companion, the commoner Quinú, complete their quest.

WILLIAM FITZGERALD JENKINS

562. Leinster, Murray, pseud. *Sidewise in Time and Other Scientific Adventures*. Chicago: Shasta Publishers, 1950.

This collection illustrates how science fiction can easily become fantasy when the crucial element of extrapolation is withdrawn and the author allows his mind to move beyond the restraints of natural law.

a. "Sidewise in Time"
b. "Proxima Centauri"
c. "A Logic Named Joe"
d. "De Profundis"
e. "The Fourth-Dimensional Demonstrator"
f. "The Power"

NORMA N. JOHNS

563. *Bodoman of Sor: [being The Saga of Dam Rabot from the Groanicles of Sor]*. [Essex, England]: B[ritish] F[antasy] S[ociety], 1977 [paper].

A parody of John Lange's Chronicles of Counter Earth (see below). A heavy-handed treatment that exploits the original's elements of sexism and sadomasochism.

DIANA WYNNE JONES

The Dalemark Series

564. *Cart and Cwidder*. London: Macmillan, 1975.

565. *Drowned Amulet*. London: Macmillan, 1977.

These first two in a projected five-volume juvenile/adult series, are set in a Medieval realm of Dalemark where the virtuous North struggles against the repressive South. The

protagonist of *Cart and Cwidder* is aided in his
escape from the South by the strange powers of
a large harp, a legacy from his recently mur-
dered father, and is accompanied in his flight
by his brother, sister, and a young noble, all
of whom must be brought to the safety of the
North. In *Drowned Amulet*, three youngsters discover that the folk gods, Old Ammet and Libby
Beer, are not just the ritualistic symbols
that everyone thinks. Aided by the awesome
powers of the god and goddess and in search of
a magical amulet, the children become embroiled
in a conflict of enormous scope. The Dalemark
series is unusually realistic and has an excellent blend of the numinous and everyday,
be they agonizing or joyous.

IVAR JORGENSON, pseud. See PAUL W. FAIRMAN

JAAN KANGILASKI

566. *The Seeking Sword*. New York: Ballantine, 1977
[paper].

An unusual combination of fantasy and horror
featuring a stone age shaman who has placed his
soul in a sword. Controlling all who handle
it, the sentient sword has survived through the
ages successfully seeking revenge on all the
descendants of an enemy tribe. The action in
the novel is set shortly after the shootings at
Kent State University and contains many topical
allusions. The modern characters are particularly realistic, and their attempts to cope
with the sword's bloody acts are well delineated
and pointedly human.

WALTER KARIG

567. *Zotz!* New York: Rinehart, 1947.

A timid professor, John Jones, teaching at a
southern theological seminary, discovers that
an ancient spell allows him to point his finger, say "zotz," and generate awesome, death-
dealing results. Much of this comic and sat-
iric fantasy concerns Jones' interaction with
a young lady, whose clothes were stripped off
by his first zotz lightning bolt, and the so-

cial, political, religious, and military esta-
blishments' attempts to cope with Jones' unusual gift.

MARVIN KAYE

568. *The Incredible Umbrella.* Garden City, NY: Doubleday, 1979.

Very much in the vein of L. Sprague de Camp
and Fletcher Pratt's Incomplete Enchanter series (see above), this highly regarded, comic
fantasy is about a banal English professor, J.
Adrian Fillmore, who buys a magic umbrella.
Before he even realizes it, the bumbershoot
transports him to the literary realms of Gilbert and Sullivan and beyond to confront
Mikado's daughter-in-law-elect, Pickwick,
Dracula, Moriarty and Sherlock Holmes, Franken-
stein, an army of evil triangles, trolls, wizards, and more.

JOSEPH E[VERIDGE] KELLEAM

569. *When the Red King Woke.* New York: Avalon Books,
1966.

A young man, Tom Blake, and his fiancee, Flo
DeLee, are transported to a realm where either
sorcery or super science (it's never made clear)
reigns. A group of the inhabitants can communicate with a mysterious being from space, the
Red King, who is englobed in a strange bubble.
Even though the Red King sleeps, he communicates
with this special group and teaches them how to
use the power of their minds to heal and create.
Unfortunately, the remainder of the inhabitants
resent the powers of their fellows and become
barbarians, even though the gifted attempt to
provide for their less fortunate fellows. A
war ensues, Flo succumbs to greed and is one of
the antagonists, and the kingdom of the Red
King falls as he awakens and dies. Tom is returned to the everyday world but is followed
by the woman he fell in love with in the fantasy realm.

570. *The Last Magician: Nine Stories from Weird Tales.*
Ed. Patrick H. Adkins. Vol. I. The David H.
Keller Memorial Library. New Orleans, LA:
P.D.A. Enterprises, 1978 [paper].

    a.   "Half a Century of Writing" [autobiograph-
        ical essay]
    b.   "The Last Magician"
    c.   "Valley of Bones"
    d.   "The Dogs of Salem"
    e.   "Lords of the Ice"
    f.   "The Damsel and Her Cat"
    g.   "The Little Husbands"
    h.   "Death of the Kraken"
    i.   "The Goddess of Zion"
    j.   "Bindings Deluxe"

    Further volumes are promised in this series:
    The Conquerors, The Evening Star, and *Seeds of
    Death: Tales of Fantasy and Horror* among others.

571. *Life Everlasting and Other Tales of Science, Fantasy, and Horror.* Comp. Sam Moskowitz and Will
Sykora. Newark, NJ: Avalon, 1947. Rpt. Westport, CT: Hyperion, 1974.

    a.   "Life Everlasting"
    b.   "The Boneless Horror"
    c.   "Unto Us a Child is Born"
    d.   "No More Tomorrows"
    e.   "The Thing in the Cellar"
    f.   "The Dead Woman"
    g.   "Heredity"
    h.   "The Face in the Mirror"
    i.   "The Cerebral Library"
    j.   "A Piece of Linoleum"
    k.   "The Thirty and One"

572. *The Sign of the Burning Heart.* Saint-Lo [France]:
Imprimerie de La Marche, 1938.

    A utopian fantasy, composed of four loosely
    connected tales, that is written very much in
    the style of James Branch Cabell. Recognized
    by many as Keller's best work.

573. *Tales from Underwood.* New York: Published for
Arkham House by Pellegrini & Cudahy, 1952.

    a.   "The Worm"
    b.   "The Revolt of the Pedestrians"
    c.   "The Yeast Men"

DAVID H[ENRY] KELLER continued

       d. "The Doorbell"
       e. "The Flying Fool"
       f. "The Psychophonic Nurse"
       g. "A Biological Experiment"
       h. "Free as the Air"
       i. "The Bridle"
       j. "Tiger Cat"
       k. "The God Wheel"
       l. "The Golden Bough"
       m. "The Jelly Fish"
       n. "The Opium Eater"
       o. "The Thing in the Cellar"
       p. "The Moon Artist"
       q. "Creation Unforgivable"
       r. "The Dead Woman"
       s. "The Door"
       t. "The Perfumed Garden"
       u. "The Literary Corkscrew"
       v. "A Piece of Linoleum"

                DOUGLAS C. KENNEY
       See HENRY R. BEARD AND DOUGLAS C. KENNEY

SUSAN ALICE KERBY, pseud. See ALICE ELIZABETH BURTON

                   GERALD KERSH

574. *On an Odd Note*. New York: Ballantine, 1958
      [paper].

       a. "Seed of Destruction"
       b. "Frozen Beauty"
       c. "Reflections in a Tablespoon"
       d. "The Crewel Needle"
       e. "The Sympathetic Souse"
       f. "The Queen of Pig Island" (original title:
               "Mistress of Porcosito")
       g. "Prophet Without Honor"
       h. "The Beggars' Stone"
       i. "The Brighton Monster" (original title:
               "The Monster")
       j. "The Extraordinarily Horrible Dummy"
               (original title: "The Whisper")
       k. "Fantasy of a Hunted Man"
       l. "The Gentleman All in Black"
       m. "The Eye" (original title: "The Murderer'
               Eye")

                      133

575. *The Water Babies: A Fairy Tale for a Land Baby.*
London: Macmillan, 1863. Rpt. New York: Garland, 1976.

A young chimney sweep is aided by the fairy queen in escaping his tormentors and his dirt. He is transformed into a water-baby (a water sprite) and is gradually purged of his rough humanity through the wonder of his experiences and his new friends. Particularly noteworthy for its settings, characters, and involved incidents that reflect Kingsley's ability to create a well-developed fantasy realm.

Bibliography

576. Stevenson, Lionel, ed. *Victorian Fiction: A Guide to Research.* Cambridge, MA: Harvard University Press, 1964.

577. Thorp, Margaret [Farrand]. *Charles Kingsley, 1819-1875.* Princeton, NJ: Princeton University Press, 1937, pp. 191-204.

578. Parrish, Morris Longstreth, and Barbara Kelsey Mann. *Charles Kingsley and Thomas Hughes First Editions (With a Few Exceptions) in the Library at Dormy House, Pine Valley, New Jersey. Described With Notes.* London: Constable, 1951.

LEONARD KIP

579. *Hannibal's Man and Other Tales.* Albany: Argus, 1878.

    a. "Hannibal's Man"
    b. "In Three Heads"
    c. "The Ghost of Grantley"
    d. "The Secret of Appolonius Septro"
    e. "Prior Polycarp's Portrait"
    f. "St. Nicholas and the Gnome"

VERNON KNOWLES

580. *Here and Otherwhere.* London: R. Holden, 1926 [not seen]. Rpt. New York: Arno Press, 1978 [not seen].

581. *The Ladder*. London: The Mandrake Press, 1929.

In this whimsical novelette, typical of Knowles' fiction, a young man releases a magical ladder sent by his seafaring brother from a far-off land. Both he and his chum ascend into the unknown and are soon followed by all the inhabitants of their village, Finchincombe. The ladder raises the deserted town to national prominence, but collapses before a curious nation can learn where it leads, and Knowles never reveals where it does go.

582. *Silver Nutmegs*. London: R. Holden, 1927 [not seen]. Rpt. New York: Arno Press, 1978 [not seen].

583. *The Street of Queer Houses and Other Tales*. New York: Boullion, Biggs, 1924. Rpt. of the London: Wells Gardner, Darton, 1925, edition by Arno Press, New York, in 1978 [not seen].

a. "The Street of Queer Houses"
b. "The Weeping God"
c. "A Matter of Characterization"
d. "The House of Yesterdays"
e. "The Three Gods"
f. "The Pendant"
g. "The Author Who Entered His MS."
h. "The Mask"
i. "The Man Who Was Troubled by His Shadow"
j. "The Book of the Thousand Answers"
k. "The Idealist"
l. "The Broken Statue"
m. "The House That Took Revenge"
n. "The Elizabethan Gown"
o. "Honeymoon Cottage"

DEAN R[AY] KOONTZ

584. *The Crimson Witch*. New York: Curtis, 1971 [paper].

A rationalized fantasy, in which a young American "hippie," having rejected the family fortune, takes an overdose of a mind-expanding drug, PBT, and is projected into a sword and sorcery realm. He is befriended by a talking dragon and becomes the paramour of the Crimson Witch, a relationship born in hate and continued in love. Aided by the dragon and the witch, Cheryn, the protagonist, Jake Turnet, invades

the palace of the dark sorcerer, Lelar, and
returns to his own world with his comrades
through a time-space portal. However, the
three find contemporary American culture too
much even for the dragon's strength and the
witch's magic. They return to the fantasy
realm, deal Lelar his final defeat, and establish the benevolent reign of Jake.

585. *The Haunted Earth*. New York: Lancer, 1973 [paper].

In this comic detective story, the Maseni, an
alien race, have come to Earth and dissolved
the barrier between the natural and the supernatural. Stereotypes, mythic and religious
figures, *numina*, and supernatural personages
all come into being and share the Earth with
mankind. In the distorted legal and social
morays of this polyglot culture, Jesse Blake,
a private investigator, and Brutus, his Hell-
Hound partner, indulge in various sexual fantasies, solve crimes involving the interaction
between normal and supernatural creatures, and
are ultimately confronted with a menace that
could only exist in this delightful, hybrid
realm.

FREDERICK ARNOLD KUMMER

586. *Gentlemen in Hades: The Story of a Damned Débutante*. London: John Long, 1932. Rpt. with
Ladies in Hades: A Story of Hell's Smart Set--
two volumes in one--as *Shades of Hades*. New
York: Arno Press, 1978 [reprinted from a 1930
New York edition that, along with this reprint,
has not been seen].

A humorous fantasy concerning the activities of
the inhabitants of Hell that is much in the
vein of John Kendrick Bangs' works (see above)
and the sequel to *Ladies in Hades* (see below).
A young lady is killed, goes to Hell, and becomes the bedmate of many of history's most
famous men.

587. *Ladies in Hades: A Story of Hell's Smart Set*.
London: John Hamilton, 1928. Rpt. with *Gentle-
men in Hades: The Story of a Damned Débutante*--
two volumes in one--as *Shades of Hades*. New
York: Arno Press, 1978 [reprinted from a 1930
New York edition that, like the reprint, has

not been seen].

A number of history's most famous women form a
club and recount history from their points of
view. Satan, in this humorous fantasy echoing
the works of John Kendrick Bangs, ultimately
must dissolve the disruptive gathering.

KATHERINE KURTZ

The Camber and Deryni Series

588. *Camber of Culdi: Volume IV in the Chronicles of
     Deryni.* New York: Ballantine Books, 1976
     [paper].

589. *Saint Camber: Volume II in the Legends of Camber
     of Culdi.* New York: Ballantine Books, 1978.

590. *Camber the Heretic: Volume III in the Legends of
     Camber of Culdi.* In progress.

591. *Deryni Rising: Volume I in the Chronicles of
     Deryni.* New York: Ballantine Books, 1970 [paper].

592. *Deryni Checkmate: Volume II in the Chronicles of
     Deryni.* New York: Ballantine Books, 1972 [paper].

593. *High Deryni: Volume III in the Chronicles of
     Deryni.* New York: Ballantine Books, 1973 [paper].

In the Deryni series (numbers 591-593 above), a
royal house defended by a young king, Kelson,
and his dead father's trusted advisor, Morgan,
a member of the half-human, persecuted, and
sorcerous Deryni race, must battle rival Deryni
(who attempt to recover the rule over humans
they once enjoyed) through powers arcane, must
resolve the rift between the human and Deryni
races through social and psychological reform,
must unify the church and state through political manipulation, and must cooperate in ad-
justing Kelson to his own, unknown Deryni
powers. While the affairs of state do dominate
a large portion of this epic series, there are
also a number of poignantly human moments. The
wedding night of Kelson's ancestor, the only
survivor of the royal Haldene line who has been
living the celibate life of a monk, is accomplished with great beauty in *Culdi of Camber.*
Also, the tragic love affair between Bronwyn

and Kevin in *Deryni Checkmate* highlights Kurtz's ability to delineate human emotion and personal sorrow.

It should be noted that the Legends of Camber of Culdi (numbers 588-590 above) occur two hundred years before Kelson's coronation and that *Culdi of Camber*, despite its misleading subtitle, was originally offered as the background novel to the Deryni series. The Legends of Camber of Culdi, the Deryni patron saint whose spectral power and guidance is evident throughout the Deryni volumes, is the biography of Camber; the history of the reinstatement of the Haldene (Kelson's) royal house; and the overthrow of the Deryni rule. This is one of the better series in all of modern fantasy and successfully rivals the achievement of Andre Norton's Witch World and Roger Zelazny's Amber series. It is complex without being confusing, effectively narrated, and based on the theme of the resolution of prejudice through rites of passage.

HENRY KUTTNER

594. *The Dark World*. New York: Ace, 1965 [paper].

Many of Kuttner's novels appear to be fantasy until the final chapter when a science-fiction resolution is offered. For much of its length, *The Dark World* is a sword and sorcery fantasy focusing on the conflict between normal men and a lost race in which wolves, horses, and eagles are as intelligent as man and do cooperate with virtuous humans. In the final chapter, it is revealed that the animals are the product of radiation emanating from a crashed alien space ship.

For those readers who like their fantasies transformed into science fiction, two similar titles are listed below.

595. *The Mask of Circe*. New York: Ace, 1971 [paper].

596. *Valley of the Flame*. New York: Ace, 1964 [paper].

R[APHAEL] A[LOYSIUS] LAFFERTY

597. *The Devil is Dead.* New York: Avon, 1971 [paper].
      Rpt. Boston: Gregg, 1977.

      A meandering and difficult narrative of a sea
      journey on a ship captained by what appears to
      be the devil. The prose and plot are involved
      and convoluted, and the major theme of appear-
      ance and reality constantly distorts the mean-
      ing of the action, making it difficult to under-
      stand. The ultimate question the novel raises
      is not whether the captain is the devil or,
      when the captain dies, if the devil is really
      dead. Rather, it is the following paradox:
      if the devil should die, then, would not evil
      be unrestrained and be far worse than it nor-
      mally is?

598. *Does Anyone Else Have Something to Add? Stories*
      About Secret Places and Mean Men. New York:
      Charles Scribner's Sons, 1974.

      a. "About a Secret Crocodile"
      b. "Mad Man"
      c. "Nor Limestone Islands"
      d. "The Man Underneath"
      e. "Boomer Flats"
      f. "This Grand Carcass Yet"
      g. "In the Garden"
      h. "Growing Hinges of the World"
      i. "Golden Trabant"
      j. "How They Gave It Back"
      k. "Maybe Jones and the City"
      l. "Seven Story Dream"
      m. "Adam Had Three Brothers"
      n. "Pig in a Pokey"
      o. "The Weirdest World"
      p. "The Ultimate Creature"

      JOHN [BATTERSBY CROMPTON] LAMBOURNE

599. *The Kingdom That Was.* London: John Murray, 1931.

      An effective condemnation of brutality among
      man and animals, which can also be considered
      a satirical beast fable. Jim Burnett, a noted
      hunter, finds himself mysteriously transported
      to a pre-Edenic realm after he has killed an
      elephant. In this pre-history, he finds him-
      self without his gun amid talking animals who
      consider humans to be at the bottom of the
      ladder of being. Coping with his intellectual

139

conceit as a modern man, Burnett must come to
terms with his own inadequacies, man's role
in this world, and the vicious regent of the
animal kingdom, the Leopard. Aided by his new-
found wife, Brown Eyes, and Mopa the Owl, he
is saved by the return of Elephant, the God-
King, and witnesses the fall from innocence in
this once utopian animal kingdom. An appendix,
"The Personal Narrative of Professor F.B.
Ellis, D.Sc., F.R.S.E., F.E.S.," recounts
Burnett's return to the modern world.

GENE LANCOUR, pseud. See GENE FISHER

ANDREW LANG
Also see H[ENRY] RIDER HAGGARD AND ANDREW LANG

600. *In the Wrong Paradise and Other Stories*. London:
Kegan Paul, Trench, 1886.

   a.   "The End of Phæacia"
   b.   "In the Wrong Paradise"
   c.   "A Cheap Nigger"
   d.   "The Romance of the First Radical"
   e.   "A Duchess's Secret"
   f.   "The House of Strange Stories"
   g.   "In Castle Perilous"
   h.   "The Great Gladstone Myth"
   i.   "My Friend the Beach-Comber"

601. *Prince Prigio*. Bristol: J.W. Arrowsmith and
London: Simpkin, Marshall, 1889.

602. *Prince Ricardo of Pantouflia: Being the Adventures
of Prince Prigio's Son*. Bristol: J.W. Arrowsmith and London: Marshall, Hamilton, Kent,
1893.

Bibliography

603. Green, Roger Lancelyn. *Andrew Lang*. London: Bodley Head, 1962, pp. 78-84.

604. Green, Roger Lancelyn. *Andrew Lang: A Critical
Biography with a Short Title Index of the Works
of Andrew Lang*. Leicester: Edmund Ward, 1946.

[ANDREW LANG] AND W[ALTER] H[ERRIES POLLOCK]

605. *He.* London: Longmans, Green, 1887 [paper].

One of the many parodies of H. Rider Haggard's *She* (see above).

JOHN F. LANGE, JR.
(Also see NORMA N. JOHNS)

The Chronicles of Counter Earth Series

606. Norman, John, pseud. *Tarnsman of Gor.* New York: Ballantine, 1966 [paper].

607. _____. *Outlaw of Gor.* New York: Ballantine, 1967 [paper].

608. _____. *Priest-Kings of Gor.* New York: Ballantine, 1968 [paper].

609. _____. *Nomads of Gor.* New York: Ballantine, 1969 [paper].

610. _____. *Assassin of Gor.* New York: Ballantine, 1970 [paper].

611. _____. *Raiders of Gor.* New York: Ballantine, 1971 [paper].

612. _____. *Captive of Gor.* New York: Ballantine, 1972 [paper].

613. _____. *Hunters of Gor.* New York: DAW, 1974 [paper].

614. _____. *Marauders of Gor.* New York: DAW, 1975 [paper].

615. _____. *Tribesmen of Gor.* New York: DAW, 1976 [paper].

616. _____. *Slave Girl of Gor.* New York: DAW, 1977 [paper].

617. _____. *Beasts of Gor.* New York: DAW, 1978 [paper].

Lange's swashbuckling series of sword and sorcery adventures are both highly popular and frequently vilified. Renamed "Buckets of Gore" by one reviewer, the series has been criticized as sexist and violent. Showing major influence from Burroughs' Mars series (see above), the Gor series is a celebration of brutality and adventure in its most unequivocal masculine form.

STERLING E. LANIER

618. *The War For the Lot: A Tale of Fantasy and Terror.* Chicago and New York: Follett, 1969.

A young boy is selected by an ancient wood spirit to lead the animal kingdom against the invasion of an army of city rats. Communicating telepathically, the boy and the animals are able to protect the "Lot," a tract of virgin wilderness. Well-plotted and suitable for juveniles.

SANDERS ANNE LAUBENTHAL

619. *Excalibur.* New York: Ballantine, 1973 [paper].

A modern Arthurian romance in which the Pendragon comes to 20th-century Mobile, Alabama, to recover Excalibur from a pre-Columbian ruin. Includes all the trappings of the legend, including a grail quest, and an excellent cast of good and evil female characters, including Morgan le Fey and Morgause of Orkney.

MARGERY LAWRENCE, pseud. See MRS. ARTHUR EDWARD TOWLE

TANITH LEE

620. *Companions on the Road.* London: Macmillan, 1975.

In a tale reminiscent of Geoffrey Chaucer's "Pardoner's Tale," three men--Kachil the thief, Feluce the arrogant soldier, and Havor the worthy captain--steal a sorcerous gold goblet from a sacked city. Pursued by the spirits of an evil count, his son, and his awesomely powerful daughter, first Kachil and then Feluce are killed while they sleep by the power of their own macabre dreams. Havor, spurned by all, is finally saved by the spirits of a young soldier and his family, for whom he has done a good turn.

621. *Death's Master*. New York: DAW, 1979 [paper].

> A companion volume to *Night's Master* (see below) which is set in the same environment and which does include appearances by Azhrarn. However, this volume revolves around the god Uhlume, Death's Master. In pursuit of happiness and immortality, major human characters embrace or challenge death. Narasen, Queen of Merh, slays a wizard, is subject to a horrible and carnal curse, bears a hermaphroditic shape-changer and demon child by a dead man, and ultimately becomes Queen and ruler of the underworld. Simmu/Shell, the unknowing hermaphrodite, becomes an adept adventurer, violates the Garden of the Golden Daughters, drinks from the Well of Immortality, establishes a city of immortals only to discover the dread of life-without-death, and is remade by Uhlume. Zhirek/Zhirem, an outcast nomad child, becomes invulnerable after being dipped into a well of immortal fire and becomes Simmu's companion and lover, but he grows hateful of Simmu and is later, as a master wizard, the prime agent in destroying the city of immortals. While these characters fill much of the action, many other minor ones--i.e., Kassafeh, Simmu's wife, and Hhabaid, princess of the sea people--have significant involvement in the action of this highly complex, darkly gothic, markedly eastern, and excellent work.

622. *Night's Master*. New York: DAW Books, 1978 [paper].

> A loosely connected series of tales divided into three books--"Life Underground," "Tricksters," and "The World's Lure"--all interconnected by the often strange and inhuman interests of Azhrarn, Prince of Demons and Night's Master. Among the tales, the most striking are the chronicles of Sivesh, a mortal child raised in the City of Demons, Druhim Vanashta, who longs to return to the mundane world and loses the grace of Azhrarn; the tale of Kazir, a minstrel, whose characterization captures the myth of Orpheus in a new and original way; the bittersweet history of Zorayas, who Azhrarn turns from hideous to supernaturally beautiful and who leads bloody conquests and performs self-serving seductions; and the master tale of the work, the death and rebirth of Azhrarn, himself. In its construction of alien setting,

character, and tone, this work compares very favorably with Sylvia Townsend Warner's *Kingdoms of Elfin* and Jack Vance's tales of the Dying Earth (see below).

623. *The Storm Lord*. New York: DAW, 1976 [paper].

An excellent portrait of a created world that suffers from extreme racism and sexism. These faults are confronted and conquered by the protagonist, Raldnor, bastard son of a high priestess and the High King of a superior race.

624. *Volkhavaar*. New York: DAW, 1977 [paper].

An excellent and highly descriptive novel reflecting Lee's continuing themes of life, death, and rebirth as a female slave and a master of dark illusion contend for the favor of a god. She, driven by love, finds a greater truth than mere supremacy. The illusionist returns to the bitterness of his squalid origins and the darkness of his inner self.

The Birthgrave Trilogy

625. *The Birthgrave*. New York: DAW, 1975 [paper].

626. *Vazkor, Son of Vazkor*. New York: DAW, 1978 [paper].

627. *Quest for the White Witch*. New York: DAW, 1978 [paper].

A two generation, mother and son, fantasy. A young woman awakes in a volcano suffering from amnesia in *The Birthgrave*. Forced into a world she neither knows nor understands, she experiences life as the mate of Vazkor, a sorcerer and conqueror. She finally discovers her true identity as an immortal and is able to use her magical powers. In *Vazkor, Son of Vazkor*, her son, who she abandoned to be raised as the son of a nomad chief, discovers his origin and goes in search of his albino mother, who he believes has ruthlessly slain his father. The search is completed in *Quest for the White Witch*, as the son comes to his full power as an immortal. The series ends with one of the few examples of justifiable incest in all of literature.

VERNON LEE, pseud. See VIOLET PAGET

628. *The Wind's Twelve Quarters.* New York: Harper &
      Row, 1975.

      The collection is particularly noteworthy since
      it contains the two seed stories for Le Guin's
      Earthsea Trilogy (*).

      a. "Semley's Necklace"
      b. "April in Paris"
      c. "The Masters"
      d. "Darkness Box"
      e. "The Word of Unbinding"*
      f. "The Rule of Names"*
      g. "Winter's King"
      h. "The Good Trip"
      i. "Nine Lives"
      j. "Things"
      k. "A Trip to the Head"
      l. "Vaster than Empires and More Slow"
      m. "The Stars Below"
      n. "The Field of Vision"
      o. "Direction of the Road"
      p. "The Ones Who Walk Away from Omelas"
      q. "The Day Before the Revolution"

      The Earthsea Trilogy

629. *A Wizard of Earthsea.* Berkeley: Parnassus, 1968.
      Rev. ed. London: Victor Gollancz, 1971.

630. *The Tombs of Atuan.* New York: Atheneum, 1971.

631. *The Farthest Shore.* New York: Atheneum, 1972.

      Le Guin's tales of the wizard Ged are among the
      most highly acclaimed of contemporary fantasies.
      Her epic and human chronicle of the training,
      maturation, and final days of the archimage is
      a well-paced narrative filled with well-research-
      ed magical lore and marked by serious explora-
      tions of the questions of identity, power, and
      ethics. In addition, her characterization of
      the sorcerous and world-wise dragons is one of
      the best in all fantasy. Suitable for juveniles.

      Bibliography

632. Bittner, James W. "A Survey of Le Guin Criticism."
      In *Ursula K. Le Guin: Voyager to Inner Lands
      and to Outer Space.* Ed. Joe DeBolt. Port
      Washington, NY, and London: Kennikat Press,
      1978.

633. Levin, Jeff. "Ursula K. Le Guin: A Select Bibliography." *Science-Fiction Studies*, 2 (1975),
204-208.

FRITZ [REUTER] LEIBER, [JR.]

634. "Conjure Wife." In *Witches Three*. New York:
Twayne, 1952, pp. 19-168. First separate book
publication: New York: Twayne, 1953. Rpt.
Boston: Gregg, 1977.

A highly suspenseful novel about a young college
professor and his witch wife. The tale begins
with his discovery and destruction of her protective charms and moves from there to an excellent climax as the young couple become the
focus of a darkly sorcerous storm. Originally
published in the April, 1943, issue of *Unknown*,
and the source of a feature length film, en-
titled *Burn Witch Burn* in the United States and
Night of the Eagle in Britain.

635. *The Mind Spider and Other Stories*. New York: Ace,
1961 [paper]. Bound dos-a-dos with Leiber's
The Big Time.

a. "The Haunted Future" (original title:
"Tranquility, or Else!")
b. "Damnation Morning"
c. "The Oldest Soldier"
d. "Try and Change the Past"
e. "The Number of the Beast"
f. "The Mind Spider"

636. *Night Monsters*. New York: Ace, 1969 [paper].
Bound dos-a-dos with Leiber's *The Green
Millennium*.

a. "The Black Gondolier"
b. "Midnight in the Mirror World"
c. "I'm Looking for Jeff"
d. "The Casket-Demon"

637. *The Night of the Wolf*. New York: Ballantine,
1966 [paper].

a. "The Lone Wolf"
b. "The Wolf Pair"
c. "Crazy Wolf"
d. "The Wolf Pack"

638. *Night's Black Agents*. Sauk City, WI: Arkham
House, 1947.

This collection is Leiber's first book, and,
while its fantasy content is restricted to
three of its ten short stories--(a) "The Man
Who Never Grew Young" and two Fafhrd and the
Gray Mouser tales, (b) The Sunken Land" and
(c) "Adept's Gambit"--it is important for the
often clumsy, but very enlightening, statements
of Leiber's philosophy and opinions. For example, his contempt for the insulating and res-
trictive nature of excessive civilization is
made very clear. The other stories in the
collection are quite correctly labelled horror
in the table of contents:

d.   "Smoke Ghost"
e.   "The Automatic Pistol"
f.   "The Inheritance"
g.   "The Hill and the Hole"
h.   "The Dreams of Albert Moreland"
i.   "The Hound"
j.   "Diary in the Snow"

The 1978 paperback reprint (New York: Berkley)
adds two horror stories that did not appear in
the first edition:

k.   "The Girl with the Hungry Eyes"
l.   "A Bit of the Dark World"

Both editions contain an interesting foreword
in which Leiber explains the birth of the
Fafred and the Gray Mouser series (see below).

639. *Shadows With Eyes*. New York: Ballantine, 1962
[paper].

a.   "A Bit of the Dark World"
b.   "The Dead Man"
c.   "The Power of the Puppets"
d.   "Schizo Jimmie"
e.   "The Man who Made Friends with Electricity"
f.   "A Deskful of Girls"

The Fafred and the Gray Mouser Series

640. *Two Sought Adventure: Exploits of Fafhrd and the
Gray Mouser*. New York: Gnome, 1957. Expanded

edition: see *Swords Against Death* (below).

a. "The Jewels in the Forest" (original title: "Two Sought Adventure")
b. "Thieves' House"
c. "The Bleak Shore"
d. "The Howling Tower"
e. "The Sunken Land"
f. "The Seven Black Priests"
g. "Claws from the Night" (original title: "Dark Vengeance")

641. *Swords and Deviltry*. New York: Ace, 1970 [paper]. Rpt. Boston: Gregg, 1977.

a. "Induction"
b. "The Snow Women"
c. "The Unholy Grail"
d. "Ill Met in Lankhmar"

642. *Swords Against Death*. New York: Ace, 1970 [paper]. Rpt. Boston: Gregg, 1977. An expansion of *Two Sought Adventure* (see above).

a. "The Circle Curse"
b. "The Jewels in the Forest"
c. "The Thieves' House"
d. "The Bleak Shore"
e. "The Howling Tower"
f. "The Sunken Land"
g. "The Seven Black Priests"
h. "Claws from the Night"
i. "Bazaar of the Bizarre"

643. *Swords in the Mist*. New York: Ace, 1968 [paper]. Rpt. Boston: Gregg, 1977.

a. "The Cloud of Hate"
b. "Lean Times in Lankhmar"
c. "Their Mistress, the Sea"
d. "When the Sea-King's Away"
e. "The Wrong Branch"
f. "Adept's Gambit"

644. *Swords Against Wizardry*. New York: Ace, 1968 [paper]. Rpt. Boston: Gregg, 1977.

a. "In the Witch's Tent"
b. "Stardock"
c. "The Two Best Thieves in Lankhmar"
d. "The Lords of Quarmall" (with Harry Otto Fischer)

FRITZ [REUTER] LEIBER, [JR.] continued

645. *The Swords of Lankhmar*. New York: Ace, 1968 [paper].
Rpt. Boston: Gregg, 1977.

The novel-length expansion of "Scylla's Daughter,"
Fantastic Stories, May 1961.

646. *Swords and Ice Magic*. New York: Ace, 1977 [paper].
Rpt. Boston: Gregg, 1977.

    a.   "The Sadness of the Executioner"
    b.   "Beauty and the Beasts"
    c.   "Trapped in the Shadowland"
    d.   "The Bait"
    e.   "Under the Thumbs of the Gods"
    f.   "Trapped in the Sea of Stars"
    g.   "The Frost Monstreame"
    h.   "Rime Isle"

647. *Rime Isle*. Chapel Hill, NC: Whispers Press, 1977.

Novel-length version of "The Frost Monstreame"
and "Rime Isle" with illustrations by Tim Kirk.

These collections and two novels are among the
most popular examples of sword and sorcery fantasy. The series is pure fun as the northern
barbarian Fafhrd and the diminutive thief the
Gray Mouser fight, connive, and love their ways
through quests, adventures, and dilemmas.
Leiber offers the best description of the series
in "Adept's Gambit" (see *Night's Black Agents*
above): "Material relating to them has, on the
whole, been scattered by annalists, since they
were heroes too disreputable for classic myth,
too cryptically independent ever to let themselves be tied to a folk, too shifty and improbable in their adventures to please the historian, too often involved with a riff-raff of
dubious demons, unfrocked sorcerers, and dis-
credited deities--a veritable underworld of
the supernatural."

Bibliography

648. Allen, Paul C. "Of Swords and Sorcery: Fafhrd &
the Gray Mouser." *Fantasy Crossroads*, No. 8
(May 1976), 40-41.

649. Allen, Paul C., and Mike Barrett. "Bibliography"
[Fafhrd & Gray Mouser stories]. *The Silver
Eel*. Evensville, TN: Robert P. Barger, 1978
[paper].

650. Lewis, Al. "Fritz Leiber: A Bibliography."
     Magazine of Fantasy and Science Fiction, July
     1969, pp. 63-68.

MURRAY LEINSTER, pseud.   See WILLIAM FITZGERALD JENKINS

C[LIVE] S[TAPLES] LEWIS

651. *The Dark Tower and Other Stories*.   Ed. Walter
     Hooper. London: Collins, 1977.

     a.   "The Dark Tower"
     b.   "The Man Born Blind"
     c.   "The Shoddy Lands"
     d.   "Ministering Angels"
     e.   "Forms of Things Unknown"
     f.   "After Ten Years"

652. *The Great Divorce: A Dream*.   London: Geoffrey
     Bles, 1945 [not seen]. Rpt. [New York]:
     Macmillan, 1969 [paper].

     At intervals, the inhabitants of Hell are
     allowed a bus trip to the outskirts of Heaven
     and are there approached by ministering friends,
     now inhabitants of the divine realm.   Each
     fallen soul is given the opportunity to under-
     stand and recant the sin he or she committed on
     earth. For the fallen, the landscape of
     Heaven's suburb seems to be as hard as glass,
     but as the fortunate few realize their errors,
     the fauna and flora become correctly soft.
     Lewis constantly uses his excellent irony and
     his knowledge of theology as many of the self-
     righteous sinners refuse to see beyond them-
     selves and choose to return to Hell.

653. *The Screwtape Letters*.   London: Geoffrey Bles,
     1942.

     Lewis' delightful creation of the correspondence
     between a greater devil in Hell with a lesser
     devil on earth. The lesser devil is in the pro-
     cess of ineptly seducing a young man into a life
     of sin. He seeks the continual advice of his
     superior as his selected victim relentlessly
     sinks into the throes of virtue. The senior
     devil's inadvertent shape shift into the form
     of a centipede, as the result of his frustra-
     tion with his demonic pupil, is one of the out-

standing comic scenes in all of fantasy.

The Space Trilogy

654. *Out of the Silent Planet*. London: Lane, 1938.

655. *Perelandra* [occasionally titled *Voyage to Venus: Perelandra* in later editions]. London: Lane, 1943.

656. *That Hideous Strength: A Modern Fairy-Tale for Grown-Ups*. London: Lane, 1945. Abridged edition as *The Tortured Planet*. New York: Avon, [1958] [paper].

Sometimes called the Ransom Trilogy after its protagonist, this is an examination of the nature of creation, life, and ethics. In the first two volumes, Ransom travels to Mars and Venus to witness the advent of life and intelligence. In the third volume, Ransom returns to Earth, and, as the Arthurian pendragon, he successfully confronts a major threat to Man, God, and existence. The series is distinguished by its extensive mythological and theological content as Lewis gives his substantial intellect full rein. Its major theme is that Man must be in accord with divine creation and elemental law if he is to be successful and happy, and throughout the series, it is made quite clear that science and technology lead Man away from his individual and cosmic destiny.

The Chronicles of Narnia

657. *The Lion, the Witch, and the Wardrobe*. London: Geoffrey Bles [not seen]. Rpt. New York: Macmillan, 1950.

658. *The Voyage of the "Dawn Treader."* London: Geoffrey Bles, 1952.

659. *The Silver Chair*. London: Geoffrey Bles, 1953.

660. *The Magician's Nephew*. New York: Macmillan; London: The Bodley Head, 1955.

661. *The Horse and His Boy*. London: Geoffrey Bles, 1954.

662. *The Last Battle: A Story for Children*. London: The Bodley Head, 1956.

The Chronicles of Narnia are among the classics of children's and juvenile literature, and have charmed many an adult. They focus on a group of children who find an enchanted realm of talking animals through the back of a wardrobe. They ally themselves with the good king of Narnia, Aslan, and the powers of virtuous magic in a titanic psychomachia that has strong allegorical, Christian elements.

Bibliography

663. Hooper, Walter. "A Bibliography of the Writings of C.S. Lewis." In *Light on C.S. Lewis*. Ed. Jocelyn Gibb. London: Geoffrey Bles, 1965, pp. 121-148.

DAVID LINDSAY

664. *Devil's Tor*. London: G.P. Putnam's Sons, 1932. Rpt. New York: Arno Press, 1978 [not seen].

While Lindsay's *A Voyage to Arcturus* (see below) has received most of the critical attention, there are those who consider *Devil's Tor* his masterwork. In Scotland, Hugh Drapier and Ingrid Fletcher discover a tomb beneath a large stone demon's head on Devil's Tor. They discover separate halves of a stone with occult and extra-dimensional powers. However, Drapier is killed and one Henry Saltfleet must complete the stone's union with bittersweet results. Much of the action is presided over by visions of a giant goddess and ancient figures.

665. *The Violet Apple & the Witch*. Ed. J.B. Pick. Chicago: Chicago Review Press, 1976 [paper].

666. *A Voyage to Arcturus*. London: Methuen, 1920. Rpt. Boston: Gregg, 1977.

A vivid and difficult novel that at times seems to defy understanding. However, it never denies wonder, and its parallel between biological alterations and perceptions is one of the most unusual in all fantasy. The excellent description of the planet Tormance, a place where physical change is a way of life, and the protagonist Maskull, an Earthling who has been persuaded to travel to this metamorphic environment, are well integrated as alien visitor and alien

place try to come to terms in the arena of truth
and perception, godhood and humanity. A classic
of macabre imagination with a unique ending as
Maskull dies and is reborn.

ERIC LINKLATER

667. *Crisis in Heaven: An Elysian Comedy*. London:
Macmillan, 1944.

668. *A Spell for Old Bones*. London: Jonathon Cape, 1949.
Rpt. New York: Arno Press, 1978 [reprinted from
a 1950 New York edition that, like the reprint,
has not been seen].

A young wastrel in ancient Scotland, Albyn,
decides that instead of working he would like
to be a poet. While his powers of verse are
never much to speak of, he does manage to seduce
the king's daughter and thus cure her of her
speechlessness. However, Albyn's seemingly
idyllic world is darkened by the presence of
the true ruler of the kingdom, the irrecusable
giant Furbister. After Albyn finds a wife for
Furbister, a neighboring giant, Od McGammon,
becomes jealous and war results. After a
pyrrhic victory for both sides, Albyn returns
to his wife and his daydreams.

Bibliography

669. Temple, Ruth Z., and Martin Tucker. *Twentieth-
Century British Literature: A Reference Guide
and Bibliography*. New York: Frederick Ungar,
1968, pp. 195-196.

JOHN URI LLOYD

670. *Etidorhpa or the End of Earth: The Strange History
of a Mysterious Being and the Account of His
Remarkable Journey*. Cincinnati: By the Author,
1895 [not seen]. 11th ed. New York: Dodd,
Mead, 1901.

Llewellyn Drury narrates the journey of the
protagonist, known only as I-Am-The-Man. Violating the rules of an occult order, I-Am-The-
Man is exiled and goes on a hollow-earth journey beginning at Paducah, Kentucky. Guided by
a nameless purblind humanoid, he passes through

vast fungi forests and over an enormous underground lake. The two travellers discuss a variety of ethic, moral, abstract, and metaphysical
issues, all of which are unified at the center
of the Earth. These issues were to be more
fully clarified in a sequel that was never
written.

Etidorhpa (Aphrodite spelled backwards) was
probably an influence on Lovecraft's *At the
Mountains of Madness*.

Bibliography

671. Burke, W.J., Will D. Howe, Irving Weiss, and Anne
      Weiss. *American Authors and Books 1640 to
      the Present*. 3rd rev. ed. New York: Crown,
      1972, p. 385.

JACK [CHANEY] LONDON

672. *Before Adam*. New York and London: Macmillan,
      1907.

      A novel of reincarnation in which a man remem-
      bers his former life as a paleolithic man.
      London admitted that his tale of racial memory
      was strongly derived from Stanley Waterloo's
      Story of Ab (1897).

673. *Curious Fragments: Jack London's Tales of Fantasy
      Fiction*. Ed. Dale L. Walker. Port Washington,
      NY, and London: Kennkat Press, 1975.

      a. "Who Believes in Ghosts!"
      b. "A Thousand Deaths"
      c. "The Rejuvenation of Major Rathbone"
      d. "Even Unto Death"
      e. "A Relic of the Pliocene"
      f. "The Shadow and the Flash"
      g. "The Enemy of All the World"
      h. "A Curious Fragment"
      i. "Goliah"
      j. "The Unparalleled Invasion"
      k. "When the World Was Young"
      l. "The Strength of the Strong"
      m. "War"
      n. "The Scarlet Plague"
      o. "The Red One"

674. *The Star Rover*. New York: Macmillan, 1915. Rpt.

as *The Jacket (The Star Rover)*. London: Mills & Boon, 1915.

A novel of social reform, this concerns a prison inmate who escapes inhuman treatment by freeing his soul from his body. In interconnected episodes, he roams the stars, reliving previous lives.

Bibliography

675. Walker, Dale L., and James E. Sisson III. *The Fiction of Jack London: A Chronological Bibliography*. El Paso, TX: Texas Western Press, 1972.

676. Woodbridge, Hensley C., John London, and George H. Tweney. *Jack London: A Bibliography*. Georgetown, CA: Talisman Press, 1966; Enl. ed. Milwood, NY: Kraus Reprint, 1973.

GABRIELLE MARGARET VERE [CAMPBELL] LONG

677. Bowen, Marjorie, pseud. *The Last Bouquet: Some Twilight Tales*. London: John Lane, The Bodley Head, 1933.

a. "The Last Bouquet"
b. "Madam Spitfire"
c. "The Fair Hair of Ambrosine"
d. "The Hidden Ape"
e. "The Avenging of Ann Leek"
f. "The Crown Derby Plate"
g. "The Perscription"
h. "Elsie's Lonely Afternoon"
i. "The Lady Clodagh"
j. "A Plaster Saint"
k. "Florence Flannery"
l. "Kecksies"
m. "The Sign-Painter and the Crystal Fishes"
n. "Raw Material"

Bibliography

678. Wagenknecht, Edward. "Bowen, Preedy, Shearing & Co.: A Note in Memory and a Checklist." *Boston University Studies in English*, 3, No. 3 (1957), 181-189.

ROBERT LORY

679. *Master of the Etrax*. New York: Dell, 1970

[paper].

In this whimsical sword and sorcery tale, Hamper, the However of Balik, searches for a magical talisman, the Etrax. Relying more on his nimble wits than his diminutive frame, he braves sorcery and monsters to stumble his way to success.

JANE [WEBB] LOUDON

680. *The Mummy! A Tale of the Twenty-Second Century.* 3 vols. London: Henry Colburn, 1827.

In a future, matriarchal society of super science, Edric reanimates the mummy of Cheops. The mummy escapes and involves itself in the court intrigue of London. Ultimately, the mummy reveals that it had been brought to life by supernatural forces, not Edric's efforts. To atone for its evil career as pharoah, the mummy must do good deeds and punish evil doers.

H[OWARD] P[HILLIPS] LOVECRAFT

681. *The Dream-Quest of Unknown Kadath.* Buffalo, NY: Shroud, 1955 [paper].

Originally written in 1926 and not published separately until this edition, this is one of Lovecraft's rare excursions outside of the realm of the horror genre, although it does contain elements of horror and certainly uses portions of the Cthulhu mythos. It is written very much in the style of Lord Dunsany (see Plunkett below) and utilizes Lovecraft's frequent protagonist, Randolph Carter. It concerns Carter's "dream-quest" through a fantastic metropolis where he meets a number of horrible and pleasing creatures. Ultimately, the traveler confronts one of the most despicable of the Cthulhu deities, Nyarlathotep, eventually falls back into his waking world, and discovers that he has been traveling through his native Boston.

Bibliography

682. Owings, Mark, with Jack L. Chalker. *The Revised H.P. Lovecraft Bibliography.* Baltimore:

Mirage Press, 1973.

MARK M. LOWENTHAL

683. *Crispan Magicker*. New York: Avon, 1979 [paper].

In this disappointingly non-descriptive sword
and sorcery novel, Crispan, the youngest and
greatest of an Order of Wizards, must go out
into a medieval realm to confront a fallen
member of the order. Crispan has spent most
of his life studying and, while he is recognized
as perhaps the greatest wizard to ever live, his
doubts are foremost in his mind as he journeys
out into an alien world to confront Vladur, a
foul necromancer. Struggling with his fears
and confused by his fascination for the sword
and warfare, Crispan finally does defeat Vladur
in a poorly described arcane duel and returns
to the Order Vladur has destroyed to find that
even its energetically preserved neutrality
could not protect it. He wanders off from the
world of men in his continuing attempt to find
himself as the novel ends.

SAM J. LUNDWALL

684. *Alice's World*. New York: Ace Books, 1971 [paper].
Bound dos-a-dos with Lundwall's *No Time for
Heroes*.

A space ship lands on Earth, long abandoned in
man's leap to the stars, and its crew discovers
a world of fairy-tale and mythological creations,
including Medea, Oistros, Venus, the Phoenix,
the Sphinx, the Valkyries, Pegasus, Yggdrasil,
the Mad Tea Party, Captain Nemo, Heracles, and
Lundwall's interesting composite, "Anycity."
All seems to be controlled and generated by the
enigmatic Alice, and all the manifestations
deny the crew's desire to return to rational
phenomenon.

RICHARD A[LLEN] LUPOFF

685. *Lisa Lane*. New York: Bobbs-Merrill, 1976.

A young girl comes to puberty and finds that
she is one of a number of "closet" werewolves.

She seeks her own identity as her minority group "comes out."

686. *Sword of the Demon*. New York: Harper & Row, 1977.

A metaphysical odyssey based in part on Japanese mythology in which the adventures of Aizen and Kishimo, as they seek the land of Tsuna, are combined with the activities of two godlike figures, neither man nor woman, as they seek an obscure goal. A highly difficult novel that in its myriad impressions and vivid sensuality can be more easily felt than understood.

ERIC VAN LUSTBADER

Sunset Warrior Trilogy

687. *The Sunset Warrior*. Garden City, NY: Doubleday, 1977.

688. *Shallows of Night*. Garden City, NY: Doubleday, 1978.

689. *Dai-San*. Garden City, NY: Doubleday, 1978.

In a subterranean and mechanized world of the far-distant future, the seeming remains of humanity seek survival and power under one of the polar caps. Ronin, blademaster and combat adept, avoids the allegiances of the underground power structure, despite the fact that he is the most highly trained student of the combat-master, the enigmatic and antagonistic Salamander. Ronin, however, escapes and discovers a world of men and magic still exists on the surface, but that the entire world is threatened by the coming of the incarnation of evil, the Dolman, and is immediately being devastated by the presence of the Dolman's four monstrous heralds, the Makkon. It is Ronin's responsibility to transport a magical scroll to the fabled isle of Ama-no-mori. In the final volume, more obscure and mythic than the first two, Ronin is transformed into a god: the final god of man, Dai-San, the Sunset Warrior. In this incarnation, he assimilates his earlier companions and their qualities and becomes the sum total of forces needed to defeat the Dolman. Lustbader's trilogy is distinguished from run-of-the-mill sword and sorcery through its positive echoes of Jack Vance's Dying Earth, by its excellent characterization, and its use of oriental philosophy and mythology. Ronin's inadvertent slaying of his sister, at the end of volume one, is an example of Lustbader's ability to bring both the positive and negative qualities of his characters to full life.

JANE DENVIL LYNCH

The Atlantis Series

690. Gaskell, Jane, pseud. *The Serpent*. London: Holder and Stoughton, 1963.

691. _____. *Atlan*. London: Holder and Stoughton, 1965.

692. _____. *The City*. London: Holder and Stoughton, 1966.

An involved series with significant political content and intrigue. All the volumes are cliff-hangers, as the Atlantean princess, Cija, spends her first seventeen years in cloistered isolation and then strikes out into the world. She becomes involved in white and black magic, marriage to a semi-human overlord, many wars and battles, court politics, and numerous relationships. After many years as a wanderer, she discovers her semi-human overlord, falls in love with him, and shares his conquest of Atlantis. Rewarding for the reader who will persevere in spite of the often overly dense prose and excessive melodrama.

RICHARD K. LYON
See ANDREW J. OFFUTT AND RICHARD K. LYON

EDWARD BULWER LYTTON
See EDWARD GEORGE EARLE BULWER-LYTTON

COLUM MacCONNELL

693. *Tark and the Golden Tide*. New York: Leisure Books, 1977 [paper].

Although advertised "in the tradition of Conan," this run-of-the-mill sword and sorcery adven-

ture is in imitation of Leiber's Fafhrd and the
Gray Mouser series (see above) as a giant barbarian with his broad sword and a diminutive
swordsman with his rapier fight their ways
through blood and beauty.

GEORGE MacDONALD

694. *At the Back of the North Wind*. London: Strahan,
1871 [issued in 1870].

Juvenile.

695. *Evenor*. [Ed. Lin Carter]. New York and London:
Ballantine, 1972 [paper].

    a.   "The Wise Woman"
    b.   "The Carasoyn"
    c.   "The Golden Key"

696. *Gifts of the Child Christ and Other Tales*. 2
vols. London: Sampson Low Marston, Searle, and
Rivington, 1882 [not seen].

697. *Gifts of the Child Christ: Fairytales and Stories
for the Childlike*. Ed. Glenn Edward Sadler.
2 vols. Grand Rapids, MI: William B. Eerdmans,
1973 [paper].

With the exceptions of *At the Back of the North
Wind, The Princess and the Goblin, The Princess
and Curdie, Phantastes,* and *Lilith*, these omnibus volumes collect and reprint all of Mac-
Donald's fairy tales and short stories, along
with an essay, "The Fantastic Imagination,"
and two poems, "The Girl that Lost Things" and
"That Holy Thing."

    a.   "The Gifts of the Child Christ"
    b.   "The History of Photogen and Nycteris"
         [alternate title: "The Day Boy and
         the Night Boy"]
    c.   "The Shadows"
    d.   "Little Daylight"
    e.   "The Golden Key"
    f.   "Cross Purposes"
    g.   "The Wise Woman, or The Lost Princess:
         A Double Story"
    h.   "The Castle: A Parable"
    i.   "Port in a Storm"
    j.   "Papa's Story [A Scot's Christmas Story]"

     k. "The Light Princess"
     l. "The Giant's Heart"
     m. "The Carasoyn"
     n. "The Gray Wolf"
     o. "The Cruel Painter"
     p. "The Broken Swords"
     q. "The Wow O'Rivven [The Bell]"
     r. "Uncle Cornelius, His Story"
     s. "The Butcher's Bills"
     t. "Birth, Dreaming, Death [The Schoolmaster's Story]"

698. *The Golden Key.* New York: Farrar, Straus and Giroux, 1967 [first published in 1867; first separate book publication?].

699. *The Light Princess.* London: Blackie & Son, 1890 [rpt. from *Dealing With the Fairies,* 1867].

700. *Lilith.* London: Chatto & Windus; New York: Dodd, Mead, 1895. Rpt. in *Phantastes and Lilith.* Grand Rapids, MI: Wm. B. Eerdmans, 1964 [paper] with an introduction by C.S. Lewis.

An allegorical journey through fairyland that was a major influence on C.S. Lewis' Narnian Chronicles (see above) and that concentrates on the archetypal themes of death, resurrection, and mutability. Vane, the protagonist, follows the mysterious Raven, the supposed ghost of an old librarian but actually Adam, into the "region of the seven dimensions." Vane becomes a primary figure, both through his foolishness and intelligence, in the psychomachia between the "lovers"--a race of innocent children--and the "bags"--wicked and fell giants. During his adventures, his major foe is the evil shape-changer, Lilith, who is ultimately redeemed through the efforts of the virtuous characters.

701. *Phantastes: A Faerie Romance for Men and Women.* London: Smith, Elder, 1858. Rpt. in *Phantastes and Lilith.* Grand Rapids, MI: Wm. B. Eerdmans, 1964 [paper] with an introduction by C.S. Lewis.

Wondrous challenges and temptations mark this allegorical quest for love and self in the land of the fairies. Anodos, the protagonist, wanders in a fantasy land governed by magic and various *numina.* In the course of his travels, he is threatened by the ogre of the ash, succored by the lady of the birch, accompanied by

the dread shadow of reality, nearly destroyed
by the archetypal wasteland, avoided by the
alabaster maiden he saves with a song, killed,
and reborn into his original mundane world with
a far greater appreciation of the harmony of
life. Despite numerous opinions to the con-
trary, MacDonald's prose is not that difficult,
and this adventure does offer the reader an
excellent sense of participation.

702. *The Portent: A Story of the Inner Vision of the
Highlanders, Commonly Called the Second Sight.*
London: Smith, Elder, 1864.

703. *The Princess and Curdie.* London: Chatto & Windus,
1883 [not seen] [issued in 1882].

Juvenile.

704. *The Princess and the Goblin.* London: [Strahan],
1872 [not seen] [issued in 1871].

Juvenile.

705. *The Wise Woman. A Parable.* London: Strahan, 1875.

Bibliography

706. Bulloch, John Malcolm. *A Centennial Bibliography
of George MacDonald.* Aberdeen: Aberdeen University Press, 1925. Rpt. with corrections in
the *Aberdeen Library Bulletin,* 5 (February
1925), 679-747.

PATRICIA A. McKILLIP

707. *The Forgotten Beasts of Eld.* New York: Atheneum,
1974.

A highly imagistic and descriptive setting
surrounds the innocent Sybel, the child and
protege of a wizard who, at his passing, left
her a company of semi-legendary beasts, all
excellent creatures. Ultimately, she must confront harsh realities and is torn between a
fosterling child and the knight who loves her.

708. *The Throme of the Erril of Sherill.* New York:
Atheneum, 1973.

In this charming and appealing juvenile, a

young man goes in search of a non-existent "throme," a song of great beauty, to win a princess. Knowing all along that he is questing a will-of-the-wisp, he travels to non-existent places and finally generates the throme from himself and his experiences after he discards the traditional garb of warfare for clothes and "weapons" that ally him with nature.

The Hed Trilogy

709. *The Riddle-Master of Hed*. New York: Atheneum, 1976.

710. *Heir of Sea and Fire*. New York: Atheneum, 1977.

711. *Harpist in the Wind*. New York: Atheneum, 1979.

Torn between his duty as the ruler of a peaceful, sleepy province and his destiny as a trained seeker of wisdom and magic, a riddle-master, Morgan, ventures out into a land where each portion of the land is ruled by a "keeper" who is in communion with the "land-magic" of his or her realm. Morgan must undergo fierce trials as he grows in his power and magic and attempts to meet the destiny imposed upon him by the three stars on his forehead and the magical harp he comes to possess. He is partially aided by his beloved, Raederle (who is the focus of the second volume). She continually seeks him as he withdraws to Erlenstar Mountain to confront the enigmatic High One, the figure who bestowed and controlled the earth-magic that each ruler possesses. Morgan finds only falsehood in the Mountain and discovers that the High One has vanished and his place usurped by a fell sorcerer. He also meets the High One's Harper, Deth, who appears a friend at one moment and an enemy at another. In the final volume, Morgan endures many archetypal tests and purifications, raises the dead, harps the wind, learns the true identity of the Harper and the majesty of his own powers, and assumes the mantel of the High One's heir. A powerful series that is among the best in contemporary fantasy!

FIONA MacLEOD, pseud. See WILLIAM SHARP

712. *The Children of the Pool and Other Stories*. London: Hutchinson, [1936].

    a.   "The Exalted Omega"
    b.   "The Children of the Pool"
    c.   "The Bright Boy"
    d.   "The Tree of Life"
    e.   "Out of the Picture"
    f.   "Change"

713. *The Great God Pan and the Inmost Light*. London: John Lane, 1894. Rpt. as *The Great God Pan*. New York: Roberts Brothers, 1894.

A young woman is possessed by Pan, indulges in many of the god's typical activities, and, as a result, attempts suicide a number of times.

714. *The Three Imposters or the Transmutations*. London: John Lane, 1895.

    a.   "Prologue"
    b.   "Adventure of the Gold Tiberius"
    c.   "The Encounter of the Pavement"
    d.   "Novel of the Dark Valley"
    e.   "Adventure of the Missing Brother"
    f.   "Novel of the Black Seal"
    g.   "Incident of the Private Bar"
    h.   "The Decorative Imagination"
    i.   "Novel of the Iron Mail"
    j.   "The Recluse of Bayswater"
    k.   "Novel of the White Powder"
    l.   "Strange Occurrence in Clerkenwell"
    m.   "History of the Young Man with Spectacles"
    n.   "Adventure of the Deserted Residence"

Bibliography

715. Danielson, Henry. *Arthur Machen: A Bibliography With Notes, Bibliographical and Critical*. London: Henry Danielson, 1923. Rpt. Ann Arbor: Plutarch Press, 1971.

716. Goldstone, Adrian, and Wesley Sweetser. *A Bibliography of Arthur Machen*. Austin: University of Texas, 1965.

JACK MANN, pseud. See E[VELYN] CHARLES VIVIAN

DON MARQUIS

717. *archy and mehitabel*. Garden City, NY: Doubleday,
      Page, 1927.

> The delightful and charming tale of the friend-
> ship and adventures of archy the cockroach (who
> types without capitals) and mehitabel the cat.

JOHN [EDWARD] MASEFIELD

718. *The Box of Delights or When the Wolves Were Running*.
      London: William Heinemann, 1935.

> Sequel to *The Midnight Folk* (see below). Both
> titles are juvenile excursions into fairy land
> and magic that may be of interest.

719. *The Midnight Folk: A Novel*. London: William
      Heinemann, 1927.

Bibliography

720. Handley-Taylor, Geoffrey. *John Masefield, O.M.:
      The Queen's Poet Laureate. A Bibliography and
      Eighty-First Birthday Tribute*. London: Cran-
      brook Tower Press, 1960.

DAVID MASON

721. *The Deep Gods*. New York: Lancer, 1973 [paper].

> The mind and personality of a twentieth-century
> man are transmigrated into the dead body of a
> man who existed long before recorded history.
> This pre-Edenic world of the far distant past
> is teetering on the edge of destruction, and the
> commonality that binds all nature together be-
> fore the Fall is in grave danger. The protagon-
> ist must confront the tragedy and deal with the
> deep gods--whales--as one of their wisest
> fellows has gone mad and threatens all creation.

722. *The Sorcerer's Skull*. New York: Lancer, 1970
      [paper].

> The sorcerer Myrdin Velis bargains successfully
> with Owen of Marrdale, warrior and thief, to
> return a strange wizard's skull to its place of
> origin. After a journey characterized by the
> excellent use of major and minor events (i.e.,
> Owen's dream of an idyllic land), Owen and his

well-delineated companions--Khitai, a "small"
wizard, and Zelsa, a beautiful tavern wench--
defeat armies of vampires and the immortal Vryhol,
when Owen destroys the true soul of Myrdin, who
is revealed as a true lord of evil.

The Kavin Series

723. *Kavin's World*. New York: Lancer, 1969 [paper].

724. *The Return of Kavin*. New York: Lancer, 1972
      [paper].

      A parallel universe, sword and sorcery pair of
      novels concerning the heroic and magical ex-
      ploits of Kavin and his ancestors. Mason's
      creation of Thuramon the magician and the wise
      dragon folk are excellent examples of imagina-
      tive skill.

Bibliography

725. Boardman, John. "In Memoriam: David Mason [1924-
      1974]." *Science Fiction Review*, 4 (1975), 13.

BRANDER MATTHEWS

726. *Tales of Fantasy and Fact*. New York: Harper &
      Brothers, 1896.

      a. "A Primer of Imaginary Geography"
      b. "The Kinetoscope of Time"
      c. "The Dream-Gown of the Japanese Ambassador"
      d. "The Rival Ghosts"
      e. "Sixteen Years Without a Birthday"
      f. "The Twinkling of an Eye"
      g. "A Confidential Postscript"

727. *With My Friends: Tales Told in Partnership*. New
      York: Longmans, Green, 1891.

      a. "The Art and Mystery of Collaboration"
             (essay)
      b. "The Document in the Case" with H.C. Bunner
      c. "Seven Conversations of Dear Jones and
             Baby Van Rensselaer" with H.C. Bunner
      d. "Edged Tools: A Tale in Two Chapters" with
             Walter Herries Pollock
      e. "Mated by Magic: A Story with a Post-
             script" with Walter Herries Pollock
      f. "One Story is Good Till Another is Told"

              with George H. Jessop
    g.   "Three Wishes" with F. Anstey, pseud.
        [Thomas Anstey Guthrie]

Bibliography

728. Howson, Roger. *The Bookshelf of Brander Matthews.*
     New York: Columbia University Press, 1931.

W[ILLIAM] SOMERSET MAUGHAM

729. *The Magician.* London: William Heinemann, 1908.

Bibliography

730. Toole, Stott R.A. *A Bibliography of the Works of*
    W. Somerset Maugham. London: Kaye & Ward, 1973.

ANDRÉ MAUROIS

731. *The Weigher of Souls.* Trans. Hamish Miles. New
    York and London: D. Appleton, 1931.

    A scientist seeks to isolate and capture the
    human soul through a series of experiments
    that end in his own frustration and a tragic
    and partial success.

WILLIAM MAYNE

732. *A Game of Dark.* London: Hamish Hamilton, 1971.

    A psychological fantasy in which a boy, haunted
    by a dream of a destructive dragon, flees his
    own lack of sympathy for his ill father and his
    disinterest in his parents' morality. In his
    medieval dream world, he is trained by a lord
    and finally faces the dreaded white worm
    (dragon). Violating his chivalric training,
    he destroys the worm by reason rather than by
    combat. It is this commitment to reason that
    allows him to leave his dream world and return
    to cope with his actual life.

RICHARD MEADE

733. *Exile's Quest.* New York: Signet, 1970 [paper].

    In this average sword and sorcery novel, a

young lord, Gallt, leads an expedition of
thieves and murderers into unknown lands to
avoid the headsman's axe and rescue a queen,
Thayna. Unfortunately, Thayna is the only
character in the world that is well developed,
and two other elements--the immortal wizard and
a magic talisman--do not live up to their imaginative potential.

734. *The Sword of Morning Star*. New York: Signet,
1969 [paper].

A young boy endures trials to secure a magic
blade and fights "half-wolves" to fulfill his
destiny in this effective sword and sorcery
work that contains interesting subplots of court
and family intrigue.

GEORGE MEREDITH

735. *The Shaving of Shagpat: An Arabian Adventure*. London: Chapman and Hall, 1856. Rev. ed. West-
minster: Archibald Constable, 1898.

Shibli Bagarag, oriental barber and hero, goes
on a quest to achieve the greatest of glories:
to shave the hairy gentleman Shagpat. Aided
by a sorceress and shape changer, Noorna bin
Noorlea, Shibli saves princesses, visits
oriental palaces and underground kingdoms, and
escapes with his wit intact in this highly
descriptive, comic, and ironic example of pseudo-
oriental fantasy.

Bibliography

736. Collie, M. *George Meredith: A Bibliography*. London:
Dawsons, 1974.

737. Forman, Maurice Buxton. *A Bibliography of the
Writings in Prose and Verse of George Meredith*.
Edinburgh: Dunedin Press, 1922. Rpt. New York:
Haskell House, 1971.

738. Forman, Maurice Buxton. *Meredithiana: Being a Supplement to the Bibliography of Meredith*. Edinburgh: n.p. [Dunedin Press?], 1924. Rpt. New
York: Haskell House, 1971.

739. Olmsted, John Charles. *George Meredith: An Annotated Bibliography 1925-1975*. New York: Garland,

1978.

A[BRAHAM] MERRITT
See also A[BRAHAM] MERRITT AND HANNES BOK

740. *Creep, Shadow.* Garden City, NY: Doubleday, Doran,
1934.

An action-laden lost-race fantasy with strong
elements of horror that is similar to many of
Merritt's works in tone and theme. In this
tale of vampiric reincarnation, the action re-
volves around an unusual eternal triangle
composed of the reincarnation of the Druid
white witch Ys; the reincarnation of Ys' lover,
Caranac; and Caranac's true love, Helen.

741. *Dwellers in the Mirage.* New York: Liveright, 1932.

Another lost-race fantasy in which the protagonist struggles with his strange consciousness of
a previous life as the long-dead hero Dwayanu.
Initially enthralled by an evil being from
another dimension who demands human sacrifices,
Leif Langdon/Dwayanu overcomes the possession
and slays the monster.

742. *The Face in the Abyss.* New York: Liveright, 1931.

Deep in the Andes, a group of greedy American
adventurers are transformed into drops of gold
when they attempt to violate the prison of
Nimir, Lord of Evil. The protagonist avoids a
like fate and joins in the successful struggle
to end Nimir's power. Despite Merritt's pseudo-
scientific explanations, events and characters
are simply too fantastic, too alien, to be
accepted as the products of extrapolation or
science fiction.

743. *The Fox Woman [and Other Stories].* New York:
Avon, 1949. Rpt. New York: Arno Press, 1978
[not seen].

a. "The Fox Woman"
b. "The People of the Pit"
c. "Through the Dragon Glass"
d. "The Drone"
e. "The Last Poet and the Robots"
f. "Three Lines of Old French"
g. "The White Road"

        h.   "When Old Gods Wake"
        i.   "The Women of the Wood"

744. *The Fox Woman*. New York: New Collectors' Group, 1946. Bound with Hannes Bok's *The Blue Pagoda*, a completion of the unfinished *The Fox Woman*.

A girl is born, possessed by the fox woman, and raised in the woman's temple after her father has been killed in an attack directed by her uncle. When she is grown, the girl journeys to America where the fox woman again asserts her control and forces the girl to kill her uncle. The girl also dies in an ensuing fire, but the fox woman restores her to life.

745. *The Moon Pool*. New York and London: G.P. Putnam's, 1919.

The search for "The Shining One," a fell monster that steals people, leads a group of explorers into an underground kingdom. There the protagonist falls in love with a high priestess, and their love destroys the Shining One and its power. However, the protagonist is ultimately marooned in the normal surface world and cannot return to his beloved.

746. *Ship of Ishtar*. New York: G.P. Putnam's Sons, 1926.

A tour-de-force by one of the early masters of fantasy. Description, event, setting, and characterization are well-handled as an American adventurer is drawn into a parallel world while staring at what seems to be an intricate and detailed ship model. On board the strange "Flying Dutchman," the Ship of Ishtar, he finds the deck evenly divided into black and white and discovers an eternal battle between the forces of good and evil as they each try to extend their portion of the ship and achieve complete sovereignty. Poorly imitated by Hannes Bok's *The Sorcerer's Ship* (New York: Ballantine, 1969), and originally published in 1924 in *Unknown Worlds*.

747. *Thru the Dragon Glass*. Jamaica, NY: ARRA Printers, 1917.

Bibliography

748. Wentz, Walter J. *A. Merritt: A Bibliography of*

A[BRAHAM] MERRITT continued

> *Fantastic Writings.* Roseville, CA: George A.
> Bibby, 1965 [paper].

A[BRAHAM] MERRITT AND HANNES BOK

749. *The Black Wheel.* New York: New Collectors' Group,
1947.

HOPE MIRRLESS

750. *Lud-in-the-Mist.* London: William Collins Sons,
1926.

> The slow-witted and weak-willed inhabitants of
> Lud-in-the-Mist are nearly destroyed by the
> evil fairies and their narcotic fruit.

J[OHN] A[MES] MITCHELL

751. *That First Affair and Other Sketches.* New York:
Charles Scribner's Sons, 1896.

    a. "That First Affair"
    b. "Mrs. Lofter's Ride"
    c. "Two Portraits"
    d. "The Man Who Vanished"
    e. "A Bachelor's Supper"

Bibliography

752. Burke, W.J., Will D. Howe, Irving Weiss, and Anne
Weiss. *American Authors and Books: 1640 to the
Present.* 3rd rev. ed. New York: Crown, 1972,
p. 434.

RICHARD MONACO

753. *Parsival or a Knight's Tale.* New York: Macmillan,
1977 [paper].

> A retelling of Chrétien de Troyes' 12th century
> French romance about a foolish boy who becomes
> a knight and proceeds to make a shambles out
> of chivalry and the Grail quest.

MICHAEL [JOHN] MOORCOCK

754. *Gloriana, or the Unfulfill'd Queen: Being a Ro-*

mance. London: Allison & Busby, 1978 [the 1978 Avon reprint adds illustrations by Elizabeth Malczynski].

In this audacious imitation of the eighteenth-century picaresque novel, Moorcock paints a highly embroidered portrait of Queen Gloriana, ruler of Albion, an area that contains America and most of Asia. Gloriana struggles to maintain her reign against the connivances of Chancellor Montfallcon. She is in great danger because Montfallcon has unleashed his most dreaded weapon, Captain Arturus Quire: Quire the seducer, Quire the wicked, Quire the cruel. Gloriana is especially vulnerable because she, like her British prototype, indulges every debauchery in pursuit of the orgasm that seems to forever escape her. However, with the future of the empire and its golden age in the balance, Quire is estranged from Montfallcon, and he and Gloriana finally find the union she desires so deeply. Quire is, then, revealed to be of unsuspected royal blood (he is truly Prince Arthur) and the realm is saved through Quire's efforts, and he and Gloriana--the "King of Vice" and the "Queen of Virtue"--are united by law as well as body.

755. *Sojan*. Manchester [England]: Savoy, 1977 [paper].

A collection of Moorcock's early sword and sorcery, which appeared in *Tarzan Adventures*, featuring Sojan, Klan the Spoiler, Dek of Noothar, and Rens Karto of Bersnol, plus four essays by Moorcock explaining the origins of two of his protagonists--Elric of Melniboné and Jerry Cornelius--and a self parody, "The Stone Thing: A Tale of Strange Parts."

a.   "The Stone Thing: A Tale of Strange Parts"
b.   "The Dying Castles: A Vignette"
c.   "Sojan the Swordsman"
d.   "Sojan, Swordsman of Zylor"
e.   "Sojan and the Sea of Demons"
f.   "Sojan and the Plain of Mystery"
g.   "Sojan and the Sons of the Snake-God"
h.   "Sojan and the Devil Hunters of Norj"
i.   "Klan the Spoiler: Urjohl of Civ ... and the Edge of the World"
j.   "Dek of Noothar: The Sword of Life" (with John Wisdom)
k.   "Rens Karto of Bersnol: In Which Sojan

Returns" (with Dick Ellingsworth)
l. "The Secret Life of Elric of Melniboné"
m. "Elric"
n. "New Worlds--Jerry Cornelius"
o. "In Lighter Vein: A Note on the Jerry
    Cornelius Tetralogy"

Dorian Hawkmoon I: The History of the Runestaff
(The Chronicles of Count Brass is a sequel to
this series--see below).

756. *The Jewel in the Skull.* New York: Lancer, 1967
      [paper]. Rev. ed. New York: DAW, 1977 [paper].

757. *Sorcerer's Amulet.* New York: Lancer, 1968 [paper].
      Rpt. as *The Mad God's Amulet.* Frogmore, Eng-
      land: Mayflower, 1969 [paper]. Rev. ed. [using
      British title] New York: DAW, 1977 [paper].

758. *Sword of the Dawn.* New York: Lancer, 1968 [paper].
      Rev. ed. New York: DAW, 1977 [paper].

759. *The Secret of the Runestaff.* New York: Lancer,
      1969 [paper]. Rpt. as *The Runestaff.* Frogmore,
      England: Mayflower, 1969 [paper]. Rev. ed.
      [using British title] New York: DAW, 1977 [paper].

See Dorian Hawkmoon II: The Chronicles of Count
Brass for annotation.

N.B. All four volumes of The History of the
Runestaff have been reissued in slightly revised form by DAW Books. The revisions include
additional material that clarifies Moorcock's
Eternal Hero theme.

Dorian Hawkmoon II: The Chronicles of Count Brass
(sequel to The Runestaff series--see above).

760. *Count Brass.* Frogmore, England: Mayflower, 1973
      [paper].

761. *The Champion of Garathorm.* Frogmore, England:
      Mayflower, 1973 [paper]. Also the third book
      in the Ericose series--see below.

762. *The Quest for Tanelorn.* Frogmore, England: May-
      flower, 1975 [paper]. Also the culminating vol-
      ume for all of Moorcock's sword and sorcery, eter-
      nal champion series.

Moorcock's four sword & sorcery series--featuring
Dorian Hawkmoon (Count Brass and Runestaff), Elric,

Erekosë, and Prince Corum--are all interrelated
within the concepts of alternate planes of existence and the eternal hero, many heroes who are
actually one fighting to preserve the virtues
of Law and the eternal balance and who are also
sent off to struggles in other dimensions.
The champion eternal's foes are the exponents
of Chaos. Needless to say, these interrelationships make for bibliographic nightmares, and
various notes are added here to clarify these
highly mythic and action-oriented series. The
protagonist of the Count Brass series and its
sequel series, The History of the Runestaff,
is Dorian Hawkmoon, or Duke von Köln. His
world is somewhere in a far-future, post-holocaust France. Hawkmoon is trying to protect
the Kamarg, an enclave against the forces of
Chaos (the dread animal-masked people of Granbre-
tan) that is ruled by Count Brass. Hawkmoon is
captured by the Granbretans and has a jewel
implanted in his forehead. If the jewel is
activated, it will destroy his brain. Thus, he
becomes their pawn until Count Brass can devise
a shield that moderates the activation of the
jewel. Much of the series is concerned with
protecting the Kamarg; trying to remove the
jewel; Hawkmoon's love affair with and marriage
to Yisselda, Count Brass's daughter, who is
abducted late in the series; and his pursuit of
an evil sorcerer.

N.B. The final volume in the Count Brass series--
The Quest for Tanelorn--is also the culminating
novel of all four of Moorcock's sword and sor-
cery series. In this volume, all four heroes--
Hawkmoon, Erekose, Elric, and Corum--are brought
together for the mixed blessing of the discovery
of their ultimate goal, the eternal city of
Tanelorn, and for the resolution of the Black
Sword (Elric), the Runestaff, and the Cosmic
Balance.

Elric: Original Series

763. *Elric of Melniboné*. London: Hutchinson, 1972.
Altered edition published as *The Dreaming City*.
New York: Lancer, 1972 [paper].

764. *The Stealer of Souls and Other Stories*. London:
Neville Spearman, 1963.

a. "The Dreaming City"

MICHAEL [JOHN] MOORCOCK continued

      b.   "While the Gods Laugh"
      c.   "The Stealer of Souls"
      d.   "Kings in Darkness"
      e.   "The Flame Bringers"

765. *The Sleeping Sorceress*. London: New English Library, 1971. Rpt. as *The Vanishing Tower*. New York: DAW, 1977. Abr. ed. New York: Lancer, 1972 [paper].

      a.   "The Torment of the Last Lord" [alternate title: "The Sleeping Sorceress"]
      b.   "To Snare the Pale Prince"
      c.   "Three Heroes with a Single Aim"

766. *The Singing Citadel*. Frogmore, UK: Mayflower, 1970 [paper]; New York: Lancer, 1970 [paper].

      a.   "The Singing Citadel"
      b.   "Master of Chaos"
      c.   "To Rescue Tanelorn . . ."
      d.   "The Greater Conqueror"

767. *Elric: The Return to Melniboné*. Brighton-Seattle, WA: Unicorn Books, 1973 [paper] [not seen].

768. *The Jade Man's Eyes*. Brighton-Seattle, WA: Unicorn Books, 1973 [paper]. Later incorporated into *The Sailor on the Seas of Fate* (see below).

769. *Stormbringer*. London: Herbert Jenkins, 1965.

      a.   "The Coming of Chaos"
      b.   "Sad Giant's Shield"
      c.   "Doomed Lord's Passing"

Elric: Revised Series

770. *Elric of Melniboné*. New York: DAW, 1976 [paper].

771. *The Sailor on the Seas of Fate*. New York: DAW, 1976 [paper]; includes revision of *The Jade Man's Eyes* (see above).

772. *The Weird of the White Wolf*. New York: DAW, 1977 [paper].

      a.   "The Dream of Earl Aubec" [original title: "Master of Chaos"]
      b.   "The Dreaming City"
      c.   "While the Gods Laugh"
      d.   "The Singing Citadel"

773. *The Vanishing Tower*. New York: DAW, 1977 [paper].
Rpt. of *The Sleeping Sorceress* (see above).

774. *The Bane of the Black Sword*. New York: DAW, 1977
[paper].

    a. "The Stealer of Souls"
    b. "Kings in Darkness"
    c. "The Flamebringers"
    d. "To Rescue Tanelorn"

775. *Stormbringer*. New York: DAW, 1977 [paper].

    a. "Dead God's Homecoming"
    b. "Black Sword's Brothers"
    c. "Sad Giant's Shield"
    d. "Doomed Lord's Passing"

Moorcock's original Elric series grew without
too much attention to series' coherency, and
the reader should appreciate that the original
Elric books listed above do not necessarily
reflect a reading order based on internal
chronology, nor can they since the original
series does skip about and overlap. Unless the
reader is a very serious Moorcock fan or scholar,
the revised and clarified DAW series is recom-
mended. However, Moorcock's Elric should not
be neglected; he is one of the most unusual
characters in all of fantasy, not just of sword
and sorcery fantasy. Elric, the last in the
line of a race of eldrich sorcerer-kings,
wanders about in a world increasingly dominated
by man, a race he views as short-lived and con-
temptible in their magic and ambitions. An
albino and congenitally weak, Elric must depend
on Stormbringer, his black rune blade, to
drink souls and give him strength. Elric's
powers, adventures, dark melancholy, fatalism,
and tendency to drink the souls of those he
loves best make him both a tragic and an alien
figure, at once admirable and repulsive.

Erekosë Series

776. *The Eternal Champion*. New York: Dell, 1970 [paper].
Rev. ed. New York: Harper & Row, 1978.

777. *Phoenix in Obsidian*. Frogmore, England: Mayflower,
1970 [paper]. Rpt. as *The Silver Warriors*.
New York: Dell, 1973 [paper].

778. *The Champion of Garathorm.* Frogmore, England: Mayflower, 1975 [paper]. Also volume two in Hawkmoon II: The Chronicles of Count Brass (see above).

Erekosë is, in a number of ways, the most enlightening of Moorcock's heroes. Unlike Hawkmoon, Elric, and Corum who are frustrated by their ignorance of their destinies, Erekosë knows that he is to be continually summoned to fight battles for mankind and Law--a task he dreads. Moreover, he is the only one of the heroes who remembers his incarnations as the Eternal Champion. For him, time as a linear series of events has ceased to exist, and he dwells in a limbo of event-oriented summonings. For example, in *The Champion of Garathrom,* he is united with his incarnation of Dorian Hawkmoon to become Ilian, Queen of Garathrom. When a group of foreign invaders are defeated, Hawkmoon returns to his proper frame, but Erekosë is doomed to go back to his shadow existence until he is summoned again. Thus, Erekosë is all of Moorcock's heroes, and he is the unifying factor in *The Quest for Tanelorn* (see Dorian Hawkmoon II: The Chronicles of Count Brass above), which is the final volume in this series, as well as all of Moorcock's Champion Eternal series (Hawkmoon, Elric, and Prince Corum).

Michael Kane Series

779. Bradbury, Edward P[owys], pseud. *Warriors of Mars.* London: Compact Books, 1965 [paper]. Rpt. as *City of the Beast.* New York: Lancer, 1971 [paper].

780. _____. *Blades of Mars.* London: Compact Books, 1965 [paper]. Rpt. as *Lord of the Spiders.* New York: Lancer, 1970 [paper].

781. _____. *Barbarian of Mars.* London: Compact Books, 1965 [paper]. Rpt. as *Masters of the Pit.* New York: Lancer, 1970 [paper].

An unfortunate reworking of Edgar Rice Burroughs' Mars series (see above).

Prince Corum Jhalen Irsei or the Prince of the Scarlet Robe Series

782. *The Knight of Swords.* New York: Berkley, 1971

[paper]. Rpt. in *The Swords Trilogy*. New York: Berkley, 1977 [paper].

783. *Queen of Swords*. New York: Berkley, 1971 [paper]. Rpt. in *The Swords Trilogy*. New York: Berkley, 1977 [paper].

784. *The King of Swords*. New York: Berkley, 1971 [paper]. Rpt. in *The Swords Trilogy*. New York: Berkley, 1977 [paper].

785. *The Bull and the Spear*. London: Allison and Busby, 1973.

786. *The Oak and the Ram*. London: Allison and Busby, 1973.

787. *The Sword and the Stallion*. London: Allison and Busby, 1974.

In a pre-history, British Isles setting, Corum, the last surviving member of a nearly immoral and contemplative race called the Vadhagh, discovers that a more primitive race (the Mabden) have been systematically eliminating the Vadhagh. Swearing vengeance, he must slay the three Chaos lords who are supporting the Mabden and who rule the various planes of existence of his world. It is interesting to note that the Chaos lord, known as the Knight of Swords, is Lord Arioch, Elric's patron (see above). In the course of his defeat of the three Chaos lords, chronicled in the first three volumes of this series, Corum loses his left hand and right eye. These are replaced by a sorcerer with the six-fingered hand of one god and the jewel eye of another; Corum uses these "new senses" in his success against the Chaos lords. It is interesting to note that in *King of Swords*, Moorcock first uses the device of a repeated episode to unify the four eternal champion series. It again tells the tale of the rescue of Jhary-a-Conel (the heroes' varied-form sidekick) that first appeared in the Elric adventure, *The Sleeping Sorceress* (see above).

In the second of the three volumes of this series, which takes place some eighty years later, Corum has retreated into contemplation and has become a god to the Mabden. He answers their summonings and helps them defeat the Fhoi Myore and renew their lands by using the talis-

mans mentioned in the titles. The volumes are
set in about 2000 B.C. and mention both the
Druids and Stonehenge.

Bibliography

788. Allen, Paul C. "Of Swords and Sorcery 5." *Fantasy
Crossroads*, No. 13 (June 1978), 31-40.

789. Callow, A.J. *The Chronicles of Moorcock: A Bibliography*. London: By the Author, 1978 [paper].

790. Moorcock, Michael. "The Eternal Champion Cycle."
In *The Eternal Champion: A Fantastic Romance*.
New York: Harper & Row, 1978, pp. 180-181.

C[ATHERINE] L[UCILE] MOORE

791. *The Best of C.L. Moore*. Ed. Lester del Rey.
Garden City, NY: Nelson Doubleday [Science Fiction Book Club], 1975.

   a.   "Introduction: Forty Years of C.L. Moore"
          (Lester del Rey)
   b.   "Shambleau"**
   c.   "Black Thirst"**
   d.   "The Bright Illusion"
   e.   "Black God's Kiss"*
   f.   "Tryst in Time"
   g.   "Greater than Gods"
   h.   "Fruit of Knowledge"
   i.   "No Woman Born"
   j.   "Daemon"
   k.   "Vintage Season"
   l.   "*Afterward*: Footnote to 'Shambleau'
          . . . and Others"

   *Jirel of Jorey stories (see below); **North-
      west Smith stories.

792. *Jirel of Joiry*. New York: Paperback Library,
1969 [paper].

   This collection would be noteworthy if only for
   the occurrence of one of the few female protagonists in fantasy in general and sword and sorcery fantasy in particular. It is, however,
   more than just that. Jirel's admirable courage
   in the face of horror and helplessness make
   her an exciting and dynamic figure, and Moore's
   description, settings, and dark devices are
   striking and original. "The Black God's Kiss,"

in which Jirel carries a very ironic gesture of affection for an enemy, is a particularly fine example of Moore's ability to endow her character with both human and superhuman characteristics. All of the short stories in this volume originally appeared in *Weird Tales* from 1934 to 1939 and first appeared in book form in *Shambleau and Others* (see below) and *Northwest of Earth* (see below). The one Jirel of Jorey story not reprinted here, "Quest of the Starstone," was written in collaboration with her husband, Henry Kuttner.

    a.   "Jirel Meets Magic"
    b.   "Black God's Kiss"
    c.   "Black God's Shadow"
    d.   "The Dark Land"
    e.   "Hellsgarde"

793. *Northwest of Earth*: New York: Gnome, 1954.

    a.   "Dust of the Gods"**
    b.   "Lost Paradise"**
    c.   "The Dark Land"*
    d.   "Julhi"**
    e.   "Hellsgarde"*
    f.   "The Cold Grey God"**
    g.   "Yvala"**

*Jirel of Jorey tales (see above); **Northwest Smith tales.

794. *Shambleau and Others*. New York: Gnome, 1953.

    a.   "The Black God's Kiss"*
    b.   "The Black God's Shadow"*
    c.   "Jirel Meets Magic"*
    d.   "Shambleau"**
    e.   "Black Thirst"**
    f.   "Scarlet Dream"**
    g.   "The Tree of Life"**

*Jirel of Jorey tales (see above); **Northwest Smith stories (see above).

CHRISTOPHER MORLEY

795. *The Arrow*. Garden City, NY: Doubleday, Page, 1927.

A young man finds an arrow that seems to change

CHRISTOPHER MORLEY continued

in size to a point where it decides. It unites
him with his lady love in a union recalling
the myth of Psyche and Cupid.

Bibliography

796. Sargent, Ralph M. "Dear Chris." *Haverford Review*, 3 (Winter 1944), 22-25.

KENNETH MORRIS

797. *The Book of Three Dragons*. New York and Toronto:
Longmans, Green, 1930. Rpt. New York: Arno
Press, 1978 [not seen].

The sequel to *The Fates of the Princes of Dyfed*
(see below) and, like its predecessor, based
on the branches of the Welsh *Mabinogion* (also
see Evangline Walton Ensley above). Manawyddan
fails in his attempt to bring the head of Bran
the Blessed to London because two protective
talismans are stolen. Manawyddan and his companions bury the head, and Manawyddan begins a
search for the talismans that leads him to the
underworld and pits him against a full comple-
ment of magic and monsters.

798. Morus, Cenydd [Welsh for Kenneth Morris], pseud.
The Fates of the Princes of Dyfed. Point Loma,
CA: Aryan Theosophical Press, 1914 [not seen].
Rpt. North Hollywood, CA: Newcastle Publishing,
1978 [paper].

Based on the first book of *The Mabinogion*.

a.   "The Sovereignty of Annwn"
b.   "The Story of Pwyll and Rhianon, or The
        The Book of the Three Trials"
c.   "The Coming of Rhianon Ren Ferch Hefeydd"
d.   "The Basket of Gwaeddfyd Newynog, and
        Gwaeddfyd Newynog Himself"
e.   "The Coming of Ab Cilcoed, and The Three
        Trials of Pwyll Pen Annwn"
f.   "The Story of Rhianon and Pryderi, or The
        Book of the Three Unusual Arts of
        Pryderi Fab Pwyll"
g.   "The Story of Dienw'r Anffodion"
h.   "The Story of Rhianon and Pryderi"
i.   "The Three Unusual Arts of Teyrnion and
        Gwri Gwallt Euryn and the Freeing of
        the Birds of Rhianon"

        j.   "The Return of Pryderi"

799. *The Secret Mountain, and Other Tales*. London: Faber & Gwyer, 1926.

        a.   "The Secret Mountain"
        b.   "Red-Peach-Blossom Inlet"
        c.   "The Last Adventure of Don Quixote"
        d.   "Slon ap Siencyn"
        e.   "The Rose and the Cup"
        f.   "Daffodil"
        g.   "The King and the Three Ascetics"
        h.   "The Saint and the Forest-Gods"
        i.   "The Divina Commedia of Evan Leyshon"
        j.   "The Apples of Knowledge"

WILLIAM MORRIS

800. *Child Christopher and Goldilind the Fair*. Hammersmith, England: Kelmscott Press, 1895.

801. *Golden Wings and Other Stories*. Van Nuys, CA: Newcastle, 1976 [paper].

A reprinting of Morris' shorter fiction that appeared in *Oxford and Cambridge Magazine*, 1856.

        a.   "Introduction" (Alfred Noyes)
        b.   "Published Works"
        c.   "The Story of the Unknown Church"
        d.   "Lindenborg Pool"
        e.   "A Dream"
        f.   "Gertha's Lovers"
        g.   "Svend and His Brethren"
        h.   "The Hollow Land"
        i.   "Golden Wings"
        j.   "Frank's Sealed Letter"
        k.   "Afterward" (Richard B. Mathews)

802. *The Story of the Glittering Plain Which Has Been Also Called the Land of Living Men or the Acre of the Undying*. Hammersmith, England: Kelmscott Press, 1891.

The protagonist, attempting to rescue his beloved, is lured into the realm of immortality. Ultimately, he must choose between eternal life without her or a normal existence with her.

803. *The Sundering Flood*. Hammersmith, England: Kelmscott Press, printed 1897, issued 1898.

This is Morris' last novel. It is edited from a unique manuscript (probably an early draft) by Morris' daughter, Mary Morris.

Two young children fall in love by looking at and talking to each other across a river called the Sundering Flood. The boy, Osberne, comes to age in a time of tumult, growing to nobility as a friend of the dwarves and wielding the magic sword Boardcleaver, given to him with his heroic manhood by a mysterious pilgrim. After his battles and trials are over, he triumphantly returns to Elfhild, his first love.

804. *The Water of the Wondrous Isles*. Hammersmith, England: Kelmscott Press, 1897.

Birdalone was stolen by a witch when she was a child. When she comes to her maidenhood, she steals an enchanted boat and sails to a number of enchanted islands. On one of them, she meets three maidens who are captives and who lament the loss of their true loves, three knights. Ultimately, after numerous battles and sorcerous dangers, Birdalone reaches the final enchanted destination, and all four women are fulfilled in love.

805. *The Well at the World's End*. Hammersmith: Kelmscott Press, 1896.

Long considered Morris' masterpiece and considered by many one of the greatest fantasy novels ever written. A young boy flees his home and comes to manhood as a ruler and a warrior in a medieval realm. Along the way, he loves two women: one gives him suffering, the other joy. His greatest challenge comes at the end of the book when he must confront the power that can be his if he drinks from a magical well.

806. *The Wood Beyond the World*. Hammersmith, England: Kelmscott Press, 1894.

Morris' first fantasy novel and something of a disappointment for anyone familiar with the interlaced and descriptive artistry of *The Well at the World's End*. *The Wood Beyond the World* is a lost-race novel in a number of ways. A young man sees a lovely girl who immediately disappears. Later, he sails to a strange island and finds the girl enslaved by a witch

in a hidden valley. They fall in love, she
slays the witch, and they become King and Queen
of another land through the fulfillment of a
prophecy.

Bibliography

807. Fredeman, William Evan. "William Morris and His
Circle: A Select Bibliography." *Journal of
the William Morris Society*, 1, No. 4 (1964),
23-33.

808. _____. "William Morris and His Circle: A Select
Bibliography of Publications, 1963-1965."
Journal of the William Morris Society, 2, No.
1 (1966), 13-26.

809. Forman, Harry Buxton. *Books of William Morris
Described With Some Account of His Doings in
Literature and in the Allied Arts*. London: F.
Hollings, 1897. Rpt. New York: Burt Franklin,
1969.

810. [Isaac, J.H.] Scott, Temple, pseud. *A Bibliography
of the Works of William Morris*. London: Bell
& Sons, 1897. Rpt. Ann Arbor, MI: Gryphon
[distributed by Gale Research], 1971.

CENYDD MORUS, pseud. See KENNETH MORRIS

MEREDITH MOTSON
See ODD BJERKE AND MEREDITH MOTSON

TALBOT MUNDY

The Jimgrim Series

811. *The Nine Unknown*. Indianapolis: Bobbs-Merrill,
1924.

812. *The Devil's Guard*. Indianapolis: Bobbs-Merrill,
1926. British edition: *Ramsden*. London:
Hutchinson, 1926 [not seen].

813. *Jimgrim*. New York, Century, 1931. Rpt. in *All
Four Winds: Four Novels of India*. London:
Hutchison, 1934, with *King--of the Khyber
Rifles* (1916), *Om: the Secret of Arbor Valley*

(1924), and *Black Light* (1930).

James Schuyler Grim ("Jimgrim"), the intrepid British adventurer and prototype of such figures as Doc Savage, joins forces with a group of multi-talented comrades--Jeff Ramsden, Chullunder, Major Robert Crosby, Jeremy Ross, and Narayan Singh--to battle the secret forces of the occult in India, the Gobi, and Egypt. With unrelenting stalwartness, they always manage to thwart these mystical and ancient plots to dominate the world. There are many more books by Mundy that chronicle the adventures of these characters, all listed in Bradford M. Day's bibliography (see below) for the interested reader and all filled with excellent examples of oriental magic, mysticism, and machination.

Bibliography

814. Day, Bradford M. *Talbot Mundy Biblio: Materials Toward a Bibliography of the Works of Talbot Mundy.* New York: Science-Fiction & Fantasy Publications, 1955 [paper]. Rev. ed. in *Bibliography of Adventure: Mundy, Burroughs, Rohmer, Haggard.* Denver, NY: Science Fiction & Fantasy Publications, 1964 [paper]. Rpt. New York: Arno, 1978.

H[AROLD] WARNER MUNN

815. *King of the World's Edge.* New York: Ace, 1966 [paper].

816. *The Ship From Atlantis.* New York: Ace, 1967 [paper]. Bound dos-a-dos with Emil Petaja's *The Stolen Sun.*

817. *Merlin's Ring.* New York: Ballantine, 1974 [paper].

The *Ship from Atlantis* is the sequel to *King of the World's Edge* and *Merlin's Ring* utilizes the same characters without sustaining the first two novels' plot. In *King of the World's Edge,* Myrdhinn and a few Britains escape the fall of the Round Table, journey to the New World (North America), and establish a settlement in opposition to the Toltecs and Mayans. In *The Ship From Atlantis,* Myrdhinn's (Merlin's) godson sails off in an Odyssey-like adventure and discovers a ship from destroyed Atlantis.

On the ship is one of the more unusual female protagonists in fantasy, Corenice, a sorceress made of metal. Both *King of the World's Edge* and *The Ship From Atlantis* are reprinted in an omnibus volume, *Merlin's Godson* (New York: Ballantine, 1976 [paper]), and it should be noted that *King of the World's Edge* made its first appearance in magazine form in 1939, some twenty-eight years before its sequel. *Merlin's Ring* is a vast epic fantasy that spans the age of Atlantis to the sixteenth century. Merlin's godson, Gwalachmai, uses his uncle's ring to endure through time and continually be reunited with his beloved, Corenice.

JOHN MYERS MYERS

818. *Silverlock*. New York: Dutton, 1949.

A fantastic jaunt through a realm called The Commonwealth. The protagonist, a transported Earthling, accompanied by his multi-named guide (Taliesin), meets a homosexual Beowulf, Circe, the Green Knight, King Arthur, the Houynyhms, and Satan, among others, as he journeys through a series of experiences and realms that seem to be drawn from all that is wondrous in myth, legend and literature.

ROBERT NATHAN

819. *So Love Returns*. New York: Alfred A. Knopf, 1958.

EDITH NESBIT, pseud. See EDITH NESBIT BRAND

HENRY WOODD NEVINSON

820. *Films of Time: Twelve Fantasies*. London: George Routledge & Sons, 1939.

a.   "The Divine Rites of Kings"
b.   "'Fame Double-Mouthed'"
c.   "His Own Obituary"
d.   "Great is Diana!"
e.   "On the Blue Danube"
f.   "How It Strikes a Contemporary"
g.   "Old Caspar"
h.   "Each is I"

      i.   "A Changeful Night"
      j.   "Cry of the Soul"
      k.   "Next Time!"
      l.   "Judgment's Dilemma"

HENRY NEWBOLT

821. *Aladore*. Edinburgh and London: William Blackwood and Sons, 1914. Rpt. Van Nuys, CA: Newcastle, 1975 [paper].

In a medieval realm, Sir Ywain meets the lovely sorceress, Aithne, in the city of Paladore. She has been granted the opportunity to visit Aladore, the magically created and enchanted counterpart of Paladore. The two find peace and love in Aladore, but they are recalled to the mundane city to defend it from invaders. They are seemingly slain, but late arrivals to the battle's aftermath find the two lovers apparently sleeping as bronze statues in the city's chapel.

Bibliography

822. "Bibliographies of Modern Authors: Sir Henry John Newbolt." *London Mercury*, 2, No. 1 (May 1920), 114-115.

"LARRY" [LAURENCE VAN COTT] NIVEN

823. *The Magic Goes Away*. New York: Ace, 1978 [paper].

In this brief, albeit heavily illustrated (by Esteban Maroto), novella, two wizards--Clubfoot and Warlock--form a company made up of the talking skull of a vanquished wizard; a voluptuous sorceress; and the last survivor of the Greek destruction of Atlantis. They go in search of the last living god to attempt to restore mana, the source of magical energy, to the world. Thwarted by the nature of the god they discover, their futures and fortunes make this a fantasy of poignant characterization, tragic in its final resolution. The Maroto illustrations are superb and well coordinated with the text.

JOHN NORMAN, pseud. See JOHN F. LANGE, JR.

ANDRE NORTON (born: ALICE MARY NORTON)

824.   *Here Abide Monsters*. New York: Atheneum, 1973.

An interesting mixture of fantasy and science
fiction that utilizes the phenomena of the
Bermuda Triangle and Charles Fort's collections
of unexplained events. Two young people pass
through a gate between worlds and join a group
of World War II British and other peoples from
various times and places. The world is ruled
by a seemingly magic people who offer the earthlings special powers. Much of the action surrounds a battle between the inhabitants and the
saucer people and the internal struggle within
the earthlings as to whether or not they will
accept the powers the inhabitants offer.

825.   *Huon of the Horn, Being a Tale of That Duke of
Bordeaux Who Came to Sorrow at the Hand of
Charlemagne and Yet Won the Favor of Oberon,
the Elf King, to His Lasting Fame and Great
Glory*. New York: Harcourt, Brace, 1949.

A novelization of the Carlovingian legend of
the youthful Duke of Bordeaux: his quests in
Saracen realms and other fell places, his
gaining of a fair wife, and the noble position
he gained in the kingdom of Faerie.

826.   *The Many Worlds of Andre Norton*. Ed. Roger Elwood.
Radnor, PA: Chilton, 1974. Rpt. as *The Book of
Andre Norton*. New York: DAW, 1975 [paper].

a.   "All Cats Are Grey"
b.   "The Gifts of Asti"
c.   "Long Live Lord Kor!"
d.   "The Long Night of Waiting"
e.   "London Bridge"
f.   "Mousetrap"
g.   "On Writing Fantasy" (essay)
h.   "Andre Norton: Loss of Faith" (essay by
        Rick Brooks)
i.   "Norton Bibliography" (in the DAW reprint,
        this has been revised by Helen-Jo
        Jakusz Hewitt)

827.   *Moon of Three Rings*. New York: Viking, 1966.

An interesting interplanetary fantasy of shape
changing and moon magic in which a young sorceress aids a young earthling by sharing her
ability to communicate with animals and to
place human souls in animal bodies. As with

many of Miss Norton's books, her allusions to a
mysterious and wondrous past add a continual
bell-like echo to her work that lends depth and
numinousity to the action. Sequel: *Exiles of
the Stars*. New York: Viking, 1971.

828. *Quag Keep*. New York: Atheneum, 1978.

A war-game enthusiast is transported into his
own game and becomes Milo Jagon, a mercenary
whose sword is sworn to Law in its struggle with
Chaos. He meets a number of other ensorcered
gamers who must serve the unknown master player's moves: a lizard-man, a bard, a cleric, a
warrior maid, an elf, and a were-boar. A native
wizard, Hystaspes, unites the group, despite
their distrust of each other, in an attempt to
destroy the master player's control. When they
do develop a spirit of friendship, they break
the master player's control, and although they
are unable to leave Greyhawk, they decide to
maintain their friendship.

829. *Wraiths of Time*. New York: Atheneum, 1976.

Tallahassee, a young Black archaeologist, is
thrown into an alternate world by a psychic
blast from an ancient ankh. She recovers next
to the dead body of her double in a realm
where the Egyptian empire and the matriarchal
empire of Meroë are united into a vast African
empire. Tallahassee must assume the burden of
her dead double, Princess Ashake, and enter
into a psychic battle against the evil Khasti,
who is trying to destroy the empire.

The Witch World Series: Simon Tregarth and Family

830. *Witch World*. New York: Ace, 1963 [paper]. Rpt.
Boston: Gregg, 1977.

831. *Web of the Witch World*. New York: Ace, 1964
[paper]. Rpt. Boston: Gregg, 1977.

832. *Three Against the Witch World: [Beyond the Mind
Barrier]*. New York: Ace, 1965 [paper]. Rpt.
Boston: Gregg, 1977.

833. *Warlock of the Witch World*. New York: Ace, 1967
[paper]. Rpt. Boston: Gregg, 1977.

834. *Sorceress of the Witch World*. New York: Ace,

ANDRE NORTON continued

1968 [paper]. Rpt. Boston: Gregg, 1977.

The Witch World Series: Wereriders

835. *The Crystal Gryphon*. New York: Atheneum, 1972.

836. *The Year of the Unicorn*. New York: Ace, 1965
[paper]. Rpt. Boston: Gregg, 1977.

837. *The Jargoon Pard*. New York: Atheneum, 1974.

The Witch World Series: Miscellaneous

838. *Spell of the Witch World*. New York: DAW, 1972
[paper]. Rpt. Boston: Gregg, 1977.

    a. "Dragon Scale Silver"
    b. "Dream Smith"
    c. "Amber Out of Quayth"

839. *Trey of Swords*. New York: Grosset & Dunlap, 1977.

    a. "Sword of Lost Battles"
    b. "Sword of Ice"
    c. "Sword of Shadow"

840. *Zarsthor's Bane*. New York: Ace, 1978 [paper].

Andre Norton's Witch World series is one of the
most celebrated in contemporary fantasy. Set
in a matriarchal world governed by a cult of
witches, it explores the human elements of fear,
self-concept, ambition, greed, and power.
While all of the tales are set in this realm,
the series is subdivided into three categories.
The major one, comprised of five novels, focuses on the transported Earthling Simon Tregarth
and his family. Saved by the Siege Perilous,
a magical transporter, from certain death on
Earth, he marries one of the normally virginal
witches, and they discover to their delight
that her powers unexpectedly remain intact.
Battling resurrected adepts from the past of
Witch World, struggling against the dreaded
scientific Kolder, and daring the threat of the
witches themselves, they and their two sons and
daughter defend themselves and their world and,
at the same time, unravel many of its long-
buried mysteries. The Wererider or shape-
changer subdivision is more romance or love
oriented than the main Tregarth division, and
it is principally concerned with the discovery

of self and the tolerance of uniqueness. The two miscellaneous short story collections and one novel deal with isolated activities outside the concerns of the other two divisions. Throughout the series, the wide and varied character of Norton's well conceived world is continually demonstrated. Well plotted and humanly characterized, all the works have an excellent spirit of adventure and romance, magic and science, and humanity and necessity.

Bibliography

841. Schlobin, Roger C. *Andre Norton: A Bibliography*. Boston: G.K. Hall, forthcoming 1979.

ALFRED NOYES

842. *The Devil Takes a Holiday*. London: John Murray, 1955.

The devil, as a Mr. Balliol, an international financer, goes to Santa Barbara for a vacation and finds that man has become so evil that, as devil, he may be out of a job.

Bibliography

843. Tobin, James Edward. "Alfred Noyes: A Corrected Bibliography." *Catholic Library World*, 15 (1945), 181-184.

CHARLES NUETZEL

844. *Swordmen of Vistar*. Reseda, CA: Powell, 1969 [paper].

A below average sword and sorcery novel concerning the love between a princess and a simple warrior. Their trials are undistinguished with the possible exception of their encounter with the Black Wizard and his comely daughter.

BJORN NYBERG. See ROBERT E[RVIN] HOWARD: Conan Series

FRITZ-JAMES O'BRIEN

845. *The Diamond Lens with Other Stories*. Ed. William

Winter. New York: Charles Scribner's Sons, 1885 [paper].

a. "The Diamond Lens"
b. "The Wondersmith"
c. "Tommatoo"
d. "Mother of Pearl"
e. "The Bohemian"
f. "The Lost Room"
g. "The Pot of Tulips"
h. "The Golden Ingot"
i. "My Wife's Tempter"
j. "What Was It?"
k. "Dake Humphrey's Dinner"
l. "Milly Dove"
m. "The Dragon Fang"

846. *The Poems and Stories of Fitz-James O'Brien.* Ed. William Winter. Boston: James R. Osgood, 1881.

Contains the same short stories as reprinted in *The Diamond Lens with Other Stories* (see above) plus forty-three poems and autobiographical recollections.

WILLIAM DOUGLAS O'CONNOR

847. *Three Tales: The Ghost, The Brazen Android, The Carpenter.* Boston and New York: Houghton, Mifflin, 1892.

LIAM O'FLAHERTY

848. *The Ecstasy of Angus.* London: Joiner and Steele, 1931. Rpt. Dublin: Wolfhound Press, 1978.

Drawing on ancient Celtic myth and Druidic lore, this is an unusual and highly imagistic retelling of the creation myth, so unusual that it was called heretic when it was first published in a limited edition in 1931. Angus, the god of love and creation, has overfilled the world with fecundity, and after a conflict with the god of the sea over domains, he is seduced by the wily Fand, an irresistible earth fairy. Although Angus has been warned that he himself must never indulge in the act of pro-creation, he cannot resist Fand. The child Genius is born of their coupling, and Angus and all the gods immediately grow old and die

LIAM O'FLAHERTY continued

　　　　as good and evil knowledge enter the ..

　　　Bibliography

849.　[Armstrong, Terence Ian Fytton]. Gawsworth, John,
　　　　pseud. *Ten Contemporaries.* 2nd Series. Lon-
　　　　don: Joiner and Steele, 1933.

ANDREW J. OFFUTT

850.　*Ardor on Aros.* New York: Dell, 1973 [paper].

　　　　An erotic spoof of Burroughs' Mars series (see
　　　　above) in which a student is transported to a
　　　　primitive, low-gravity realm and must use his
　　　　unusual abilities and cunning to defeat various
　　　　wizards, strange beings, and odd plants. Much
　　　　of the cause of his troubles and his amorous
　　　　difficulties arises from violating tradition
　　　　when he saves a young princess from rape and
　　　　then unknowingly shames her by failing to
　　　　avail himself of her generous charms.

851.　*The Black Sorcerer in the Black Castle.* Aberdeen,
　　　　MD: Hall Publications, 1976 [paper].

　　　　A sword and sorcery parody with particular
　　　　emphasis on the works of Robert E. Howard. It
　　　　originally appeared in *If,* December 1966, as
　　　　"The Forgotten Gods of Earth."

852.　*Chieftain of Andor.* New York: Dell, 1976 [paper].

　　　　A sword and sorcery novel with a larger-than-
　　　　usual dose of sexuality. The hero is a con-
　　　　temporary man whose mind is transported into
　　　　the body of an inhabitant of a barbarian planet.

853.　*Messenger of Zhuvastou.* New York: Berkley, 1973
　　　　[paper].

　　　　A light-hearted, rollicking, and carnal sword
　　　　and sorcery fantasy which is very reminiscent
　　　　of Stashoff's Gramarye series (see below). A
　　　　young wastrel searches for his brother's slayer,
　　　　a young woman of cunning and evil, on a world
　　　　where modern technology is prohibited. During
　　　　his quest, he is, of course, involved in all
　　　　the mechanisms of the sword and sorcery tale.
　　　　The references to contemporary science-fiction
　　　　writers should not be overlooked, especially

the one to Robert A. Heinlein on page 144.

ANDREW J. OFFUTT AND RICHARD K. LYON

854. *Demon in the Mirror*. New York: Pocket Books, 1978 [paper].

The daughter of a pirate captain consorts with royalty and wizards to reassemble the body of a necromancer, a task she has undertaken to save her brother. To fully succeed, she must finally confront a creature that is only half-human and that survives by drinking souls.

CLAUDE HOUGHTON OLDFIELD

855. Houghton, Claude, pseud. *Three Fantastic Tales*. London: Frederick C. Joiner, 1934.

a. "The Man Who Hated Everybody"
b. "The Madness of Christopher Curlew"
c. "The Strange Case of Mr. Anatole Pickering"

856. _____. *The Fantastic Adventure*. Mobile, AL: Nobody, 1881.

JOHN OLDREY

857. *The Devil's Henchman*. London: Methuen, 1926.

A lost-race fantasy with strong elements of the occult and some of super science, this is the history of the final psychomachia between the earthly representatives of the evil god Set and those of the virtuous goddess Isis. Many contemporary evils are attributed to Set, including Karl Marx.

FRANK OWEN

858. *The Porcelain Magician: A Collection of Oriental Fantasies*. New York: Gnome Press, 1948.

a. "The Fan"
b. "The Inverted House"
c. "The Latern Maker"
d. "The Porcelain Magician"
e. "The Purple Sea"
f. "The Old Man Who Swept the Sky"

g. "Doctor Shen Fu"
h. "Pale Pink Porcelain"
i. "The Rice Merchant"
j. "The Blue City"
k. "The Fountain"
l. "Monk's Blood"
m. "The Golden Hour of Kwah Fan"
n. "The Wind That Tramps the World"

NORVELL W. PAGE

859. *Flame Winds.* New York: Berkley, 1969 [paper].

This novel and its sequel, *Sons of the Bear-God* (see below), were originally published in 1939 in *Unknown.* They focus on the exploits of the swashbuckling figure of Prestor John and his conflicts with men and wizards. *Flame Winds* has a pseudo-historical introduction that discusses the first-century myths of Prestor John and the possibilities of his actual existence.

860. *Sons of the Bear-God.* New York: Berkley, 1969 [paper].

Bibliography

861. Allen, Paul C. "Of Swords & Sorcery No. 3." *Fantasy Crossroads,* No. 10-11 [March 1977), 42-46.

VIOLET PAGET

862. Lee, Vernon, pseud. *Pope Jacynth to Which Are Added Ariadne in Mantua and other Romance Inventions.* Collection of British Authors, Vol. 3866. Leipzig: Bernhard Tauchnitz, 1906 [paper]. A reprint edition.

a. "Pope Jacynth"
b. "Prince Alberic and the Snake Lady"
c. "A Wedding Chest"
d. "The Lady and Death"
e. "St. Eudæmon and His Orange Tree"
f. "The Featureless Wisdom"
g. "Ariadne in Mantua"

863. _____. *The Snake Lady and Other Stories.* Ed. Horace Gregory. New York: Grove Press, 1954 [paper].

This is a reprint edition. Most of Paget's

works were written and first published in the
late-nineteenth century.

a. "Prince Alberic and The Snake Lady"
b. "A Wedding Chest"
c. "Amour Dure"
d. "Dionea"
e. "A Wicked Voice"
f. "The Legend of Madame Krasinska"
g. "A Seeker of Pagan Perfection"
h. "The Virgin of the Seven Daggers"

ALEXEI AND CORY PANSHIN

864. *Earth Magic.* New York: Ace Books, 1978 [paper].

Originally published in *Fantastic Stories*, 1973,
as "Son of Black Morca," this is a slow-moving
heroic fantasy that focuses on the brutally
orphaned son of the barbaric chieftain, Black
Morca. With the bumbling wizard Oliver, Morca's
son, Haldene, seeks to avenge his father's death,
but is possessed by the goddess Libera and
becomes her agent and consort.

[LUCY PEACOCK]

865. Anonymous. *The Adventures of the Six Princesses
of Babylon, in their Travels to the Temple of
Virtue: An Allegory.* London: Printed for the
Author by T. Bensley, 1785.

Bibliography

866. Watson, George, ed. *The New Cambridge Bibliography of English Literature.* Cambridge:
Cambridge University Press, 1971, II (1660-
1800), 1007, 1010, 1025.

MERVYN [LAURENCE] PEAKE

The Gormenghast Trilogy

867. *Titus Groan.* London: Eyre and Spottiswoode, 1946.

868. *Gormenghast.* London: Eyre and Spottiswoode, 1950.

869. *Titus Alone.* London: Eyre and Spottiswoode, 1959.

Peake's Gormenghast Trilogy, long one of the more

curious fantasies, centers on the labyrinth of
Castle Gormenghast, its inhabitants, and its
77th Lord, Titus. Darkly Gothic, fatalistic,
and ritualistic, it chronicles Titus's youth,
rebellion, adventures and rite of passage as
he discovers that, no matter how far he travels,
he cannot escape his birthplace and domain.
The 1968 Eyre and Spottiswoode edition of *Titus
Groan* has a brief introduction by Anthony
Burgess.

Bibliography

870. Batchelor, John. *Mervyn Peake: A Bibliographical
and Critical Exploration.* London: Gerald Duckworth, 1974.

EDWARD PEARSON

871. *Chamiel.* New York: Pocket Books, 1974 [paper].

A retelling of Lucifer's rebellion and of the
great battle between his armies and the forces
of Heaven.

MARIO [ANDREW] PEI

872. *Swords of Anjou.* New York: J. Day, [1953].

A retelling of the *Chanson de Roland* by a well-
known linguistics scholar. Two sons of Geoffrey
of Anjou, followers of Roland, accompany Ganelon
during his treacherous parley with the Saracens.
They both fall in love with foreign women, one
a Saracen, the other a Visigoth. Thrown into
prison because of their involvement with the
Saracen woman, they are reported dead. However,
they escape and one of the women goes to
Charlemagne to warn him of Ganelon's treachery.
Unfortunately, Charlemagne believes Ganelon's
tale that the two paladins are dead and judges
the woman insane. Pei's objective in this tale
was to add love to the otherwise militaristic
Chanson de Roland.

EMIL PETAJA

The Kalevala Series

873. *Saga of Lost Earths.* New York: Ace, 1966 [paper].

874. *The Star Mill*. New York: Ace, 1966 [paper].

875. *The Stolen Sun*. New York: Ace, 1967 [paper].
Bound dos-a-dos with H. Warner Munn's *The Ship
From Atlantis*.

876. *Tramontane*. New York: Ace, 1967 [paper]. Bound
dos-a-dos with Michael Moorcock's *The Wreaks
of Time*.

877. *The Time Twister*. New York: Dell, 1968 [paper].

Using genetic memory, the Jungian collective
unconscious, and the Finnish legends of the
Kalevala, Petaja creates an interesting combination of science fiction and fantasy as the
characters take on the identities of the
Kalevala's main figures--Lemminkainen, Ilmarinen,
Wainomoinen, Kullervo, Ukko, Louhi, and Hiisi--
and are involved in psychomachias that span
ages, societies, and galaxies.

ALEXANDER M[OORE] PHILLIPS

878. *The Mislaid Charm*. Philadelphia: Prime Press,
1947.

A "Walter Mitty" type, Henry A. Pickett, becomes
the unknowing bearer of the charm that belongs
to a group of opinionated gnomes from Northern
Pennsylvania. While the gnomes search, the
charm develops a personality of its own, albeit
a half-witted one, and begins to test its
powers with Henry the victim of its humorous
hedonism and whim. In the process, he becomes
totally drunk and is trapped in a bar with an
African motif when the sentient charm brings
all the decorations to life. Fortunately, he
is saved by a beautiful, statuesque woman who
the gnomes "curse" him to marry when they recover the charm.

EDEN PHILLPOTTS

879. *Alcyone (A Fairy Story)*. London: Ernest Benn,
1930.

880. *The Apes*. London: Faber and Faber, [1929].

881. *Arachne*. London: Faber and Gwyer, 1927.

882. *Circe's Island and The Girl & the Faun*. London: Grant Richards, 1925 [actually issued in 1926].

883. *Evander*. London: Grant Richards, 1919.

884. *The Flint Hart: A Fairy Story*. London: Smith, Elder, 1910.

885. *The Girl and the Faun*. London: Cecil Palmer and Hayward, 1916.

886. *The Lavender Dragon*. London: Grant Richards, 1923.

    A dragon flies about the countryside rescuing the downtrodden from their wretched lives. He brings them to a utopian community he has created and benevolently rules. When he dies after a battle with a wicked dragon who has threatened his kingdom, he is deeply mourned by his "subjects" who he has taught to be self-sufficient.

887. *The Miniature*. London: Watts, 1926.

888. *Pan and the Twins*. London: Grant Richards, 1922.

889. *The Transit of the Red Dragon and Other Tales*. Bristol: J.W. Arrowsmith and London: Simpkin, Marshall, Hamilton, Kent, 1903.

    a. "The Heart of the Scorpion"
    b. "The Transit of the Red Dragon"
    c. "The Mystery of the Toadstone"

890. *The Treasures of Typhon*. London: Grant Richards, 1924.

    Bibliography

891. Hinton, Percival. *Eden Phillpotts: A Bibliography of First Editions*. Birmingham: Greville Worthington, 1931.

    EDWARD JOHN MORETON DRAX PLUNKETT,
    LORD DUNSANY

892. Lord Dunsany. *The Blessing of Pan*. London and

New York: G.P. Putnam's Sons, 1927.

The magic of Pan draws upon and gives magic to a country village until even the pastor is drawn to a pagan site and performs as a Druid priest.

893. _____. *The Book of Wonder: A Chronicle of Little Adventures at the Edge of the World*. London: William Heinemann, 1912.

    a. "The Bride of the Man-Horse"
    b. "The Distressing Tale of Thangobrind the Jeweller, And of the Doom that Befell Him"
    c. "The House of the Sphinx"
    d. "The Probable Adventure of the Three Literary Men"
    e. "The Injudicious Prayers of Pombo the Idolator"
    f. "The Loot of Bombasharna"
    g. "Miss Cubbidge and the Dragon of Romance"
    h. "The Quest of the Queen's Tears"
    i. "The Hoard of the Gibbelins"
    j. "How Nuth Would Have Practised His Art Upon the Gnoles"
    k. "How One Came, as was Foretold, to the City of Never"
    l. "The Coronation of Mr. Thomas Shap"
    m. "Chu-bu and Sheemish"
    n. "The Wonderful Window"

894. _____. *The Charwoman's Shadow*. London and New York: G.P. Putnam's Sons, 1926.

A young sorcerer frees a charwoman's shadow, which has been magically taken from her, and restores her opportunity to lead a fruitful life. This is an excellent transformation of a mundane idea into a glowing fantasy that occurs in the same setting as *The Chronicles of Don Rodriguez* (see below).

895. _____. *The Chronicles of Don Rodriguez*. London and New York: G.P. Putnam's Sons, 1922. Later American title: *Don Rodriguez: Chronicles of Shadow Valley*.

A picaresque tale set in a fictional Spanish Golden Age. Its principal characters are an innocent, energetic, and amorous adventurer; his servant; and a professor of magic.

896. _____. *The Curse of the Wise Woman*. London:
      William Heinemann, 1933.

      Set in the Irish countryside, this is the tale
      of a young gentleman and the mystic effect the
      love and fear of the Irish bog has on him, his
      servants, grooms, and neighbors. Among other
      things, it leads them all to an animosity to-
      ward strangers and outsiders.

897. _____. *A Dreamer's Tales*. London: George Allen
      and Sons, 1910.

      a.   "Poltarnees, Beholder of Ocean"
      b.   "Blagdaross"
      c.   "The Madness of Andelsprutz"
      d.   "Where the Tides Ebb and Flow"
      e.   "Bethmoora"
      f.   "Idle Days on the Yann"
      g.   "The Sword and the Idol"
      h.   "The Idle City"
      i.   "The Hashish Man"
      j.   "Poor Old Bill"
      k.   "The Beggars"
      l.   "Carcassonne"
      m.   "In Zaccarath"
      n.   "The Field"
      o.   "The Day of the Poll"
      p.   "The Unhappy Body"

898. _____. *Fifty-One Tales*. London: Elkin Mathews,
      1915. Rpt. as *Food of Death: Fifty-One Tales*.
      Hollywood, CA: Newcastle, 1974 [paper].

      a.   "The Assignation"
      b.   "Charon"
      c.   "The Death of Pan"
      d.   "The Sphinx at Gizeh"
      e.   "The Hen"
      f.   "Wind and Fog"
      g.   "The Raft-Builders"
      h.   "The Workman"
      i.   "The Guest"
      j.   "Death and Odysseus"
      k.   "Death and the Orange"
      l.   "The Prayer of the Flowers"
      m.   "Time and the Tradesman"
      n.   "The Little City"
      o.   "The Unpasturable Fields"
      p.   "The Worm and the Angel"
      q.   "The Songless Country"
      r.   "The Latest Thing"

s.   "The Demagogue and the Demi-Monde"
t.   "The Giant Poppy"
u.   "Roses"
v.   "The Man with the Golden Ear-rings"
w.   "The Dream of King Karna-Vootra"
x.   "The Storm"
y.   "A Mistaken Identity"
z.   "The True History of the Hare and the
         Tortoise"
aa.   "Alone the Immortals"
bb.   "A Moral Little Tale"
cc.   "The Return of Song"
dd.   "Spring in Town"
ee.   "How the Enemy Came to Thlunrana"
ff.   "A Losing Game"
gg.   "Taking Up Piccadilly"
hh.   "After the Fire"
ii.   "The City"
jj.   "The Food of Death"
kk.   "The Lonely Isle"
ll.   "The Sphinx in Thebes (Massachusetts)"
mm.   "The Reward"
nn.   "The Trouble in Leafy Green Street"
oo.   "Furrow-Maker"
pp.   "Lobster Salad"
qq.   "The Return of the Exiles"
rr.   "Nature and Time"
ss.   "The Song of the Blackbird"
tt.   "The Messengers"
uu.   "The Three Tall Sons"
vv.   "Compromise"
ww.   "What We Have Come To"
xx.   "The Tomb of Pan"
yy.   "The Poet Speaks with Earth"

"The Poet Speaks with Earth" is omitted from
the Newcastle reprint.

899.   _____. *The Fourth Book of Jorkens*. London:
       Jarrolds, [1947?] [not seen]. Sauk City, WI:
       Arkham House, 1948.

a.   "Making Fine Weather"
b.   "Mgamu"
c.   "The Haunting of Halahanstown"
d.   "The Pale-Green Image"
e.   "Jorkens Leaves Prison"
f.   "The Warning"
g.   "The Sacred City of Krakovlitz"
h.   "Jorkens Practises Medicine and Magic"
i.   "Jarton's Disease"
j.   "On the Other Side of the Sun"

k. "The Rebuff"
l. "Jorkens' Ride"
m. "The Secret of the Sphinx"
n. "The Khamseen"
o. "The Expulsion"
p. "The Welcome"
q. "By Command of Pharaoh"
r. "A Cricket Problem"
s. "A Life's Work"
t. "The Ingratiating Smile"
u. "The Last Bull"
v. "The Strange Drug of Dr. Caber"
w. "A Deal with the Devil"
x. "Strategy at the Billards Club"
y. "Jorkens in Witch Wood"
z. "Lost"
aa. "The English Magnifico"
bb. "The Cleverness of Dr. Caber"
cc. "Fairy Gold"
dd. "A Royal Dinner"
ee. "A Fight with Knives"
ff. "Out West"
gg. "In A Dim Room"

900. _____. *The Gods of Pegāna*. London: Elkin Mathews, 1905 [not seen]. Rpt. London: Pegana Press, 1911.

a. "The Gods of Pegāna"
b. "Of the Making of the Worlds"
c. "Of the Game of the Gods"
d. "The Chaunt of the Gods"
e. "The Sayings of Kib"
f. "Concerning Sish (The Destroyer of Hours)"
g. "The Sayings of Slid (Whose Soul is by the Sea)"
h. "The Deeds of Mung (Lord of All Deaths Between Pegana and the Rim)"
i. "The Chaunt of the Priests"
j. "The Sayings of Limpang-Tung (The God of Mirth and of Melodious Minstrels)"
k. "Of Yoharneth-Lahai (The God of Little Dreams and Fancies)"
l. "Of Roon, the God of Going and the Thousand Home Gods"
m. "The Revolt of the Home Gods of Dorozhand (Whose Eyes Regard the End)"
n. "The Eye in the Waste"
o. "Of the Thing that Is Neither God nor Beast"
p. "Yonath the Prophet"
q. "Yug the Prophet"

    r.   "Alhireth-Hotep the Prophet of the Calamity
         that Befell Yūn-Ilāra by the Sea, and
         of the Building of the Tower of the
         Ending of Days"
    s.   "Of How the Gods Whelmed Sidith"
    t.   "Of How Imbaun Became High Prophet in
         Aradec of All the Gods Save One"
    u.   "Of How Imbaun Met Zodrak Pegāna"
    v.   "The Sayings of Imbaun"
    w.   "Of How Imbaun Spake of Death to the King"
    x.   "Of Ood"
    y.   "The River"
    z.   "The Bird of Doom and the End"

901.   _____. *The King of Elfland's Daughter*. London:
      G.P. Putnam's Sons, 1924.

A major influence on many contemporary fantasy
authors--notably L. Sprague de Camp, Fritz
Leiber, and H.P. Lovecraft--and considered
Dunsany's greatest novel. Alveric, an adven-
turous prince from the Vale of Erl, takes an
elf-princess as his bride. However, she can
no more remain in the lands of men than a flower
can live in ice. After bearing Alveric a son,
Orion, she returns to the land of fairy.
Alveric, armed with a magical sword formed from
seventeen thunderbolts, pursues her. Thwarted
by elfin magic, his love nonetheless proves to
be the greater power, and finally his father-
in-law reunites the lovers by making Erl part
of fairyland. While Dunsany's prose is often
difficult, there are moments of glowing description, and the themes of alienation, love,
and the effect of alien knowledge are given
effective shape through the language and the
characters.

902.   _____. *The Little Tales of Smethers and Other
      Stories*. London: Jarrolds, 1952.

    a.   "The Two Bottles of Relish"
    b.   "The Shooting of Constable Slugger"
    c.   "An Enemy of Scotland Yard"
    d.   "The Second Front"
    e.   "The Two Assassins"
    f.   "Kriegblut's Disguise"
    g.   "The Mug in the Gambling Hell"
    h.   "The Clue"
    i.   "Once Too Often"
    j.   "An Alleged Murder"
    k.   "The Waiter's Story"

l. "A Trade Dispute"
m. "The Pirate of the Round Pond"
n. "A Victim of Bad Luck"
o. "The New Master"
p. "A New Murder"
q. "A Tale of Revenge"
r. "The Speech"
s. "The Lost Scientist"
t. "The Unwritten Thriller"
u. "In Ravancore"
v. "Among the Bean Rows"
w. "The Death-Watch Beetle"
x. "Murder by Lightning"
y. "The Murder in Netherby Gardens"
z. "The Shield of Athene"

903. _____. *Mr. Jorkens Remembers Africa*. London and
Toronto: William Heinemann, 1934. American
title: *Jorkens Remembers Africa*.

a. "The Lost Romance"
b. "The Curse of the Witch"
c. "The Pearly Beach"
d. "The Walk to Lingham"
e. "The Escape From the Valley"
f. "One August in the Red Sea"
g. "The Bare Truth"
h. "What Jorkens Has to Put Up With"
i. "Ozymandias"
j. "At the End of the Universe"
k. "The Black Mamba"
l. "In the Garden of Memorie"
m. "The Slugly Beast"
n. "Earth's Secret"
o. "The Persian Spell"
p. "Stranger Than Fiction"
q. "The Golden Gods"
r. "The Correct Kit"
s. "How Ryan Got Out of Russia"
t. "The Club Secretary"
u. "A Mystery of the East"

904. _____. *The Story of Mona Sheehy*. London and
Toronto: William Heinemann, 1939.

The fairy faith of Ireland inspires Mona
Sheehy to believe the rumor that she is the
daughter of the fairy queen of Shee. While
others lock their doors, Mona takes her greatest pleasures in being out and about in the
dusk and dark.

905. _____. *The Sword of Welleran and Other Stories.*
London: George Allen and Sons, 1908.

    a. "The Sword of Welleran"
    b. "The Fall of Babbulkund"
    c. "The Kith of the Elf-Folk"
    d. "The Highwaymen"
    e. "In the Twilight"
    f. "The Ghosts"
    g. "The Whirlpool"
    h. "The Hurricane"
    i. "The Fortress Unvanquishable, Save for
       Sacnoth"
    j. "The Lord of Cities"
    k. "The Doom of La Traviata"
    l. "On the Dry Land"

906. _____. *Tales of Three Hemispheres.* Boston: Luce,
1919. Rpt. Philadelphia: Owlswick Press, 1976,
from a 1922 edition with an introduction by
H.P. Lovecraft.

    a. "The Last Dream of Bwona Khubla"
    b. "The Postman of Otford"
    c. "The Prayer of Boob Aheera"
    d. "East and West"
    e. "A Pretty Quarrel"
    f. "How the Gods Avenged Meoul Ki Ning"
    g. "The Gifts of the Gods"
    h. "The Sack of Emeralds"
    i. "The Old Brown Coat"
    j. "An Archive of the Older Mysteries"
    k. "A City of Wonder"
    l. "Beyond the Fields We Know: Publishers'
       [sic] Note"
         1. "First Tale: Idle Days on the Yann"
         2. "Second Tale: A Shop on Go-By Street"
         3. "Third Tale: The Avenger of Per-
           dondaris"

907. _____. *Tales of Wonder.* London: Elkin Matthews,
1916. American title: *The Last Book of Wonder.*

    a. "A Tale of London"
    b. "Thirteen at Table"
    c. "The City on Mallington Moor"
    d. "Why the Milkman Shudders When He Perceives
       the Dawn"
    e. "The Bad Old Woman in Black"
    f. "The Bird of the Difficult Eye"
    g. "The Long Porter's Tale"
    h. "The Bureau D'Echange de Maux"

EDWARD JOHN MORETON DRAX PLUNKETT, LORD DUNSANY continued

     i.   "A Story of Land and Sea"
     j.   "The Loot of Loma"
     k.   "A Tale of the Equator"
     l.   "A Narrow Escape"
     m.   "The Watch-Tower"
     n.   "The Secret of the Sea"
     o.   "How Plash-Goo Came to the Lane of None's Desire"
     p.   "The Three Sailors' Gambit"
     q.   "How Ali Came to the Black Country"
     r.   "The Exile's Club"
     s.   "The Three Infernal Jokes"

    Bibliography

908. Amory, Mary. *Biography of Lord Dunsany*. London: Collins, 1972.

WALTER HERRIES POLLOCK.
See ANDREW LANG AND W[ALTER] H[ERRIES POLLOCK]

ELIZABETH MARIE POPE

909. *The Perilous Gard*. Boston: Houghton Mifflin, 1974.

A young girl, Kate Sutton, is exiled by her beautiful sister to Elvenwood Hall, a keep with dark, supernatural associations. She encounters a young man enduring a self-imposed exile of guilt: he had lost his sister to a fairy well. After offering himself in exchange as a willing human sacrifice, his sister is recovered, but Kate accepts the bondage of the fairy folk in the "hollow hill" to rescue him. During their time underground, Kate and her young man, Christopher Heron, discover each other and themselves, and Kate finds a new beauty to replace her awkwardness and insecurity.

TIM POWERS

910. *The Drawing of the Dark*. New York: Ballantine, 1979 [paper].

In sixteenth-century Vienna, an aging soldier of fortune is drawn away from his job as a bouncer in an inn by Merlin to aid in bringing back the spirit of King Arthur.

911. *Atlantis*. London: MacDonald, 1954.

> A continuation of the adventures of Homer's
> Odysseus. After the seige of Troy, Odysseus'
> innate restlessness drives him to further ad-
> ventures in the west. He seeks and discovers
> Atlantis and then goes on to discover the New
> World.

912. *A Glastonbury Romance*. New York: Simon and
Schuster, 1932.

913. *Morwyn: or, The Vengeance of God*. London:
Cassell, 1937. Rpt. New York: Arno, 1976.

> A retired army captain falls in love with the
> daughter of a vivisector. When all three are
> struck by a divinely directed meteor, the father
> is killed and the two lovers are transported to
> Hell. While in Hell, the two lovers are be-
> friended by the ancient Welsh poet, Taliesin.
> They need his protection as they are accosted
> by first the ghost of the father and then the
> spirits of all the sadists and vivisectors in
> Hell. The onslaught becomes so dire that they
> must awaken Merlin, who visits their own sins
> on the ghosts. They are then joined by So-
> crates and one of the ancient judges of the
> Golden Age, free one of the ancient Titans
> from his suffering, and return home. One of
> the few examples of didactic fantasy.

Bibliography

914. Thomas, Dante. *A Bibliography of the Writings of
John Cowper Powys, 1872-1963*. Mamaroneck, NJ:
Paul P. Appel, 1975.

T[HEODORE] F[RANCIS] POWYS

915. *Mr. Weston's Good Wine*. London: Chatto & Windus,
1927.

> God goes incognito as an agreeable wine merchant.

916. *Unclay*. London: Chatto & Windus, 1931.

> John Death loses his talisman, a parchment that
> enables him to claim lives, "to unclay." With-
> out it, he becomes merely an irrestible seducer
> of young women in the English village he has

T[HEODORE] F[RANCIS] POWYS continued

       retired to for the time that he is indisposed.

    Bibliography

917. Riley, Peter. *A Bibliography of T. F. Powys*.
       Hastings [England]: R.A. Brimmell, 1967.

FLETCHER PRATT
Also see L[YON] SPRAGUE DE CAMP AND FLETCHER PRATT

918. "Blue Star." In *Witches Three*. [Ed. Fletcher
      Pratt.] New York: Twayne, 1952, pp. 225-423.
      First separate publication: New York: Ballan-
      tine, 1969 [paper].

      Three men dream and their dreams become the
      setting for this politically oriented fantasy.
      Rodvard and the witch Lalette become embroiled
      in various political and revolutionary activi-
      ties. Lalette possesses a talisman, the blue
      star, which will allow her lover to distinguish
      the emotions of others. Rodvard is encouraged
      by a political group to falsely court Lalette.
      However, he falls in love with her in spite of
      himself and his comrades, and they both flee
      from numerous groups that desire their power.

919. Fletcher, George U., pseud. *The Well of the Uni-
      corn*. New York: William Sloan, 1948. Rpt.
      New York: Garland, 1975.

      Considered one of the classics of contemporary
      fantasy, in this sword and sorcery adventure,
      Airar Avarson and the enchanter Meliboe toget-
      her weld the free fishers, the star captains,
      and the Imperial Children of the Well into a
      strong force that repels the invading Vulkings
      and preserves democratic rule. At the end of
      the book, Airar and Meliboe come to the magical
      well and must decide if the peace a draft of
      its water promises is worth the price that it
      demands: the loss of free will and aggression.

FLETCHER PRATT AND L[YON] SPRAGUE DE CAMP
Also see L[YON] SPRAGUE DE CAMP AND FLETCHER PRATT

920. *Land of Unreason*. New York: Henry Holt, 1942.

      Fred Barber, an American diplomat, becomes a
      "changeling" after he leaves scotch whiskey,

rather than milk, out for the "little people."
In this humorous adventure, he later discovers
that he is the reincarnation of Frederick Bar-
barossa in the eternal battle between good and
the multiple guises of evil. Barber's principal
weapon in the tale is a magic rose. The 1979
Dell paperback edition reprints Edd Cartier's
original illustrations for the shortened version
that appeared in the October, 1941, issue of
Unknown Worlds. The first edition, as cited
above, includes a tease at the end: the first
eighteen pages of the *Incomplete Enchanter*.

921. *Tales from Gavagan's Bar*. New York: Twayne, 1953.
Enl. ed. Philadelphia: Owlswick, 1978.

a.   "The Gift of God"
b.   "Corpus Delectable"
c.   "The Better Mousetrap"
d.   "Elephas Frumenti"
e.   "Beasts of Bourbon"
f.   "The Love-Nest"
g.   "The Stone of the Sages"
h.   "'Where to, Please?'"
i.   "The Palimpsest of St. Augustine"
j.   "More Than Skin Deep"
k.   "No Forwarding Address"
l.   "When the Night Wind Howls"
m.   "My Brother's Keeper"
n.   "A Dime Brings You Success"
o.   "The Rape of the Lock"
p.   "Here, Putzi!"
q.   "Gin Comes in Bottles"
r.   "The Black Ball"
s.   "The Green Thumb"
t.   "Caveat Emptor"
u.   "The Eve of St. John"
v.   "The Ancestral Amethyst"

The enlarged 1978 edition adds a previously
unpublished story--(w) "There'd Be Thousands
in It"--and an essay by de Camp explaining the
genesis of the stories.

E[DGAR] HOFFMAN PRICE

922. *Far Lands Other Days*. Chapel Hill, NC: Carcosa,
1975.

a.   "The Word of Santiago"
b.   "The Peacock's Shadow"

       c.   "Gray Sphinx"
       d.   "Makeda's Cousin"
       e.   "Satan's Garden"
       f.   "Queen of the Lilin"
       g.   "The Dreamer of Atlânaat"
       h.   "A Jest and a Vengeance"
       i.   "Wolves of Kerak"
       j.   "The Hand of Wrath"
       k.   "One Step from Hell"
       l.   "Web of Wizardry"
       m.   "Saladin's Throne-Rug"
       n.   "Allah Sends a Reaper"
       o.   "Khosru's Garden"
       p.   "Hasheesh Wisdom"
       q.   "Snake Goddess"
       r.   "House of the Monoceros"
       s.   "You Can't Eat Glory"
       t.   "Woman in the Case"
       u.   "Heart of a Thief"
       v.   "Kiss of Sekhmet"
       w.   "Vengeance in Samarra"
       x.   "Selene Walks by Night"
       y.   "Prayer to Satan"
       z.   "A King is Next to God"
       aa.   "Shadow Captain"
       bb.   "Peach Blossom Paradise"
       cc.   "The Hands of Janos"
       dd.   "The Shadow of Saturn"
       ee.   "The Infidel's Daughter"

923.   *Strange Gateways*. Sauk City, WI: Arkham House,
       1967.

       a.   "The Fire and the Flesh"
       b.   "Graven Image"
       c.   "The Stranger from Kurdistan"
       d.   "The Rajah's Gift"
       e.   "The Girl from Samarcand"
       f.   "Tarbis of the Lake"
       g.   "Bones for China"
       h.   "Well of the Angels"
       i.   "Strange Gateway"
       j.   "Apprentice Magician"
       k.   "One More River"
       l.   "Pale Hands"

       CHARLES HARRY CLINTON PRICE-GORDON
         See FREDERICK WILLIAM ROLFE AND
       CHARLES HARRY CLINTON PRICE-GORDON

924. *The Other Place and Other Stories of the Same Sort.*
Melbourne, London, and Toronto: William Heinemann, 1953.

    a. "The Other Place"
    b. "The Grey Ones"
    c. "Uncle Phil on TV"
    d. "Guest of Honor"
    e. "Look After the Strange Girl"
    f. "The Statues"
    g. "The Leadington Incident"
    h. "Mr. Strenberry's Tale"
    i. "Night Sequence"

Bibliography

925. Day, Allen Edwin. "J.B. Priestley: A Checklist."
Bulletin of Bibliography, 28 (April-June 1971),
42-48.

926. _____. *J.B. Priestley: An Annotated Bibliography.*
New York: Garland, forthcoming 1979.

927. Jones, I. Alun. "The First Editions of J.B.
Priestley." *Bookman*, 80 (April 1931), 46.

SEABURY [GRANDIN] QUINN

928. *Is the Devil a Gentleman? The Best Fiction of
Seabury Quinn.* Baltimore, MD: Mirage, 1970.

    a. "Uncanonized"
    b. "The Globe of Memories"
    c. "Glamour"
    d. "The Gentle Werewolf"
    e. "The Cloth of Madness"
    f. "The Merrow"
    g. "Is the Devil a Gentleman?"
    h. "Masked Ball"
    i. "Bon Voyage, Michele"

929. . . . *Roads.* Sauk City, WI: Arkham House, 1948.

A delightful reconstruction of the origin and
life of Santa Claus generated from legend,
fact, fancy, and imagination.

Bibliography

930. A Quinn bibliography, by Mark Owings, is appended
to *Is the Devil a Gentleman?* (see above).

931. *Harkfast! The Making of the King.* London: Con-
       stable, 1976 [not seen]. Rpt. London: Sphere
       Books, 1977 [paper].

       A Druid magically summons a young boy and endows
       him with the powers and skills he will need to
       replace a dead king. Set in post-Roman Britain,
       this is in many ways as realistic and brutal as
       Henry Treece's *The Green Man* (see below), and
       the supernatural and natural elements are skill-
       fully blended in this chronicle of the maturation
       of the protagonist's often painfully necessary
       kingly skills. The novel ends with the youth
       preparing to gain a throne and his gathering of
       appropriate companions and officers, seeming to
       promise a sequel.

RUDOLFE RASPE.   See ANONYMOUS ANTHOLOGIES: BARON MUHAUSEN

QUINN READE

932. *Quest of the Dark Lady.* New York: Belmont Tower,
       1969 [paper].

       An average sword and sorcery novel with more
       than its share of gore. A slave girl, a
       traitor, and a king's advisor go in search of
       an immortal dark lady, who, when married to
       their king, will acquire her full sorcerous
       powers.

JAMES RICE.   See WALTER BESANT AND JAMES RICE

FREDERICK WILLIAM ROLFE [BARON CORVO] AND
CHARLES HENRY CLINTON PRICE-GORDON

933. Prospero and Caliban, pseud. *Hubert's Arthur,
       Being Certain Documents Found Among the Literary
       Remains of Mr. N.C., Here Produced by Prospero
       and Caliban.* London, Toronto, Melbourne, and
       Sidney: Cassell, 1935. Rpt. New York: Arno
       Press, 1978 [not seen].

       An alternate history novel that assumes that
       Prince Arthur, the nephew of Richard the Lion
       Hearted, is denied his right to the throne of
       England by the usurper John Lackland. After
       becoming the ruler of Jerusalem by marriage,

Arthur gains the cooperation of the King of France and conquers England, regaining his rightful place. His reign is challenged by Prince Henry, but Arthur defeats him and rules for many years until his epic passing.

Bibliography

934. Woolfe, Cecil. *A Bibliography of Frederick Rolfe. Baron Corvo.* Rev. ed. London: Rupert Hart-Davis, 1972.

GEORGE WILLIAM RUSSELL

935. A.E., pseud. *The Avatars: A Futurist Fantasy.* London: Macmillan, 1933.

936. _____. *The Mask of Apollo and Other Stories.* Dublin: Whaley, and London: Macmillan [1904].

    a. "The Mask of Apollo"
    b. "The Cave of Lilith"
    c. "The Story of a Star"
    d. "A Dream of Angus Oge"
    e. "The Meditation of Ananda"
    f. "The Midnight Blossom"
    g. "The Childhood of Apollo"

Bibliography

937. Denson, Alan. *Printed Writings of George W. Russell (Æ): A Bibliography with Notes on his Pictures and Portraits.* Evanston, IL: Northwestern University Press, 1961.

FRED SABERHAGEN

The Broken Lands Trilogy

938. *The Broken Lands.* New York: Ace, 1968.

939. *The Black Mountains.* New York: Ace, 1971 [paper].

940. *Changeling Earth.* New York: DAW, 1973 [paper].

As this trilogy opens, science and technology are suppressed, and, in fact, negated by an ancient device to prevent another nuclear holocaust. Magic reigns supreme, and society has returned to a pre-industrial level. The con-

flict between science and magic and the redis-
covery of the scientific past form the nucleus
of most of the action, and finally the world is
re-enlightened, the suppressive device destroyed, and magic banished.

BLANCE BLOOR SCHLEPPEY

941. *The Soul of a Mummy and Other Stories.* [Indiana-
polis?]: By the Author, 1908.

a. "The Soul of a Mummy"
b. "Hearts and Crafts"
c. "The Devil's Sonata"
d. "Just Jake"
e. "Mrs. Mainwaring's Second Marriage"
f. "The Mad Master"
g. "The Heart of Esculapius"
h. "The Nector of a Thousand Years"
i. "Marvin's Ghost"
j. "The Gnawbone Culture Club"
k. "A House and a Reincarnation"

OLIVE SCHREINER

942. *Dreams.* Boston: Roberts Brothers, 1891.

a. "The Lost Joy"
b. "The Hunter"
c. "The Gardens of Pleasure"
d. "In a Far-Off World"
e. "Three Dreams in a Desert"
f. "A Dream of Wild Bees"
g. "In a Ruined Chapel"
h. "Life's Gifts"
i. "The Artist's Secret"
j. "I Thought I Stood"
k. "The Sunlight Lay Across My Bed"

Bibliography

943. Watson, George, ed. *The New Cambridge Bibliography
of English Literature.* Cambridge: Cambridge
University Press, 1969, III (1800-1900), 1077.

G. FIRTH SCOTT

944. *The Last Lemurian: A Westralian Romance.* London:
James Bowden, 1898. Rpt. New York: Arno Press,

G. FIRTH SCOTT continued

1978 [not seen].

The Hatter and Dick Halwood travel to Lemuria
and encounter the last queen, Tor Ymmothe, who
has been condemned to wander in a series of
caves for thousands of years to do penance for
the sins of her race. She guards a sealed tomb
that contains the body of a comatose princess,
waiting for the return of her beloved. Halwood
thinks he recognizes the girl, opens the tomb,
and as her body falls into dust, she tells him
to seek her elsewhere in the world. A volcano
erupts, killing all except Halwood and destroying the remnants of Lemuria. He returns to
civilization, and when he seeks out the Hatter's
now orphaned daughter, he finds her the image
of the princess he had discovered in Lemuria.

WILLIAM SHARP

945.   MacLeod, Fiona, pseud. *The Sin-Eater, The Washer
of the Ford, and Other Legendary Moralities*.
New York: Duffield, 1910.*

Reprints some of the contents of *The Washer of
the Ford* (see below).

a.   "Prologue--From Iona"
b.   "The Sin-Eater"
c.   "The Ninth Wave"
d.   "The Judgment o' God"
e.   "The Harping of Cravetheen"
f.   "Silk o' the Kine"
g.   "Ula and Urla"
h.   "The Washer of the Ford"
i.   "St. Bride of the Isles"
j.   "The Fisher of Men"
k.   "The Last Supper"
l.   "The Dark Nameless One"
m.   "The Three Marvels of Hy"
n.   "The Woman with the Net"
o.   "Cathal of the Woods"
p.   "The Song of the Sword"
q.   "The Flight of the Culders"
r.   "Mircath"
s.   "The Sad Queen"
t.   "The Laughter of Scathach the Queen"
u.   "Ahèz the Pale"
v.   "The King of Ys and Dahut the Red"

*N.B. An earlier edition has been cited which
contains some of the contents of this volume:

The *Sin-Eater and Other Tales and Episodes.*
Chicago: Stone & Kimball, 1895. A bibliographic
history of the volumes, title changes, and contents is provided on pages 448-9 of the 1910
edition cited above.

946. The *Washer of the Ford: And Other Legendary Moralities.* Edinburgh: Patrick Geddes and Colleagues
and Chicago: Stone & Kimball, 1896 [joint pub-
lication].

a. "The Washer of the Ford"
b. "Muime Chriosd"
c. "The Fisher of Men"
d. "The Last Supper"
e. "The Dark Nameless One"
f. "The Three Marvels of Hy"
g. "The Annir-Choille"
h. "The Shadow-Seers"
i. "The Song of the Sword"
j. "The Flight of the Culders"
k. "Mircath"
l. "The Laughter of Scathach the Queen"
m. "Ula and Urla"

Bibliography

947. Watson, George, ed. *The New Cambridge Bibliography
of English Literature.* Cambridge: Cambridge
University Press, 1969, III (1800-1900), 1064-
1065.

RICHARD S[HARPE] SHAVER

948. *I Remember Lemuria and The Return of Sathanas.*
Evanston, IL: Venture Books, 1948.

A combination of two highly descriptive stories:
the first is told as a reminiscence of the ad-
vanced science of Lemuria, and the second is a
"biography" of Satan and his minions who are
rendered impotent by the fantastic science of
the "Aesir." *I Remember Lemuria* and related
tales first appeared in *Amazing Stories,* 1945-
1947, and caused quite a turmoil by being presented as factual accounts. *I Remember Lemuria*
was also reprinted as "The Hidden World" in *The
Shaver Mystery* (1961). The reprint was also
presented as fact, and it was used as justifi-
cation by various pseudo-scientific cults both
in the 1940's and 1960's. The July, 1958, is-

217

sue of *Fantastic* featured a final tale, "The
Dream Makers," and a number of essays on the
Shaver phenomenon.

MICHAEL SHEA

949. *A Quest for Simbilis*. New York: DAW, 1974 [paper].

Based on Jack Vance's theme of the dying earth
(see below), this is an above average sword and
sorcery, quest novel. A liege lord and his
larcenous companion seek the master mage
Simbilis only to find him strangely turned from
the world and involved in one of the degenerate
pursuits of a world that has lost its vitality.

CARL SHERRELL

950. *Arcane*. New York: Jove/HBJ, 1978 [paper].

Based on the ancient Tarot cards, this unusual
novel is cyclical in structure and begins with
the arrival of a fool in a small, medieval
town and ends with the awakening to wisdom of
the fool's son, himself an innocent. In the
process, there is a bitter political struggle;
an empire rises and falls; and the first fool
becomes a wise man, marries a goddess, bears
children, and is raised to the god-like status
of a master sorcerer.

951. *Raum*. New York: Avon, 1977 [paper].

Raum, an earl of Hell, is summoned by a wizard.
When the wizard is slain, Raum is free to walk
the earth. Initially cutting a path of blood
and conquest through the world, he seeks Camelot
and Merlin to discover the true nature of himself, the world, Satan, and Hell. As he experiences the world and life, he becomes more
and more human and less demonic. As the novel
progresses, he finds both love and despair as
his demonic nature is totally erased. A swashbuckling work that is also marked by a strong
element of tragedy and poignancy, and that promises a sequel.

952.   *The Book of Skulls.* New York: Charles Scribner's
       Sons, 1972.

       Four students, inspired and directed by the re-
       discovery of a long-lost manuscript, "The Book
       of Skulls," go in search of immortality, know-
       ing full well that two of them must die.

   Bibliography

953.   Tuck, Donald H. "Robert Silverberg: Bibliography."
       The Magazine of Fantasy and Science Fiction,
       April 1974, pp. 81-88.

                     CLIFFORD D[ONALD] SIMAK

954.   *The Enchanted Pilgrimage.* New York: Berkley, 1975.

       A pilgrimage of marvels and a search for know-
       ledge are the frames as Mark Cornwall joins
       forces with a rafter goblin, a creature called
       the Gossiper, his true-love Mary, a motorcyclist,
       and various other excellent figures to search
       out the wise Old Ones. While the conclusion is
       not what the characters anticipate, or the read-
       er for that matter, the narrative of the quest
       and journey does make good reading.

955.   *The Fellowship of the Talisman.* New York: Ballan-
       tine Books, 1978.

       Simak's second fantasy, which has marked simil-
       arities to his first (see above) in structure
       and plot and which echoes Irving Wallace's *The
       Word: A Novel* (New York: Simon & Schuster, 1972).
       Simak's protagonist, Duncan of the House of
       Standish, must transport a manuscript, thought
       to be a first-hand account of the life of Christ,
       to London for verification. Set in a twentieth-
       century England, where progress has stopped at
       the Middle Ages, Duncan must cross through the
       dreaded hoard, a communion of demons and fell
       spirits who devastate the countryside and re-
       tard man's development at cyclical intervals.
       Duncan gathers a fellowship--a giant man-at-
       arms, who grew up with him; a war horse; a war
       dog; a banshee; the little people; a homeless
       ghost; a friendly and repentant demon; and a
       beautiful, young sorceress and her aged mount,
       a griffin--but he never does discover if the
       document (talisman) is genuine although he does

use it to scatter the dread hoard as they swarm
in their regeneration of evil.

Bibliography

956. Owings, Mark. *The Electric Bibliograph, Part 1:
     Clifford D. Simak*. Baltimore: Alice & Jay
     Haldeman, 1971 [paper].

MAY SINCLAIR

957. *Uncanny Stories*. London: Hutchinson, 1923 [not
     seen]; New York: Macmillan, 1923.

     a. "Where Their Fire is Not Quenched"
     b. "The Token"
     c. "The Flaw in the Crystal"
     d. "The Nature of the Evidence"
     e. "If the Dead Knew"
     f. "The Victim"
     g. "The Finding of the Absolute"

UPTON SINCLAIR

958. *It Happened to Didymus*. New York: Sagamore Press,
     1958.

     The dilemmas created when an angel gives a
     contemporary man the power to perform miracles.

959. *The Milennium: A Comedy of the Year 2000*. 3 vols.
     Little Book Nos. 590-592. Girard, KA: Haldeman-
     Julius, 1924 [paper]; Pasadena: by the author,
     1924 [simultaneous publication?].

     Originally appeared in 1914 as "The Milennium:
     A Story" in sixteen installments in *Appeal to
     Reason*.

960. *Our Lady: A Story*. London: T. Werner Laurie, 1938.

     A fictional and compassionate biography of
     Marya, the mother of Jesus.

961. *Prince Hagen: A Phantasy*. Boston: L.C. Page,
     1903. Rpt. New York: Arno Press, 1978 [not
     seen].

     A satirical fantasy in which the narrator is
     carried off to Nibelheim, the Teutonic under-

world, and is given the unfortunate chore of educating Prince Hagen, the King's spoiled, 800-year-old son. Hagen proves to be an apt pupil, and he puts his education to use by becoming a politician, first in Tammany Hall, initially as a Democrat, finally as a Republican. He becomes the toast of New York, becomes engaged to a socially prestigious debutante, but is killed before the enormity of his political machinations can be fulfilled.

Bibliography

962. Gottesman, Ronald. *Upton Sinclair: An Annotated Checklist.* [Kent, OH]: Kent State University Press, 1973.

ISAAC BASHEVIS SINGER

963. *A Crown of Feathers and Other Stories.* New York: Farrar, Straus and Giroux, 1973.

a. "A Crown of Feathers"
b. "A Day in Coney Island"
c. "The Captive"
d. "The Blizzard"
e. "Property"
f. "The Lantuch"
g. "The Son from America"
h. "The Briefcase"
i. "The Cabalist of East Broadway"
j. "The Bishop's Robe"
k. "A Quotation from Klopstock"
l. "The Magazine"
m. "Lost"
n. "The Prodigy"
o. "The Third One"
p. "The Recluse"
q. "A Dance and a Hop"
r. "The Egotist"
s. "The Beard"
t. "The Dance"
u. "On a Wagon"
v. "Neighbors"
w. "Grandfather and Grandson"

964. *The Fools of Chem and Their Holiday.* Trans. Isaac Bashevis Singer. New York: Farrar, Straus and Giroux, 1973.

A group of wise men, led by Gronam Ox, the first

Sage of Chem, bring civilization to their community and also bring all the sufferings attendant to society.

965. *A Friend to Kafka and Other Stories*. [Ed. Robert
Giroux]. New York: Farrar, Straus & Giroux,
1970.

    a.   "A Friend to Kafka"
    b.   "Guests on a Winter Night"
    c.   "The Key"
    d.   "Dr. Beeber"
    e.   "Stories from Behind the Stove"
    f.   "The Cafeteria"
    g.   "The Mentor"
    h.   "Pigeons"
    i.   "The Chimney Sweep"
    j.   "The Riddle"
    k.   "Altele"
    l.   "The Joke"
    m.   "The Primper"
    n.   "Schloimele"
    o.   "The Colony"
    p.   "The Blasphemer"
    q.   "The Wager"
    r.   "Fate"
    s.   "Powers"
    t.   "Something is There"

966. *Passions and Other Stories*. New York: Farrar,
Straus and Giroux, 1975.

    a.   "Hanka"
    b.   "Old Love"
    c.   "Errors"
    d.   "The Admirer"
    e.   "Sabbath in Portugal"
    f.   "The Yearning Heifer"
    g.   "The Witch"
    h.   "Sam Palka and David Vishkover"
    i.   "A Tutor in the Village"
    j.   "The New Year Party"
    k.   "A Tale of Two Sisters"
    l.   "A Pair"
    m.   "The Fatalist"
    n.   "Two Markets"
    o.   "The Gravedigger"
    p.   "The Sorcerer"
    q.   "Moishele"
    r.   "Three Encounters"
    s.   "The Adventure"
    t.   "Passions"

967. *Short Friday and Other Stories.* [Ed. Robert
     Giroux]. New York: Farrar, Straus and Giroux,
     1964.

     a. "Taibele and Her Demon"
     b. "Big and Little"
     c. "Blood"
     d. "Alone"
     e. "Esther Kreindel the Second"
     f. "Jachid and Jechidah"
     g. "Under the Knife"
     h. "The Fast"
     i. "The Last Demon"
     j. "Yentl the Yeshiva Boy"
     k. "Three Tales"
     l. "Zeidlus the Pope"
     m. "A Wedding in Brownsville"
     n. "I Place My Reliance on No Man"
     o. "Cunegunde"
     p. "Short Friday"

968. *Zlateh the Goat and Other Stories.* Trans. Isaac
     Bashevis Singer and Elizabeth Shub. New York:
     Harper & Row, 1966.

     a. "Juvenile: Fool's Paradise"
     b. "Grandmother's Tale"
     c. "The Snow of Chelm"
     d. "The Mixed-up Feet and the Silly Bride-
         groom"
     e. "The First Shlemiel"
     f. "The Devil's Trick"
     g. "Zlateh the Goat"

                    CLARK ASHTON SMITH

969. *The Double Shadow and Other Fantasies.* [n.p.:
     Auburn Journal Print, 1933] [paper].

     a. "The Voyage of King Euvoran"
     b. "The Maze of the Enchanter"
     c. "The Double Shadow"
     d. "A Night in Malneant"
     e. "The Devotee of Evil"
     f. "The Willow Landscape"

970. *Genius Loci and Other Tales.* Sauk City, WI: Ark-
     ham House, 1948.

     a. "Genius Loci"
     b. "The Willow Landscape"

    c.   "The Phantoms of the Fire"
    d.   "The Eternal World"
    e.   "Vulthoom"
    f.   "A Star-Change"
    g.   "The Primal City"
    h.   "The Disinterment of Venus"
    i.   "The Satyr"
    j.   "The Garden of Adompha"
    k.   "The Charnel God"
    l.   "The Black Abbot of Puthuum"
    m.   "The Weaver in the Vault"

971. *Hyperborea*. Ed. Lin Carter. New York: Ballantine, 1971 [paper].

    a.   "The Muse of Hyperborea, *a Prose Poem*"
    b.   "The Seven Geases"
    c.   "The Weird of Avoosl Wuthoqquan"
    d.   "The White Sybil"
    e.   "The Testament of Athammaus"
    f.   "The Coming of the White Worm"
    g.   "Ubbo-Sathla"
    h.   "The Door to Saturn"
    i.   "The Ice-Demon"
    j.   "The Tale of Satampra Zeiros"
    k.   "The Theft of Thirty-Nine Girdles"
    l.   "The Abominations of Yondo"
    m.   "The Desolation of Soom"
    n.   "The Passing of Aphrodite"
    o.   "The Memnons of the Night"
    p.   "Notes on the Commoriom Myth-Cycle" (Lin Carter)

972. *Lost Worlds*. Sauk City, WI: Arkham House, 1944.

    a.   "The Tale of Satampra Zeiros"
    b.   "The Door to Saturn"
    c.   "The Seven Geases"
    d.   "The Coming of the White Worm"
    e.   "The Last Incantation"
    f.   "A Voyage to Sfanomoë"
    g.   "The Death of Malygris"
    h.   "The Holiness of Azedarac"
    i.   "The Beast of Averoigne"
    j.   "The Empire of the Necromancers"
    k.   "The Isle of the Torturers"
    l.   "Necromancy in Naat"
    m.   "Xeethra"
    n.   "The Maze of Maal Dweb"
    o.   "The Flower-Women"
    p.   "The Demon of the Flower"
    q.   "The Plutonian Drug"
    r.   "The Planet of the Dead"

    s.   "The Gorgon"
    t.   "The Letter from Mohaun Los"
    u.   "The Light from Beyond"
    v.   "The Hunters from Beyond"
    w.   "The Treader of the Dust"

973. *Out of Space and Time.* Sauk City, WI: Arkham
    House, 1942.

    a.   "The End of the Story"
    b.   "A Rendezvous in Averoigne"
    c.   "A Night in Malnéant"
    d.   "The City of the Singing Flame"
    e.   "The Uncharted Isle"
    f.   "The Second Interment"
    g.   "The Double Shadow"
    h.   "The Chain of Aforgomon"
    i.   "The Dark Eidolon"
    j.   "The Last Hieroglyph"
    k.   "Sadastor"
    l.   "The Death of Ilalotha"
    m.   "The Return of the Sorcerer"
    n.   "The Testament of Athammaus"
    o.   "The Weird of Avoosl Wuthoqquan"
    p.   "Ubbo-Sathla"
    q.   "The Monster of the Prophecy"
    r.   "The Vaults of Yoh-Vombis"
    s.   "From the Crypts of Memory"
    t.   "The Shadows"

974. *Poseidonis.* Ed. Lin Carter. New York: Ballantine,
    1973 [paper].

    a.   "The Muse of Atlantis"
    b.   "The Last Incantation"
    c.   "The Death of Malygris"
    d.   "Tolometh"
    e.   "The Double Shadow"
    f.   "A Voyage to Sfanomoë"
    g.   "A Vintage from Atlantis"
    h.   "Atlantis: a poem"
    i.   "In Lemuria"
    j.   "An Offering to the Moon"
    k.   "The Uncharted Isle"
    l.   "Lemurienne"
    m.   "The Epiphany of Death"
    n.   "In Cocaigne"
    o.   "Symposium of the Gorgon"
    p.   "The Venus of Azombeii"
    q.   "The Isle of Saturn"
    r.   "The Root of Ampoi"
    s.   "The Invisible City"

      t.   "Amithaine"
      u.   "The Willow Landscape"
      v.   "The Shadows"

975.   *Tales of Science and Sorcery*. Sauk City, WI: Arkham House, 1964.

      a.   "Master of the Asteroid"
      b.   "The Seed from the Sepulcher"
      c.   "The Root of Ampoi"
      d.   "The Immortals of Mercury"
      e.   "Murder in the Fourth Dimension"
      f.   "Seedling of Mars"
      g.   "The Maker of Gargoyles"
      h.   "The Great God Atwo"
      i.   "Mother of Toads"
      j.   "The Tomb-Spawn"
      k.   "Schizoid Creator"
      l.   "Symposium of the Gorgon"
      m.   "The Theft of Thirty-Nine Girdles"
      n.   "Morthylla"

976.   *Xiccarph*. Ed. Lin Carter. New York: Ballantine, 1972 [paper].

      a.   "The Maze of Maal Dweb"
      b.   "The Flower-Women"
      c.   "Vulthoom"
      d.   "The Dweller in the Gulf"
      e.   "The Vaults of Yoh-Vombis"
      f.   "The Doom of Antarion"
      g.   "The Demon of the Flower"
      h.   "The Monster of the Prophecy"
      i.   "Sadastor"
      j.   "From the Crypts of Memory"

977.   *Zothique*. Ed. Lin Carter. New York: Ballantine, 1970 [paper].

      a.   "Zothique"
      b.   "Xeethra"
      c.   "Necromancy in Naat"
      d.   "The Empire of the Necromancers"
      e.   "The Master of the Crabs"
      f.   "The Death of Ilalotha"
      g.   "The Weaver in the Vault"
      h.   "The Witchcraft of Ulua"
      i.   "The Charnel God"
      j.   "The Dark Eidolon"
      k.   "Morthylla"
      l.   "The Black Abbot of Puthuum"
      m.   "The Tomb-Spawn"

n. "The Last Hieroglyph"
o. "The Isle of Torturers"
p. "The Garden of Adompha"
q. "The Voyage of King Euvoran"
r. "Epilogue: The Sequence of the Zothique Tales" (Lin Carter)

Bibliography

978. Cockcroft, Thomas G.L. *The Tales of Clark Ashton Smith: A Bibliography*. Melling, Lower Nutt, New Zealand: Thomas G.L. Cockcroft, 1951 [paper].

ERNEST BRAMAH SMITH

979. Bramah, Ernest, pseud. *The Wallet of Kai Lung*. London: Grant Richards, 1900.

980. _____. *Kai Lung's Golden Hours*. London: Grant Richards, 1922.

981. _____. *Kai Lung Unrolls His Mat*. London: Grant Richards, 1928.

982. _____. *The Return of Kai Lung*. New York: Sheridan, 1937.

983. _____. *Kai Lung Beneath the Mulberry-Tree*. London: Grant Richards, 1940.

984. _____. *Kai Lung: Six: Uncollected Tales from Punch*. Ed. William While. Tacoma, WA: Non-Profit Press, 1974.

a. "The Story of Lam-Hoo and the Reward of Merit"
b. "The Story of Chung Pun and the Miraculous Peacocks"
c. "The Story of Yuen Yong and the Empty Soo-Shong Chest"
d. "The Story of Sing Tsung and the Exponent of Dark Magic"
e. "The Story of Kwey Chao and the Grateful Song Bird"
f. "The Story of Li Pao, Lucky Star and the Intruding Stranger"

985. _____. *Moon of Much Gladness: Related by Kai Lung*. London: Cassell, 1932 [not seen].

All of the witty and comic Kai Lung volumes

are structurally arranged as tale collections, much like *The Thousand Nights and One Night* and *The Canterbury Tales*. They are all set in a completely fictional China inhabited by dragons, maidens, adventurers, and magicians. Much of the charm of the tales is created by the conversion of supposed oriental homelies, tales, and parables into the English idiom.

Bibliography

986. White, William. "Ernest Bramah: A First Checklist." *Bulletin of Bibliography*, 22 (May/August 1958), 127-131.

987. _____. "Some Uncollected Authors XXXVII: Ernest Bramah, 1869?-1942." *Book Collector*, 13, No. 1 (1964), 54-63.

988. _____. "Ernest Bramah [Smith] in Periodicals, 1890-1972." *Bulletin of Bibliography*, 32 (1975), 33-34, 44.

NANCY SPRINGER

989. *The Book of Suns.* New York: Pocket Books, 1977 [paper].

A well-told narrative in which two youths, a prince and a peasant, become blood brothers in a magical, medieval setting. They become the leaders of the fairy folk and scattered bands of virtuous people in a tyrannized and poisoned kingdom and overthrow the prince's evil father. In the process, they come to terms with their own mystical destinies, their loves, and their unexpected common parentage.

A. SQUARE, pseud. See EDWIN ABBOTT ABBOTT

CHRISTOPHER STASHEFF

The Gramarye Series

990. *The Warlock In Spite of Himself.* New York: Ace Books, 1969 [paper]. Rpt. New York: Garland, 1975.

991. *King Kobold.* New York: Ace Books, 1971 [paper].

Like Poul Anderson's award-winning short story, "The Queen of Air and Darkness," and David Bischoff's *Nightworld* (see above), Stasheff's series is an example of the use of fantasy devices and characters within a science-fiction work. Rodney d'Armand (later Rod Gallowglass) is an intergalactic agent sent to the planet of Gramarye to return the planet to a benevolent star empire. Accompanied by his cybernetic and epileptic horse, Fess, he encounters what appear to be witches, were-creatures, elves, and a young sorcerous queen in a series of outrageous, humorous, and wondrous contacts. All is accounted for through extra-sensory talents in this spoof of space opera. A third volume was to appear from Granada Publishing in England in late 1977.

CHRISTINA [ELLEN] STEAD

992. *The Salzburg Tales.* New York and London: Appleton-Century, 1934.

a. "The Personages"
b. "The Marionettist"
c. "Guest of the Redshields"
d. "Don Juan in the Arena"
e. "The Gold Bride"
f. "The Centenarist's Tales (I)"
g. "The Deacon of Rottenhill"
h. "The Death of Svend"
i. "In Doulcemer"
j. "Silk-Shirt"
k. "The Centenarist's Tales (II)"
l. "The Mirror"
m. "The Sparrow in Love"
n. "The Divine Avenger"
o. "The Triskelion"
p. "Lemonias"
q. "The Centenarist's Tales (III)"
r. "The Sensitive Goldfish"
s. "The Amenities"
t. "A Russian Heart"
u. "Fair Women"
v. "The Centenarist's Tales (IV)"
w. "The Prodigy"
x. "Gaspard"
y. "Morpeth Tower"
z. "Sappho"

CHRISTINA [ELLEN] STEAD continued

aa.	"The Little Old Lady"
bb.	"The Centenarist's Tales (V)"
cc.	"Antinoüs"
dd.	"To the Mountain"
ee.	"On the Road"
ff.	"A Colin, a Chloë"
gg.	"The Centenarist's Tales (VI)"
hh.	"Speculation in Lost Causes"
ii.	"The Death of the Bee"
jj.	"Day of Wrath"
kk.	"Poor Anna"
ll.	"The Wunder Gottes"
mm.	"Overcote"
nn.	"The Centenarist's Tales (VII)"
oo.	"The Epilogue"

Bibliography

993. Watson, George, ed. *The New Cambridge Bibliography of English Literature*. Cambridge: Cambridge University, 1972, IV (1900-1950), 742.

JAMES STEPHENS

994. *The Crock of Gold*. London: Macmillan, 1912.

Irish myths and imaginary creatures are combined in this magical romp that was the inspiration for the musical *Finian's Rainbow*.

995. *The Demi-Gods*. London: Macmillan, 1914.

Bibliography

996. Bramsbäck, Birgit. *James Stephens: A Literary and Bibliographical Study*. Uppsala: A-B Lunde-
quista, 1959.

997. Pyle, Hilary A. *James Stephens: His Work and An Account of His Life*. London: Routledge & Kegan Paul, 1965, pp. 183-191.

FRANCIS STEVENS, pseud.   See GERTRUDE BARROWS BENNETT

"FRANK" [FRANCIS] R[ICHARD] STOCKTON

998. *The Bee-Man of Orn and Other Fanciful Tales*. New York: Charles Scribner's Sons, 1887.

a.   "The Bee-Man of Orn"

"FRANK" [FRANCIS] R[ICHARD] STOCKTON continued

      b. "The Griffith and the Minor Canon"
      c. "Old Pipes and the Dryad"
      d. "The Queen's Museum"
      e. "Christmas Before Last; or, the Fruit of
          the Fragile Palm"
      f. "Prince Hassak's March"
      g. "The Battle of the Third Cousins"
      h. "The Banished King"
      i. "The Philopena"

999. *The Lady or the Tiger? and Other Stories.* New
      York: Charles Scribner's Sons, 1884.

      a. "The Lady, or the Tiger?"
      b. "The Transferred Ghost"
      c. "The Spectral Mortgage"
      d. "Our Archery Club"
      e. "That Same Old 'Coon"
      f. "His Wife's Deceased Sister"
      g. "Our Story"
      h. "Mr. Tolman"
      i. "On the Training of Parents"
      j. "Our Fire-Screen"
      k. "A Piece of Red Calico"
      l. "Every Man His Own Letter-Writer"

1000. *The Magic Egg and Other Stories.* New York: Charles
      Scribner's Sons, 1907.

      a. "The Magic Egg"
      b. "His Wife's Deceased Sister"
      c. "The Widow's Cruise"
      d. "Captain Eli's Best Ear"
      e. "Love Before Breakfast"
      f. "The Staying Power of Sir Rohan"
      g. "A Piece of Red Calico"
      h. "The Christmas Wreck"
      i. "My Well and What Came Out of It"
      j. "Mr. Tolman"
      k. "My Unwilling Neighbor"
      l. "Our Archery Club"

1001. *The Story-teller's Pack.* New York: Charles Scrib-
      ner's Sons, 1897.

      a. "A Few Words to Begin With"
      b. "The Magic Egg"
      c. "The Staying Power of Sir Rohan"
      d. "The Widow's Cruise"
      e. "Love Before Breakfast"
      f. "The Bishop's Ghost and the Printer's Baby"
      g. "Captain Eli's Best Ear"
      h. "As One Woman to Another"

    i.   "My Well and What Came Out of It"
    j.   "Stephen Skarridge's Christmas"
    k.   "My Unwilling Neighbor"

Bibliography

1002. Griffin, Martin Ignatius Joseph. *Frank R. Stockton: A Critical Bibliography*. Philadelphia: University of Pennsylvania Press, 1939, pp. 149-173.

HUBERT STRASSL

Magira-War Game Series

1003. Walker, Hugh, pseud. *Reiter in der Finsternis*. Rastatt, West Germany: Erich Pabel Verlag, 1975 [not seen]. Rpt. as *War-Gamers' World: [Magira I]*. Trans. Christine Priest. New York: DAW Books, 1978 [paper].

1004. _____. *Das Heer der Finsternis*. Rastatt, West Germany: Erich Pabel Verlag, 1975 [not seen]. Translated and published by DAW Books as *Army of Darkness*. Trans. Christine Priest. New York: DAW Books, 1978 [paper].

1005. _____. *Boten der Finsternis*. Rastatt, West Germany: Erich Pabel Verlag, 1976 [not seen]. Rpt. as *Messengers of Darkness*. Trans. Christine Priest. New York: DAW Books, 1979 [paper].

A series of novelizations of the fantasy war games that are popular in many clubs and gatherings in both the United States and Europe. A war-gamer becomes a part of his own fantastic creation as Strassl recreates a war-game that grew out of the meetings of a German-Austrian fan club called "FOLLOW." For a similar work, see Andre Norton's *Quag Keep* (above).

THEODORE STURGEON
(born EDWARD HAMILTON WALDO)

1006. *Caviar*. New York: Ballantine, 1955.

    a.   "Bright Segment"
    b.   "Microcosmic God"
    c.   "Ghost of a Chance"
    d.   "Prodigy"

　　　e.　"Medusa"
　　　f.　"Blabbermouth"
　　　g.　"Shadow, Shadow on the Wall"
　　　h.　"Twink"

1007.　*E Pluribus Unicorn: A Collection of Short Stories.*
　　　New York: Abelard, 1953.

　　　a.　"The Silken-Swift"
　　　b.　"The Professor's Teddy-Bear"
　　　c.　"Bianca's Hands"
　　　d.　"A Saucer of Loneliness"
　　　e.　"The World Well Lost"
　　　f.　"It Wasn't Syzygy"
　　　g.　"The Music"
　　　h.　"Scars"
　　　i.　"Fluffy"
　　　j.　"The Sex Opposite"
　　　k.　"Die, Maestro, Die!"
　　　l.　"Cellmate"
　　　m.　"A Way of Thinking"

　　　Also includes an appendix listing Sturgeon's
　　　science fiction and fantasy in anthologies.

1008.　*Sturgeon is Alive and Well . . . A Collection of*
　　　Short Stories. New York: G. P. Putnam's Sons,
　　　1971.

　　　a.　"To Here and the Easel"
　　　b.　"Slow Sculpture"
　　　c.　"It's You!"
　　　d.　"Take Care of Joey"
　　　e.　"Crate"
　　　f.　"The Girl Who Knew What They Meant"
　　　g.　"Jorry's Gap"
　　　h.　"It was Nothing--Really!"
　　　i.　"Brownshoes"
　　　j.　"Uncle Fremmis"
　　　k.　"The Patterns of Dorne"
　　　l.　"Suicide"

1009.　*Thunder and Roses: Stories of Science-Fiction and*
　　　Fantasy. Ed. Groff Conklin. London: Michael
　　　Joseph, 1957.

　　　a.　"Mewhu's Jet"
　　　b.　". . . And My Fear is Great . . ."
　　　c.　"Minority Report"
　　　d.　"The Hurkle is a Happy Beast"
　　　e.　"Thunder and Roses"
　　　f.　"Bulkhead"

     g.   "Tiny and the Monster"
     h.   "A Way Home"

     A Way Home (see below) is an expanded version of this collection.

1010.   *A Way Home: Stories of Science Fiction and Fantasy*. Ed. Groff Conklin. New York: Funk & Wagnalls, 1955. Abr. ed. see *Thunder and Roses* . . . above.

     a.   "Unite and Conquer"
     b.   "Special Aptitude"
     c.   "Mewhu's Jet"
     d.   "Hurricane Trio"
     e.   "'. . . And My Fear is Great . . .'"
     f.   "Minority Report"
     g.   "The Hurkle is a Happy Beast"
     h.   "Thunder and Roses"
     i.   "Bulkhead"
     j.   "Tiny and the Monster"
     k.   "A Way Home"

1011.   *Without Sorcery: Thirteen Tales*. [Philadelphia]: Prime Press, 1948. Abr. ed. as *Not Without Sorcery*. New York: Ballantine, 1961 [paper]-- contents as asterisked.

     a.   "The Ultimate Egoist"
     b.   "It"*
     c.   "Poker Face"*
     d.   "Shottle Bop"
     e.   "Artnan Process"*
     f.   "Memorial"
     g.   "Ether Breather"*
     h.   "Butyl and the Breaker"*
     i.   "Brat"*
     j.   "Two Percent Inspiration"*
     k.   "Cargo"*
     l.   "Maturity"
     m.   "Microcosmic God"

Bibliography

1012.   Moskowitz, Sam. "Fantasy and Science Fiction by Theodore Sturgeon." *The Magazine of Fantasy and Science Fiction*, September 1962, pp. 56-61.

JA[ME]S F[RANK] SULLIVAN

1013.   *Queer Side Stories*. London: Downey, 1900.

a. "The Story of the King's Idea"
b. "Impossibility"
c. "The End of War"
d. "Moozeby"
e. "The Identity of Mr. Push"
f. "Old Joe's Picnic"
g. "The Birth-Rate"
h. "Mr. Hay"
i. "The Beauty College Co."
j. "The Unbelievers' Club"
k. "The Judge's Penance"
l. "The Man with a Malady"
m. "A Use for Genius"
n. "The Thinner Out"
o. "The Dwindling Hour"
p. "The Disadvantages of Mind"
q. "Abraham Fleeter's Weariness"
r. "The Astral Thruppe"

THOMAS BURNETT SWANN

1014. *The Dolphin and the Deep.* New York: Ace, 1968
[paper].

a. "The Dolphin and the Deep"
b. "The Manor of Roses"
c. "The Murex"

1015. *The Goat Without Horns.* New York: Ballantine,
1971 [paper].

Narrated by a dolphin, the protagonist's best
friend, this is the pseudo-historical tale of
an English woman, Elizabeth, who marries a
barbaric "Carib" king in the West Indies, bears
him a daughter, and retires to her bed as an
invalid. Charles Sorley, the protagonist, is
brought from England to tutor the daughter,
Jill, and becomes Elizabeth's lover. Elizabeth's
husband and the king, Curt, is a member of a
shark cult and possesses an elixir of youth
with which he has bought his wife's love. Curt
and the cult members are "devolving," and in the
final climatic scene, Curt changes into a shark
to destroy Charles. Charles, however, is saved
when his dolphin friend kills the were-shark.
Elizabeth and Jill return to England, but
Charles chooses to remain with his dolphin
friend on the island.

1016. *The Gods Abide*. New York: DAW, 1976 [paper].

> In a fourth-century, Christianized Mediterranean,
> Ashtoreth/Stella, the mother goddess, is making
> her last attempts to save her followers and
> creatures from the hostile Yahweh, the Christian
> "Desert King." The three protagonists--Tute-
> linà, Nod, and Dyland--discover they are corn
> sprites and flee Christian tyranny to Britain,
> but find that their adversaries have preceded
> them. Fortunately, Astoreth creates a sanc-
> tuary, a "Not-World," where they will be safe
> from even Yahweh.

1017. *Green Phoenix*. New York: DAW, 1972 [paper].

> Mellonia, a dryad, falls in love with Aeneas,
> who, along with his followers and son, has
> fled the Trojans. Aeneas, hoping to found a
> new Troy, runs afoul of Volumna, Queen of the
> Dryads. After exposing Volumna's deceit--she
> has convinced the dryads that if they take a
> certain drug and go to a certain tree they will
> mate with a god when, in actuality, the male(s)
> is a foul faun(s)--Aeneas is slain. Volumna,
> however, is rejected by her followers after
> she tries to slay Aeneas' son, Ascanius.
> Mellonia is elected the new queen and an alli-
> ance is formed with the Greeks. The sequel to
> *Lady of the Bees* (see below), which contains
> Swann's short story "Love is a Dragonfly"
> (*Magazine of Fantasy and Science Fiction*, March
> 1972).

1018. *How Are the Mighty Fallen*. New York: DAW, 1974
       [paper].

> In a fictional Biblical Israel, King Saul has
> denounced his immortal and beautiful queen,
> Ahinoam, who is a winged Siren and a worshipper
> of Ashtoreth. While Saul fills his time with
> the more orthodox Rizpah, Ahinoam's son, Jona-
> than (actually fathered secretly by a Siren
> drone), has been accepted as Saul's heir.
> Jonathan, however, secretly has rejected the
> god Yahweh (see *The Gods Abide* above) and wor-
> ships Ashtoreth. Jonathan is condemned to
> death by breaking Saul's edict not to eat or
> drink after a battle. However, Nathan, Jona-
> than's armor bearer and friend, is slain instead
> as a scapegoat. Meanwhile, the guilt fostered
> by Yahweh's prophets is slowly driving Saul mad,

and Jonathan is becoming the lover of David,
Saul's harpist, and training David to be a warrior, a fortunate move since David must act in
Jonathon's stead against the giant Goliath.
Jonathon remains with the crazed Saul, partially
out of loyalty and mostly to protect his mother
and sisters, but is slain by the Philistines.
David can only watch since Rizpah's revelation
of his and Jonathon's homosexual relationship
has caused his exile. Ahinoam and David plead
with the Witch of Endor to raise Jonathon from
the dead, but his spirit can only call for
David to unify Israel and refuses to return.
However, David is given a sign that Jonathon's
spirit has been claimed by Ashtoreth.

1019. *Lady of the Bees.* New York: Ace, 1976 [paper].

Set in fictional Latium, this is the tale of
how the dryad Mellonia (the eternal dryad who
appears with Aeneas in Swann's *Green Phoenix*
[see above]) and her companion, the young faun
Sylvan, assist Remus and Romulus in regaining
their usurped throne. An enlargement of the
novelette "Where is the Bird of Fire?" (see
below).

1020. *The Minikins of Yam.* New York: DAW, 1976 [paper].

Filled with the marvelous creatures and cons-
tructs that are so typical of Swann's works,
this is a pseudo-historical novel about a young
pharaoh whose father had banished magic from
the realm. He joins with the minikin Immortelle,
who proudly announces that she holds the rank
of "whore," to discover the source of droughts
and plagues that have descended on his kingdom.
He discovers that it was his father's anti-
magic edict that is the cause through its rejection of his succubus mother and the female
principle of generation.

1021. *Moondust.* New York: Ace, 1968 [paper].

Rahab-Moondust, a female winged sprite whose
race has been enslaved by the subterranean
Fennecs, is sent to the Biblical city of
Jericho as a changeling to be impregnated.
After she has intercourse with an Israelite
spy, she disappears and her human brother, Bard,
and his friend, Zeb, seek her in the Fennecs'
underground world. Bard is captured and

threatened with castration, but Rahab saves
him. She is, however, sentenced to compete in
a mortal battle called "wind war." Even though
she emerges triumphant, Zeb's pet hyena kills
the leader of the Fennecs, and all must flee.
As they escape, they collapse the Fennec tunnels,
making the walls of Jericho "tumble down."

1022. *The Not-World*. New York: DAW, 1975 [paper].

Dierdre, an invalid and a novelist, finds unexpected adventures in the Not-World, a wooded
remnant of the Celtic past peopled with things
and creatures ancient and magical. Her quest
for the imprisoned and seemingly youthful adventurer Dylan leads her to revelations of the
mind and soul, the active versus the passive
life, in this last bastion against the creeping
mechanization of the oncoming Industrial Revo-
lution. As always in Swann's fiction, science,
technology, and civilization are seen as evil
threats to wonder and magic.

1023. *Queens Walk in the Dusk*. Forest Park, GA: Heri-
tage Press, 1977.

In many ways, the background story for *Green
Phoenix* (see above) that relates the tale of
the tragic death of Dido, Aeneas' mistress and
Queen of Carthage. Mixed in this tale of vi-
ciousness and cruelty are Nereid Electra,
Dido's twisted mother, and Iarbus, the Elephant
King, whose deep jealousy is the immediate
cause of Dido's death. This volume includes a
memoir by Gerald Page.

1024. *The Tournament of Thorns*. New York: Ace, 1976
[paper].

In three interconnected adventures--"Stephen,"
"John," and "Lady Mary"--three children flee a
feudal manor and seek adventure. After encounters with the dread mandrakes and the blessed
unicorn, they arrive finally at the Manor of
Roses. When they leave the lady of the manor
and her graciousness, she discovers that she,
too, is a mandrake and opens her doors to the
strangely human creatures. Incorporates "The
Manor of Roses" (see *The Dolphin and the Deep*
above) and "The Stalking Trees" (*Magazine
of Fantasy and Science Fiction*, January 1973).

1025. *The Weirwoods.* New York: Ace, 1967 [paper].

> A continuing example of Swann's elegant use of
> mythology, description, and sensuality as the
> weir-man Vel is rescued from his human enslavers
> by the sorceress Vegoia and an army of cats.
> In the process a town is destroyed; the Etrurian
> princess Tanaquil loses her father and finds
> reality and love; and the gifted musician Arnth
> discovers the difference between supernatural
> and mortal love, confronts the reality of muta-
> bility, and ends his ceaseless wanderings.

1026. *Where is the Bird of Fire?* New York: Ace, 1970
      [paper].

      a. "Where is the Bird of Fire?"*
      b. "Vashti"
      c. "Bear"

      *Expanded into *Lady of the Bees* (see above).

1027. *Will-o-the-Wisp.* London: Corgi, 1977 [not seen].

1028. *Wolfwinter.* New York: Ballantine, 1972 [paper].

> A highly complex novel that centers on Erinna,
> one of Sappho's young companions on the Isle of
> Lesbos. Erinna is seduced by a satyr, but is
> married to a Sybarite by her father. Her hus-
> band exposes the obviously alien child, and she
> runs away to recover it. After being saved
> from a white wolf by a white-skinned trader
> (actually a zombie who hunts souls for Hades),
> she sets up house-keeping with the faun (Skim-
> mer) who recovered her child. Meanwhile, her
> first satyr lover reappears, although he is
> aged, and the quickly maturing Skimmer begins
> to foster a mutual desire between he and Erinna.
> However, as soon as Erinna accepts Skimmer, the
> white trader reappears, demanding the soul of
> Erinna and the child. If he is denied, he
> threatens to destroy a race of healers, the
> Telesphori, who are friends to the fauns. Des-
> pite warnings, Erinna goes with him but substi-
> tutes her soul for the child's. She is saved
> from Cerberus and Hades when Aphrodite admires
> her selfless love, and she returns to Skimmer
> for a few poignant years before he dies; she
> ultimately becomes a sybil.

THOMAS BURNETT SWANN continued

The Minotaur Novels

1029. *Cry Silver Bells*. New York: DAW Books, 1977 [paper].

Although the last written, the chronological
setting of this novel is the earliest of Swann's
"Minotaur" novels (see *Day of the Minotaur* and
The Forest of Forever below). A young brother
and sister, thief and whore by profession, are
banished from Egypt to the Land of the Beasts
(Crete). There they meet and are allied with
Zoe the Dryad and Silver Bells the Centaur.
When the group is exiled to the sea by the centaur king, the two young people are captured by
the Tritons, the sea people, and Silver Bells
is also enslaved when he tries to rescue them.
Zoe leads a force--including Eunostos, Silver
Bells' son--and saves all three from the dread
Sphynx. Silver Bells, however, is poisoned by
the Sphynxes at the victory banquet, paving the
way for Eunostos' role as the last centaur.

1030. *The Forest of Forever*. New York: Ace Books, 1971
[paper].

Second of Swann's Minotaur novels and probably
his best statement of his "beast-folk" and his
belief in the unity of nature, this is composed
of two interconnected tales featuring the young
Eunostos, the last minotaur; Zoe, the voluptuous
dryad of Crete; and Kora, the ethereal dryad.
In the first tale, "Eunostos," the young minotaur courts Kora, who is distracted by her
wondrous dreams of a fair prince and his city,
and rescues her and Zoe from the evil bee queen,
Saffron, who has kidnapped the two dryads to
draw Eunostos into her fatal love embrace. In
the second part, "Aeacus," Eunostos and Kora
are to be wed. However, Kora rescues a young
brother of the King of Crete, Aeacus, and while
nursing him back to health, she realizes that
he is the young man of her dreams, they marry,
and Kora bears two children. Aeacus, however,
realizes that his children are the only heirs
to the throne of Crete, and he flees with them
and returns to Crete. Zoe and Eunostos attempt
to rescue the children, but fail, and Kora per-
ishes with her tree in a fire she herself has
set.

1031. *Day of the Minotaur*. New York: Ace, 1966 [paper].

Originally published in *Science Fantasy* (Nos.

67-69) as "The Blue Monkeys," in 1964-5, this
is the last tale in Swann's Minotaur novels.
Eunostos, the last centaur, rescues two Cretan
children, Thea and Icarus, from the Achaeans
and their blood sacrifice. In love with the
prudish Thea and a father to the vital Icarus,
Eunostos saves Icarus from the eldrich lust of
the Queen of the Bees, but the Bee people lead
the Achaens into the forest, allow them to
destroy it, capture Thea, and slay all the
centaurs save Eunostos. While Icarus and
Eunostos are able to defeat the Achaens with
the poisonous blue monkeys and save Thea, they
realize they can no longer stay in the forest,
and they sail for the *Islands of the Blest*.

RABINDRANATH TAGORE

1032. *Hungry Stones and Other Stories*. [Trans. C.F.
Andrews and others]. London: Macmillan, 1916.

a. "The Hungry Stones"
b. "The Victory"
c. "Once There Was a King"
d. "The Home-coming"
e. "My Lord, the Baby"
f. "The Kingdom of Cards"
g. "The Devotee"
h. "Vision"
i. "The Babus of Nayanjore"
j. "Living or Dead?"
k. "'We Crown Thee King'"
l. "The Renunciation"
m. "The Cabuliwallah"

Bibliography

1033. Anon. *A Centenary Volume. Rabindranath Tagore,
1861-1961*. New Delhi: Sahitya Akadmi, 1961,
pp. 504-519.

JAMES THURBER

1034. *The Wonderful O*. New York: Simon and Schuster,
1957.

Thurber's amazing combination of wit, nonsense,
wisdom and insight in this tale of pirates, a
non-existent treasure, an island, gentle people, a princess, and the elimination of the

JAMES THURBER continued

> letter "o."
>
> Two other collections of Thurber's unique fic-
> tion that should be of interest to fantasy
> enthusiasts are *Fables for Our Time and Famous
> Poems Illustrated.* New York and London: Harper
> and Brothers [1940], and *Further Fables for Our
> Time.* New York: Simon and Schuster, 1956.

Bibliography

1035. Bowden, James T. *James Thurber: A Bibliography.*
Columbus, OH: Ohio State University Press, 1969.

PETER VALENTINE TIMLETT

The Atlantis Series

1036. *The Seedbearers.* London: Quartet Books, 1974
[paper].

1037. *The Power of the Serpent.* New York: Bantam Books,
1976 [paper].

> The first two books in what is billed as a
> trilogy that centers on the nature and fall of
> Atlantis and moves to the settlement of Great
> Britain. The action is marked throughout by
> the struggle between good and evil, the spirit-
> ual and the temporal, and among various power
> groups and religions. The content tends toward
> the sensational, while the narrative tends to-
> ward the slow.

J[OHN] R[ONALD] R[EUEL] TOLKIEN
(also see HENRY N. BEARD AND DOUGLAS C. KENNEY)

1038. *Farmer Giles of Ham:* [a quote in Elfin] *or in the
Vulgar Tongue: The Rise and Wonderful Adven-
tures of Farmer Giles, Lord of Tame, Count of
Worminghall and King of the Little Kingdom.*
London: George Allen and Unwin, 1949.

> Ægidius Ahenobarbus Julius Agricola de Hammo,
> or Farmer Giles of Ham in the vulgar tongue,
> is believed to have chased a giant from his
> village in this light tale. He even receives
> a gift of a sword, Caudimordax ("vulgarly
> Tailbiter"), from the king. When a dragon,
> Chrysophylax the Rich, finds the tales of the

supposedly frightened giant attractive (despite
the flies--Giles' blunderbuss), he too decides
to journey to the land of men to satisfy his
hunger. Giles is drafted to fight the dragon
and is successful primarily because of Tailbiter's
sentient reaction to dragons and his own blind luck.
Ultimately, Giles makes his dog proud of him
and forces the cowed Chrysophylax to yield most
of his hoard to Giles and his neighbors.

1039. *Tree and Leaf*. London: G. Allen and Unwin, 1964.

    a.   "Leaf by Niggle"
    b.   "On Fairy-Stories" [essay]

1040. *The Silmarillion*. Ed. Christopher Tolkien. Boston: Houghton Mifflin, 1977.

This posthumous collection of tales and legends
provides the history of the First Age in Tolkien's
cosmos, the age that precedes the Middle Earth
of *The Hobbit* and The Lord of the Rings Trilogy.
As such, it is the history of the Elves rather
than of the intermingled races of Middle Earth.
It is the history of Morgoth, the first Dark
Lord, and the High Elves as they struggle to
recover the Silmarils from Morgoth. The Silmarils hold the light of the Trees of Valinor
and are keys to the power of good. Yet, this
volume contains far more than the conflict between Morgoth and the High Elves, and those who
have gained admittance to Tolkien's fantasy
realm through the Rings Trilogy will find many
questions answered (i.e., why Galadriel and
Elrond remain on Middle Earth after their companions have long passed on) and more than a
few left as mysteries. Additional sections,
beside (a) "Quenta Silmarillion," include (b)
"The Ainulindalë," a creation myth; (c) "The
Valaquenta," a description of the nature of the
gods; (d) "The Akallabêth," the tale of the
fall of Nūmenor (an Atlantis myth); and (e) "Of
the Rings of Power and the Third Age," the
chronicle of the making of the rings of power
that figure so prominently in Middle Earth.

1041. *Smith of Wootton Major*. London: George Allen and Unwin, 1967.

A light tale in which a master cook journeys
into the realm of faery, returns with a silver
star, and leaves it as a legacy when he vanish-

es. The star is passed on to a new person every twenty-four years by way of a special cake and with the help of the King of Faery, who poses as first an apprentice cook and later as the master cook. Most of the tale is devoted to a blacksmith and his family who are enriched by the star, but who must pass it on at the end of the tale. *Smith of Wootton Major* is especially interesting for its anticipation of the passing of the One Ring in The Lord of the Rings Trilogy.

1042. *The Tolkien Reader*. New York: Ballantine, 1966 [paper].

    a.   Peter S. Beagle. "Tolkien's Magic Ring" [essay]
    b.   "The Homecoming of Beorhtnoth Beorhthelm's Son" [play]
    c.   "Tree and Leaf"
        1. "On Fairy-Stories" [essay]
        2. "Leaf by Niggle"
    d.   "Farmer Giles of Ham"
    e.   "The Adventures of Tom Bombadil and Other Verses from The Red Book" [poem]

The Lord of the Rings

1043. *The Hobbit or There and Back Again*. London: Allen and Unwin, 1937. Rev. ed. London: Allen and Unwin, 1951. 2nd Rev. ed. London: Allen and Unwin, 1966.

1044. *The Fellowship of the Ring: Being the First Part of the Lord of the Rings*. London: Allen and Unwin, 1954. 2nd ed. Boston: Houghton Mifflin, 1967. Rev. ed. New York: Ballantine, 1965 [paper].

1045. *The Two Towers: Being the Second Part of the Lord of the Rings*. London: Allen and Unwin, 1954. 2nd ed. Boston: Houghton Mifflin, 1967. Rev. ed. New York: Ballantine, 1965 [paper].

1046. *The Return of the King: Being the Third Part of the Lord of the Rings*. London: Allen and Unwin, 1955. 2nd ed. Boston: Houghton Mifflin, 1967. Rev. ed. New York: Ballantine, 1965 [paper].

Tolkien's Lord of the Rings series stands as the uncontested masterpiece of contemporary fantasy. Its struggle between good and evil;

its focus on the diminutive heroes Frodo and
Samwise; its brilliantly drawn sorcerer, Gan-
dalf, and master necromancer, Sauron; and its
many villains, noble king, magical characters,
geography, description, characterization, and
created languages and songs make the series a
work of high moment and rich experience. *The
Hobbit* is the background work for the Trilogy
that comprises the main action. In it, Bilbo
discovers the one ring, the powerful talisman that
is the stake in the later struggle between the
fell and the virtuous.

Bibliography

1047. Carpenter, Humphrey. *Tolkien: A Biography*. Boston: Houghton Mifflin, 1977.

1048. West, Richard C. *Tolkien Criticism: An Annotated
Checklist*. [Kent, OH]: Kent State University
Press, 1970.

MRS. ARTHUR EDWARD TOWLE

The Dr. Miles Pennoyer Stories

1049. Lawrence, Margery, pseud. *Number Seven, Queer
Street: Being Some Stories Taken from the Pri-
vate Casebook of Dr. Miles Pennoyer, Recorded
by His Friend and Occasional Assistant, Jerome
Latimer*. London: R. Hale, 1945 [not seen].
Rpt. Sauk City, WI: Mycroft & Moran, 1969.

a. "The Case of the Bronze Door"
b. "The Case of the Haunted Cathedral"
c. "The Case of Ella McLeod"
d. "The Case of the White Snake"
e. "The Case of the Moonchild"

1050. _____. *Master of Shadows: [Being Four Strange
Stories from the Casebook of Dr. Miles Pennoyer,
Psychic Doctor. Recorded by His Friend and
Occasional Assistant Jerome Latimer]*. London:
Robert Hale, 1959.

a. "Saloozy"
b. "Circus Child"
c. "The Woman on the Stairs"
d. "The Twisted Christ"

Along with John Burke's Dr. Caspian and Bromwen

Powys and Randall Garrett's Lord Darcy, among others, Towle's Dr. Pennoyer is a psychic detective who follows the traditional pattern: super, gifted individual is aided by sidekick in penetrating mystery, usually with occult content. The evil forces are unknown to the world-at-large, but wield enormous power. The detective, with the support of the powers of good, saves the world. For an interesting departure from this formula, see James Gunn's *The Magicians* (above). Other notable collections, by Towle, that demonstrate the intrusion of fantasy into the mystery form, are *Nights of the Round Table* (1926); its sequel, *The Terraces of Night* (1932); and *The Floating Cafe and Other Stories* (1936).

HENRY TREECE

1051. *The Green Man*. London: Bodley Head, 1966.

Set in sixth-century Northern Europe and inspired by Danish chronicle, this is one of the most brutal, barbaric, and savage fantasies ever written. Much of the reason for this is that Treece rejects the symbolism of ritual and returns to actualities. For example, instead of a fertility ritual in which the queen blesses the fields, in this work the queen is stripped nude and dragged across the fields by horses. Distinctive features, aside from the blood and brutality, are the appearances of the senile Beowulf and King Arthur and a most unusual conclusion.

LOUIS AND JACQUELYN TRIMBLE

1052. *Guardians of the Gate*. New York: Ace, 1972 [paper].

An average sword and sorcery novel in which the male and female protagonists fulfill a prophecy and summon the forces necessary to good's conquest of evil.

JOHN TURMAN

1053. *Saxon and the Sorceress*. Austin, TX: Morganland Press [the Author], 1978 [paper].

A privately-printed, sword and sorcery novel

that is destined to be published by a major
press. Saxon, a discontented young man, is
transported into a magical realm by the evil
sorceress Lylora, who is aided by her medium
or familiar, Witha, a Doberman Pinscher. An
innocent, Saxon does not realize that Lylora
expects that he will become an archimage and
her willing servant. Saxon, unlike the other
adepts in this world, does not possess magic,
but extrasensory perception. Thus, in this
post-holocaust setting where science and pro-
jectile weapons have been prohibited by a group
of six departed master adepts, Saxon's powers
are not understood. Finally, Saxon allies himself with the virtuous forces after he has
gained mental communication with a large and
caustic cat, Oskar, and been aided by the
virtuous sorceress, Shyla. Turman effectively
characterizes the minor figures, both human and
animal, and handles both the militaristic and
magical aspects of the novel well. Its ending
is an effective cliff hanger as Saxon falls
fully under the power of Lylora. Two more volumes are promised in this evolving series.

AMOS TUTUOLA

1054. *The Palm-Wine Drinkard and His Dead Palm-Wine
Tapster in the Dead's Town.* London: Faber,
1952 [not seen]. Rpt. New York: Grove, 1953.

Tutuola is particularly interesting because of
his use of African folklore. In the volume,
he draws upon Yoruba myths and legends as the
young protagonist is involved in a cyclic pattern of episodes after he has gone into the
underworld to find a dead friend. Other works
of interest to the fantasist are *Abaiyi and his
Inherited Poverty* (1967), *The Brave African
Huntress* (1958), *The Feather Woman of the Jungle*
(1962), *My Life in the Bush with Ghosts* (1954),
and *Simbi and the Satyr of the Dark Jungle*
(1955)--all first published in London by Faber
and Faber.

Bibliography

1055. Collins, Harold R. *Amos Tutuola.* New York:
Twayne, 1969.

MARK TWAIN, pseud.   See SAMUEL LANGHORNE CLEMENS

JOHN UPDIKE

1056.   *The Centaur.*   New York: Alfred A. Knopf, 1963.

A modern rendition of the myth of Chiron, the
wisest of centaurs, who, mortally wounded but
unable to die because of his immortality,
sacrificed eternal life to save Prometheus.
In this retelling, Chiron is a teacher of science
at Olinger High School; Prometheus is his fif-
teen-year-old son. Set in Pennsylvania during
the winter of 1947 and narrated by the son,
Chiron's torment is a well-blended combination
of myth and realism.

Bibliography

1057.   Olivas, Michael A.   *An Annotated Bibliography of
John Updike Criticism, 1967-1973, and a Checklist of His Works.*   New York: Garland Press,
1975.

1058.   Sokoloff, B.A., and David E. Arnason, eds.   *John
Updike: A Comprehensive Bibliography.*   Norwood,
PA: Norwood, 1973.

1059.   Taylor, C. Clarke.   *John Updike: A Bibliography.*
Kent, OH: Kent State University Press, 1968.

DAVE VAN ARNAM

1060.   *The Players of Hell.*   New York: Belmont, 1968
[paper].   Bound with William Tenn's *A Lamp for
Medusa.*

An unusually striking fantasy--involving a
thief, a professional soldier, and a reawakened
god--that is distinguished by its excellent
mythic and magical elements.

1061.   *Wizard of Storms.*   New York: Belmont, 1970 [paper]
[not seen].   Rpt. Manchester, England: PBS Limited, 1972 [paper].

The sequel to *The Players of Hell* although it
does not sustain the quality of its predecessor
due to weak characterization. Zantain, the reawakened, immortal sorcerer, has mandated a
search for magic talismans to restore and ampli-
fy his powers. Much of the novel is occupied

248

DAVE VAN ARNAM continued

> by this quest and by the struggle between
> Qurvel, the Wizard of Storms, and Zantain's
> three unusual servants.

HENRY VAN DYKE

1062. *The Blue Flower*. New York: Charles Scribner's
Sons, 1902.

    a. "The Blue Flower"
    b. "The Source"
    c. "The Mill"
    d. "Spy Rock"
    e. "Wood-Magic"
    f. "The Other Wise Man"
    g. "A Handful of Clay"
    h. "The Lost Word"
    i. "The First Christmas-Tree"

Bibliography

1063. Van Dyke, Tertius. *Henry Van Dyke: A Biography*.
New York and London: Harper & Brothers, 1935,
pp. 427-433.

A[LFRED] E[LTON] VAN VOGT

1064. *The Book of Ptath*. Reading, PA: Fantasy Press,
1947. Rpt. New York: Garland, 1975.

> An army captain, transported to Gondwanaland
> in the distant future, becomes a demigod. He
> falls under the evil control of the goddess
> Ineznia, but after completing seven magical
> tasks, his full powers are awakened and he des-
> troys her. Originally published in *Unknown*
> (October 1943), this edition is the first book
> released by the Fantasy Press.

Bibliography

1065. Van Vogt, A.E. *Reflections of A.E. Van Vogt:
The Autobiography of a Science Fiction Giant,
With a Complete Bibliography*. Lakemont, GA:
Fictioneer Books, 1975.

[JOHN] "JACK" [HOLBROOK] VANCE

1066. *The Dying Earth*. New York: [Hillman Periodicals],

1950 [paper]--the first two "chapters" are re-
versed in this edition and corrected in the
1962 Lancer and subsequent editions.

A collection of six loosely connected tales,
unified by their common setting: Vance's vision
of the earth in the far-distant future when the
sun is going dark and mankind has lost its vitality. Each story focuses on various protagonists as they move through this eldritch environment assured of their dooms. Indulgent and de-
cadent, they seek their pleasures and live out
their pointless lives amid sorcery, degenerate
science, monstrosities, beauty, and cruelty.
For a related work, see Michael Shea's *A Quest
for Simbilis* above.

a. "Mazirian the Magician"
b. "Turjan of Miir"
c. "T'sais"
d. "Liane the Wayfarer"
e. "Ulan Dhor"
f. "Guyal of Sfere"

1067. *The Eyes of the Overworld*. New York: Ace Books,
1966. Rpt. Boston: Gregg Press, 1976.

Linked by its setting to *The Dying Earth*, this
"semi-sequel" is composed of seven interrelated
short stories that have as their protagonist
Cugel the Clever. Cugel, a master thief and
sorcerer, seeks a magic lens and doles out suffering and cruelty to all he encounters as he
travels to his own goal. Ironically, he considers everyone a dupe until his own appropriate
end.

a. "The Overworld"
b. "Cil"
c. "The Mountains of Magnatz"
d. "The Sorcerer Pharesm"
e. "The Pilgrims"
f. "The Cave in the Forest"
g. "The Manse of Iucounu"

For Vance's other Dying Earth tales--"The Bag-
ful of Dreams," "The Seventeen Virgins," and
"Morreion"--see the title index to this volume.

Bibliography

1068. Allen, Paul C. "Of Swords and Sorcery." *Fantasy*

Crossroads, 9 (August 1976), 25-27.

1069. Levack, [Daniel] J H [sic], and Tim Underwood, comps. *Fantasms: A Bibliography of the Literature of Jack Vance.* San Francisco and Columbia, PA: Underwood/Miller, 1978.

VERCORS, pseud. See JEAN BRULLER

GORE VIDAL

1070. *Kalki: A Novel.* New York: Random House, 1978.

Kalki, the Hindu god whose arrival on Earth means the destruction of all mankind except his followers, appears to have materialized in the guise of an ex-G.I., and a specialist in germ warfare, Kelly. Teddy Ottinger, the world's best female pilot and journalist, infiltrates Kalki's inner circle to discover his true nature. Through a combination of social satire and mythology, the novel unravels Kalki's true nature and reveals that Kalki is indeed Siva the Destroyer.

Bibliography

1071. Bruccoli, Mathew J., and C.E. Frazer Clark, eds. *First Printings of American Authors: Contributions Toward Definitive Checklists.* Detroit: Gale Research, 1978, II, 321-333.

GEORGE SYLVESTER VIERECK AND PAUL ELDRIDGE

The Wandering Jew Trilogy

1072. *My First Two Thousand Years: The Autobiography of the Wandering Jew.* New York: Macaulay, 1928.

1073. *Salome: The Wandering Jewess: My First Two Thousand Years of Love.* New York: Horace Liveright, 1930.

1074. *The Invincible Adam.* New York: Horace Liveright, 1932 [not seen].

Filled with fictional portraits of historical characters--Jesus, Mary Magdelene, Nero, Prestor John, Attila, Mohammed, Charlemagne, Don Juan, Leonardo de Vinci, Spinoza, Einstein, Lenin, and others--this is a fictional autobiography of the Jew that Christ cursed to wander through eternity. However, Cartaphilus or Isaac Laguedam is not the traditional suffering penitent; rather, he is an elegant young rake in the tradition of Don Juan and Casanova, whose love affair with the equally unusual Salome unifies this chronicle.

EVELYN CHARLES H. VIVIAN

The Gees Series

1075. Mann, Jack, pseud. *Maker of Shadows*. London: Wright & Brown, [1938]. Rpt. New York: Arno, 1976 [not seen].

One of a number of novels under the Mann pseudonym featuring the occult detective Gregory "Gees" (pronounced "G's") George Gordon Green and an example of a work that occupies the shadowy area between fantasy and horror. "Gees" is directed by a friend to visit Margaret Aylenar, whose daughter is under the spell of an immortal and ancient priest, Gamel MacMorn. MacMorn, having built his house within an ancient stone ring and about an altar of blood sacrifice, renews his life through the ages with the blood of his victims, turning them into pitiable shadows who must do his bidding. Before "Gees" defeats MacMorn and his evil dark goddess, he experiences an evening with a lamia that is notable for its sensuous detail. *Maker of Shadows* is notable for its use of ancient mythologies, especially Welsh, and for its portrait of the aging, but beautiful, Margaret Aylenar, the last bastion against the evil of MacMorn, who lives within a rectangle of Rowan trees, the Ygdrasil of Norse mythology. Sequel: *The Glass Too Many* (see below).

1076. _____ . *The Ninth Life*. London: Wright & Brown, [1939].

Another of Vivian's horror-fantasy novels concerning the occult detective Gregory "Gee's" George Gordon Green. In this case, "Gees," in trying to save a friend from a "slinky" woman, becomes involved with her himself. Cleo Kefra is one of the original Egyptian priestesses of the cat goddess Sekhmet and has lived and re-mained beautiful through the ages as a result of a compact she made with the goddess. Given nine lives through periodic sacrifices that she is unaware of, she has gathered magical lore through all her lifetimes. The brutal deaths of two children by what appears to be the claws of a large cat are what draws "Gees" further into the adventure and to its strong conclusion when it becomes clear that Cleo is not the villain and the goddess Sekhmet makes an appearance.

Other Gees' novels follow:

1077. _____. *Gees' First Case*. London: Wright & Brown, 1936.

A straight-forward, non-fantastic mystery.

1078. _____. *Grey Shapes*. London: Wright & Brown, 1937.

"Gees" battles werewolves.

1079. _____. *Nightmare Farm*. London: Wright & Brown, [1937].

1080. _____. *The Kleinert Case*. London: Wright & Brown, 1938 [not seen].

1081. _____. *Her Ways Are Death*. London: Wright & Brown, [1939].

"Gees" confronts a witch.

1082. _____. *The Glass Too Many*. London: Wright & Brown, [1940].

The sequel to *Maker of Shadows*.

Bibliography

1083. Hagen, Ordean A. *Who Done It? A Guide to Detective, Mystery and Suspense Fiction*. New York and London: R.R. Bowker, 1969, pp. 261 (as Jack Mann, pseud.), 387.

KARL EDWARD WAGNER

The Kane Series

1084. *Darkness Weaves With Many Shades*. Abr. ed. Rese-

da, CA: Powell, 1970 [paper]. Cmpt. ed. New
York: Warner, 1978 [paper].

1085. *Death Angel's Shadow: [Three Tales of Kane].* New
York: Warner, 1973 [paper].

    a. "Reflections for the Winter of My Soul"
    b. "Cold Light"
    c. "Mirage"

1086. *Bloodstone.* New York: Warner, 1975 [paper].

1087. *Dark Crusade.* New York: Warner, 1976 [paper].

1088. *Night Winds.* New York: Warner, 1978 [paper].

    a. "Undertow"
    b. "Two Suns Setting"
    c. "The Dark Muse"
    d. "Raven's Eyrie"
    e. "Lynortis Reprise"
    f. "Sing a Last Song of Valdese"

Like Michael Moorcock's Elric and Carl Sherrell's
Raum (see above), Wagner's protagonist Kane is
at least partially evil. In these sword and
sorcery adventures, his redemptive quality is
that his selfishness and greed bring about the
destruction of greater evils than himself.

Bibliography

1089. Allen, Paul C. "Of Swords & Sorcery." *Fantasy
Crossroads,* No. 9 (August 1976), 25-27.

ARTHUR EDWARD WAITE

1090. *The Quest of the Golden Stairs: A Mystery of King-
hood in Faërie.* London: Theosophical House,
1927 [not seen]. Rpt. Hollywood, CA: Newcastle,
1974 [paper].

An allegorical dream fantasy that has significant similarities to George MacDonald's *The
Golden Key* (see 698 above) and Edmund Cooper's
The Firebird (see 236 above) and that is a pop-
ularization of Waite's mystic and cabalistic
philosophy. A young prince, Starbeam, journeys
through a fairy land to discover his lady,
crown, fame, fortune, and, most significantly,
his inner self.

This is a highly imagistic and descriptive tale
that explores the full social, political, and
magical aspects of "Faërie" as they are dis-
closed through Starbeam's trials and revelations.

HUGH WALKER, pseud. See HUBERT STRASSL

EVANGELINE WALTON, pseud. See EVANGELINE WALTON ENSLEY

SYLVIA TOWNSEND WARNER

1091. *Kingdoms of Elfin.* New York: Viking, 1977.

A collection of sixteen short stories that
chronicles the history, geography, and life of
the often cruel and capricious elves and their
human changelings. A fine example of the creation of "un-human" and alien beings.

a. "The One and the Other"
b. "The Five Black Swans"
c. "Elphenor and Weasel"
d. "The Blameless Triangle"
e. "The Revolt at Brocéliande"
f. "The Mortal Milk"
g. "Beliard"
h. "Visitors to a Castle"
i. "The Power of Cookery"
j. "Winged Creatures"
k. "The Search for an Ancestress"
l. "The Climate of Exile"
m. "The Late Sir Glamie"
n. "Castor and Pollux"
o. "The Occupation"
p. "Foxcastle"

1092. *Lolly Willows; or the Loving Huntsman.* London:
Chatto and Windus, 1926.

The charming biography of Lolly Willows, a woman who willfully decides to become a witch.
After Lolly breaks free from her family, she
moves to Great Mop in Buckinghamshire, drawn
as though by some faint and lovely music. She
is content there among the beech-woods, but her
happiness is threatened by the arrival of
nephew Titus, a young man from Oxford who has
come to write a book. Calling on a considerate
and understanding Satan, she becomes a witch.

With a kitten for a familiar and the power to
curdle the milk Titus uses for his nightly
Ovaltine, she soon has him dissatisfied, engaged,
and packed off to London. With Titus' departure,
she is again independent and glories with Satan
in his numerous domestic guises.

Bibliography

1093. Watson, George, ed. *The New Cambridge Bibliography
of English Literature*. Cambridge: Cambridge
University Press, 1972, IV (1900-1950), 762-763.

MANLY WADE WELLMAN

1094. *Who Fears the Devil?* Sauk City, WI: Arkham House,
1963.

A collection of loosely connected short stories,
most of which were published in *The Magazine of
Fantasy and Science Fiction* in "somewhat different form," that are set in the North Carolina
mountains and feature that group commonly known
as "hillbillies." The protagonist, identified
only as John, uses his silver-stringed guitar
to conquer overt and terrifying evil and magic.
All the stories have a heroic and whimsical
charm, especially in their female characters,
that blends well with their significant elements
of horror.

a. "John's My Name"*
b. "O Ugly Bird!"
c. "Why They're Named That"*
d. "One Other"
e. "Then I Wasn't Alone"*
f. "Shiver in the Pines"
g. "You Know the Tale of Hoph"*
h. "Old Devlins was A-Waiting"
i. "Find the Place Yourself"*
j. "The Desrick on Yandro"
k. "The Stars Down There"*
l. "Vandy, Vandy"
m. "Blue Monkey"*
n. "Dumb Supper" [original title: "Call Me
      From the Valley"]
o. "I Can't Claim That"*
p. "The Little Black Train"
q. "Who Else Could I Count On"*
r. "Walk Like a Mountain"
s. "None Wiser for the Trip"*

       t.   "On the Hills and Everywhere"
       u.   "Nary Spell"*
       v.   "Nine Yards of Other Cloth"

      *Brief introductions spoken by John the Minstrel
      to each tale that follows.

H[ERBERT] G[EORGE] WELLS

1095. *The Sea Lady: A Tissue of Moonshine.* London:
      Methuen, 1902 [not seen]. Rpt. Westport, CT:
      Hyperion, 1976 [paper].

      A young British aristocrat, Fred Bunting, res-
      cues a young girl who appears to be drowning.
      However, she turns out to be a mermaid. The
      family adopts her with comic results as the
      young "girl" views staid, middle-class British
      life from her free and pagan perspective.
      Fred falls in love with her. As a result, he
      begins to see a visionary and sensual world
      beyond his own experience, and he abandons his
      traditional plans for a new life as the novel
      ends and the mermaid returns to the sea.

1096. *The Wonderful Visit.* London: J.M., Dent, 1895.
      Rpt. New York: Arno Press, 1978 [not seen].

      Inexplicably, an angel falls to earth into a
      small English town. He cannot adjust to earth-
      ly values and circumstances, and his actions
      and appearance draw the increasing hatred of
      the townspeople. Befriended only by the town
      vicar (who originally shot him down while
      hunting), he becomes increasingly human, falls
      in love with a servant girl, and is consumed
      in flames when he tries to save her from a
      burning house. However, their souls are united,
      and this combination of tragedy and comedy
      does have a happy ending. For an interesting
      contrast, see Carl Sherrell's *Raum* above.

Bibliography

1097. Hammond, J.R. *Herbert George Wells: An Annotated
      Bibliography of His Works.* New York: Garland,
      1977.

1098. Mullen, R.D. "An Annotated Survey of Books and
      Pamphlets by H.G. Wells." In *H.G. Wells and
      Modern Science Fiction.* Ed. Darko Suvin with

Robert Philmus. Lewisburg, NJ: Bucknell University Press and London: Associated University Presses, 1977, pp. 223-268.

DENNIS WHEATLEY

1099. *The Devil Rides Out*. London: Hutchinson, 1934 [not seen]. Rpt. London: Arrow Books, 1954, with a new edition in 1969 [paper].

All of Wheatley's books are more occult and weird fiction than fantasy, but his canon contains enough sorcerous lore to be of interest to some fantasy readers and his books have been lauded as classics of their type. In much the same manner as Evelyn Charles H. Vivian's "G's" series and John Burke's Dr. Caspian books (see above), Wheatley's fiction focuses on the psychic detective, his faithful retainers, exotic environments, and macabre villains and situations. *The Devil Rides Out*, which utilizes the same characters as *Gateway to Hell* (see below), pits three protagonists against a Satanic coven and elemental evil. Before everyone is threatened with the loss of soul and before the dread Talisman of Set is destroyed, a beautiful young woman is resurrected, an angelic child is saved from being the principal sacrifice in a Black Mass, and a treasured comrade is saved from the Devil's work--all in an unexpected *deus ex machina*. Other titles in Wheatley's large canon are cited below without annotation.

1100. *Gateway to Hell*. London: Hutchinson, 1970 [not seen]. Rpt. London: Arrow Books, 1972 [paper].

1101. *The Haunting of Toby Jugg*. London: Hutchinson, 1948 [not seen]. Rpt. London: Arrow Books, 1959 [paper].

1102. *The Irish Witch*. London: Hutchinson, 1973 [not seen]. Rpt. London: Arrow Books, 1975 [paper].

1103. *The Ka of Gifford Hillary*. London: Hutchinson, 1965 [not seen]. Rpt. London: Arrow Books, 1961, with a new edition in 1969 [paper].

1104. *The Satanist*. London: Hutchinson, 1960 [not seen]. Rpt. London: Arrow Books, 1962, with a new edition in 1969 [paper].

DENNIS WHEATLEY continued

1105. *Strange Conflict*. London: Hutchinson, 1941 [not seen]. Rpt. London: Arrow Books, 1959, with a new edition in 1969 [paper].

1106. *They Used Dark Forces*. London: Hutchinson, 1964 [not seen]. Rpt. London: Arrow Books, 1966, with a new edition in 1969 [paper].

1107. *To the Devil--A Daughter*. London: Hutchinson, 1953 [not seen]. Rpt. London: Arrow Books, 1956, with a new edition in 1969 [paper].

EDWARD LUCAS WHITE

1108. *Lukundoo and Other Stories*. New York: George H. Doran, 1927.

    a. "Lukundoo"
    b. "Floki's Blade"
    c. "The Picture Puzzle"
    d. "The Snout"
    e. "Alfandega"
    f. "The Message on the Slate"
    g. "Amina"
    h. "The Pig-Skin Belt"
    i. "The House of the Nightmare"
    j. "Sorcery Island"

1109. *The Song of the Sirens and Other Stories*. New York: E.P. Dutton, 1919.

    a. "The Song of the Sirens"
    b. "Iarbas"
    c. "The Right Man"
    d. "Dodona"
    e. "The Elephant's Ear"
    f. "The Fasces"
    g. "The Swimmers"
    h. "The Skewbald Panther"
    i. "Disvola"
    j. "The Flambeau Brackett"

Bibliography

1110. Burke, W.J., Will D. Howe, Irving Weiss, and Anne Weiss. *American Authors and Books: 1640 to the Present*. 3rd rev. ed. New York: Crown, 1972, p. 687.

1111. *The Elephant and the Kangaroo*. New York: G.P.
       Putnam's Sons, 1947.

       A humorous and light fantasy based on an impend-
       ing second flood, and featuring the Archangel
       Michael, who arrives down the chimney of the
       O'Callaghan's farm in Ireland and announces to
       Mr. White, a free-thinking bachelor, and Mr.
       and Mrs. O'Callaghan that they are to repopulate
       the earth.

1112. *Mistress Masham's Repose*. New York: G.P. Putnam's
       Sons, 1946.

       A group of Lilliputians, originally brought as
       freaks to England after Gulliver's voyage, are
       protected by a ten-year-old heiress, Maria, from
       her wicked governess and the overly pious vicar.
       However, it is the "little people" who ultimately
       save Maria, and she finally learns to let them
       live their own lives.

       The Once and Future King Series

1113. *The Sword in the Stone*. New York: G.P. Putnam's
       Sons, 1938.

1114. *The Witch in the Wood* [retitled "The Queen of Air
       and Darkness" in *The Once and Future King*]. New
       York: G.P. Putnam's Sons, 1939.

1115. *The Ill-Made Knight*. New York: G.P. Putnam's Sons,
       1940.

1116. *The Once and Future King*. London: Collins, 1958.

1117. *The Book of Merlyn: The Unpublished Conclusion to
       "The Once and Future King."* Austin: University
       of Texas Press, 1977.

       The best contemporary treatment of the Arthurian
       legend, far exceeding the pseudo-historical
       treatment by Mary Stewart in *The Crystal Cave* and
       The Hollow Hills. White's characterization and
       modern view of the lives of Arthur, Merlin, and
       all the other figures of Camelot are filled with
       humor, joy, sadness, cruelty, pathos, and trag-
       edy. His use of contemporary psychological
       explanations and his introduction of modern ana-
       chronisms give a unique perspective, none more
       striking than Merlin, the wizard who is living
       backwards, remembering the future and forgetting

the past. *The Once and Future King* is an omnibus volume, collecting revisions of *The Sword in the Stone* (with two new chapters), *The Witch in the Wood* (retitled "The Queen of Air and Darkness"), *The Ill-Made Knight*, and adding a new section, "The Candle in the Wind." *The Book of Merlyn* was written in 1940-1941 and supposedly not published because of paper shortages during World War II. However, there is more credence to the view that neither White nor his publisher thought enough of his heavily political and bitter attack on mankind to pursue its publication.

Bibliography

1118.   Crane, John K. *T.H. White*. New York: Twayne Publishers, 1974.

WILLIAM ANTHONY PARKER WHITE

1119.   Boucher, Anthony, pseud. *The Compleat Werewolf and Other Stories of Fantasy and Science Fiction*. New York: Simon and Schuster, 1969.

   a.   "The Compleat Werewolf"
   b.   "The Pink Caterpillar"
   c.   "Q.U.R."
   d.   "Robine"
   e.   "Snulbug"
   f.   "Mr. Lupescu"
   g.   "They Bite"
   h.   "Expedition"
   i.   "We Print the Truth"
   j.   "The Ghost of Me"

Bibliography

1120.   Offord, Lenore Glen, comp. *A Boucher Portrait: Anthony Boucher as Seen by His Friends and Colleages . . . And A.* [sic] *Boucher Bibliography Compiled by J.R. Christopher with D.W. Dickensheet and R.E. Briney*. White Bear Lake, MN: The Armchair Detective, n.d.

LEONARD WIBBERLEY

1121.   *The Quest of Excalibur*. New York: G.P. Putnam's Sons, 1959.

   A light and witty novel concerning the return

of King Arthur, Cibber Brown and his companion's
search for Excalibur in a Rolls Royce, and an
attempt to cure all the ills of modern-day
England.

MARY E. WILKINS, pseud. See MARY E. WILKINS [FREEMAN]

CHARES W.S. WILLIAMS

1122. *All Hallow's Eve.* London: Faber & Faber, 1945.

Set in a dual environment of post-World War II
London and the city of the dead, this novel's
action is primarily concerned with the interface of these two places--one real, one meta-
physical--that are unified by a painting by
Jonathon Dayton, one of the characters. The
novel is dominated by Simon the Clerk, seemingly
a religious fanatic, but actually a master sorcerer who has other images of himself scattered
throughout the world. His goals are world
domination and control of the city of the dead.
Simon seeks to gain this domination through the
sacrifice of his daughter, Betty, but the in-
tervention of the spirit of a dead woman, Lester
Furnival, through her husband and Dayton, his
brother, brings Simon's plans to an elaborate
end on All Hallow's Eve. Love, balance, and
unity are restored in this, the last of Williams'
published novels.

1123. *Descent Into Hell.* London: Faber & Faber, 1937.
Rpt. Grand Rapids, MI: William B. Eerdmans,
1965 [paper].

Williams explores the variety of love, both
selfless and selfish, in this study of the
overlap between the worlds of life and death.
Set in Battle Hill, an old Roman battle ground,
two people--the young Pauline Anstruther and
the middle-aged Lawrence Wentworth--are the
focus of a struggle that spans time as it examines the vulgarities and sublimities of human
passions, fears, and interrelationships.

1124. *The Greater Trumps.* London: Victor Gollancz, 1932
[not seen]. Rpt. Grand Rapids, MI: William B.
Eerdmans, 1976 [paper].

The discovery of the original deck of Tarot

cards causes Henry Lee, a young lawyer, to attempt to unite them with a set of golden figures
he owns that move in the Great Dance of the
World. As the guardian of the figures, Lee and
his beloved Nancy Coningsby try to take the cards
from her father, Lothair. With the cards and
figures joined, Lee expects to be able to see
and control the future. After creating a storm
to cause Lothair's death and gain the cards,
Lee loses control of the storm, and Sybil, a
woman of great power due to her commitment to
the divinity of love and Lothair's sister, must
rescue Lothair and recover the cards. Uniting
Henry Lee and Nancy, Sybil becomes a curative
vision of Joanna, another character who has been
insane; the storm is quelled; and the cards are
scattered and peace is restored.

1125. *Many Dimensions*. London: Victor Gollancz, 1931
[not seen]. Rpt. Grand Rapids, MI: William B.
Eerdmans, 1965 [paper].

A young Englishman, Sir Giles Tumulty, has man-
aged to obtain the crown of Suleiman ben Daood
from a member of the family that has been guard-
ing it in Persia for several hundred years.
The crown contains a miraculous stone, which
contains the letters of the tetragrammaton, and
has the power to cure and move people through
time and space. Most significantly, the stone
has the power to reproduce itself, with each
reproduction having the powers of the original.
The disasters and graces that follow demonstrate
the danger of the supernatural in the natural
world as Chloe Burnett, a young woman, accepts
the *geis* of reuniting the stone with its repro-
ductions, but only at great price as she is
transfigured and finally dies, no longer having
a place in the mundane world.

1126. *The Place of the Lion: A New Novel*. London: Victor
Gollancz, 1931 [paper]. Rpt. Grand Rapids, MI:
William B. Eerdmans, 1965 [paper].

A student of the Principles of Creation succeeds
in drawing the personified and elemental forms
of emotions into the world: the Lion of Strength,
the Butterfly of Beauty, the Serpent of Subtlety,
the Eagle of Knowledge, the Lamb of Innocence,
the Pterodactyl of False Knowledge, etc. These
Elementals are uncontrollable and begin to draw
their qualities from any person or substance

that is not in complete harmony. As a result,
both people and things are absorbed, and much of
the immediate environment is destroyed. Anthony
Durrant, the only character who is in balance
and who possesses self-knowledge and self-mas-
tery, goes to the source of the elements and,
in a reinactment of Adam's naming of animals
and things in Eden, gains control of the Elementals and returns them to their proper places in
cosmic order.

1127. *Shadows of Ecstacy*. London: Victor Gollancz, 1933
[not seen]. Rpt. Grand Rapids, MI: William B.
Eerdmans, 1965.

The first novel that Williams wrote, even though
it was published fifth, is a conflict between
the forces of ecstasy, championed by Nigel
Considine, and the forces of reason, led by Sir
Bernard Travers. Considine gathers the forces
of Africa to overthrow Europe, the bastion of
reason, and to find immortality through rebirth
for himself. Considine, after having consider-
able success, is killed by a greedy henchman,
and both the characters and the reader are left
wondering what the world would have been like if
Considine had lived and gained the success he
seemed to be capable of achieving.

1128. *War in Heaven*. London: Victor Gollancz, 1930.
Rpt. Grand Rapids, MI: William B. Eerdmans,
1965 [paper].

The Grail is discovered in a church in Castra
Parvulorum and becomes the center of a struggle
between a group of Satanists and a group of
saintly and pious men. After the chaos of
possessions, black magic, and a variety of rituals, the guardian of the Grail, Prestor John,
appears (as he has several times before) in the
full glory of his powers, destroys the necro-
mancers, and saves the virtuous. The next
morning, a mass is said using the Grail, and as
it ends, the Grail passes from the world.

Bibliography

1129. Glenn, Lois. *Charles W.S. Williams: A Checklist*.
[Kent, OH]: Kent State University Press, 1975.

JAY WILLIAMS

1130. *The Hero from Otherwhere.* New York: Dell, 1972
[paper].

An interesting juvenile in which two totally
different young boys are called to the principal's office only to be confronted by two wizards. The boys are told that they have been
chosen to confront the dread wolf Fenris, the
incarnation of fear materialized through the
singing of a master poet, Woding. Journeying
to "Otherwhere," the boys become involved with
their own mutual animosities, a demonic shape
changer, a professor of screaming, and a good
witch before they must confront the total evil
of Fenris.

"JACK" [JOHN STEWART] WILLIAMSON

1131. *Darker Than You Think.* Reading, PA: Fantasy
Press, 1948. Rpt. New York: Garland, 1975.

Probably the best werewolf tale ever told. The
young and confused protagonist, the startlingly
alluring heroine, and the gothic allusions to
an ancient battle between mankind and a race of
sorcerous shape changers give this novel con-
siderable impact as the shape changers--homo
superiors--begin to rise again. First published
in *Unknown,* December 1940.

1132. *Reign of Wizardry.* New York: Lancer, 1964 [paper].

A retelling of Theseus' single-handed conquest
of Crete in the form of an only average sword
and sorcery tale. Theseus must not only physi-
cally conquer the forces of Crete and Talos,
its bronze guardian, but he must also defeat
its dread black magic and its shape changing
king, Minos. He does this with the help of
Ariadne, Minos' daughter, who has fallen in
love with him.

JOHN ANTHONY BURGESS WILSON

1133. Burgess, Anthony, pseud. *The Eve of St. Venus.*
London: Sedgewick and Jackson, 1964.

Venus interrupts a wedding and claims the groom.
He possesses her briefly before her power as
the goddess of love comes to the fore, and she

consecrates the original union. In a foreword
to the American edition (New York: W.W. Norton,
1970), Wilson explains the use of Burton's *Anatomy of Melancholy* (part 3, section 2) as a
source for the novel and indicates that it was
first written in 1950.

Bibliography

1134. Boytinck, Paul. *Anthony Burgess: An Enumerative
Bibliography With Selected Annotations.* Norwood, PA: Norwood Editions, 1974.

1135. Rosa, Alfred F., and Paul A. Eschhloz. *Contemporary
Fiction in America and England, 1950-1970: A
Guide to Information Sources.* Detroit: Gale
Research, 1976, pp. 101-102.

GENE WOLFE

1136. *The Devil in the Forest.* Chicago: Follett, 1976
[not seen]. Rpt. New York: Ace, 1977 [paper].

A highly introspective and strange story in
which a boy's journey through the forest and
his encounters with Wat the Highwayman, Mother
Cloot the Witch, and the Barrow Man, among
others, are parallels or reflections of his
own inner development and maturation.

ELINOR [HOYT] WYLIE

1137. *The Orphan Angel.* New York: Alfred A. Knopf,
1926.

Based on the premise that the poet Percy
Shelley did not die in the Bay of Spezzia but
was saved from drowning and taken to America
aboard the ship Witch of the West. Renamed
Shiloh by his rescuer, David Butternut, Shelley
becomes an able seaman and travels about America
aiding David in his search for the sister of a
man he killed.

1138. *The Venetian Glass Nephew.* New York: George H.
Doran, 1925.

Bibliography

1139. Blanck, Jacob. *Merle Johnson's American First Edi-*

ELINOR [HOYT] WYLIE continued

> *tions.* Rev. and enl. ed. Waltham, MA: Mark
> Press, 1965, pp. 551-553.

1140. Burke, W.J., Will D. Howe, Irving Weiss, and Anne
Weiss. *American Authors and Books: 1640 to the
Present Day.* 3rd rev. ed. New York: Crown,
1972, p. 713.

ROGER ZELAZNY

1141. *Isle of the Dead.* New York: Ace Books, 1969
[paper]. Rpt. Boston: Gregg, 1976 [not seen].

> What begins as a seeming science fiction novel
> about a world-scaper or planet-maker turns
> ultimately to divine possession and manifesta-
> tion. Francis Sandow, his life prolonged
> through cryostasis, is the only Earthman trained
> by the alien and ancient Pei'ans to use the
> power of his mind to create worlds. Part of
> his final initiation is the selection of a pat-
> ron deity from Pei'an pantheon of gods. Sandow
> selects Shimbo of Darktree, Shrugger of Thunders.
> While Sandow has been aware of some empathy with
> the god during his acts of creation and has
> wondered why Shimbo's images glow whenever he
> enters a Pei'an shire, Sandow has never thought
> too much of the shadowy and numinous presence.
> His reactions change markedly, however, when a
> Pei'an enemy, a failure as a world scaper,
> seeks revenge by restoring a number of Sandow's
> past friends, his wife, and his greatest enemy
> to life by using stolen recall tapes, methods
> of recording a person's personality and cells
> after death. When Sandow goes to a planet he
> has created, Illyria, to confront the Pei'an,
> he discovers that the world is polluted and his
> enemy has been possessed by Belion, the enemy
> of his patron, Shimbo. In a clash of enormous
> powers, the two gods use the bodies of the ant-
> agonists to resolve their own conflict. As is
> typical with Zelazny, Shadow emerges as a sar-
> donic and human protagonist who chooses his
> own future after the god has had his way.

1142. *Jack of Shadows.* New York: Walker, 1971.

> A highly mythic work that combines magic and
> science as Jack of Shadows, a sorcerer or
> "power" and a darkside dweller on a world with
> no rotation, uses both computers and sorcery to
> gain revenge against his fellow darksiders.

Destroying the machinery and magic that holds
the world still, he dramatically changes the
world order.

The Amber Series

1143. *Nine Princes in Amber*. New York: Doubleday, 1970.

1144. *The Guns of Avalon*. New York: Doubleday, 1972.

1145. *The Sign of the Unicorn*. New York: Doubleday, 1975.

1146. *The Hand of Oberon*. New York: Doubleday, 1976.

1147. *The Courts of Chaos*. New York: Doubleday, 1978.

Zelazny's popular Amber Series focuses on mythical patterns, magic, political intrigue, and
the nature of reality. The only true reality
is Amber, whose ruling family creates all other
places, "shadow," with their minds. When
Oberon, the family's patriarch, disappears, the
various children plot against each other for
the crown. Corwin, the protagonist, finds himself one of the prime candidates and struggles
against his kin. However, it soon becomes clear
that Amber's struggle is not within but without
as the mysterious Courts of Chaos threaten
Amber's order and the primeval pattern that is
its unifying essence. The series draws heavily
on the Tarot cards and the Grail legend (from
Jesse Weston's *From Ritual to Romance*) for
much of its material.

Bibliography

1148. Yoke, Carl. *A Reader's Guide to Roger Zelazny*.
West Linn, OR: Starmont House, 1979 [paper].

ANTHOLOGIES

BRIAN W. ALDISS, ed.

1149. *Best Fantasy Stories.* London: Faber and Faber, 1962 [paper].

a. Michael Joyce. "Perchance to Dream"
b. Ray Bradbury. "In a Season of Calm Weather"
c. Alexander Lernet-Holenia. "Baron Bagge"
d. John Collier. "Incident on a Lake"
e. Angus Wilson. "Mummy to the Rescue"
f. Brian W. Aldiss. "Intangibles Inc."
g. Jack Finney. "Cousin Len's Wonderful Adjective Cellar"
h. Charles Beaumont. "You Can't Have Them All"
i. "Saki" [H.H. Munro]. "The Story-Teller"
j. Robert Lindner. "The Jet-Propelled Couch"

ANONYMOUS

1150. *Sometimes, Never: Three Tales of Imagination.* London: Eyre & Spottiswoode, 1956.

a. William Golding. "Envoy Extraordinary"
b. John Wyndham, pseud. [John Beynon Harris]. "Consider the Ways"
c. Mervyn Peake. "Boy in Darkness"

ANONYMOUS: BARON MUCHAUSEN

1151. Bangs, John Kendrick. *Mr. Munchausen: Being a True Account of Some of the Recent Adventures Beyond the Styx of the Late Hieronymus Carl Friedrich, sometime Baron Munchausen of Baden-werder, as Originally Reported for the Sunday Edition of the Gehenna Gazette by its Special Interviewer the Late Mr. Ananias formerly of Jerusalem and now First Transcribed from the Columns of that Journal.* Boston: Noyes, Platt, 1901.

1152. *The Singular Adventures of Baron Munchausen by*

ANONYMOUS: BARON MUCHAUSEN continued

> *Rudolfe Raspe and Others: A Definitive Text.*
> Ed. John Carswell. 2nd & enl. ed. New York:
> Limited Editions Club, 1952.
>
> a. "The Singular Adventures of Baron Munchau-
>   sen"
> b. "A Sequel to the Singular Adventures of
>   Baron Munchausen"
>
> plus a descriptive bibliography.

1153. *The Singular Travels, Campaigns, Voyages, and*
       Sporting Adventures of Baron Munnikhouson,
       Commonly Pronounced Munchausen: As He Relates
       them Over a Bottle, when Surrounded by His
       Friends: A New Edition Considerably Enlarged,
       and Ornamented with Four Views, Engraved from
       the Baron's Drawings. Oxford [England]: The
       University Press, 1786.

       Bibliography

1154. Wackermann, Erwin. *Münchhausiana: Bibliographie*
       der Münchhausen - Ausgaben und Münchhausiaden
       mit einen Beitrag zur Geschichte der frühen
       Ausgaben. Stuttgart: Verlag Fritz Eggert,
       1969.

                   ANONYMOUS: WONDER CLUB

1155. Halidom, M.Y., pseud. *Tales of the Wonder Club.*
       Rev. ed. London: Thomas Burleigh, 1903 [al-
       though this is called a revised edition on the
       title page, it is the first edition of a work
       that is most probably the work of a number of
       authors].

       a. "A Peep at the Wonder Club"
       b. "The Phantom Flea--The Lawyer's Story"
       c. "The Spirit Lovers--The Doctor's Story"
       d. "The Mermaid Place; or Captain Though-
           yard's Dream"
       e. "The Headless Lady--The Artist's First
           Story"
       f. "The Demon Guide; or, The Gnome of the
           Mountain--The Geologist's Story"
       g. "The Landlord's Daughter's Tale--The
           Pigmy Queen: A Fairy Tale"
       h. "The Haunted Stage Box--The Tragedian's
           Story"
       i. "The Spirit Leg--The Analytical Chemist's

        Story"
j. "Lost in the Catacombs--The Antiquary's
        Story"

1156. Dryasdust, pseud. *Tales of the Wonder Club.* London: Harrison & Sons, [1899, 1900?] [not seen].

1157. Halidom, M.Y., pseud. *Tales of the Wonder Club.* Second Series. New & Rev. ed. London: Thomas Burleigh, 1904 [not seen].

1158. _____. *The Last of the Wonder Club [Tales of the Wonder Club.* Third Series].* London: Thomas Burleigh, 1905 [not seen].

JONATHON BACON AND STEVE TROYANOVICH, eds.

1159. *Omniumgathum: An Anthology of Verse by Top Authors in the Field of Fantasy.* Lamoni, IA: Stygian Isle Press, 1976 [paper].

This fan publication is the only volume of collected fantasy verse. Includes poetry by Manly Wade Wellman, A. Merritt, H.P. Lovecraft, H. Warner Munn, Hannes Bok, Mervyn Peake, Stanley Weinbaum, Andre Norton, Robert E. Howard, Michael Moorcock, Poul Anderson, Clark Ashton Smith, William Hodgson, Frank Belknap Long, Emil Petaja, August Derleth, Roger Zelazny, and Brian Lumley.

D[ONALD] R[OYNOLD] BENSON, ed.

1160. *The Unknown: 11 Stories.* New York: Pyramid Books, 1963 [paper].

a. Henry Kuttner. "The Misguided Halo"
b. Nelson S. Bond. "Prescience"
c. Theodore Sturgeon. "Yesterday Was Monday"
d. L. Sprague de Camp. "The Gnarly Man"
e. Fritz Leiber. "The Bleak Shore"
f. H.L. Gold. "Trouble with Water"
g. Malcolm Jameson. "Double and Redoubled"
h. Manly Wade Wellman. "When It Was Moonlight"
i. Robert Arthur. "Mr. Jinx"
j. Anthony Boucher. "Snulbug"
k. Frederic Brown. "Armageddon"

Stories originally published in *Unknown* and *Unknown Worlds.*

271

D[ONALD] R[OYNOLD] BENSON continued

1161. *Unknown Five*. New York: Pyramid, 1964 [paper].

    a. Isaac Asimov. "Author! Author!"
    b. Cleve Cartmill. "The Bargain"
    c. Theodore Sturgeon. "The Hag Séleen"
    d. Alfred Bester. "Hell is Forever"
    e. Jane Rice. "The Crest of the Wave"

ROBERT H. BOYER AND KENNETH J. ZAHORSKI, eds.

1162. *Dark Imaginings: A Collection of Gothic Fantasy*.
New York: Dell, 1978 [paper].

A classroom oriented anthology that treads the
fine line between horror and fantasy. It is
divided into two sections: Gothic high fantasy
and Gothic low fantasy.

    a. George MacDonald. "Cross Purposes"
    b. A. Merritt. "The Woman of the Wood"
    c. Robert E. Howard. "The Mirrors of Tuzun
        Thune"
    d. C.L. Moore. "Werewoman"
    e. Clark Ashton Smith. "The Enchantress of
        Sylaire"
    f. Fritz Leiber. "The Unholy Grail"
    g. Poul Anderson. Excerpt from *Three Hearts
        and Three Lions*.
    h. Ursula K. Le Guin. "Darkness Box"
    i. Arthur Conan Doyle. "The Brown Hand"
    j. William H. Hodgson. "The Inhabitants of
        the Middle Islet"
    k. H. Rider Haggard. "Smith and the Pharaohs"
    l. Algernon Blackwood. "The Dance of Death"
    m. H.P. Lovecraft. "The Haunter of the Dark"
    n. T.H. White. "The Troll"
    o. Ray Bradbury. "The Crowd"
    p. Peter Beagle. "Lila the Werewolf"

1163. *The Fantastic Imagination: An Anthology of High
Fantasy*. New York: Avon, 1977 [paper].

A well-conceived selection of "High Fantasy"--
fantasy dealing with cosmic issues and characters of high stature--that contains both short
stories and self-contained excerpts from novels.
Each selection is preceded by a brief biograph-
ical-bibliographical introduction.

    a. Johann Ludwig Tieck. "The Elves"
    b. Lord Dunsany. "The Sword of Welleran"
    c. George MacDonald. "The Light Princess"

ROBERT H. BOYER AND KENNETH J. ZAHORSKI continued

    d. John Buchan. "The Grove of Ashtaroth"
    e. J.B. Cabell. "The Music From Behind the
        Moon"
    f. Frank R. Stockton. "The Accommodating
        Circumstance"
    g. H.E. Bates. "The Peach Tree"
    h. Alexander Grin. "The Loquacious Goblin"
    i. J.R.R. Tolkien. "Riddles in the Dark"
        [from *The Hobbit*]
    j. C.S. Lewis. "The Magician's Book" [from
        The Voyage of the "Dawn Treader"]
    k. C.S. Lewis. "The Dufflepuds Made Happy"
        [from *The Voyage of the "Dawn Treader"*]
    l. Mark Van Doren. "The Tall One"
    m. Lloyd Alexander. "The Foundling"
    n. Peter S. Beagle. "Come Lady Death"
    o. Ursula Le Guin. "The Rule of Names" [seed
        story for *The Wizard of Earthsea*]
    p. Sylvia Townsend Warner. "Beliard"

1164. *The Fantastic Imagination II: An Anthology of High
      Fantasy.* New York: Avon, 1978 [paper].

    a. George MacDonald. "The Golden Key"
    b. Barry Pain. "The Glass of Supreme Moments"
    c. Frank R. Stockton. "Old Pipes and the
        Dryad"
    d. Lord Dunsany. "The Kith of the Elf-folk"
    e. Kenneth Morris. "Red-Peach-Blossom Inlet"
    f. Selma Lagerlöf. "The Legend of the Christ-
        mas Rose"
    g. Evangeline Walton Ensley. "Above Ker-Is"
    h. Eric Linklater. "The Abominable Imprecca-
        tion"
    i. C.L. Moore. "Jirel Meets Magic"
    j. David H. Keller. "The Thirty and One"
    k. Ursula K. Le Guin. "April in Paris"
    l. Joan Aiken. "A Harp of Fishbones"
    m. Lloyd Alexander. "The Smith, the Weaver,
        and the Harper"
    n. Patricia McKillip. [from] "The Throme of
        the Erril of Sherill"
    o. Sylvia Townsend Warner. "Elphenor and
        Weasel"
    p. Vera Chapman. "Crusader Damosel"

RAY[MOND DOUGLAS] BRADBURY, ed.

1165. *The Circus of Dr. Lao and Other Improbable Stories.*
      New York: Bantam, 1956 [paper].

    a. Charles G. Finney. "The Circus of Dr. Lao"

b. Nigel Kneale. "The Pond"
c. E.B. White. "The Hour of Letdown"
d. Roald Dahl. "The Wish"
e. Shirley Jackson. "The Summer People"
f. Nathaniel Hawthorne. "Earth's Holocaust"
g. Loren Eiseley. "Buzby's Petrified Woman"
h. Oliver LaFarge. "The Resting Place"
i. Henry Kuttner. "Threshold"
j. James H. Schmitz. "Greenface"
k. John Seymour Sharnik. "The Limits of
   Walter Horton"
l. Robert Coates. "The Man Who Vanished"

1166. *Timeless Stories from Today and Tomorrow.* New
York: Bantam Books, 1952 [paper].

a. Robert M. Coates. "The Hour After Westerly"
b. Henry Kuttner. "Housing Problem"
c. Walter Van Tilburg Clark. "The Portable
   Phonograph"
d. Sidney Carroll. "None Before Me"
e. Ludwig Bemelmans. "Putzi"
f. Shirley Jackson. "The Demon Lover"
g. Christine Noble Govan. "Miss Winters and
   the Wind"
h. Helen Eustis. "Mr. Death and the Redheaded Woman" [original title: "The Rider
   on the Pale Horse"]
i. Nigel Kneale. "Jeremy in the Wind"
j. John Kier Cross. "The Glass Eye"
k. John Steinbeck. "Saint Katy the Virgin"
l. Josephine W. Johnson. "Night Flight"
m. John B.L. Goodwin. "The Cocoon"
n. Wessel Hyatt Smitter. "The Hand"
o. Roald Dahl. "The Sound Machine"
p. J.C. Furnas. "The Laocoön Complex"
q. Christopher Isherwood. "I am Waiting"
r. William Sansom. "The Witnesses"
s. John Cheever. "The Enormous Radio"
t. Hortense Calisher. "Heartburn"
u. E.B. White. "The Supremacy of Uruguay"
v. Ray Bradbury. "The Pedestrian"
w. Sidney Carroll. "A Note for the Milkman"
x. Jean Hrolda. "The Eight Mistresses"
y. Franz Kafka. "In the Penal Colony"
z. Russell Maloney. "Inflexible Logic"

WHIT BURNETT AND MARTHA FOLEY, eds.

1167. *The Flying Yorkshireman: Novellas.* New York and

WHIT BURNETT AND MARTHA FOLEY continued

London: Harper & Brothers, 1938.

a. Eric Knight. "The Flying Yorkshireman"
b. Helen Hull. "Snow in Summer"
c. Albert Maltz. "Season of Celebration"
d. Rachel Maddux. "Turnip's Blood"
e. I.J. Kapstein. "The Song the Summer Evening Sings"

TERRY [GENE] CARR, ed.

1168. *Into the Unknown: Eleven Tales of Imagination*.
Nashville, Camden, New York: Thomas Nelson,
1973.

a. Ray Bradbury. "McGillahec's Brat"
b. Robert Silverberg. "As Is"
c. John Wyndham. "Technical Slip"
d. Vance Aandahl. "Beyond the Game"
e. Terry Carr. "Touchstone"
f. Harlan Ellison. "Are You Listening?"
g. Jorge Luis Burges. "The Lottery in Babylon"
h. Hilary Bailey. "Dogman of Islington"
i. J.G. Ballard. "The Drowned Giant"
j. Carol Carr. "Inside"
k. James E. Gunn. "The Old Folks"

1169. *New Worlds of Fantasy*. New York: Ace, 1967 [paper].

a. Roger Zelazny. "Divine Madness"
b. John Brunner. "Break the Door of Hell"
c. Jorge Luis Borges. "The Immortal"
d. R.A. Lafferty. "Narrow Valley"
e. Ray Russell. "Comet Wine"
f. Katherine MacLean. "The Other"
g. Mildred Clingerman. "A Red Heart and Blue Roses"
h. Terry Carr. "Stanley Toothbrush"
i. Thomas M. Disch. "The Squirrel Cage"
j. Peter S. Beagle. "Come Lady Death"
k. Curt Clark. "Nackles"
l. J.G. Ballard. "The Lost Leonardo"
m. Keith Roberts. "Timothy"
n. Avram Davidson. "Basilisk"
o. Alfred Gillespie. "The Evil Eye"

1170. *New Worlds of Fantasy #2*. New York: Ace, 1970
[paper].

a. Robert Sheckley. "The Petrified World"

    b. Keith Roberts. "The Scarlet Lady"
    c. Avram Davidson. "They Loved Me in Utica"
    d. Jorge Luis Borges. "The Library of Babel"
    e. B.J. Bayley. "The Ship of Disaster"
    f. Joanna Russ. "Window Dressing"
    g. Harry Harrison. "By the Falls"
    h. Kris Neville. "The Night of the Nickel Beer"
    i. David Redd. "A Quiet Kind of Madness"
    j. Roger Zelazny. "Museum Piece"
    k. Terry Carr. "The Old Man of the Mountains"
    l. Britt Schweitzer. "En Passant"
    m. Wilmar H. Shiras. "Backward, Turn Backward"
    n. Thomas M. Disch. "His Own Kind"
    o. Katherine MacLean. "Perchance to Dream"
    p. Leonid Andreyeff. "Lazarus"
    q. R.A. Lafferty. "The Ugly Sea"
    r. Robert Bloch. "The Movie People"

1171. *#3: New Worlds of Fantasy*. New York: Ace, 1971 [paper].

    a. Peter S. Beagle. "Farrell and Lila the Werewolf"
    b. R.A. Lafferty. "Adam Had Three Brothers"
    c. Avram Davidson. "Big Sam"
    d. Edgar Pangborn. "Longtooth"
    e. Fritz Leiber. "The Inner Circles"
    f. Victor Contoshi. "Von Goom's Gambit"
    g. Zenna Henderson. "Through a Glass--Darkly"
    h. Roger Zelanzy. "The Stainless Steel Leech"
    i. Terry Carr. "Sleeping Beauty"
    j. Robert Bloch. "The Plot is the Thing"
    k. Jorge Luis Borges. "Funes the Memorious"
    l. J.G. Ballard. "Say Goodbye to the Wind"
    m. William M. Lee. "A Message from Charity"

1172. *The Others*. Greenwich, CT: Fawcett, 1969 [paper].

    a. Philip K. Dick. "Roog"
    b. Daphine Du Maurier. "The Blue Lenses"
    c. Richard Matheson. "Shipshape Home"
    d. Ray Nelson. "Eight O'Clock in the Morning"
    e. R.A. Lafferty. "The Six Fingers of Time"
    f. Damon Knight. "Be My Guest"
    g. Robert A. Heinlein. "They"

1173. *Step Outside Your Mind*. London: Dennis Dobson, 1967.

    a. Roger Zelazny. "Divine Madness"

    b. John Brunner. "Break the Door of Hell"
    c. Jorge Luis Borges. "The Immortal"
    d. R.A. Lafferty. "Narrow Valley"
    e. Ray Russell. "Comet Wine"
    f. Katherine MacLean. "The Other"
    g. Mildred Clingerman. "A Red Heart and Blue
       Roses"
    h. Terry Carr. "Stanley Toothbrush"
    i. Thomas M. Disch. "The Squirrel Cage"
    j. Peter S. Beagle. "Come Lady Death"
    k. Curt Clark. "Nackles"
    l. J.G. Ballard. "The Lost Leonardo"
    m. Keith Roberts. "Timothy"
    n. Avram Davidson. "Basilisk"
    o. Alfred Gillespie. "The Evil Eye"

1174. *Year's Finest Fantasy*. New York: Berkley, 1978
    [paper].

    a. Harlan Ellison. "Jeffty is Five"
    b. Jack Vance. "The Bagful of Dreams"
    c. Stephen King. "The Cat from Hell"
    d. Steven Utley and Howard Waldrop. "Black
       as the Pit, From Pole to Pole"
    e. Woody Allen. "The Kugelmass Episode"
    f. Avram Davidson. "Manatee Gal Ain't You
       Coming Out Tonight"
    g. Raylyn Moore. "Getting Back to Before
       It Began"
    h. T. Corghessan Boyle. "Descent of Man"
    i. Julian Reid. "Probability Storm"
    j. Robert Ackerman. "Growing Boys"

LIN[WOOD VROOMAN] CARTER, ed.

1175. *Discoveries in Fantasy*. New York: Ballantine,
    1972 [paper].

    A historical anthology of neglected fantasy
    originally published from 1900 to 1931.

    a. Ernest Bramah [Smith]. "The Vision of Yin"
    b. Ernest Bramah [Smith]. "The Dragon of
       Chang Tao"
    c. Richard Garnett. "The Poet of Panopolis"
    d. Richard Garnett. "The City of Philosophers"
    e. Donald Corley. "The Bird with the Golden
       Beak"
    f. Donald Corley. "The Song of the Tombe-
       laine"
    g. Eden Phillpotts. "The Miniature"

1176. *Dragons, Elves, and Heroes*. New York: Ballantine, 1969 [paper].

Excerpts from the following epics, sagas, and romances, except as noted:

a. *Beowulf*
b. *The Volsunga Saga*
c. *The Mabinogion*
d. Rudyard Kipling. "Puck's Song"
e. *The Grettir Saga*
f. *The Poems of Ossian*
g. *Le Morte d'Arthur*
h. *Tom O'Bedlam's Song*
i. *The Kiev Cycle*
j. *The Kalevala*
k. *Maundervile's Travels*
l. William Shakespeare. *The Tempest*
m. Edmund Spenser. *The Faerie Queene*
n. *The Gesta Romanorum*
o. *Palmerin of England*
p. *The Shah-Namah*
q. Robert Browning. "Child Roland to the Dark Tower Came"
r. Voltaire. *The Romances*
s. Alfred Lord Tennyson. "The Horns of Elfland"

1177. *Flashing Swords! #1*. Garden City, NY: Nelson Doubleday [Science Fiction Book Club], 1973.

This series contains stories written by an informal collection of writers known as The Swordsmen and Sorcerers' Guild of America, "S.A.G.A." While Andrew Offutt's *Swords Against Darkness* series contains more sword and sorcery tales, these volumes contain more quality.

a. Fritz Leiber. "The Sadness of the Executioner"
b. Jack Vance. "Morreion"
c. Poul Anderson. "The Merman's Children"
d. Lin Carter. "The Higher Heresies of Oolimar"

1178. *Flashing Swords! #2*. Garden City, NY: Nelson Doubleday [Science Fiction Book Club], 1973.

a. L. Sprague de Camp. "The Rug and the Bull"
b. Michael Moorcock. "The Jade Man's Eyes"
c. Andre Norton. "The Toads of Grimmerdale"
d. John Jakes. "Ghoul's Garden"

LIN[WOOD VROOMAN] CARTER continued

1179. *Flashing Swords! #3: Warriors and Wizards.* New
York: Dell, 1976 [paper].

    a. L. Sprague de Camp. "Two Yards of Dragon"
    b. Andre Norton. "Spider Silk"
    c. Fritz Leiber. "The Frost Monstreme"
    d. Lin Carter. "The Curious Custom of the
       Turjan Seraad"
    e. Avram Davidson. "Caravan to Illiel"

1180. *Flashing Swords! #4: Barbarians and Black Magicians.*
New York: Dell, 1977 [paper].

    a. Jack Vance. "The Bagful of Dreams"
    b. Poul Anderson. "The Tupilak"
    c. John Jakes. "Storm in a Bottle"
    d. Katherine Kurtz. "Swords Against the
       Marluk"
    e. Michael Moorcock. "The Lands Beyond the
       World"

1181. *Great Short Novels of Adult Fantasy.* Vol. I.
New York: Ballantine, 1972 [paper].

    a. Fletcher Pratt and L. Sprague de Camp.
       "Wall of Serpents" [see de Camp and
       Pratt, *The Incomplete Enchanter,* above]
    b. Anatole France. "The Kingdom of the Dwarfs"
    c. Robert W. Chambers. "The Maker of Moons"
    d. William Morris. "The Hollow Land"

1182. *Great Short Novels of Adult Fantasy.* Vol. II.
New York: Ballantine, 1973 [paper].

Four novellas published from 1858 to 1923.

    a. George MacDonald. "The Woman in the
       Mirror"
    b. Robert W. Chambers. "The Repairer of
       Reputations" [from *The King in Yellow*]
    c. Ernest Bramah Smith. "The Transmutation
       of Ling"
    d. Eden Phillpotts. "The Lavender Dragon"

1183. *Kingdoms of Sorcery.* Garden City, NY: Doubleday,
1976.

The Forerunners of Fantasy

    a. Voltaire. "The History of Babouc the
       Scythian"
    b. William Beckford. "The Palace of Subter-
       ranean Fire"

c.   George MacDonald. "The Witch Woman"

Fantasy as Saga

d.   William Morris. "The Folla of the Mountain
     Door"
e.   E.R. Eddison. "A Night-Piece of Ambre-
     merine." [from *Mistress of Mistresses*]
f.   Fletcher Pratt. "Dr. Meliboë the Enchanter"
     [from *The Well of the Unicorn*]
g.   Fritz Leiber. "The Two Best Thieves in
     Lankhmar" [from *Swords Against Wizardry*]

Fantasy as Parable

h.   Edgar Allan Poe. "Shadow and Silence"
i.   Clark Ashton Smith. "Fables from the Edge
     of Night"
j.   Robert H. Barlow. "The Tomb of the God"

Fantasy as Anecdote

k.   T.H. White. "Merlyn vs. Madame Mim" [from
     The Once and Future King]
l.   L. Sprague de Camp. "The Owl and the Ape"
m.   Lin Carter. "The Twelve Wizards of Ung"

Fantasy as Epic

n.   C.S. Lewis. "Deep Magic from the Dawn of
     Time" [from *The Lion, the Witch, and
     the Wardrobe*]
o.   J.R.R. Tolkien. "The Bridge of Khazad-
     Dum" [from *The Fellowship of the Ring*]
p.   Richard Adams. "The Story of the Blessing
     of El-Ahraihad" [from *Watership Down*]

1184.   *The Magic of Atlantis*. New York: Lancer, 1970
        [paper].

A group of short stories that focuses on the
many wonders of Atlantis as it lived and died.

a.   Robert E. Howard. "The Mirrors of Tuzun
     Thune"
b.   Henry Kuttner. "The Spawn of Dagon"
c.   L. Sprague de Camp. "The Eye of Tandyla"
d.   Lin Carter. "The Seal of Zoan Sathla"
e.   Edmond Hamilton. "The Vengeance of Ulios"
f.   Clark Ashton Smith. "The Death of Malygris"
g.   Nictzin Dyalhis. "The Heart of Atlantan"

1185. *New Worlds for Old*. New York: Ballantine, 1971
[paper].

A gathering of late nineteenth and twentieth-
century makers of imaginary worlds.

a. William Beckford. "Zulkais and Kalilah"
b. Edgar Allan Poe. "Silence: A Fable"
c. George MacDonald. "The Romance of Photo-
gen and Nycteris"
d. Oscar Wilde. "The Sphinx"
e. Lord Dunsany. "The Fall of Babbulkund"
f. H.P. Lovecraft. "The Green Meadow"
g. Gary Myers. "The Feast in the House of
the Worm"
h. Lin Carter. "Zingazar"
i. George Sterling. "A Wine of Wizardry"
j. Robert E. Howard. "The Garden of Fear"
k. C.L. Moore. "Jirel Meets Magic"
l. Clifford Ball. "Duar the Accursed"
m. Clark Ashton Smith. "The Hashish-Eater"
n. Mervyn Peake. "The Party at Lady Cusp-
Canine's"
o. Lin Carter. "The Sword of Power"

1186. *Realms of Wizardry*. Garden City, NY: Doubleday,
1976.

Fantasy as Legend

a. Lord Dunsany. "The Hoard of the Gibbelins"
b. H.P. Lovecraft. "The Doom that Came to
Sarnath"
c. Robert Bloch. "Black Lotus"
d. Gary Myers. "The Gods of Earth"

Fantasy as Satire

e. Richard Garnett. "The City of Philosophers"
f. James Branch Cabell. "Some Ladies and
Jurgen"
g. Donald Corley. "The Book of Lullume"

Fantasy as Romance

h. H. Rider Haggard. "The Descent Beneath
Kor"
i. A. Merritt. "The Whelming of Cherkis"
[from *The Metal Monster*]
j. Hannes Bok. "How Orcher Broke the Koph"
[from *The Sorcerer's Ship*]

Fantasy as Adventure Story

k. Robert E. Howard. "Swords of the Purple
        Kingdom" [from *King Kull*]
l. Clifford Ball. "The Goddess Awakes"
m. C.L. Moore and Henry Kuttner. "Quest of
        the Starstone"

New Directions in Fantasy

n. Jack Vance. "Liane the Wayfarer" [from
        The Dying Earth]
o. Michael Moorcock. "Master of Chaos"
p. Roger Zelazny. "Thelinde's Song"

1187. *The Year's Best Fantasy Stories*. New York: DAW,
        1975 [paper].

An annual series with a sword and sorcery emphasis; readers should be cautioned that the selections only partially represent a selection of
the "year's best." A number of the stories in
each volume are specially commissioned and have
not appeared elsewhere. Each volume contains
an appendix surveying the year's best fantasy.

a. Marion Zimmer Bradley. "The Jewel of
        Arwen"
b. Lloyd Alexander. "The Sword Dyrnwyn"
c. Robert E. Howard. "The Temple of Abomina-
        tion"
d. Clark Ashton Smith. "The Double Tower"
e. Fritz Leiber. "Trapped in the Shadowland"
f. Lin Carter. "Black Hawk of Valkarth"
g. Hannes Bok. "Jewel Quest"
h. L. Sprague de Camp. "The Emperor's Fan"
i. Pat McIntosh. "Falcon's Mate"
j. Charles R. Saunders. "The City of Madness"
k. Jack Vance. "The Seventeen Virgins"

1188. *The Year's Best Fantasy Stories: 2*. New York:
        DAW, 1977 [paper].

a. Tanith Lee. "The Demoness"
b. Thomas Burnett Swann. "The Night of the
        Unicorn"
c. Pat McIntosh. "Cry Wolf"
d. Fritz Leiber. "Under the Thumbs of the
        Gods"
e. Paul Spencer. "The Guardian of the Vault"
f. L. Sprague de Camp. "The Lamp from
        Atlantis"

g. Gary Myers. "Xiurhn"
h. Lin Carter. "The City in the Jewel"
i. Walter C. DeBill, Jr. "In 'Ygiroth"
j. Clark Ashton Smith and Lin Carter. "The
   Scroll of Morloc"
k. C.A. Cador. "Payment in Kind"
l. Avram Davidson. "Milord Sir Smiht, the
   English Wizard"

1189. *The Year's Best Fantasy Stories: 3.* New York: DAW,
1977 [paper].

a. L. Sprague de Camp. "Eudoric's Unicorn"
b. Gardner F. Fox. "Shadow of a Demon"
c. Pat McIntosh. "Ring of Black Stone"
d. George R.R. Martin. "The Lonely Songs of
   Laren Dorr"
e. Karl Edward Wagner. "Two Suns Setting"
f. Clark Ashton Smith. "The Stairs in the
   Crypt"
g. Raul Garcia Capella. "The Goblin Blade"
h. C.J. Cherryh. "The Dark King"
i. Lin Carter. "Black Moonlight"
j. Gary Myers. "The Snout in the Alcove"
k. George R. Saunders. "The Pool of the Moon"

1190. *The Year's Best Fantasy Stories: 4.* New York:
DAW, 1978 [paper].

a. Poul Anderson. "The Tale of Hauk"
b. Grail Undwin [pseud.?]. "A Farmer on the
   Clyde"
c. Clark Ashton Smith. "Prince Alcouz and
   the Magician"
d. Robert E. Howard and Andrew J. Offutt.
   "Nekht Semerkeht"
e. Lin Carter. "The Pillars of Hell"
f. Philip Coakley. "Lok the Depressor"
g. Avram Davidson. "Hark! Was That the
   Squeal of an Angry Thoat?"
h. Pat McIntosh. "The Cloak of Dreams"
i. Phyllis Eisenstein. "The Land of Sorrow"
j. Tanith Lee. "Odds Against the Gods"
k. Ramsey Campbell. "The Changer of Names"

1191. *The Young Magicians.* New York: Ballantine, 1969
[paper].

An excellent representation of contemporary
heroic fantasy writers.

a. William Morris. "Rapunzel"

    b. Lord Dunsany. "The Sword of Welleran"
    c. E.R. Eddison. "In Valhalla"
    d. James Branch Cabell. "The Way of Ecben"
    e. H.P. Lovecraft. "The Quest of Iranon"
    f. H.P. Lovecraft. "The Cats of Ulthar"
    g. Clark Ashton Smith. "The Maze of Maal
        Dweb"
    h. Lin Carter. "The Whelming of Oom"
    i. Lin Carter. "Azlon"
    j. A. Merritt. "Through the Dragon Glass"
    k. Robert E. Howard. "The Valley of the
        Worm"
    l. L. Sprague de Camp. "Heldendammerung"
    m. L. Sprague de Camp. "Ka the Appalling"
    n. Jack Vance. "Turjan of Miir" [from *The
        Dying Earth*, see above)
    o. J.R.R. Tolkien. "Once Upon a Time"
    p. J.R.R. Tolkien. "The Dragon's Visit"
    q. C.S. Lewis. "Narnian Suite"

M.L. CARTER, ed.

1192. *Demon Lovers and Strange Seductions*. Greenwich,
     CT: Fawcett, 1972 [paper].

    a. J. Sheridan LeFanu. "Ultor de Lacy"
    b. Arthur Machen. "The Great God Pan"
    c. Marion Z[immer] Bradley. "The Wind People"
    d. Jerome Bixby. "Can Such Beauty Be?"
    e. Algernon Blackwood. "The Glamour of the
        Snow"
    f. Robert Hichens. "How Love Came to Pro-
        fessor Guildea"
    g. Robert Bloch. "The Thinking Cap"
    h. Fredric Brown. "Too Far"
    i. Winston Marks. "The Naked People"
    j. Theodore Sturgeon. "A Touch of Strange"

JOHNATHAN COTT, ed.

1193. *Beyond the Looking Glass: Extraordinary Works of
     Fantasy and Fairy Tale* [from the Nineteenth
     Century]. New York: Stonehill, 1973.

    a. Leslie Fiedler. "Introduction"
    b. John Ruskin. "The King of the Golden
        River or The Black Brothers"
    c. Tom Hood. "Petsetilla's Posy"
    d. Mrs. Clifford. "Wooden Toby: An Anyhow
        Story"
    e. Mary de Morgan. "Through the Fire"

JOHNATHAN COTT continued

    f.   Mary de Morgan. "The Wanderings of Aras-
         mon"
    g.   Maggie Brown. "Wanted--A King"
    h.   Mark Lemon. "Tinykin's Transformations"
    i.   George MacDonald. "The Golden Key"
    j.   George MacDonald. "The Day Boy and the
         Night Girl"
    k.   Christina Rossetti. "Goblin Market"

[WILLIAM L. CRAWFORD, ed.]

1194. *The Garden of Fear and Other Stories of the Bizarre and Fantastic.* Los Angeles, CA: Crawford, 1945 [paper].

    a.   Robert E. Howard. "The Garden of Fear"
    b.   L.A. Eshbach. "The Man with the Hour
         Glass"
    c.   H.P. Lovecraft. "Celephais"
    d.   Miles J. Breuer. "Mars Colonizes"
    e.   David H. Keller. "The Golden Bough"

L[YON] SPRAGUE DE CAMP, ed.

1195. *The Fantastic Swordsmen.* New York: Pyramid, 1967
[paper].

    a.   Robert Bloch. "Black Lotus"
    b.   Lord Dunsany. "The Fortress Unvanquishable
         Save for Sacnoth"
    c.   Robert E. Howard and L. Sprague de Camp.
         "Drums of Tombalku"
    d.   John Jakes. "The Girl in the Gem"
    e.   Henry Kuttner. "Dragon Moon"
    f.   H.P. Lovecraft. "The Other Gods"
    g.   Michael Moorcock. "The Singing Citadel"
    h.   Luigi de Poscailis. "The Tower"

1196. *The Spell of Seven: Stories of Heroic Fantasy.*
New York: Pyramid, 1965 [paper].

    a.   Fritz Leiber. "Bazaar of the Bizarre"
    b.   Clark Ashton Smith. "The Dark Eidolon"
    c.   Lord Dunsany. "The Hoard of the Gibbelins"
    d.   L. Sprague de Camp. "The Hungry Hercynian"
    e.   Michael Moorcock. "Kings in Darkness"
    f.   Jack Vance. "Mazirian the Magician" [from
         The Dying Earth]
    g.   Robert E. Howard. "Shadows in Zamboula"

1197. *Swords and Sorcery: Stories of Heroic Fantasy.*
New York: Pyramid, 1963 [paper].

a. Poul Anderson. "The Valor of Cappen Varra"
b. Lord Dunsany. "Distressing Tale of Thango-
brind the Jeweller"
c. Robert E. Howard. "Shadows in the Moonlight"
d. Henry Kuttner. "The Citadel of Darkness"
e. Fritz Leiber. "When the Sea King's Away"
f. H.P. Lovecraft. "The Doom That Came to
Sarnath"
g. C.L. Moore. "Hellsgarde"
h. Clark Ashton Smith. "The Testament of
Athammaus"

1198. *Warlocks and Warriors.* New York: G.P. Putnam's
Sons, 1970.

a. Ray Capella. "Turutal"
b. Lin Carter. "The Gods of Niom Parma"
c. Robert E. Howard. "The Hills of the Dead"
d. Henry Kuttner. "Thunder in the Dawn"
e. Fritz Leiber. "Thieves' House"
f. C.L. Moore. "Black God's Kiss"
g. Lord Dunsany. "Chu-bu and Sheemish"
h. Clark Ashton Smith. "The Master of the
Crabs"
i. H.G. Wells. "The Valley of Spiders"
j. Roger Zelazny. "The Bells of Shoredan"

THOMAS M[ICHAEL] DISCH AND CHARLES NAYLOR, eds.

1199. *Strangeness: A Collection of Curious Tales.* New
York: Charles Scribner's Sons, 1977.

a. Shirley Jackson. "The Beautiful Stranger"
b. Virginia Woolf. "Solid Objects"
c. Brian Aldiss. "Where the Lines Converge"
d. Italo Calvino. "All at One Point"
e. Sarah Orne Jewett. "The Waiting Place"
f. Philip José Farmer. "Sketches Among the
Ruins of My Mind"
g. Joan Aiken. "Elephant's Ear"
h. Joyce Carol Oates. "Bodies"
i. M. John Harrison. "Running Down"
j. Thomas M. Disch. "The Roaches"
k. Russell Fitzgerald. "The Last Supper"
l. William Sansom. "Among the Dahlias"
m. Pamela Zoline. "The Holland of the Mind"
n. John Sladek. "Elephant with Wooden Leg"

    o.   Thomas Mann. "The Wardrobe"

GEORGE ERNSBERGER, ed.
See DONALD A[LLEN] WOLLHEIM AND GEORGE ERNSBERGER, eds.

EDMUND J. FARRELL, THOMAS E. GAGE, JOHN
PFORDRESHER, AND RAYMOND J. RODRIGUES, eds.

1200. *Fantasy: Shapes of Things Unknown*. Glenview, IL:
Scott, Foresman, 1974 [paper].

    a. John Collier. "Thus I Refute Beelzy"
    b. J.C. Furnas. "The Laocoön Complex"
    c. Daphne du Maurier. "The Blue Lense"
    d. Mary Chase. "Harvey"
    e. E.F. Benson. "Mrs. Amworth"
    f. Saki, pseud. [H.H. Munro]. "Gabriel-
        Ernest"
    g. Manly Wade Wellman. "Oh Ugly Bird"
    h. A.M. Burrage. "The Green Scarf"
    i. Richard Matheson. "Born of Man and Woman"
    j. George Langelaan. "The Fly"
    k. Theodore Sturgeon. "Talent"
    l. Hortense Calisher. "Heartburn"
    m. Jack Conroy. "The High Divers"
    n. Phil Squires. "Pecos Bill"
    o. Whitfield Cook. "The Portable Mrs.
        Tillson"
    p. H.L. Gold. "The Man with English"
    q. Charles Beaumont. "Free Dirt"
    r. John Collier. "The Chaser"
    s. Edgar Allan Poe. "The Masque of the Red
        Death"
    t. Richard Matheson. "Prey"
    u. Vladimir Grigoriev. "The Horn of Plenty"
    v. H.G. Wells. "The Magic Shop"

JULIUS FAST, ed.

1201. *Out of this World: An Anthology*. New York: Penguin Books, 1944 [paper].

    a. John Collier. "Evening Primrose"
    b. Saki [H.H. Munro]. "Laura"
    c. Eric Knight. "Sam Small's Tyke"
    d. Robert Arthur. "Satan and Sam Shay"
    e. John Kendrick Bangs. "A Disputed Author-
        ship"
    f. Nelson S. Bond. "Mr. Mergenthwirker's

JULIUS FAST continued

          Lobblies"
    g. H.G. Wells. "A Vision of Judgment"
    h. John Collier. "Thus I Refute Beelzy"
    i. Stephen Vincent Benét. "The King of Cats"
    j. Oscar Wilde. "The Canterville Ghost"
    k. Julius Fast. "My Friend Merton"
    l. Arch Oboler. "And Adam Begot"
    m. Lord Dunsany. "The Club Secretary"
    n. Jack London. "The Scarlet Plague"

MARJORIE FISCHER AND ROLFE HUMPHRIES, eds.

1202. *Pause to Wonder: Stories of the Marvelous, Myster-
       ious, and Strange.* New York: Julian Messner,
       1944.

    a. Ralph Hodgson. "Reason"
    b. Virginia Woolf. "A Haunted House"
    c. Frank R. Stockton. "The Philosophy of
        Relative Existences"
    d. Liam O'Flaherty. "Birth"
    e. F. Scott Fitzgerald. "The Curious Case
        of Benjamin Button"
    f. Irwin Shapiro. "Strong But Quirky"
    g. Frank O'Conner. "The Man Who Stopped"
    h. William Butler Yeats. "A Man and His
        Boots"
    i. Walter de la Mare. "Off the Ground"
    j. John Buchan. "The Rime of True Thomas"
    k. Ralph Bates. "The Haunted Man"
    l. Ambrose Bierce. "A Horseman in the Sky"
    m. Arthur Machen. "The Bowman"
    n. Livy. "Before the Battle at Lake Trasi-
        menus"
    o. William March. "Private Martin Passy"
    p. Ernest Rhys. "Ballad of the Buried Sword"
    q. G[ilbert] K[eith] Chesterton. "The Perfect
        Game"
    r. Oscar Wilde. "The Canterville Ghost"
    s. W.W. Jacobs. "The Rival Beauties"
    t. Edward Lear. "The Dong with the Luminous
        Nose"
    u. Pliny. "A Haunted House"
    v. Frank R. Stockton. "The Transferred Ghost"
    w. Charles Erskine Scott Wood. "A Beautiful
        Maiden"
    x. Ambrose Bierce. "An Imperfect Conflagra-
        tion"
    y. Henry Yelvington. "The Phantom Fence Rider
        of San Miguel"
    z. Roy Helton. "Old Christmas"

aa. Henry James. "The Real Right Thing"
bb. Finley Peter Dunne. "The Quick and the
    Dead"
cc. David Garnett. "Lady Into Fox"
dd. J[ohn] M[illington] Synge. "Charley
    Lambert"
ee. Washington Irving. "The Bold Dragoon"
ff. Wilfrid Wilson Gibson. "The Vixen"
gg. Anon. "A Blazing Starre Seene in the
    West"
hh. D.H. Lawrence. "The Last Laugh"
ii. Geoffrey Household. "Dionysus and the Pard"
jj. Ovid. "Story of Pygmalion"
kk. John Collier. "The Chaser"
ll. Herodotus. "King Cheops' Daughter"
mm. Sylvia Townsend Warner. "Nelly Trim"
nn. E.M. Forster. "The Story of the Siren"
oo. James Thurber. "The Unicorn in the Garden"
pp. Charles Erskine Scott Wood. "Mount Shasta"
qq. W.B. Yeats. "The Wisdom of the King"
rr. Virgil. "Orpheus and Eurydice"
ss. Cotton Mather. "A True Account"
tt. Robert Frost. "The Witch of Coös"
uu. Mark Twain. "Extract from Captain Storm-
    field's Visit to Heaven"
vv. Alfred Henry Lewis. "Colonel Sterett
    Relates Marvels"
ww. Lucian. "A True Story"
xx. T.S. Eliot. "Macavity: The Mystery Cat"
yy. William March. "Private Roger Jones"
zz. Sergeant Bill Davidson. "Tall Tales of
    the G.I.s"
aaa. Julius Caesar. "The Elks"
bbb. Ludwig Bemelmans. "Sacre du Printemps"
ccc. John Steinbeck. "The Elf in Algiers"
ddd. Donald Cowie. "Lord Deliver Us"
eee. Winifred Holtby. "The Voice of God"
fff. W. Somerset Maugham. "The Judgment Seat"
ggg. Christina Stead. "The Sensitive Goldfish"
hhh. Orson Welles. "Panic"
iii. H.H. Munro ["Saki"]. "The Soul of
    Laploshka"
jjj. Ludwig Bemelmans. "'No Trouble At All'"
kkk. Robert Graves. "Welsh Incident"
lll. G.K. Chesterton. "The Angry Street: A
    Bad Dream"
mmm. Heywood Broun. "Artist Unknown"
nnn. Anon. "A Miracle of St. Scothinus"
ooo. Antonia White. "The Saint"
ppp. Osbert Sitwell. "The Silence of God"
qqq. Anon. "A Miracle of St. Goar"
rrr. J.M. Synge. "Building the Church"
sss. William March. "Private Edward Romano"

MARJORIE FISCHER AND ROLFE HUMPHRIES continued

    ttt. Lady Gregory. "Blessed Patrick of the
         Bells"
    uuu. Bede. "How Caedmon Learned to Sing"
    vvv. Samuel Lover. "King O'Toole and St. Kevin"
    www. H.G. Wells. "The Man Who Could Work Mira-
         cles"
    xxx. Elizabeth Goudge. "A Shepherd and A Shep-
         herdess"
    yyy. Max Beerbohm. "The Case of Prometheus"
    zzz. E.M. Forster. "The Road from Colonus"
    aaaa. John Bunyan. "Mr. Valiant Summoned"
    bbbb. Ovid. "Philemon and Baucis"
    cccc. Liam O'Flaherty. "The Fairy Goose"
    dddd. John Masefield. "The Passing Strange"

BARTHOLD FLES, comp.

1203. *The Saturday Evening Post Fantasy Stories*. New
    York: Avon, 1951 [paper].

    a. D.V. Gallery, Rear Admiral, USN. "The
       Enemy Planet"
    b. Grace Amundson. "The Child Who Believed"
    c. Noel Langley. "Scene for Satan"
    d. Will F. Jenkins. "Doomsday Deferred"
    e. Willard Temple. "The Eternal Duffer"
    f. Gerald Kersh. "Note on Danger B"
    g. Paul Gallico. "The Terrible Answer"
    h. Wilbur Schramm. "The Voice in the Ear-
       phones"
    i. Conrad Richter. "Doctor Hanray's Second
       Chance"

GARRETT FORD, ed.

1204. *Science and Sorcery*. Los Angeles: Fantasy Publish-
    ing, [1953] [not seen]. Rpt. New York: Zebra,
    1978 [paper].

    a. Cordwainer Smith, pseud. [Paul M.A. Line-
       barger]. "Scanners Live in Vain"
    b. Isaac Asimov and Frederick Pohl. "The
       Little Man on the Subway"
    c. Alfred Coppel, Jr. "What Goes Up"
    d. Ed Earl Repp. "Kleon of the Golden Sun"
    e. Leo Page. "How High on the Ladder?"
    f. Robert Ernest Gilbert. "Footprints"
    g. Ray Bradbury. "The Naming of Names"
    h. Henry Hasse. "The Eyes"
    i. Stanton A. Coblentz. "The Scarlet Lunes"

    j.   George R. Cowie. "Demobilization"
    k.   John Martin Leahy. "Voices From the Cliff"
    l.   Sam Moskowitz. "The Lost Chord"
    m.   R.H. Deutsch. "The Watchers"
    n.   J.T. Oliver. "The Peaceful Martian"
    o.   Arthur J. Burks. "Escape to Yesterday"

THOMAS E. GAGE, ed. See EDMUND J. FARRELL, et al., eds.

VIC GHIDALIA, ed.

1205. *The Devil's Generation*. New York: Lancer, 1973
    [paper].

    a.   Ray Bradbury. "Black Ferris"
    b.   Henry Kuttner. "Call Him Demon"
    c.   Richard Matheson. "Mother By Protest"
    d.   Robert Bloch. "Floral Tribute"
    e.   August Derleth. "The Place in the Woods"
    f.   Robert Silverberg. "Hole in the Air"
    g.   Anthony Boucher. "Mr. Lupescu"
    h.   Clifford D. Simak. "Day of Truce"
    i.   Algernon Blackwood. "The Other Wing"

1206. *Wizards and Warlocks*. New York: Manor, 1972
    [paper].

    a.   Robert Bloch. "The Secret of Sebek"
    b.   Mark Schorer and August Derleth. "The
        Left Wing"
    c.   Clark Ashton Smith. "The Necromantic
        Tale"
    d.   L. Ron Hubbard. "Battle of Wizards"
    e.   Nathaniel Hawthorne. "Young Goodman
        Brown"
    f.   M.R. James. "Casting the Runes"
    g.   Richard Marsh. "The Disappearance of Mrs.
        Macrecham"
    h.   Bruce Elliott. "So Sweet as Magic . . ."
    i.   E. Hoffman Price. "Apprentice Magician"

[DONALD M. GRANT, ed.]

1207. *Swordsmen and Supermen*. New York: Centaur, 1972
    [paper].

An outstanding group of five new and reprinted
examples of sword and sorcery fantasy. The
Crombie tale, concerning a questing shape-

[DONALD M. GRANT] continued

     changer, is a particular treat.

     a.   Robert E. Howard. "Meet Cap'n Kidd"
     b.   Jean D'Esme. "The Death of a Hero"
     c.   Darrel Crombie. "Wings of Y'vrn"
     d.   Arthur D. Howden Smith. "The Slave of
          Marathon"
     e.   Lin Carter. "How Sargoth Lay Siege to
          Zaremm"

     PETER HAINING, comp.

1208. *Weird Tales: A Facsimile of the World's Most
      Famous Fantasy Magazine.* Jersey, [London]:
      Neville Spearman, 1976.

     a.   Edmond Hamilton. "The Man Who Returned"
     b.   Robert E. Howard. "Black Hound of Death"
     c.   August W. Derleth. "The Shuttered House"
     d.   Seabury Quinn. "Frozen Beauty"
     e.   H.P. Lovecraft. "Beyond the Wall of Sleep"
     f.   Clark Ashton Smith. "The Garden of
          Adompha"
     g.   Virgil Finlay. "The Horns of Elfland"
     h.   Henry Kuttner. "Beyond the Phoenix"
     i.   G.G. Pendarves. "The Black Monk"
     j.   Henry S. Whitehead. "The Passing of a
          God"
     k.   Reader's Letters (1939). "The Eyrie"
     l.   Manly Wade Wellman. "The Valley Was Still"
     m.   Anon. "True Psychic Experiences: It Hap-
          pened to Me"
     n.   Nictzin Dyalhis. "Heart of Atlantan"
     o.   Anon. "Calling All Fantasy Fans"
     p.   Fritz Leiber. "The Phantom Slayer"
     q.   Anon. "Weird Tales Club"
     r.   Robert Bloch. "The Beasts of Barsac"
     s.   Ray Bradbury. "Bang! You're Dead!"
     t.   Anon. "Stay Tuned for Terror"
     u.   Reader's Letters (1954). "The Eyrie"
     v.   Theodore Sturgeon. "Cellmate"
     w.   H.P. Lovecraft. "The Familiars"
     x.   Algernon Blackwood. "Roman Remains"
     y.   Eric Frank Russell. "Displaced Person"
     z.   H. Russell Wakefield. "From the Vasty
          Deep"
     aa. Mary Elizabeth Counselman. "The Shot
          Tower Ghost"
     bb. Alison V. Harding. "Take the Z-Train"
     cc. Lee Brown Coye. "Weirdisms"
     dd. Margaret St. Clair. "The Little Red Owl"
     ee. Anthony M. Rud. "Ooze"

GEORGE HAY, ed.

1209. *Hell Hath Fury: An "Unknown" Anthology*. London:
Neville Spearman, 1963.

a. Cleve Cartmill. "Hell Hath Fury"
b. Fritz Leiber, Jr. "The Bleak Shore"
c. P. Schuyler Miller. "The Frog"
d. Jane Rice. "The Refugee"
e. L. Ron Hubbard. "The Devil's Rescue"
f. Robert Bloch. "The Cloak"
g. A.M. Phillips. "The Extra Bricklayer"

ROBERT HOSKINS, ed.

1210. *Swords Against Tomorrow*. Toronto: Signet, 1970
[paper].

a. Poul Anderson. "Demon Journey" [original
title: "Witch of the Demon Seas"]
b. Fritz Leiber. "Bazaar of the Bizarre"
c. Lin Carter. "Vault of Silence"
d. John Jakes. "Devils in the Walls"
e. Leigh Brackett. "Citadel of Lost Ships"

ROLFE HUMPHRIES, ed.
See MARJORIE FISCHER AND ROLFE HUMPHRIES, eds.

MARVIN KAYE, ed.

1211. *Fiends and Creatures*. New York: Popular Library,
1975 [paper].

a. Robert Bloch. "Enoch"
b. Donald A. Wollheim. "Babylon: 70 M."
c. John Kendrick Bangs. "A Midnight Visitor"
d. Tennessee Williams. "The Vengeance of
Nitocris"
e. Lord Dunsany. "The Three Infernal Jokes"
f. M.R. James. "An Episode of Cathedral
History"
g. Eugene D. Goodwin. "Damned Funny"
h. Ray Bradbury. "Interim"
i. La Motte Fouqué. "The Bottle Imp"
j. Richard Matheson. "Cresendo"
k. Fritz Leiber, Jr. "In the X-Ray"
l. Charles Baudelaire. "The Generous Gambler"
m. Charles Dickens. "Captain Murderer"
n. Ivan Turgenev. "Bubnoff and the Devil"
o. Dick Baldwin. "The Shadow Watchers"
p. Edward D. Hoch. "The Faceless Thing"

PHILIP J. KLASS, ed.

1212. Tenn, William, pseud., ed. *Children of Wonder*.
New York: Simon & Schuster, 1953 [not seen].
Rpt. as *Outsiders: Children of Wonder*. *21 Re-
markable and Fantastic Tales*. Garden City, NY:
Permabooks [Doubleday], 1954 [paper].

    a.   D.H. Lawrence. "The Rocking Horse Winner"
    b.   C.M. Kornbluth. "The Words of Guru"
    c.   Theodore Sturgeon. "Baby is Three"
    d.   Ray Bradbury. "Small Assassin"
    e.   E.M. Forster. "The Story of a Panic"
    f.   Lewis Padgett. "The Piper's Son"
    g.   Truman Capote. "Miriam"
    h.   A.E. Coppard. "Adam and Eve and Pinch Me"
    i.   Mary-Alice Schnirring. "Child's Play"
    j.   Saki, pseud. [H.H. Munro]. "The Open
        Window"
    k.   Grahame Grene. "The End of the Party"
    l.   Jane Rice. "The Idol of the Flies"
    m.   Judith Merril. "That Only a Mother"
    n.   Richard Matheson. "Born of Man and Woman"
    o.   Murray Leinster. "Keyhole"
    p.   Poul Anderson. "Terminal Quest"
    q.   Katherine MacLean. "The Origin of the
        Species"
    r.   Wilmar H. Shires. "In Hiding" [from *Chil-
        dren of the Atom*]
    s.   Aldous Huxley. "The Hatchery" [from *Brave
        New World*]
    t.   William Tenn, pseud. [Philip J. Klass].
        "Errand Boy"
    u.   Stephen Vincent Benét. "Nightmare for
        Future Reference: A Narrative Poem"

DAMON KNIGHT, ed.

1213. *The Dark Side*. Garden City, NY: Doubleday [Science
Fiction Book Club], 1965.

Selections stress the gothic element of heroic
fantasy.

    a.   Ray Bradbury. "The Black Ferris"
    b.   Robert A. Heinlein. "They"
    c.   James Blish. "Mistake Inside"
    d.   H.L. Gold. "Trouble with Water"
    e.   Peter Phillips. "C/O Mr. Makepeace"
    f.   Avram Davidson. "The Golem"
    g.   H.G. Wells. "The Story of the Late Mr.
        Elvesham"
    h.   Theodore Sturgeon. "It"

    i.   Anthony Boucher. "Nellthu"
    j.   Richard McKenna. "Casey Agonistes"
    k.   T.L. Sherred. "Eye for Iniquity"
    l.   Fritz Leiber. "The Man Who Never Grew Young"

1214. *The Golden Road: Great Tales of Fantasy and the Supernatural.* New York: Simon and Schuster, 1973.

    a.   John Collier. "Are You Too Late or Was I Too Early"
    b.   R.A. Lafferty. "Entire and Perfect Chrysolite"
    c.   Kate Wilhelm. "Jenny with Wings"
    d.   H.G. Wells. "The Truth About Pyecraft"
    e.   C.M. Kornbluth. "The Words of Guru"
    f.   Robert Arthur. "Postpaid to Paradise"
    g.   Arthur Machen. "The White People"
    h.   Mark Twain. "Extract from Captain Stormfield's Visit to Heaven"
    i.   Alfred Bester. "Will You Wait?"
    j.   Stephen Vincent Benét. "The King of Cats"
    k.   Ursula K. Le Guin. "The Word of Unbinding"
    l.   Robert A. Heinlein. "Magic, Inc."
    m.   Zenna Henderson. "Anything Box"
    n.   Heywood Broun. "Artist Unknown"
    o.   Venard McLaughlin. "The Silence"
    p.   H.P. Lovecraft. "The Dream Quest of Unknown Kadath"
    q.   Algis Budrys. "The Weeblies"
    r.   Oliver Onions [pseud. for George Oliver]. "Phantas"
    s.   Larry Niven. "Not Long Before the End"

GOGO LEWIS, ed. See SEON MANLEY AND GOGO LEWIS, eds.

[GEORGE LOCKE, ed.]

1215. *At the Mountains of Murkiness and Other Parodies.* [London]: Ferret Fantasy, 1973 [paper].

    a.   "Moll Bourne: The Mystery of a Handsome Cad (Fergus Hume)"
    b.   "Mr. M---: The Rontgen Ray-der (Conan Doyle)"
    c.   "'Duds' The Great Rumgin (Arthur Machen and Others)"
    d.   Arthur A. Sykes. "The Great Pan-Demon (Arthur Machen)"
    e.   George Forrest. "The Deathless Queen

            (Rider Haggard)"

f.   Jules Castier. "The Finding of Laura (H.G. Wells)"

g.   "Dodo: The Red Mark (Conan Doyle)"

h.   Stanley Huntley. "A Trip to the South Pole (Jules Verne)"

i.   Arthur C. Clarke. "At the Mountains of Murkiness (H.P. Lovecraft)"

1216. *The Land of the Unseen: Lost Supernatural Stories, 1828-1902.* [London]: Ferret Fantasy, 1973 [paper].

a.   Anon. "Sir Gawen; or, the Hag on the Heath"

b.   Alexandre Dumas. "The Pale Lady"

c.   Abraham Stoker. "The Crystal Cup"

d.   Kate Dodd. "Where Angels Fear to Tread"

e.   George Temple. "In an Inn"

f.   Edwin Lester Arnold. "The Splendid Dead"

g.   Ernest Favenc. "The Land of the Unseen"

ANNE McCAFFREY, comp.

1217. *Alchemy and Academe: A Collection of Original Stories Concerning Themselves with Transmutations, Mental and Elemental, Alchemical and Academic.* Garden City, NY: Doubleday, 1970.

a.   John Updike. "The Dance of the Solids" [poem]

b.   Sonya Dorman. "A Mess of Porridge"

c.   Carol Emshwiller. "The Institute"

d.   R.A. Lafferty. "Condillac's Statue"

e.   L. Sprague de Camp. "The Sorcerers" [poem]

f.   Norman Spinrad. "The Weed of Time"

g.   Samuel R. Delany. "Night and the Loves of Joe Dicostanzo"

h.   Daphine Castell. "Come Up and See Me"

i.   Joe Hensley. "Shut the Last Door"

j.   Avram Davidson. "Big Sam"

k.   James Blish. "More Light"

l.   Joanna Russ. "The Man Who Could Not See Devils"

m.   Betsy Curtis. "The Key to Out"

n.   Robert Silverberg. "Ringing the Changes"

o.   David Telfair. "In a Quart of Water"

p.   Gene Wolfe. "Morning-Glory"

q.   Virginia Kidd. "Ascension: A Workday Arabesque" [poem]

r.   Keith Laumer. "The Devil You Don't"

ANNE McCAFFREY continued

    s. Josephine Saxon. "The Triumphant Head"
    t. Peter Tate. "Mainchance"

        SEON MANLEY AND GOGO LEWIS, eds.

1218. *Ladies of Fantasy: Two Centuries of Sinister Stor-
       ies by the Gentle Sex.* New York: Lothrop, Lee
       & Shepard, 1975.

    a. E[dith] Nesbit [Brand]. "The Pavilion"
    b. Joan Aiken. "Searching for Summer"
    c. Mary Elizabeth Counselman. "The Unwanted"
    d. Dorothy Salisbury Davis. "The Muted Horn"
    e. Grazia Deledda. "The Sorcerer"
    f. Madame Blavatsky. "The Ensouled Violin"
    g. Jane Roberts. "The Red Wagon"
    h. Grena J. Bennett. "The Tilting Island"
    i. C.L. Moore. "Doorway Into Time"
    j. Lady Eleanor Smith. "No Ships Pass"

1219. *Sisters of Sorcery: Two Centuries of Witchcraft
       Stories by the Gentle Sex.* New York: Lothrop,
       Lee & Shepard, 1976.

    a. Dorothy L. Sayers. "The Cyprian Cat"
    b. Andre Norton. "Through the Needle's Eye"
    c. Ethel Marriot-Watson. "The Witch of the
        Marsh"
    d. Clara Florida Guernsey. "The Silver
        Bullet (A Story of Old Nantucket)"
    e. Lady Wilde. "The Horned Woman"
    f. Lady Gregory. "Herb-Healing"
    g. Jean Stafford. "The Warlock"
    h. Elizabeth P. Hall. "The Witch: A Tale
        of the Dark Ages"
    i. Seon Manley. "Letter from Massachusetts:
        1688"
    j. Sarah Good. "The Salem Witches and Their
        Own Voices: Examination of Sarah Good"
    k. Mrs. Volney E. Howard. "The Midnight
        Voyage of the Seagull (A Tradition of
        Salem)"
    l. Margaret Irwin. "The Book"
    m. Doris Lessing. "No Witchcraft for Sale"

        LEO MARGULIES, ed.

1220. *The Ghoul Keepers.* New York: Pyramid, 1961 [paper].

    a. Robert Bloch. "The Sorcerer's Apprentice"

    b. Theodore Sturgeon. "The Martian and the Moron"
    c. Edmond [Moore] Hamilton. "The Isle of the Sleeper"
    d. Helen W. Kassom. "Please Go 'way and Let Me Sleep"
    e. Ray Bradbury. "The Lake"
    f. Harry Altshuler. "The Witch in the Fog"
    g. L. Sprague de Camp and Fletcher Pratt. "Where the Night Wind Howls"
    h. Seabury Quinn. "Clare de Lune"
    i. Henry Kuttner. "Spawn of Dragons"

1221. *Weird Tales: Stories of Fantasy.* New York: Pyramid, 1964 [paper].

    a. Edmond Hamilton. "The Man Who Returned"
    b. Fritz Leiber, Jr. "Spider Mansion"
    c. Robert Bloch. "A Question of Etiquette"
    d. Nictzin Dyalhis. "The Sea Witch"
    e. H.P. Lovecraft. "The Strange High House in the Mist"
    f. August W. Derleth. "The Drifting Snow"
    g. Frank Belknap Long, Jr. "The Body-Masters"
    h. Robert E. Howard. "Pigeons From Hell"

1222. *Worlds of Weird.* New York: Pyramid, 1965 [paper].

    a. Seabury Quinn. "Roads"
    b. Nictzin Dyalhis. "The Sapphire Goddess"
    c. Robert E[rwin] Howard. "The Valley of the Worm"
    d. Edmond Hamilton. "He That Hath Wings"
    e. Clark Ashton Smith. "Mother of Toads"
    f. David H. Keller. "The Thing in the Cellar"
    g. Frank Belknap Long. "Giants in the Sky"

DOUGLAS MENVILLE AND MICHAEL BURGESS, eds.

1223. Menville, Douglas and R. Reginald, pseud., eds. *Dreamers of Dreams: An Anthology of Fantasy.* New York: Arno Press, 1978.

    a. John Kendrick Bangs. "The Affliction of Baron Humpfelhimmel"
    b. Laurence Housman. "The Blind God"
    c. George MacDonald. "The Gray Wolf"
    d. Bram Stoker. "The Invisible Giant"
    e. Guy Boothby. "A Professor of Egyptology"
    f. Andrew Lang. "The End of Phaeacia"
    g. Kenneth Morris. "The Last Adventures of Don Quixote"

    h.   Mervyn Peake. "Same Time, Same Place"
    i.   J[ohn] A[mes] Mitchell. "That First Affair"
    j.   Edward Everett Hale. "The Queen of Cali-
         fornia"
    k.   Edwin Lestern Arnold. "Rutherford the
         Twice-Born"
    l.   Lord Dunsany. "The Journey of the King"
    m.   H.E. Bates. *The Seekers* (London: John and
         Edward Bumpus, 1926).

1224. _____. *They: Three Parodies of H. Rider Haggard's*
      She. New York: Arno Press, 1978.

    a.   [Andrew Lang and Walter Herries Pollock].
         He (London: Longmans, Green, 1887).
    b.   [John De Morgan]. *He, A Companion to She.*
         Being the History of the Adventures of
         J. Theodosius Aristophano on the Island
         of Rapa Nui in Search of His Immortal
         Ancestor (Munro's Library, Vol. 50, No.
         72. New York: Norman L. Munro, 1887).
    c.   [John De Morgan]. *"It."* *A Wild, Weird*
         History of the Marvelous, Miraculous,
         Phantasmagorial Adventure in Search of
         He, She, and Jess, and Leading to the
         Finding of "It" (Munro's Library, Vol.
         50, No. 726. New York: Norman L. Munro,
         1887).

1225. _____. *Worlds of Never: Three Fantastic Novels.*
      New York: Arno Press, 1978.

    a.   John Kendrick Bangs. *Alice in Blunderland:*
         An Iridescent Dream (New York: Doubleday,
         Page, 1907).
    b.   [Lucy Peacock]. *The Adventures of the Six*
         Princesses of Babylon, in Their Travels
         to the Temple of Virtue: An Allegory
         (London: By the Author, 1785).
    c.   Bert Leston Taylor and W.C. Gibson. *The*
         Log of the Water Wagon or The Cruise
         of the Good Ship "Lithia" (Boston: H.M.
         Caldwell, 1905).

                  JANE MOBLEY, ed.

1226. *Phantasmagoria: Tales of Fantasy and the Super-*
      natural. Garden City, NY: Anchor-Doubleday,
      1977 [paper].

      The Wondrous Fair: Magical Fantasy

                       299

    a.   Anon. "Arthur and Gorlagon"
    b.   George MacDonald. "The Golden Key"
    c.   Lord Dunsany. "The Fortress Unvanquish-
         able Save for Sacnoth"
    d.   Theodore Sturgeon. "The Silken Swift"
    e.   Robert Bloch. "The Dark Isle"
    f.   Jorge Luis Borges. "The Rejected Sorcerer"
    g.   Nicholas Stuart Gray. "According to
         Tradition"
    h.   Andre Norton. "The Gifts of Asti"
    i.   Ursula K. Le Guin. "The Rule of Names"
    j.   Sylvia Townsend Warner. "Winged Creatures"
    k.   Peter S. Beagle. "Sia"

The Passing Strange: Supernatural Fiction

    l.   J. Sheridan Le Fanu. "An Account of Some
         Strange Disturbances in Aungier Street"
    m.   Algernon Blackwood. "Confession"
    n.   Oliver Onions. "The Beckoning Fair One"
    o.   M.R. James. "Oh, Whistle, and I'll Come
         to You, My Lad"
    p.   Peter S. Beagle. "Come Lady Death"
    q.   Elizabeth Jane Howard. "Three Miles Up"
    r.   Doris Betts. "Benson Watts is Dead and in
         Virginia"

CHARLES NAYLOR, ed.
See THOMAS M[ICHAEL] DISCH AND CHARLES NAYLOR, eds.

WILLIAM F[RANCIS] NOLAN, ed.

1227. *Three to the Highest Power: Bradbury, Oliver,
      Sturgeon.* New York: Avon, 1968 [paper].

    a.   Ray Bradbury. "The Lost City of Mars"
    b.   Theodore Sturgeon. "One Foot and the
         Grave"
    c.   Chad Oliver. "The Marginal Man"

    . Each selection is preceded by an overview of
    the author's career and followed by a checklist
    of his science fiction and fantasy.

ANDREW J. OFFUTT, ed.

1228. *Swords Against Darkness.* New York: Zebra Books,
      1977 [paper].

    a.   Robert E. Howard and Andrew Offutt. "Nekht

Semerkeht"
b. Poul Anderson. "The Tale of Hauk"
c. George W. Proctor. "The Smile of Oisia"
d. Bruce Jones. "Pride of the Fleet"
e. Manly Wade Wellman. "Straggler from
    Atlantis"
f. Richard L. Tierney. "The Ring of Sef"
g. Raul Garcia Capella. "Largarut's Bane"
h. David Drake. "Dragon's Teeth"
i. Ramsey Campbell. "The Sustenance of Hoak"

1229. *Swords Against Darkness II*. New York: Zebra
       Books, 1977 [paper].

a. Andre Norton. "Sword of Unbelief"
b. Ramsey Campbell. "The Changer of Names"
c. Manly Wade Wellman. "The Dweller in the
    Temple"
d. David M. Harris. "The Coming of Age in
    Zamora"
e. Richard L. Tierney. "The Scroll of Thoth"
f. Taneth Lee. "Odds Against the Gods"
g. Dennis More. "On Skellig Michael"
h. Andrew J. Offutt. "Last Quest"

1230. *Swords Against Darkness III*. New York: Zebra,
       1978 [paper].

a. Ramsey Campbell. "The Pit of Wings"
b. Richard L. Tierney. "The Sword of Sparta-
    cus"
c. Wayne Hooks. "Servitude"
d. David C. Smith. "Descales' Skull"
e. Tanith Lee. "In the Balance"
f. David Madison. "Tower of Darkness"
g. David Drake. "The Mantichore"
h. Kathleen Resch. "Revenant"
i. Jon DeCles. "Rite of Kings"
j. Robert E. Vardeman. "The Mating Web"
k. Manly Wade Wellman. "The Quest of Dzing-
    anji"
l. Darrell Schweitzer. "The Hag"
m. Geo. W. Proctor. "A Kingdom Won"
n. M.A. Washil. "Swordslinger"
o. Poul Anderson. "On Thud and Blunder"

GERALD W. PAGE, ed.

1231. *Nameless Places*. Sauk City, WI: Arkham House,
       1975.

a. A.A. Attanasio. "Glimpses"

    b. Thomas Burnett Swann. "The Night of the Unicorn"
    c. Brian Ball. "The Warlord of Kul Satu"
    d. G.N. Gabbard. "More Things"
    e. Robert Aickman. "The Read Road to the Church"
    f. Gary Myers. "The Gods of Earth"
    g. Robert E. Gilbert. "Walls of Yellow Clay"
    h. Scott Edelstein. "Businessman's Lament"
    i. Joseph F. Pumilia. "Dark Vintage"
    j. David A. English. "Simaitha"
    k. Stephen Goldin. "In the Land of Angra Mainyu"
    l. Gerald W. Page. "Worldsong"
    m. Brian Lumley. "What Dark God?"
    n. Bob Maurers. "The Stuff of Heroes"
    o. Joseph Payne Brennan. "Forringer's Fortune"
    p. Denys Val Baker. "Before the Event"
    q. Walter C. DeBill, Jr. "In 'Ygiroth"
    r. Ramsey Campbell. "The Lost Hand"
    s. Lin Carter. "Out of the Ages"
    t. David Drake. "Awakening"
    u. Lin Carter. "In the Vale of Pnath"
    v. Carl Jacobi. "Chameleon Town"
    w. Scott Edelstein. "Botch"
    x. David Drake. "Black Iron"
    y. E. Hoffman Price. "Selene"
    z. Ramsey Campbell. "The Christmas Present"
    aa. Arthur Byron Cover. "Lifeguard"

GERALD W. PAGE AND HANK REINHARDT, eds.

1232. *Heroic Fantasy*. New York: DAW Books, 1979 [paper].

    a. Andre Norton. "Sand Sister"
    b. Galad Elflandsson. "The Valley or the Sorrows"
    c. Don Walsh. "Ghoul's Head"
    d. "First Commentary: Swords and Swordplay"*
    e. Adrian Cole. "Astral Stray"
    f. E.C. Tubb. "Blood in the Mist"
    g. "Second Commentary: Armor"*
    h. Tanith Lee. "The Murderous Dove"
    i. Charles R. Saunders. "Death in Jukun"
    j. H. Warner Munn. "The De Pertriche Ring"
    k. "Third Commentary: Courage and Heroism"*
    l. Gerald W. Page. "The Hero Who Returned"
    m. Darrell Schweitzer. "The Riddle of the Horn"
    n. Hank Reinhardt. "The Age of the Warrior"
    o. A.E. Silas. "The Mistaken Oracle"
    p. F. Paul Wilson. "Demonsong"

GERALD W. PAGE AND HANK REINHARDT continued

  q. Manly Wade Wellman. "The Seeker in the
    Fortress"

  *Commentaries are by Page and Reinhardt.

    JOHN PFORDRESHER, ed.
  See EDMUND J. FARRELL, et al., eds.

    ERIC S. RABKIN, ed.

1233. *Fantastic Worlds: Myths, Tales, and Stories.* New
   York and Oxford: Oxford University Press, 1979.

  a. "Genesis"
  b. "Blackfoot Genesis"
  c. "The Eye of the Giant"
  d. Amos Tutuola. "How I Brought Death Into
    the World"
  e. Ovid. "The Myth of Actaeon"
  f. Ovid. "The Myth of Narcissus"
  g. Ovid. "The Myth of Philomela"
  h. "The Ghost Wife"
  i. "The Magic Swan Geese"
  j. Chinua Achebe. "Why Tortoise's Shell is
    Not Smooth"
  k. Joel Chandler Harris. "How Mr. Rabbit
    Was Too Sharp for Mr. Fox"
  l. Esther Shephard. "Paul Bunyon on the
    Columbia"
  m. Jakob and Wilhelm Grimm. "Little Red-cap"
  n. Jakob and Wilhelm Grimm. "The Sleeping
    Beauty"
  o. Jakob and Wilhelm Grimm. "Hansel and
    Grethel"
  p. Hans Christian Andersen. "The Tinderbox"
  q. George MacDonald. "The Tale of Cosmo"
  r. J.R.R. Tolkien. "Leaf by Niggle"
  s. Joseph Addison. "Our Ideas of Time"
  t. E.T.A. Hoffmann. "Ritter Gluck"
  u. Edgar Allan Poe. "The Oval Portrait"
  v. Lewis Carroll. "The Garden of Live Flowers"
  w. James Thurber. "The Secret Life of Walter
    Mitty"
  x. Norton Juster. "The Royal Banquet"
  y. E.T.A. Hoffmann. "The Sandman"
  z. Edgar Allan Poe. "The Black Cat"
  aa. H.P. Lovecraft. "The Picture in the House"
  bb. Joseph Sheridan LeFanu. "The Hand"
  cc. Ambrose Bierce. "The Moonlite Road"
  dd. M.R. James. "Lost Hearts"
  ee. William Morris. "Golden Wings"

ERIC S. RABKIN continued

    ff. Lord Dunsany [Plunkett]. "The Sword of
          Welleran"
    gg. Sylvia Townsend Warner. "The Five Black
          Swans"
    hh. Edgar Allan Poe. "The Facts in the Case
          of M. Valdemar"
    ii. Nathaniel Hawthorne. "The Birthmark"
    jj. H.G. Wells. "The Star"
    kk. Kurt Vonnegut, Jr. "Epicac"
    ll. Jack Finney. "The Third Level"
    mm. Arthur C. Clarke. "The Star"
    nn. Franz Kafka. "The Judgment"
    oo. Franz Kafka. "A Common Confusion"
    pp. Bruno Schulz. "Cockroaches"
    qq. Jorge Luis Borges. "Pierre Menard, Author
          of the Quixote"
    rr. Julio Cortázar. "Axolotl"
    ss. Tommaso Landolfi. "Pastoral"
    tt. Italo Calvino. "All at One Point"
    uu. Peter Bichsel. "There is No Such Place
          as America"
    vv. Donald Barthelme. "The Piano Player"
    ww. Richard Brautigan. "Homage to the San
          Francisco YMCA"
    xx. Robert Coover. "The Marker"
    yy. Spencer Holst. "The Zebra Storyteller"

R. REGINALD, pseud. See DOUGLAS MENVILLE
    AND MICHAEL BURGESS, eds.

HANK REINHARDT
See GERALD M. PAGE AND HANK REINHARDT, eds.

ERNEST RHYS AND C[ATHERINE] A[MY] DAWSON SCOTT, eds.

1234. *Thirty and One Stories by Thirty and One Authors.*
    London: Thornton Butterworth, 1923.

    a. I. Zangwill. "The Sabbath Breaker"
    b. Mary E. Mann. "The Blue Beads"
    c. H.G. Wells. "The Door in the Wall"
    d. Catherine Wells. "Fear"
    e. Ernest Bramah [Smith]. "The Story of
        Chang Tao"
    f. E.Œ. Somerville and Martin Ross. "The
        Whiteboys"
    g. Arnold Bennett. "The Fortune Teller"
    h. May Sinclair. "The Collector"
    i. A.T. Quiller Couch. "Statement of Gabriel
        Foot, Highwayman"

j. Grace Rhys. "Destiny and a Dog"
k. H.D. Lowry. "The Man in the Room"
l. E. Colburn Mayne. "The Turret Room"
m. John Galsworthy. "A Strange Thing"
n. Jane Findlater. "The Pictures"
o. W.W. Jacobs. "Fine Feathers"
p. C.A. Dawson Scott. "My Honoured Master"
q. A.E. Coppard. "Clorinda Walks in Heaven"
r. Rebecca West. "In a City That is Now
   Ploughed Fields"
s. R.B. Cunninghame Graham. "Mektub"
t. George R. Malloch. "The Flower"
u. E.R. "The Mare Without a Name"
v. F. Tennyson Jesse. "Why Senath Married"
w. Perceval Gibbon. "The Connoisseur"
x. Clemence Housman. "The Drawn Arrow"
y. Stacy Aumonier. "The Great Unimpression-
   able"
z. E.M. Goodman. "The Last Lap"
aa. E. Grant Watson. "Out There"
bb. Violet Hunt. "His Widows"
cc. John Russell. "The Price of the Head"
dd. Mary Webb. "Blessed are the Meek"
ee. G.K. Chesterton. "The Invisible Man"

RAYMOND J. RODRIGUES, ed.
See EDMUND J. FARRELL, et al., eds.

MAXIMILLAN J[OSEF] RUDWIN, ed.

1235. *Devil Stories: An Anthology*. New York: Alfred A.
Knopf, 1921.

a. Francis Oscar Mann. "The Devil in a Nun-
   nery: A Mediaeval Tale"
b. Niccolò Machiavelli. "Belphagor, or the
   Marriage of the Devil"
c. Washington Irving. "The Devil and Tom
   Walker"
d. Wilhelm Hauff. "From the Memoirs of
   Satan"
e. Nikolái Vasilévich Gógol. "St. John's
   Eve"
f. William Makepeace Thackeray. "The Devil's
   Wager"
g. William Makepeace Thackeray. "The Painter's
   Bargain"
h. Edgar Allan Poe. "Bon-Bon"
i. Anon. "The Printer's Devil"
j. Fernán Caballero. "The Devil's Mother-in-
   Law"

305

k. Charles Pierre Baudelairè. "The Generous Gambler"
l. Alphonse Daudet. "The Three Low Masses"
m. Frederick Beecher Perkins. "Devil-Puzzlers"
n. Charles Deulin. "The Devil's Round: A Tale of Flemish Golf"
o. Guy de Maupassant. "The Legend of Mont St.-Michel"
p. Richard Garnett. "The Demon Pope"
q. Richard Garnett. "Madam Lucifer"
r. Anatole France. "Lucifer"
s. Maxim Górky. "The Devil"
t. John Masefield. "The Devil and the Old Man"

STUART DAVIS SCHIFF, ed.

1236. *Whispers: An Anthology of Fantasy and Horror.* Garden City, NY: Doubleday, 1977.

a. Karl Edward Wagner. "Sticks"
b. David Drake. "The Barrow Troll"
c. Fritz Leiber. "The Glove"
d. Robert Bloch. "The Closer of the Way"
e. William F. Nolan. "Dark Winner"
f. Hugh B. Cave. "Ladies in Waiting"
g. Dennis Etchison. "White Moon Rising"
h. Richard Christian Matheson. "Graduation"
i. Ray Russell. "Mirror, Mirror"
j. Brian Lumley. "The House of Cthulhu"
k. John Crowley. "Antiquities"
l. James Sallis and David Lunde. "The Scallion Stone"
m. Robin Smyth. "The Inglorious Rise of the Catsmeat Man"
n. Charles E. Fritch. "The Pawnshop"
o. Robert Aickman. "Le Miroir"
p. Joseph Payne Brennan. "The Willow Platform"
q. Manly Wade Wellman. "The Dakwa"
r. David Campton. "Goat"
s. Ramsey Campbell. "The Chimney"

HANS STEFAN SANTESSON, ed.

1237. *The Mighty Barbarians: Great Sword and Sorcery Heroes.* New York: Lancer, 1969 [paper].

a. Fritz Leiber. "When the Sea King's Away"
b. L. Sprague de Camp. "The Stronger Spell"
c. Henry Kuttner. "Dragon Moon"

    d.   Lin Carter. "Thieves of Zangabol"
    e.   Robert E. Howard. "A Witch Shall Be Born"

1238. *The Mighty Swordsmen.* New York: Lancer, 1970
     [paper].

    a.   Lin Carter. "Keeper of the Emerald Flame"
    b.   Roger Zelazny. "The Bells of Shoredan"
    c.   John Brunner. "Break the Door of Hell"
    d.   Robert E. Howard. "Beyond the Black River"
    e.   Björn Nyberg. "The People of the Summit"
    f.   Michael Moorcock. "The Flame Bringers"

    C[ATHERINE] A[MY] DAWSON SCOTT, ed.
See ERNEST RHYS AND C[ATHERINE] A[MY] DAWSON SCOTT, eds.

    JEREMY SCOTT, ed.

1239. *The Mandrake Root: An Anthology of Fantastic Tales.*
    London: Jarrolds, 1946.

    a.   James Joyce. "Everlasting Fire"
    b.   Algernon Blackwood. "The Man Who Was
        Milligan"
    c.   Richard Hughes. "The Stranger"
    d.   Dorothy K. Haynes. "Changeling"
    e.   D.H. Lawrence. "The Last Laugh"
    f.   Thomas Ingoldsby. "The Leech of Folkestone"
    g.   Edward Bulwer-Lytton. "The Haunted and
        the Haunters"
    h.   Fred Marnau. "The Wrinkled Women of St.
        Nepomuk"
    i.   Arthur Calder-Marshall. "Pickle My Bones"
    j.   Alex Comfort. "The Lemmings"
    k.   Thomas De Quincey. "Confessions of an
        English Opium-Eater"
    l.   Guy de Maupassant. "The Horla"
    m.   Virginia Woolf. "The Lady in the Looking
        Glass: A Reflection"
    n.   William Sansom. "The Peach-House-Potting-
        Shed"
    o.   Wrey Gardiner. "The White House"
    p.   Olive Schreiner. "Who Knocks at the Door"
    q.   Stella Benson. "An Air-Raid Seen from
        Above"
    r.   H.H. Munro ["Saki"]. "The Open Window"
    s.   Richard Garnett. "The Bell of Saint
        Euschemon"
    t.   E.M. Forster. "The Story of a Panic"
    u.   M.R. James. "'Oh, Whistle and I'll Come,
        My Lad'"

    v.   T.F. Powys. "No Room"
    w. Pamula Hansford Johnson. "Altarwise by
         Owl-Light"
    x.   Walter de la Mare. "Winter"
    y.   J. Sheridan Le Fanu. "The Familiar"
    z.   James Laver. "Mr. Hopkins and Galatea"
   aa. John Atkins. "The Diary of William Car-
         penter"
   bb. Osbert Sitwell. "The Greeting"

ROBERT SILVERBERG, ed.

1240. *Lost Worlds, Unknown Horizons: Nine Stories of
      Science Fiction.* Nashville and New York:
      Thomas Nelson, 1978.

    a.   H.G. Wells. "The Country of the Blind"
    b.   Jack Finney. "The Third Level"
    c.   Clark Ashton Smith. "The City of the
         Singing Flame"
    d.   Fritz Leiber. "The Sunken City"
    e.   Edward Page Mitchell. "The Balloon Tree"
    f.   H.P. Lovecraft. "The Doom That Came to
         Sarnath"
    g.   Edgar Allan Poe. "A Tale of the Ragged
         Mountains"
    h.   Oliver Onions. "Phantas"
    i.   Robert Silverberg. "Trips"

[KURT SINGER, comp.]

1241. *Bloch and Bradbury. Ten Masterpieces of Science
      Fiction.* New York: Tower, 1969 [paper].

    a.   Robert Bloch.   "The Shadow from the Steeple"
    b.   Ray Bradbury.   "The Watchers"
    c.   Robert Bloch.   "The Grinning Ghoul"
    d.   Robert Bloch.   "Mannikans of Horror"
    e.   Ray Bradbury.   "Fever Dream"
    f.   Robert Bloch.   "The Druidic Dream"
    g.   Ray Bradbury.   "The Dead Man"
    h.   Robert Bloch.   "A Question of Etiquette"
    i.   Ray Bradbury.   "The Handler"
    j.   Robert Bloch.   "The Man Who Cried Wolf!"

PHILIP VAN DOREN STERN, ed.

1242. *The Moonlight Traveler: Great Tales of Fantasy and
      Imagination.* Garden City, NY: Doubleday, Doran,

1943. Rpt. as *Great Tales of Fantasy and Imagination*. New York: Washington Square Press,
1954 [paper].

a. E.M. Forster. "The Celestial Omnibus"
b. James Stephens. "Desire"
c. Max Beerbohm. "Enoch Soames"
d. H.G. Wells. "The Man Who Could Work
    Miracles"
e. Robert Louis Stevenson. "The Bottle Imp"
f. A.E. Coppard. "Adam and Eve and Pinch Me"
g. W. Somerset Maugham. "Lord Mountdrago"
h. Walter de la Mare. "All Hallows"
i. Lord Dunsany. "Our Distant Cousins"
j. Jan Struther. "Cobbler, Cobbler, Mend My
    Shoe"
k. Stella Benson. "The Man Who Missed the
    Bus"
l. Eric Knight. "Sam Small's Better Half"
m. Conrad Aiken. "Mr. Arcularis"
n. F. Scott Fitzgerald. "Diamonds as Big as
    the Ritz"
o. Edgar Allan Poe. "William Wilson"
p. Stephen Vincent Benét. "The Curfew Tolls"
q. Ralph Straus. "The Most Maddening Story
    in the World"
r. Oliver Onions. "Phantas"
s. O. Henry. "Roads of Destiny"
t. Rudyard Kipling. "'Wireless'"
u. "Saki" [H.H. Munro]. "The Music on the
    Hill"

PHIL[IP DUFFIELD] STONG, ed.

1243. *The Other Worlds*. New York: Wilfred Funk, 1941.
       A later edition, titled *The Other Worlds: 25
       Modern Stories of Mystery and Imagination*, was
       published in New York by the Garden City Pub-
       lishing Company in 1942.

a. Thorp McClusky. "The Considerate Hosts"
b. Michael Fessier. "The Man in the Black
    Hat"
c. Mindret Lord. "Naked Lady"
d. Ralph Milne Farley. "The House of Ecstacy"
e. Paul Ernst. "Escape"
f. John Jessel. "The Adaptive Ultimate"
g. Walker G. Everett. "The Woman in Gray"
h. Lester del Rey. "The Pipes of Pan"
i. Virginia Swain. "Aunt Cassie"
j. Theodore Sturgeon. "A God in a Garden"

k. Donald Bern. "The Man Who Knew All the
    Answers"
l. Eando Binder. "Adam Link's Revenge"
m. David Wright O'Brien. "Truth is a Plague"
n. Murray Leinster. "The Fourth-Dimensional
    Demonstrator"
o. Harry Bates. "Alas, All Thinking!"
p. Kelvin Kent [Henry Kuttner]. "The Comedy
    of Eras"
q. Mindred Lord. "A Problem for Biographers"
r. H.P. Lovecraft. "In the Vault"
s. Manly Wade Wellman. "School for the Un-
    speakable"
t. Seabury Quinn. "The House Where Time Stood
    Still"
u. John Flanders, pseud. [Jean Ray]. "The
    Mystery of the Lost Guest"
v. Manly Wade Wellman. "Song of the Slaves"
w. August Derleth. "The Panelled Room"
x. Henry Kuttner. "The Graveyard Rats"
y. August Derleth and Mark Schorer. "The
    Return of Andrew Bentley"

WILLIAM TENN, pseud., ed. See PHILIP J. KLASS, ed.

STEVE TROYANOVICH, ed.
See JONATHAN BACON AND STEVE TROYANOVICH, eds.

HERBERT VAN THAL, ed.

1244. *Famous Tales of the Fantastic.* New York: Hill
       and Wang, 1965.

a. Ray Bradbury. "Invisible Boy"
b. Mary Coleridge. "The King is Dead, Long
    Live the King"
c. Sir Arthur Conan Doyle. "The Speckled
    Band"
d. Romain Gary. "Comrade Pigeon"
e. Leslie Poles Hartley. "The Crossways"
f. Sir Arthur Quiller-Couch ('Q'). "The
    Roll-Call of the Reef"
g. William Sansom. "The Ballroom"
h. Robert Louis Stevenson. "The Bottle Imp"
i. Herbert George Wells. "The Magic Shop"
j. Nathaniel Hawthorne. "Rappaccini's
    Daughter"
k. Washington Irving. "The Adventure of the
    German Student"

EDWARD WAGENKNECHT, ed.

1245. *Six Novels of the Supernatural*. New York: Viking
Press, 1944.

    a.   Mrs. Oliphant. "A Beleaguered City"
    b.   Walter de la Mare. "The Return"
    c.   Frances Hodgson Burnett. "The White People"
    d.   Arthur Machen. "The Terror"
    e.   Mary Johnston. "Sweet Rocket"
    f.   Robert Nathan. "Portrait of Jennie"

GAHAN WILSON, ed.

1246. *First World Fantasy Awards*. Garden City, NY:
Doubleday, 1977.

Fantasy and horror honored by the First World
Fantasy Awards (1975), "The Howards"; a number
of the panel discussions and speeches that oc-
curred at the awards convention; and an essay,
"Toward a Greater Appreciation of H.P. Lovecraft," by Dirk Mosig. The fiction only is
cited here.

    a.   Robert Bloch. "The Bat is My Brother"
    b.   Robert Bloch. "Beatles"
    c.   Patricia McKillip. Excerpt from *The For-
gotten Beasts of Eld* (see above)
    d.   Robert Aickman. "Pages from a Young Girl's
Journal"
    e.   T.E.D. Klein. "The Events at Poroth Farm"
    f.   Sterling E. Lanier. "A Father's Tale"
    g.   Karl Edward Wagner. "Sticks"
    h.   Manly Wade Wellman. "Come Into My Parlor"
    i.   Manly Wade Wellman. "Fearful Rock"
    j.   Fritz Leiber. "The Bait"
    k.   Dave Drake. "The Shortest Way"
    l.   Dennis Etchison. "The Soft Wall"
    m.   Joseph Payne Brennan. "The Abandoned
Boudoir"
    n.   H. Warner Munn. "Cradle Son for a Baby
Werewolf"
    o.   Walter Shedlofsky. "Guillotine"
    p.   David Riley. "The Farmhouse"

DONALD A. WOLLHEIM, ed.

1247. *Swordsmen in the Sky*. New York: Ace, 1964 [paper].

    a.   Poul Anderson. "Swordsman of Lost Terra"
    b.   Andre Norton. "People of the Crater"

    c. Leigh Brackett. "The Moon That Vanished"
    d. Otis Adelbert Kline. "A Vision of Venus"
    e. Edith Hamilton. "Kaldar, World of Antares"

    DONALD A. WOLLHEIM AND GEORGE ERNSBERGER, eds.

1248. *The Avon Fantasy Reader*. New York: Avon, 1969
       [paper].

       This volume and its successor (see below) re-
       print selections from Wollheim's *Avon Fantasy
       Reader* series (1947-1951).

       a. Robert E. Howard. "The Witch from Hell's
           Kitchen"
       b. C.L. Moore. "Black Thirst"
       c. Algernon Blackwood. "A Victim of Higher
           Space"
       d. Nictzin Dyalhis. "The Sapphire Siren"
       e. William Hope Hodgson. "A Voice in the
           Night" (from *Men of Deep Waters*)
       f. Thorp McClusky. "The Crawling Horror"
       g. Manly Wade Wellman. "The Kelpie"

1249. *The 2nd Avon Fantasy Reader*. New York: Avon,
       1969 [paper].

       a. Robert E. Howard. "The Blonde Goddess of
           Bal-Sagoth"
       b. C.L. Moore. "Shambleau"
       c. Zealia Brown Bishop. "The Curse of Yig"
       d. Clark Ashton Smith. "Ubbo-Sathla"
       e. Donald Wandrei. "The Painted Mirror"
       f. Edward Lucas White. "Amina"
       g. Robert Bloch. "The Black Kiss"
       h. Laurence Manning and Fletcher Pratt. "The
           City of the Living Dead"
       i. Sax Rohmer. "The Curse of a Thousand
           Kisses"

              KENNETH J. ZAHORSKI, ed.
    See ROBERT H. BOYER AND KENNETH J. ZAHORSKI, eds.

AUTHOR, COMPILER, EDITOR, AND TRANSLATOR
INDEX

This Index includes all authors, compilers, editors, and translators cited in the entries. Numbers refer to entry code numbers. Letters designate items within the entry.

Keller, David H[enry] continued 1222-f
Kenney, Douglas 78
Kent, Kelvin. See Kuttner, Henry
Kent, Leonard J., ed. and trans. 504
Kerby, Susan Alice, pseud. See Burton, Alice Elizabeth
Kersh, Gerald 574, 1203-f
Kidd, Virginia 1217-q
King, Stephen 1174-c
Kingsley, Charles 575-578
Kip, Leonard 579
Kipling, Rudyard 1176-d, 1242-t
Kirkpatrick, Brownlee Jean 383
Klass, Philip J. 1060, 1212-t
Klass, Philip J., ed. 1212
Klein, T.E.D. 1246-e
Kline, Otis Adelbert 1247-d
Knapp, Lawrence 353
Knight, Elizabeth C., ed. and trans. 504
Knowles, Vernon 580-583
Koontz, Dean R[ay] 584-585
Kornbluth, C[yril] M. 1212-b, 1214-e
Kneale, Nigel 1165-b, 1166-i
Knight, Damon 1172-f
Knight, Damon, ed. 1213-1214
Knight, Eric 1167-a, 1201-c, 1242-1
Kummer, Frederick Arnold 586-587
Kurtz, Katherine 588-593, 1180-d
Kuttner, Henry 594-596; 116--a; 1165-i; 1166-b; 1184-b; 1186-m; 1195-e; 1197-d; 1198-d; 1205-b; 1208-h; 1220-i; 1237-c; 1243-p, x

LaFarge, Oliver 1165-h

Lafferty, R[aphael] A[loysius] 597-598, 1169-d, 1170-q, 1171-b, 1172-e, 1173-d, 1214-b, 1217-d
Lagerlöf, Selma 1164-f
Lambourne, John [Battersby Crompton] 599
Lancour, Gene, pseud. See Fisher, Gene
Landolfi, Tommaso 1233-ss
Lang, Andrew 467, 600-605, 1223-f, 1224-a
Lange, John F., Jr. 563, 606-617
Langelaan, George 1200-j
Langley, Noel 1203-c
Lanier, Sterling E. 618, 1246-f
Laubenthal, Sanders Anne 619
Laumer, Keith 1217-r
Laver, James 1239-z
Lawrence, D.H. 1202-hh, 1212-a, 1239-e
Lawrence, Margery, pseud. See Towle, Mrs. Arthur Edward
Leaky, John Martin 1204-k
Lear, Edward 1202-t
Leber, Hermann, ed. 501-502
Lee, Tanith 620-627, 1188-a, 1190-j, 1229-f, 1230-e, 1232-h
Lee, Vernon, pseud. See Paget, Violet
Lee, William M. 1171-m
Le Fanu, Joseph Sheridan 1192-a, 1226-1, 1233-bb, 1239-y
Le Guin, Ursula K[roeber] 628-633, 1162-h, 1163-o, 1164-k, 1214-k, 1226-i
Leiber, Fritz [Reuter, Jr.] 634-650, 693, 901, 1160-e, 1162-f, 1171-e, 1177-a, 1179-c, 1183-g, 1187-e, 1188-d, 1196-a, 1197-e, 1198-e, 1208-p, 1209-b, 1210-b, 1211-k, 1213-1, 1221-b, 1236-c, 1237-a, 1240-d, 1246-j
Leinster, Murray, pseud. See Jenkins, William Fitzgerald

324

Vercors, pseud. See
    Bruller, Jean
Vidal, Gore 1070-1071
Viereck, George Sylvester
    1072-1074
Virgil 1202-rrr
Vivian, Evelyn Charles
    H. 1075-1083, 1099
Voltaire 1176-r, 1183-a
Vonnegut, Kurt, Jr.
    1233-kk

Wackermann, Erwin 1154
Wagenknecht, Edward
    287, 678, 1245
Wagner, Karl Edward
    1084-1089, 1189-e,
    1236-a, 1246-g
Wagner, Karl Edward, ed.
    532-534, 554
Waite, Arthur Edward 1090
Wakefield, H. Russell
    1208-z
Waldo, Edward Hamilton
    See Sturgeon, Theodore
Waldrop, Howard 1174-d
Walker, Dale L. 673, 675
Walker, Hugh, pseud.
    See Strassl, Hubert
Wallace, Irving 955
Walsh, Don 1232-c
Walsh, Thomas P. 51
Walton, Evangeline, pseud.
    See Ensley, Evange-
    line Walton
Wandrei, Donald 1249-e
Warner, Sylvia Townsend
    622, 1091-1093, 1163-p,
    1164-0, 1202-mm,
    1226-j, 1233-gg
Washil, M.A. 1230-n
Waterloo, Stanley 672
Watson, E. Grant 1234-aa
Watson, George, ed. 2,
    34, 225, 285, 409,
    545, 866, 943, 947,
    933, 1093
Webb, Mary 1234-dd
Weinbaum, Stanley 275,
    1159
Weiss, Anne 362, 484,
    671, 752, 1110, 1140

Weiss, Irving 362, 484,
    671, 752, 1110, 1140
Weixlmann, Joseph John 52
Welles, Oscar 1202-hhh
Wellman, Manly Wade 1094-r;
    1159; 1160-h; 1200-g;
    1208-l; 1228-e; 1229-c;
    1230-k; 1232-g; 1236-g;
    1243-s, v; 1246-h, i;
    1248-g
Wells, Catherine 1234-d
Wells, H[erbert] G[eorge]
    1095-1098, 1198-i, 1200-v,
    1201-g, 1202-www, 1213-g,
    1214-d, 1215-f, 1233-jj,
    1234-c, 1240-a, 1242-d,
    1244-i
Wells, Stuart W., III
    112-N.B.
Wentz, Walter J. 748
West, Rebecca 1234-r
West, Richard C. 1048
Weston, Jesse 1147
Wheatley, Dennis 1099-1107
White, Antonia 1202-ooo
White, E.B. 1165-c, 1166-u
White, Edward Lucas 1108-
    1110, 1249-f
White, James 298
White, T[erence] H[anbury]
    1111-1118, 1162-n, 1183-k
White, William 986-988
White, William Anthony
    Parker 1119-1120, 1160-j,
    1205-g, 1213-i
Whitehead, Henry S. 1208-j
Wibberley, Leonard 1121
Wilde, Lady 1219-e
Wilde, Oscar 1185-d,
    1201-j, 1202-r
Wilhelm, Kate 1214-c
Wilkins, Mary E. See Free-
    man, Mary E. Wilkins
Williams, Charles W.S.
    1122-1129
Williams, Jay 1130
Williams, Sidney Herbert
    309
Williams, Tennessee 1211-d
Williamson, "Jack" [John
    Steward] 1131-1132
Wilson, Angus 1149-e
Wilson, F. Paul 323, 1232-p

Wilson, Gahan, ed. 1246
Wilson, John Anthony Bur-
    gess, 869, 1133-1135
Winter, William, ed.
    845-846
Wisdom, John 755-j
Wolfe, Gene 1136, 1217-p
Wollheim, Donald A. 517,
    1211-b
Wollheim, Donald A., ed.
    1247-1249
Wood, Charles Erskine
    Scott 1202-w, pp
Woodbridge, Hensley C. 676
Woodward, Wayne. See
    Bok, Hannes
Woolf, Virginia 1199-b,
    1202-b, 1239-m
Woolfe, Cecil 934
Wylie, Elinor [Hoyt]
    1137-1140
Wymer, Thomas 354
Wyndham, John, pseud.
    See Harris, John Beynon

Yeats, William Butler
    1202-h, gg
Yelvington, Henry 1202-y
Yoke, Carl 1148

Zahorski, Kenneth J., ed.
    1162-1164
Zangwill, I. 1234-a
Zeeman, Denise Avril 339
Zelazny, Roger 1141-1148,
    1159, 1169-a, 1170-j,
    1171-h, 1173-a, 1186-p,
    1198-j, 1238-b
Zoline, Pamela 1199-m

This index includes all titles of individual volumes and short stories, with their variants, and cross-references substantive references in the annotations. Numbers refer to entry code numbers. Letters designate items within the entries.

"Apples of Knowledge, The" 799-j
"Apprentice Magician" 923-j, 1206-i
"April in Paris" 628-b, 1164-k
"April 2000: The Third Expedition" 124-a
"April 2005: Usher II" 121-o, 124-e
"April 2003: The Musicians" 124-c
"April 2003: Way in the Middle of the World" 121-m,
    124-d
"April 2026: The Long Years" 121-v
"April Witch, The" 119-c
"Arabesque: The Mouse" 245-1
Arabian Tale . . ., An 82
Arachne 881
Arcane 950
"Archive of the Older Mysteries, An" 906-j
archy and mehitabel 717
Ardor on Aros 850
"Are You Listening?" 324-1, 1168-f
"Are You Too Late or Was I Too Early" 228-e, 231-d,
    1214-a
"Argonauts, The" 431-1
"Ariadne in Mantua" 862-g
"Arise, Sir — — !" 88-n
"Armageddon" 1160-k
"Armaments Race" 219-d
Army of Darkness 1004
Arrow, The 795
"Art and Mystery of Collaboration, The" 727-a
"Arthur and Gorlagon" 1226-a
Arthur Machen: A Bibliography . . . 715
Artificial Princess, The 363
"Artist Unknown" 1202-mmm, 1214-n
"Artist's Secret, The" 942-i
"Artnan Process" 1011-e
"Artushof, Der" 501-e(6)
"As Is" 1168-b
"As One Woman to Another" 1001-h
"Ascension: A Workday Arabesque" 1217-q
"Asleep: With Still Hands" 324-e
Assassin of Gor 610
"Assignation, The" 898-a
"Astral Stray" 1232-e
"Astral Thruppe, The" 1013-r
"At Covent Garden" 88-s
"At First Sight" 291-d
At the Back of the North Wind 694
"At the Cemetery" 481-t
"At the End of the Universe" 903-j
At the Mountains of Madness 670, 1215-i
At the Mountains of Murkiness and Other Parodies 1215
"At the Mountains of Murkiness (H.P. Lovecraft)" 1215-i
"At the Mouse Circus" 325-n
"At the World's Edge" 525-f
Atlan 691

"Beyond the Black River" 516-b, 526-c, 534-a, 1238-d
"Beyond the Fields We Know: Publishers' [sic] Note"
    906-1
"Beyond the Game" 1168-d
Beyond the Golden Stair 112
Beyond the Looking Glass . . . 1193
"Beyond the Phoenix" 1208-h
"Beyond the Wall of Sleep" 1208-e
"Bianca's Hands" 1007-c
Bibliographia Oziana . . . 72
"Bibliographies of Modern Authors: Sir Henry John
    Newbolt" 822
*Bibliography of Adventure: Mundy, Burroughs, Rohmer,
    Haggard* 466, 814
Bibliography of Arthur Machen, A 716
Bibliography of E.M. Forster, A 383
Bibliography of Frederick Rolfe. Baron Corvo, A 934
Bibliography of Ronald Firbank, A 370
*Bibliography of the First Editions of The Works of
    Maurice Baring, A* 46
Bibliography of the Works of F. Anstey 456
*Bibliography of the Works of Mark Twain, Samuel Langhorne
    Clemens, A* 223
Bibliography of the Works of Max Beerbohm, A 90
Bibliography of the Works of Robert Graves, A 436
*Bibliography of the Works of Sir Henry Rider Haggard
    1856-1925* 465
Bibliography of the Works of W. Somerset Maugham, A 730
Bibliography of the Works of William Morris, A 810
*Bibliography of the Writings in Prose and Verse of George
    Meredith* 737
"Bibliography of the Writings of C.S. Lewis, A" 663
*Bibliography of the Writings of John Cowper Powys, 1872-
    1963, A* 914
Bibliography of the Writings of Norman Douglas . . ., A
    315
Bibliography of William Beckford . . ., A 83
"Big and Little" 967-b
"Big Black and White Game, The" 119-1
"Big Game" 246-p
"Big Game Hunt" 219-b
"Big Sam" 1171-c, 1217-j
Big Time, The 635
"Bills, M.D." 39-b
Binary Star No. 2 323
"Bindings Deluxe" 570-j
Biography of Lord Dunsany 908
"Biological Experiment, The" 573-g
"Bird and the Girl, The" 481-z
"Bird of Doom and the End, The" 900-z
"Bird of Prey" 228-ii, 232-1, 233-r
"Bird of the Difficult Eye, The" 907-f
"Bird of Travel, The" 292-g
"Bird with the Golden Beak, The" 258-n, 1175-e

338

"Charon" 898-b
Charwoman's Shadow, The 894
"Chaser, The" 228-xx, 232-x, 233-k, 1200-r, 1202-kk
"Chaunt of the Gods, The" 900-d
"Chaunt of the Priests, The" 900-i
"Cheap Knowledge" 432-e
"Cheap Nigger, A" 600-c
"Checklist Bibliographies of Modern Authors: James
    Hilton" 492
"Checklist of the Writings of Edward Everett Hales, A"
    472
"'Cheefou'" 249-g
"Cheese" 250-r, 253-r
"Cheese-Cutter Hat Man, The" 254-b
"Cheque-Mate" 254-r
"Cherry Soul, The" 113-d
"Cherry Tree, The" 247-c
Chessman of Mars, The 157
"Chesterton Bibliography Continued" 218
Chesterton Continued. A Bibliographical Supplement 217
Chieftain of Andor 852
"Child, The" 54-c
Child Christopher and Goldilind the Fair 800
"Child Roland to the Dark Tower Came" 1176-q
"Child Who Believed, The" 1203-b
"Childhood of Apollo, The" 936-g
"Children of Asshur, The" 536-d
Children of Llyr . . ., The 331
Children of the Atom 1212-r
"Children of the Night" 510-d
"Children of the Pool, The" 712-b
Children of the Pool and Other Stories, The 712
Children of Wonder 1212
"Child's Play" 1212-i
Chimera 50
"Chimney, The" 1236-s
"Chimney Sweep, The" 965-i
"Chinfeather" 253-o
Chivalry 173
"Choice of a Bride, The" 502-a(14)
"Christmas Before Last; or, the Fruit of the Fragile
    Palm" 998-e
"Christmas Present, The" 1231-z
"Christmas Wreak, The" 1000-h
Chronicles of Don Rodriguez, The 894, 895
Chronicles of Fairy Land 540
Chronicles of Moorcock: A Bibliography, The 789
"Chu-bu and Sheemish" 893-m, 1198-g
"Chun wa" 45-j
"Cil" 1067-b
Circe's Island and The Girl & the Faun 882
"Circle Curse, The" 642-a
Circle of Light 475-478
"Circus Child" 1050-b

343

Fellowship of the Ring . . . , The 1044, 1183-o
Fellowship of the Talisman, The 955
Ferret Fantasy's Christmas Annual for 1973 490
"Fête Galante" 45-p
"Fever Dream" 122-f, 1241-i
"Few Words to Begin With, A" 1001-a
Fiction of Jack London: A Chronological Bibliography, The
   675
"Field, The" 897-n
"Field of Vision, The" 628-n
Fiends and Creatures 1211
"Fiery Dive, The" 28-a
Fiery Dive and Other Stories, The 28
"Fifteen Annas in the Rupee" 258-m
Fifth Son of the Shoemaker, The 257
Fifty-One Tales 898
"Fight with Knives, A" 899-ee
Fighting Man of Mars, A 159
"Figs" 259-d
Figures of Earth: A Comedy of Appearances 169
Films of Time: Twelve Fantasies 820
"Find the Place Yourself" 1094-i
"Finding of Laura (H.G. Wells), The" 1215-f
"Finding of the Absolute, The" 957-g
"Finding of the Graiken, The" 499-c
"Finding of the Princess, The" 431-e, 432-u
Fine and Private Place, A 73-a, 74
"Fine Feathers" 1234-o
"Finger of Fate, The" 417-n
Finian's Rainbow 994
"Finish Touch, The" 508-e
"Fire and the Flesh, The" 923-a
"Fire Balloons, The" 120-i, 124-b
"Fire of Beauty" 80-e
"Firebird, The" 236, 444, 1090
Fires of Isis 281
"First Christmas-Tree, The" 1062-i
"First Commentary: Swords and Swordplay" 1232-d
First Editions of A.E. Coppard . . . , The 255
"First Editions of J.B. Priestley, The" 927
First Editions of Philip José Farmer, The 353
"First Night of Lent, The" 118-e, 122-n
First Printings of American Authors . . . 77, 244, 401,
   1071
"First Shlemiel, The" 968-e
"First Tale: Idle Days on the Yann" 906-l(1)
First Whisper of "The Wind in the Willows," The 433
First World Fantasy Awards 1246
Fish Dinner in Memison, A 320
"Fisher of Men, The" 945-j, 946-c
"Five Black Swans, The" 1091-b, 1233-gg
Five Children and It 129
Five Novelist Poets 30
"Flag of Peace, The" 508-m

361

"Hatred of the Queen: A Story of Burma, The" 80-d
"Haunted and the Haunters, The" 1239-g
Haunted Earth, The 585
"Haunted Future, The" 635-a
"Haunted Harpsichord, The" 542-k
"Haunted House, A" (Pliny) 1202-u
"Haunted House, A" (Woolf) 1202-b
Haunted Jester, The 258
"Haunted Man, The" 1202-k
"Haunted Stage Box--The Tragedian's Story, The" 1155-h
"Haunter of the Dark, The" 1162-m
"Haunting of Halahanstown, The" 899-c
"Haunting of the Lady Shannon, The" 499-g
Haunting of Toby Jugg, The 1101
Haven, The 299
"Hawk of Basti" 536-b
"Hawks Over Shem" 519-b, 522-a
He 603, 1224-a
He, A Companion to She . . . 1224-b
"He That Hath Wings" 1222-d
"Headless Lady--The Artist's First Story, The" 1155-e
"Headpiece, The" 122-k
Heads of Cerberus, The 98
"Heart of a Thief" 922-u
"Heart of Atlantan, The" 1184-g, 1208-n
"Heart of Esculapius, The" 941-g
"Heart of the Scorpion, The" 889-a
"Heartburn" 1166-t, 1200-1
"Hearts and Crafts" 941-b
Heartsease 303
"Heavenly Choir, The" 483-f
"Heilige Serpion, Der" 501-e(1)
Heir of Sea and Fire 710
"Heldendammerung" 1191-1
"Helix from Beyond, The" 387-a
"Hell Hath Fury" 1209-a
Hell Hath Fury: An "Unknown" Anthology 1209
"Hell Hath No Fury" 227-f, 228-pp, 233-y
"Hell is Forever" 1161-d
"Hellsgarde" 792-e, 793-e, 1197-g
"Hen, The" 898-e
Henry Brocken . . . 289
Henry Fielding . . . 357
Henry Van Dyke: A Biography 1063
Her Ways Are Death 1081
"Herb-Healing" 1219-f
Herbert George Wells: An Annotated Bibliography . . .
   1097
Here Abide Monsters 823
Here and Otherwhere 580
"Here, Putzi!" 921-p
"Hereditary Memories" 481-i
"Heredity" 571-g
Hero from Otherwhere, The 1130

376

"Milly Dove" 845-l
"Milord Sir Smiht, the English Wizard" 1188-l
"Mind Spider, The" 635-f
Mind Spider and Other Stories, The 635
"Mines of Falun, The" ("Die Bergwerke zu Falun") 500-h, 501-e(7), 504-e
Miniature, The 887, 1175-g
Minikins of Yam, The 1020
"Ministering Angels" 651-d
"Ministrel, The" 44-e
"Minority Report" 1009-c, 1010-f
"Miracle of St. Goar, A" 1202-qqq
"Miracle of St. Scothinus, A" 1202-nnn
"Mirages" 1085-c
"Mircath" 945-r, 946-k
"Miriam" 1212-g
"Miroir, Le" (Aickman) 1236-o
"Mirror, The" (Stead) 992-l
Mirror Magic 140
"Mirror, Mirror" 1236-i
Mirror of Dreams . . . 425
"Mirror That Remembered (Mathematics), The" 490-d
"Mirrors of Tuzun Thune, The" 517-b, 1162-c, 1184-a
"Misguided Halo, The" 1160-a
Mislaid Charm, The 878
Miss Carter and the Ifrit 167
"Miss Cubbidge and the Dragon of Romance" 893-g
"Miss Duveen" 287-e, 292-d
"Miss Gentilbelle" 79-a
"Miss Jonathon" 540-b
"Miss Miller" 295-g
"Miss Milly" 254-f
"Miss Thing and the Surrealist" 263-i
"Miss Winters and the Wind" 1166-g
"Missing" 287-m, 288-b
"Missing Idol, The" 483-c
"Mistake Inside" 1213-c
"Mistaken Identity, A" 898-y
"Mistaken Oracle, The" 1232-o
"Mr. Andrews" 381-c
"Mr. Arcularis" 1242-m
"Mr. Arson" 273-f, 275
"Mr. Death and the Redheaded Woman" 1166-h
"Mr. Hay" 1013-h
"Mr. Hopkins and Galatea" 1239-z
"Mr. Jinx" 1160-i
Mr. Jorkens Remembers Africa 903
"Mr. Kempe" 288-a
"Mr. Lupescu" 1119-f, 1205-g
"Mr. M---: The Rontgen Ray-der (Conan Doyle)" 1215-b
"Mr. Mergenthwirker's Lobblies" 1201-f
Mr. Munchausen . . . 1151
"Mr. Strenberry's Tale" 924-h
"Mr. Tolman" 999-h, 1000-j

"Mr. Valiant Summoned" 1202-aaaa
Mr. Weston's Good Wine 915
"Mrs. Amworth" 1200-e
"Mrs. Lofter's Ride" 751-b
"Mrs. Mainwaring's Second Marriage" 941-e
Mistress Masham's Repose 1112
"Mistress of Death" 513-c
Mistress of Mistresses 319, 1183-e
"Mistress of Porcosito" 574-f
"Mixed-Up Feet and the Silly Bridegroom, The" 968-d
"Mock Sun, A" 542-d
"Modern Sinbad, The" 471-e
"Moishele" 966-q
"Moll Bourne: The Mystery of a Handsome Cad (Fergus
    Hume)" 1215-a
"Mom" 326-d
"Monk's Blood" 858-l
Monk's Magic 282
"Monster, The" 574-i
"Monster of the Prophecy, The" 973-q, 976-h
Montagne morte de la vie, La 100
"Moon Artist, The" 573-o
Moon Endureth: Tales and Fancies, The 144
"Moon Fancies" 540-e
Moon Magic . . . 374
Moon of Gomrath, The 403
Moon of Much Gladness: Related by Kai Lung 985
Moon of Skulls, The 535
"Moon of Skulls, The" 535-a
Moon of Three Rings 827
"Moon of Zembabwei, The" 530-c
Moon Pool, The 745
"Moon That Vanished, The" 1247-c
Moondust 1021
*Moonlight Traveler: Great Tales of Fantasy and Imagina-
    tion, The* 1242
"Moonlite Road, The" 1233-cc
"Moozeby" 1013-d
"Moral Little Tale, A" 898-bb
"Mordecai and Cocking" 246-f
More 88
"More Light" 1217-k
"More Than Skin Deep" 921-j
"More Things" 1231-d
"Morning-Glory" 1217-p
"Morpeth Tower" 992-y
"Morris in Chains" 243-c
"Morrison" 1177-b
"Mortal Milk, The" 1091-f
Morte d'Arthur, Le 1176-g
"Morthylla" 975-n, 977-k
Morwyn: or, the Vengeance of God 913
"Most Maddening Story in the World, The" 1242-q
"Mother By Protest" 1205-c

"Mother of Pearl" 845-d
"Mother of Toads" 975-i, 1222-e
"Mount Shasta" 1202-pp
"Mountains of Magnatz, The" 1067-c
"Mouse and Lion" 471-d
"Mousetrap" 826-f
"Movie People, The" 1170-r
"Moving Spirit" 219-i
"Muddle of the Woad, The" 413-c
"Mug in the Gambling Hall, The" 902-g
"Muime Chriosd" 946-b
Mummy! . . ., The 680
"Mummy to the Rescue" 1149-e
Münchhausiana: Bibliographie . . . 1154
"Munitions" 27-i
Murder and Magic 413
"Murder by Lightning" 902-x
"Murder in Netherby Gardens, The" 902-y
"Murder in the Fourth Dimension" 975-e
"Murderer, The" 119-h
"Murderer' Eye, The" 574-m
"Murderers, The" 79-m
"Murderous Dove, The" 1232-h
"Murex, The" 1014-c
"Muriel" 400-h
"Muse of Atlantis, The" 974-a
"Muse of Hyperborea . . ., The" 971-a
"Museum Piece" 1170-j
"Music, The" 1007-g
"Music from Behind the Moon, The" 171-c, 1163-e
"Music on the Hill, The" 1242-u
"Music, When Soft Voices Die" 263-n
"Musicians, The" 124-c
"Mutabile Semper" 430-c
"Muted Horn, The" 1218-d
"My Brother's Keeper" 921-m
"My Cousin from France" 541-i
"My Cousin's Corner Window" 502-d(1)
My First Two Thousand Years . . . 1072
"My Friend Merton" 1201-k
"My Friend the Beach-Comber" 600-i
"My Hearth" 27-k
"My Honoured Master" 1234-p
"My Hundredth Tale" 251-h
My Life in the Bush with Ghosts 1054
"My Lord, the Baby" 1032-e
"My Maiden Brief" 417-f
"My Own Experience" 101-f
"My Platonic Sweetheart" 222-e
"My Tussle with the Devil" 27-a
My Tussle with the Devil and Other Stories 27
"My Unwilling Neighbor" 1000-k, 1001-k
"My Well and What Came Out of It" 1000-i, 1001-i
"My Wife's Tempter" 845-i

"Mysterious Kôr" 113-1
"Mysterious Stranger, The" 222-a
Mysterious Stranger: A Romance, The 221
Mysterious Stranger and Other Stories, The 222
"Mystery of Joe Morgan, The" 101-b
"Mystery of the Derelict, The" 495-h
"Mystery of the East, A" 903-u
"Mystery of the Lost Guest, The" 1243-u
"Mystery of the Toadstone, The" 889-c
"Myth of Actaeon, The" 1233-e
"Myth of Narcissus, The" 1233-f
"Myth of Philomela, The" 1233-g

"Nachricht von den neuesten Schicksalen des Hundes
    Berganza" ("Report on the Latest Fortunes of the
    Dog Berganza") 501-a(5)
"Nackles" 1169-k, 1173-k
"Nada" 542-s
"Naked Lady" 1243-c
"Naked People, The" 1192-i
"Name on the Stone, The" 481-p
"Nameless Isle, The" 525-e
"Nameless One, The" 248-f
Nameless Places 1231
"Names in the Black Book" 510-c
"Naming of Names, The" 121-n, 1204-g
"Nap, The" 287-o, 288-d
"Narnian Suite" 1191-q
"Narrow Escape, A" 907-1
"Narrow Valley" 1169-d, 1173-d
"Nary Spell" 1094-u
"Nature and Time" 898-rr
"Nature of the Evidence, The" 957-d
"Necromancy in Naat" 972-1, 977-c
"Necromantic Tale, The" 1206-c
"Nector of a Thousand Years, The" 941-h
"Neighbors" 963-v
"Neil Miller Gunn" 454
"Nekht Semerkeht" 1190-d, 1228-a
"Nellthu" 1213-i
"Nelly Trim" 1202-mm
"Neon" 325-f
Nerinda (1901) 313
"Nest of Singing Birds, A" 295-j
New Cambridge Bibliography of English Literature, The
    2, 34, 225, 285, 409, 545, 866, 943, 947, 993, 1093
"New Dispensation, The" 508-g
"New Master, The" 902-o
"New Murder, A" 902-p
New Wizard of Oz, The 57
New Worlds for Old 1185
New Worlds of Fantasy 1169
New Worlds of Fantasy [#3] 1171

Phantasiestücke in Callots Manier (Fantasy Pieces in the
    Manner of Callot) 501-a
Phantasmagoria: Tales of Fantasy and the Supernatural
    1226
Phantasmion 224
Phantastes . . . 701
Phantastes and Lilith 700-701
"Phantom Fence Rider of San Miguel, The" 1202-y
"Phantom Flea--The Lawyer's Story, The" 1155-b
"Phantom Slayer, The" 1208-p
"Phantom Warriors, The" 531-g
"Phantoms of the Fire, The" 970-c
"Philemon and Baucis" 1202-bbbb
"Philopena, The" 998-i
"Philosophy of Relative Existences, The" 1202-c
"Phoenix" 324-d
Phoenix and the Carpet, The 133
Phoenix and the Mirror . . ., The 267
Phoenix in Obsidian 777
"Phoenix Land" 324-d
"Phoenix on the Sword, The" 516-d, 527-c
Phra the Phoenician 32
"Physic" 287-t, 295-c
"Piano Player, The" 1233-vv
"Pickle My Bones" 1239-i
"Picnic, The" 291-g
"Picture in the House, The" 1233-aa
"Picture Puzzle, The" 1108-c
"Pictures, The" 1234-n
Pictures in the Fire 231
"Pictures in the Fire" 228-i, 231-l
"Piece of Linoleum, A" 571-j, 573-v
"Piece of Red Calico, A" 999-k, 1000-g
"Pierre Menard, Author of the Quixote" 1233-qq
"Piffingcap" 245-d
"Pig in a Pokey" 598-n
"Pig-Skin Belt, The" 1108-h
"Pigeons" 965-h
Pigeons from Hell 510
"Pigeons from Hell" 510-a, 1221-h
"Pilgrims, The" 1067-e
"Pillars of Chambalor" 556-d
"Pillars of Hell, The" 1190-e
"Pink Caterpillar, The" 1119-b
"Pink May" 113-j
"Piper's Son, The" 1212-f
"Pipes of Pan, The" 1243-h
"Pirate of the Round Pond, The" 902-m
"Pit-a-Pat" 254-s
"Pit of Wings" 1230-a
"Pitll Pawob Division, The" 324-h
"Place in the Woods, The" 1205-e
Place of the Lion . . ., The 1126
"Place With No Name, The" 324-i, 325-o

"Stanley Toothbrush" 1169-h, 1173-h
"Star, The" (Clarke) 1233-mm
"Star, The" (Wells) 1233-jj
"Star-Change, A" 970-f
Star Mill, The 874
Star Rover, The 674
"Stardock" 644-b
Starfollowers of Coramonde, The 265
"Star-Worshipper, The" 134-a
"Stars Below, The" 628-m
"Stars Down There, The" 1094-k
"Statement of Gabriel Foot, Highwayman" 1234-i
"Statues, The" 924-f
"Stay Tuned for Terror" 1208-t
"Staying Power of Sir Rohan, The" 1000-f, 1001-c
"Stealer of Souls, The" 764-c, 774-a
Stealer of Souls and Other Stories, The 764
"Steel Cat, The" 228-11, 231-n
Step Outside Your Mind 1173
"Stephen Skarridge's Christmas" 1001-j
"Stephen Vincent Benét: A Bibliography" 95
"Sticks" 1236-a, 1246-g
"Stocks and Stones" 144-i
Stolen Sun, The 816, 875
Stone Cage, The 437
"Stone of the Sages, The" 921-g
"Stone Thing: A Tale of Strange Parts, The" 755-a
"Stories from Behind the Stove" 965-e
"Storm, The" 898-x
"Storm in a Bottle" 1180-c
Storm Lord, The 623
Stormbringer 769, 775
"Story by Angela Poe, A" 94-d
"Story of a Panic, The" 380-a, 1212-e, 1239-t
"Story of a Siren, The" 381-e
"Story of a Star, The" 935-c
Story of Ab 672
"Story of Chang Tao, The" 1234-e
"Story of Chung Pun and the Miraculous Peacocks, The"
    984-b
"Story of Dienw'r Anffodion, The" 798-g
"Story of Kwey Chao and the Grateful Song Bird, The"
    984-e
"Story of Lam-Hoo and the Reward of Merit, The" 984-a
"Story of Land and Sea, A" 907-i
"Story of Li Pao, Lucky Star and the Intruding Stranger,
    The" 984-f
Story of Mona Sheehy, The 904
"Story of Pwylla and Rhianon . . ., The" 798-b
"Story of Pygmalion" 1202-jj
"Story of Rhianon and Pryderi . . ., The" 798-h
"Story of Rhianon and Pryderi, or The Book of the Three
    Unusual Arts of Pryderi Fab Pwyll" 798-f

411

Tales of the Wonder Club   1156
Tales of the Wonder Club.   Rev. ed.   1155
Tales of the Wonder Club.   Second Series.   1157
Tales of Three Hemispheres   906
Tales of Wonder   907
"Talisman, The"   287-d, 295-d
"Tall One, The"   1163-1
Tall Stones, The   192
"Tall Tales of the G.I.s"   1202-zz
"Tanil"   246-m
"Tapsters' Tapestry"   248-n
"Tarbis of the Lake"   923-f
Tark and the Golden Tide   693
Tarnsman of Gor   604
Tarzan Adventures   755
"Taverel Manor"   512-d
"Tax Payer, The"   121-e
"Tears of the Madonna"   79-o
"Technical Slip"   1168-c
Tempest, The   1176-1
"Temple of Abomination, The"   1187-c
Temple of the Sun, The   192
"Temptation of St. Ivo, The"   400-c
Ten Contemporaries . . .   55, 135
Ten Contemporaries . . . .   Second Series.   26, 235,
    849
"Tender Age, The"   231-w
"Terminal Quest"   1212-p
Terraces of Night, The   1050
"Terrible Answer, The"   1203-g
"Terror, The"   1245-d
"Terror of the Water Tank, The"   499-e
"Tery, The"   323
"Testament of Athammaus, The"   971-e, 973-n, 1197-h
"That First Affair"   751-a, 1223-i
That First Affair and Other Sketches   751
That Hideous Strength . . .   444, 656
"That Holy Thing"   697
"That Only a Mother"   1212-m
"That Same Old 'Coon"   999-e
"Theft of Thirty-Nine Girdles, The"   971-k, 975-m
"Their Mistress, the Sea"   643-c
"Thelinde's Song"   1186-p
"Then I Wasn't Alone"   1094-e
"There is No Such Place as America"   1233-uu
"There Was an Old Woman"   116-v, 117, 123
"There Will Come Soft Rains"   121-w
"There'd Be Thousands in It"   921-w
"They"   1172-g, 1213-b
"They Bite"   1119-g
"They Loved Me in Utica"   1170-c
They: Three Parodies of H. Rider Haggard's She   1224
They Used Dark Forces   1106
"Thief, The"   45-u

"Tobias Martin, Master Cooper, and His Men" ("Meister
   Martin der Küfner und seine Gesellen") 500-g, 502-a,
   502-a(12)
"Token, The" 957-b
Tolkien: A Biography 1047
Tolkien Criticism: An Annotated Checklist 1048
"Tolkien's Magic Ring" 1042-a
"Tolometh" 974-d
Tom O'Bedlam's Song 1176-h
"Tomb of the God, The" 1183-j
"Tomb-Spawn, The" 975-j, 977-m
"Tomb of Pan, The" 898-xx
Tombs of Atuan, The 630
"Tombstone, The" 116-f, 117
"Tommatoo" 845-c
"Too Far" 1192-h
Too Many Magicians 414
"Torment of the Last Lord, The" 765-a
Tortured Planet, The 656
Touch of Nutmeg and More Unlikely Stories, The 233
"Touch of Nutmeg Makes It, The" 228-g, 233-a
"Touch of Strange, A" 1192-j
"Touched With Fire" 123-c
"Touchstone" 1168-e
Tournament of Thorns, The 1024
"Tower, The" 1195-h
"Tower of Darkness" 1230-f
"Tower of the Elephant, The" 517-d, 520-b
"Town Where No One Got Off, The" 122-h
"Trade Dispute, A" 902-l
"Tragic Wall, The" 542-l
"Train, The" 79-g
Tramontane 876
"Tranquility, or Else!" 635-a
"Transferred Ghost, The" 999-b, 1202-v
"Transformation of Bayal the Porcupine, The" 56-n
"Transit of the Red Dragon, The" 889-b
Transit of the Red Dragon and Other Tales, The 889
"Transmutation of Ling, The" 1182-c
"Trapped in the Sea of Stars" 646-f
"Trapped in the Shadowland" 646-c, 1187-e
"Traveler, The" 116-i, 117
Traveler in Black, The 142
"Treader of the Dust, The" 972-w
"Treasure of the Labyrinth, The" 386-b
"Treasure of Tranicos, The" 516-c, 527-a
"Treasure of Vasco Gomez, The" 94-e
Treasures of Typhon, The 890
"Tree, The" 287-g, 292-k
Tree and Leaf 1038, 1042-c
"Tree of Life, The" (Machen) 712-d
"Tree of Life, The" (Morris, K.) 794-g
Trey of Swords 839
Tribesmen of Gor 615

419

"Wolf Pack, The" 637-d
"Wolf Pair, The" 637-b
Wolfwinter 1028
"Wolves Beyond the Border" 527-b
"Wolves of Kerak" 926-i
"Woman in Gray, The" 1243-g
"Woman in the Case" 922-t
"Woman in the Mirror, The" 1182-a
"Woman in the Witch-Wood, The" 386-c
"Woman of the Wood, The" 1162-b
"Woman on the Stairs, The" 1050-c
"Woman Versus Women" 248-h
"Woman Who Loved Chopin, The" 542-q
"Woman With the Net, The" 945-n
"Women of the Wood, The" 743-i
"Wonderful Death of Dudley Stone, The" 123-e
"Wonderful Ice Cream Suit, The" 122-e
Wonderful O, The 1034
Wonderful Visit, The 1096
"Wonderful Window, The" 893-n
Wonderful Wizard of Oz, The 57
"Wondersmith, The" 845-b
"Wondrous Wise Man, The" 56-f
Wood Beyond the World, The 806
"Wood Magic" (Buchan) 144-m
"Wood-Magic" (Van Dyke) 1062-e
"Wooden Toby: An Anyhow Story" 1193-d
Word: A Novel, The 955
"Word of Santiago, The" 922-a
"Word of Unbinding, The" 628-e, 1214-k
"Words of Guru, The" 1212-b, 1214-e
"Working With the Little People" 326-b
"Workman, The" 898-h
"World Well Lost, The" 1007-e
World's Desire, The 467
Worlds of Never: Three Fantastic Novels 1225
Worlds of Weird 1222
"Worlds to Kill" 324-n
"Worldsong" 1231-1
"Worm, The" 573-a
"Worm and the Angel, The" 898-p
Worm Ouroboros . . . , The 318
"Wow O'Rivven . . . , The" 697-q
Wraiths of Time 829
"Wreak of the Wastrel, The" 525-r
Wreaks of Time 876
Wrexham's Romance 424, 429
"Wrinkled Women of St. Nepomuk, The" 1239-h
"Writer and the Prince, The" 195-j
*Writings of Alfred Edgar Coppard: A Bibliography,
    The* 256
"Wrong Branch, The" 643-e
"Wunder Gottes, The" 992-11